D0982917

# Modern Drama in America and England, 1950-1970

## AMERICAN LITERATURE, ENGLISH LITERATURE, AND WORLD LITERATURES IN ENGLISH: AN INFORMATION GUIDE SERIES

Series Editor: Theodore Grieder, Curator, Division of Special Collections, Fales Library, New York University

Associate Editor: Duane DeVries, Associate Professor, Polytechnic Institute of New York, Brooklyn

*Other books on American and English literature in this series:*

CONTEMPORARY FICTION IN AMERICA AND ENGLAND, 1950-1970—*Edited by Alfred F. Rosa and Paul A. Echholz*

CONTEMPORARY POETRY IN AMERICA AND ENGLAND, 1950-1975—*Edited by Martin E. Gingerich**

AUTHOR NEWSLETTERS AND JOURNALS—*Edited by Margaret C. Patterson*

AFRO-AMERICAN POETRY AND DRAMA, 1760-1975—*Edited by William P. French, Michel J. Fabre, Amritjit Singh, and Genevieve Fabre*

AMERICAN DRAMA TO 1900—*Edited by Walter J. Meserve*

ENGLISH DRAMA TO 1660—*Edited by Frieda Elaine Penninger*

ENGLISH DRAMA, 1660-1800—*Edited by Frederick M. Link*

ENGLISH DRAMA AND THEATRE, 1800-1900—*Edited by L.W. Connolly and J.P. Wearing*

ENGLISH DRAMA, 1900-1950—*Edited by E.H. Mikhail*

*in preparation

---

The above series is part of the

## GALE INFORMATION GUIDE LIBRARY

The Library consists of a number of separate series of guides covering major areas in the social sciences, humanities, and current affairs.

General Editor: Paul Wasserman, Professor and former Dean, School of Library and Information Services, University of Maryland

Managing Editor: Denise Allard Adzigian, Gale Research Company

# Modern Drama in America and England, 1950-1970

## A GUIDE TO INFORMATION SOURCES

---

*Volume 34 in the American Literature, English Literature, and World Literatures in English Information Guide Series*

**Richard H. Harris**

*Director of Drama and Literature*
*WBAI-FM in New York*
*and*
*Adjunct Assistant Professor of English*
*York College of the City University of New York*

***Gale Research Company***
*Book Tower, Detroit, Michigan 48226*

**Library of Congress Cataloging in Publication Data**

Harris, Richard Hough.
Modern drama in America and England, 1950-1970.

(American literature, English literature, and world literatures in English information guide series ; v. 34) (Gale information guide library)
Includes indexes.
1. American drama—20th century—Bibliography.
2. English drama—20th century—Bibliography.
I. Title. II. Series.
Z1231.D7H36 [PS351] 016.822'914 74-11524
ISBN 0-8103-1218-2 AACR2

With Love,
To Helen and Lin

# VITA

Richard H. Harris is director of drama and literature at WBAI-FM in New York, and adjunct assistant professor of English at York College of the City University of New York. He received his B.A. degree from Iona College in New Rochelle, New York, and his M.A. and Ph.D. from Columbia University. Academic honors awarded him include a Woodrow Wilson Fellowship.

Harris is the producer of numerous theatre works for radio. His works in this field have received grants from the New York State Council on the Arts and National Public Radio as well as a citation from the Corporation for Public Broadcasting.

# CONTENTS

# INTRODUCTION

The intent of this volume is to assist the student and scholar in finding information and opinion about plays published between 1950 and 1970 by English and American playwrights. While the focus is on this period, an effort has been made to provide coverage of some of the more recent theatrical developments.

The volume is divided into two parts--a selected reading list of secondary sources and a bibliographic guide to works of playwrights. Part 1 contains bibliographical and critical sections listing bibliographies of the genre, collections of critical essays, and articles on a variety of theatrical topics not related to a specific playwright.

Part 2 is devoted to the works of 255 playwrights and the criticism their work has stimulated. The listing of plays extends through 1975 although the reader will find citations of critical essays on only those works published from 1950 through 1970. To keep the chronological guidelines of this volume in manageable form, this rule has been followed: plays performed before 1950 but published between 1950 and 1975 are listed; plays performed between 1950 and 1975 although not published until after 1975 are not listed.

Performance history and publication history are often quite disparate. Plays, particularly those from Off and Off Off Broadway, live primarily on stage and publication is frequently an afterthought. Additionally, American publishers are considerably slower than their English counterparts in bringing theatrical events to the printed page. Thus, this volume records a history of printed play texts and criticisms, not performance histories. Where two or more plays are published in a year, then performance history has been used to establish priority. For detailed information on performance history, the reader is directed to James Vinson's CONTEMPORARY DRAMATISTS (New York: St. Martin's, 1973), an invaluable reference guide. For comprehensive coverage of black drama, the reader should consult a companion volume in this series, AFRO-AMERICAN POETRY AND DRAMA, edited by William French, Michel Fabre, Amritjit Singh, and Genevieve Fabre (Detroit: Gale Research Co., 1979).

# Introduction

Since this book includes both English and American plays and playwrights, American publication is the sole listing for American plays, and similarly with English, except for those rare cases where there is a three or more year difference between English and American publication of a play, or where the first publication is in the other country. Each play's first publication is cited. Where that is in a magazine, the subsequent book publication, if any, is also cited. If the first publication is in a collection, other publishing history, if any, is included. Acting editions have not been cited unless they are either a revised text, the only nonperiodical text available, or if their publication antedates regular book publication. However, acting editions, even if not cited in this book, are generally recommended to anyone looking for a more precise notion of a play's theatrical reality or for textual alterations made during a play's run.

After the listing of plays in order of publication date, followed by collaborations and collections, is a list of bibliographies that exist for a given author's works. There then follows a selected list, again in chronological order, of the playwright's nontheatrical writings that may be of interest.

The final section of a playwright's entry lists criticism. In alphabetical order, but chronologically within the works of a given critic, is a selection of the reviews, essays, and books written about an author's 1950 to 1970 works.

No one compiling such a book could fail to be impressed by the dangers involved. Can a full-length book or a complicated article be summarized in one paragraph without distortion? Brevity certainly poses one problem, but personal bias presents an even more serious one. Which two people could read the same essay and be left with the same impression? After several years of work on this book, I cannot say that I know the answers; I can say that I have been consistently aware of these questions. It is my hope that readers of this book will find it a useful stepping-stone. The critics and scholars I summarize and interpret certainly deserve lengthy perusal, just as the plays listed merit the closest critical scrutiny.

As the years 1950 to 1970 saw immense theatrical passion and veritable revolutions of style, so this book is an encapsulation of an extraordinary era of theatrical history. Reading and writing about the plays, playwrights, and critics of this era has been an enriching, even daunting, experience.

November 1981<br>
New York City

# LIST OF ABBREVIATIONS

| | |
|---|---|
| AL | AMERICAN LITERATURE |
| AM | AMERICA |
| BO | BOTTEGHE OSCURE |
| C | CRITIQUE |
| CE | COLLEGE ENGLISH |
| CL | COMPARATIVE LITERATURE |
| CQ | CAROLINA QUARTERLY |
| CR | CRITICAL REVIEW |
| CRQ | CRITICAL QUARTERLY |
| DC | DRAMA CRITIQUE |
| DR | DALHOUSIE REVIEW |
| DS | DRAMA SURVEY |
| EN | ENCORE |
| ENC | ENCOUNTER |
| ER | EVERGREEN REVIEW |
| ES | ESQUIRE |
| ETJ | EDUCATIONAL THEATRE JOURNAL |
| G | GAMBIT |
| HC | HOLLINS CRITIC |
| HR | HUDSON REVIEW |
| KR | KENYON REVIEW |
| MD | MODERN DRAMA |
| MLN | MODERN LANGUAGE NOTES |
| MLQ | MODERN LANGUAGE QUARTERLY |

| | |
|---|---|
| MLS | MODERN LANGUAGE SURVEY |
| MP | MODERN PHILOLOGY |
| MR | MASSACHUSETTS REVIEW |
| NR | NEW REPUBLIC |
| NTM | NEW THEATRE MAGAZINE |
| NWW | NEW WORLD WRITING |
| NYRB | NEW YORK REVIEW OF BOOKS |
| P | POETRY |
| P& P | PLAYS AND PLAYERS |
| PL | PLAYERS |
| PMLA | PUBLICATIONS OF THE MODERN LANGUAGE ASSOCIATION |
| PO | POETICS |
| PR | PARTISAN REVIEW |
| PS | PRAIRIE SCHOONER |
| QJS | QUARTERLY JOURNAL OF SPEECH |
| QRL | QUARTERLY REVIEW OF LITERATURE |
| RA | RAMPARTS |
| S | SHOW |
| SH | SHENANDOAH |
| SP | STUDIES IN PHILOLOGY |
| SR | SEWANEE REVIEW |
| TA | THEATRE ARTS |
| TCL | TWENTIETH CENTURY LITERATURE |
| TDR | TULANE DRAMA REVIEW, then THE DRAMA REVIEW (1955-56-- .) |
| TEQ | TEXAS QUARTERLY |
| TF | THEATREFACTS |
| TQ | THEATRE QUARTERLY |
| TR | TRANSATLANTIC REVIEW |
| VV | VILLAGE VOICE |
| WS | WISCONSIN STUDIES IN CONTEMPORARY LITERATURE |
| YT | YALE/THEATRE |

# A SELECTED SECONDARY SOURCE READING LIST

# BIBLIOGRAPHICAL READING LIST

Adelman, Irving, and Rita Dworkin. MODERN DRAMA: A CHECKLIST OF CRITICAL LITERATURE ON 20TH CENTURY PLAYS. Metuchen, N.J.: Scarecrow Press, 1967.

> Useful checklists of criticism, but by no means comprehensive. See also Carpenter, below.

Blum, Daniel, and John Willis, eds. THEATRE WORLD. Vols. 6-27. New York and Philadelphia: Greenberg, Chilton, and Crown Presses, 1950-70.

> Valuable series of yearbooks of the American theatre; listings are chronological, giving cast and production information, with photographs, length of run, and cast changes. The emphasis is on Broadway, but much space is given to non-Broadway and non-New York productions in the later volumes. The photographs are uncommonly engrossing.

THE BRITISH MUSEUM. DEPARTMENT OF PRINTED BOOKS. GENERAL CATALOGUE OF PRINTED BOOKS. 263 vols. London: Trustees, 1959-66.

> This monumental set, with its various ongoing supplements to date, is an invaluable guide to the holdings of the British Library (formerly the British Museum). See Eugene Sheehy's GUIDE TO REFERENCE BOOKS (9th ed., Chicago: ALA, 1976) for more detailed information about the various sequences and cumulations of the BM CATALOGUE.

Brockett, Oscar G., et al. A BIBLIOGRAPHICAL GUIDE TO RESEARCH IN SPEECH AND DRAMATIC ARTS. Glenview, Ill.: Scott, Foresman, 1963.

> Far too broad in scope.

Carpenter, Charles A. "The New Bibliography of Modern Drama Studies." MD, 12 (May 1969), 49-56.

> A brief survey of the growth of drama bibliography since 1946

prefaces a scathing review of the inadequacies of Adelman and Dworkin work (see above).

Cheshire, David. THEATRE: HISTORY, CRITICISM, AND REFERENCE. London: Clive Bingley, 1967.

This brief bibliographical essay on theatre history is the best and most readable introduction to research on the subject.

Chicorel, Marietta, ed. CHICOREL THEATER INDEX TO PLAYS IN ANTHOLOGIES, PERIODICALS, DISCS AND TAPES. New York: Chicorel, 1970.

This book, and its companion volume published in 1971, provide a comprehensive list of periodicals and anthologies in which a reader may find a play. Thus, if one wishes to find where ZOO STORY has been reprinted, this is the place to search. A third volume, published in 1972, focuses on English publications.

Coleman, Arthur, and Gary R. Tyler. DRAMA CRITICISM: A CHECKLIST OF INTERPRETATION SINCE 1940 OF ENGLISH AND AMERICAN PLAYS. Vol. 1. Denver, Colo.: Swallow, 1966.

Erratic, with many misspellings of both titles and authors.

Connor, John M., and Billie M. Connor, eds. OTTEMILLER'S INDEX TO PLAYS IN COLLECTIONS PUBLISHED BETWEEN 1900 AND MID-1970. 5th ed. Metuchen, N.J.: Scarecrow, 1971.

Handy, one-volume index, not very strong on English collections, but more available in libraries than the CHICOREL INDEX (see above).

DRAMATIC CRITICISM INDEX: A BIBLIOGRAPHY OF COMMENTARIES ON PLAYWRIGHTS FROM IBSEN TO THE AVANT-GARDE. Ed. Paul F. Breed and Florence M. Sniderman. Detroit: Gale Research Co., 1972.

Unannotated checklist, with some curious omissions.

Dukore, Bernard F. A BIBLIOGRAPHY OF THEATRE ARTS PUBLICATIONS IN ENGLISH, 1963. New York: American Educational Theatre Association, 1965.

A valuable bibliography, unfortunately not continued as an annual publication.

Hartnoll, Phyllis, ed. THE OXFORD COMPANION TO THE THEATRE. 3rd ed. London: Oxford University Press, 1967.

Contemporary theatre is this volume's weakest feature.

Ireland, Norma Olin. INDEX TO FULL LENGTH PLAYS 1944 TO 1964. Boston: F.W. Faxon, 1965.

A peculiar work which indexes PURLIE VICTORIOUS under "Cotton" as well as "Negroes."

Keller, Dean H. INDEX TO PLAYS IN PERIODICALS. Rev. ed. Metuchen, N.J.: Scarecrow Press, 1979.

This provides information about plays published in 140 different periodicals; it is divided into author and title indexed sections.

Logasa, Hannah. AN INDEX TO ONE-ACT PLAYS FOR STAGE, RADIO AND TELEVISION. 4th and 5th Supplements. Boston: F.W. Faxon, 1958, 1966.

Preponderantly children's plays.

Lowe, Claudia Jean. A GUIDE TO REFERENCE AND BIBLIOGRAPHY FOR THEATRE RESEARCH. Columbus: Ohio State University Press, 1971.

A brief compilation, half of which is devoted to general bibliographical reference, that is most useful for directions to other more extensive sources.

NATIONAL UNION CATALOG, PRE-1956 IMPRINTS. London: Mansell, 1968-- .

This catalog is now alphabetically into the U.S. entries in some 685 volumes. Completed in 1980, it is the most comprehensive resource for the holdings of U.S. libraries up to 1955.

It is at present supplemented by NATIONAL UNION CATALOG 1956-67 cumulations for 1968-72 and 1973-77. After the most recent five-year cumulation, there are one-month volumes, three-month cumulations (January-March, April-June, etc.), and annual volumes thereafter until the next five-year cumulation appears. These post-1955 cumulations have been issued by various publishers. See Eugene Sheehy's GUIDE TO REFERENCE BOOKS (9th ed, Chicago: ALA, 1976) for more detailed information on Library of Congress catalogs and the NATIONAL UNION CATALOG.

NEW YORK THEATRE CRITICS REVIEWS. N.p., n.d. Vols. 11-31.

The opening night reviews from major New York dailies from 1950 to 1970 are collected here. As the number of papers decreased, television reviews were added. This is an indispensable, handy reference tool.

NEW YORK TIMES DIRECTORY OF THE THEATER. Intro. Clive Barnes. New York: Arno, 1973.

The index to the eight volumes of collected drama reviews from the NEW YORK TIMES from 1920 to 1970.

Patterson, Charlotte A., comp. PLAYS IN PERIODICALS: AN INDEX TO ENGLISH LANGUAGE SCRIPTS IN TWENTIETH CENTURY JOURNALS. Boston: G.K. Hall, 1970.

Because it omits such periodicals as KENYON REVIEW and EVERGREEN REVIEW, this is a less useful guide than the Keller collection (see above).

Perry, Ted, ed. PERFORMING ARTS RESOURCES. Vol. 1. New York: Drama Book Specialists, 1974.

Eighteen articles describing the contents and locations of public and private collections of theatrical materials throughout the United States. This is an excellent source for the scholar seeking to discover what a particular city's libraries might have to offer. Unhappily, there is no index.

Salem, James M., ed. A GUIDE TO CRITICAL REVIEWS. Part 1: AMERICAN DRAMA, 1909-1969. 2nd ed. Metuchen, N.J.: Scarecrow Press, 1973.

An indispensable bibliography of newspaper and periodical reviews of American plays on the American stage, listed by playwright, production, and periodical, not by author of the review. The VILLAGE VOICE is the most glaring omission from the periodicals indexed. The volume indexes reviews but not "critical articles from scholarly journals."

______. A GUIDE TO CRITICAL REVIEWS. Part 3: BRITISH AND CONTINENTAL DRAMA FROM IBSEN TO PINTER. Metuchen, N.J.: Scarecrow Press, 1968.

Less complete and of less interest than the entry above, since this guide gives only American reviews of New York productions of British drama. Again, only reviews, not critical essays, are indexed.

Schoolcraft, Ralph Newman. PERFORMING ARTS BOOKS IN PRINT: AN ANNOTATED BIBLIOGRAPHY. New York: Drama Books Specialists, 1973.

This volume has one major asset and one major flaw: the asset is the inclusion of every kind of performing art from the circus through television; the flaw is the completely uncritical annotations, which nonetheless are quite complete. Supplements are issued four times a year.

Simon, Bernard, comp. SIMON'S DIRECTORY OF THEATRICAL MATERIALS, SERVICES AND INFORMATION. 4th ed. Introd. Jo. Mielziner. New York: Package Publicity Service, 1970.

A guide to rental and purchase of scenery, lighting, props, costumes, for all fifty states and Canada.

Stevenson, Isabelle, ed. THE TONY AWARDS. New York: Arno Press, 1975.

Prefaced by a short history of the American Theatre Wing, this is a list of Tony winners from 1947 to 1974.

Stratman, Carl J., C.S.V. BIBLIOGRAPHY OF THE AMERICAN THEATRE, EXCLUDING NEW YORK CITY. Chicago: Loyola University Press, 1967.

Arranged by state, in alphabetical order, are books, articles, and theses on all phases of American theatre outside New York. Those activities encompassed include arena theatre, children's theatre, Chinese theatre, minstrels, repertory theatre, university theatre, and some nineteen other categories. Invaluable.

# CRITICAL READING LIST

Abel, Lionel. METATHEATRE: A NEW VIEW OF DRAMATIC FORM. New York: Hill and Wang, 1963.

A collection of argumentative essays asserting that tragedy ended with the Greeks and that the characteristic form of subsequent Western drama is metatheatre; this form features plays within plays, self-dramatizing, dreams, and plays in which life itself is seen as a play. The volume is an example of an interesting thesis expanded out of all proportion. See also Cohn's CURRENTS, and "The death of tragedy," from Sontag's AGAINST INTERPRETATION, below.

Addenbrooke, David. THE ROYAL SHAKESPEARE COMPANY: THE PETER HALL YEARS. London: William Kimber, 1974.

A history, with interviews and statistics.

Adler, Henry. "To Hell with Society." TDR, 4 (May 1960), 53-76.

A wordy comment on the Kenneth Tynan-Eugene Ionesco debate, more an attack upon Tynan than a defense of Ionesco.

"Alice in Wonderland, Performed by the Manhattan Project, Directed by Andre Gregory." TDR, 14 (September 1970), 94-104.

Sixteen photographs.

Allsop, Kenneth. THE ANGRY DECADE: A SURVEY OF THE CULTURAL REVOLT OF THE NINETEEN-FIFTIES. With a rev. intro. by the author. London: Peter Owen, 1964.

A generally unsympathetic survey of dissident British writers of the fifties suggesting that they lack broad enough visions to encompass the true difficulties of modern life. The book's virtue is its scope; Allsop has done his homework. Less happy is the style into which the book often sinks. Jean Genet, for example, is characterized as "the conscientious Wild Man from Borneo of French drama."

Anderson, Michael. "Dionysus and the Cultured Policeman." TDR, 11 (Summer 1967), 99-104.

A thoughtful study of the relationship between ritual and drama.

Anonymous. "Ex-Village Play Director Guilty in Air-Raid Case." VV, 28 December 1955, p. 3.

A report on the arrest of Judith Malina for not taking shelter during a nationwide air raid drill.

______. "Theatre Worker." OBSERVER, 15 March 1959, p. 4.

Profile of Joan Littlewood.

Armstrong, William A., ed. EXPERIMENTAL DRAMA. London: G. Bell and Sons, 1963.

Ten essays, nine of them based on lectures given at the University of London in 1962, form an excellent introduction to post-war British drama. Armstrong's essay on the financial and production forces which controlled the pre-1956 theatre is particularly useful.

Ashmore, Jerome. "Interdisciplinary Roots of the Theater of the Absurd." MD, 14 (May 1971), 72-83.

The philosophical roots of the Absurd are traced back to the Greeks, in a demonstration that absurdist theatre is neither a trivial nor a recent development.

Bagley, Beth. "El Teatro Campesino: Interviews with Luis Valdez." TDR, 11 (Summer 1967), 70-80.

The Farm Workers Theater is discussed by its founder.

Balio, Tino, and Robert G. McLaughlin. "The Economic Dilemma of the Broadway Theatre: A Cost Study." ETJ, 21 (March 1969), 81-100.

A supplement to the Baumol and Bowen volume, below.

Barry, Jackson G. "Jose Quintero: The Director as Image Maker." ETJ, 14 (March 1962), 15-22.

A description of Quintero's rehearsal techniques that captures his suggestive, intuitive method of inspiring his actors.

Baumol, William J., and William G. Bowen. PERFORMING ARTS--THE ECONOMIC DILEMMA: A STUDY OF PROBLEMS COMMON TO THEATER, OPERA, MUSIC AND DANCE. New York: Twentieth Century Fund, 1966.

The major survey of its kind. See also Balio and McLaughlin, above.

Beck, Julian. THE LIFE OF THE THEATRE: THE RELATION OF THE ARTIST TO THE STRUGGLE OF THE PEOPLE. San Francisco: City Lights, 1972.

One hundred twenty three meditations, reflections, journal entries, and poems by the cofounder of the Living Theatre. Most of the pieces were written while the company was in exile overseas during the late 1960s and early 1970s.

Beck, Julian, and Judith Malina. "All the World's a Prison." VV, 4 September 1957, p. 4. Rpt. in THE VILLAGE VOICE READER: A MIXED BAG FROM THE GREENWICH VILLAGE NEWSPAPER. Eds. Daniel Wolf and Edwin Fancher. New York: Grove Press, 1963, pp. 135-36.

Reflecting on their thirty-day jail stint, Beck and Malina suggest that while prison robs mankind of volition, paradoxically only in prison, where men are free of greed, is there altruistic love and communal feeling.

Bentley, Eric. IN SEARCH OF THEATER. New York: Knopf, 1953.

Eric Bentley's critical writings, from THE PLAYWRIGHT AS THINKER (1946) onwards, all but singlehandedly created serious American dramatic criticism. So intellectually persuasive are his criticisms of American and British drama of the late forties and the fifties that his basic assessment of their worth has not yet been satisfactorily reappraised. The titles of two of the chapters of this volume, "Boredom in New York" and "Gentility in London," give an idea of Bentley's stance.

______. "MY FAIR LADY." MD, 1 (September 1958), 135-36.

The Lerner version of PYGMALION distorts the ending and blunts the play's unromantic Shavian spirit. This was originally a BBC broadcast.

______. "The Psychology of Farce." In LET'S GET A DIVORCE: AND OTHER PLAYS. Ed. Eric Bentley. New York: Hill and Wang, 1958.

This is an early, scaled-down version of the essay on farce in THE LIFE OF THE DRAMA, below.

______. THE LIFE OF THE DRAMA. New York: Atheneum, 1964.

Based on the 1960-61 Norton lectures at Harvard, the book is in two parts: "Aspects of a Play" and "Different Kinds of Plays." Bentley's only full-fledged attempt at defining the basic elements of theatre art is readable, persuasive, generally psychological in its approach, and much the best book of its kind.

______. THE THEATRE OF COMMITMENT, AND OTHER ESSAYS ON DRAMA IN OUR SOCIETY. New York: Atheneum, 1967.

Consisting of seven essays, with a note on their provenance, this volume takes its title from the last essay, a defense of THE DEP-

UTY and polemical, propagandistic theatre in general.

_____. THE THEORY OF THE MODERN STAGE: AN INTRODUCTION TO MODERN THEATRE AND DRAMA. Harmondsworth, Engl.: Penguin, 1968.

Part one of this anthology treats "Ten Makers of Modern Theatre." Part two is called "Towards a Historical Over-View." Much of the material in this valuable collection had never been previously anthologized.

_____. WHAT IS THEATRE?, INCORPORATING THE DRAMATIC EVENT AND OTHER REVIEWS 1944-1967. New York: Atheneum, 1968.

This reprint combines Bentley's two volumes of NEW REPUBLIC drama criticism from the years 1952 to 1956, minus three longer essays relocated to his THEATRE OF COMMITMENT (above); twelve additional reviews from 1944 to 1967 fill out the volume. Witty and erudite, these collected reviews represent a standard of critical intelligence rarely matched by subsequent writers in the field.

_____, ed. THE STORM OVER THE DEPUTY. New York: Grove Press, 1964.

A collection of thirty responses to Rolf Hochuth's controversial play about Pius XII that ranges far beyond theatrical to historians and philosophers.

_____. THIRTY YEARS OF TREASON: EXCERPTS FROM HEARINGS BEFORE THE HOUSE COMMITTEE ON UN-AMERICAN ACTIVITIES, 1938-1968. New York: Viking, 1971.

Engrossing, dramatic excerpts from the testimony of, among many others, Elia Kazan, Arthur Miller, Lillian Hellman, Joseph Papp, and Clifford Odets. Bentley later adapted much of this material into a theatre piece, ARE YOU NOW OR HAVE YOU EVER BEEN (1977).

_____. THEATRE OF WAR: COMMENTS ON 32 OCCASIONS. New York: Viking, 1972.

This is a collection of introductions, prefaces, essays, and journalism of varied and often unspecified provenance, although the date of each item is given. The volume is divided into three parts: "The Life of Modern Drama," "The Drama of Modern Life," and "Living Theatre in a Dying World." The book documents Bentley's activities as theatrical producer and cultural dissident, and his gradual detachment from theatrical involvement. His comments of Jerzy Grotowski and the Living Theatre are of particular interest.

Bermel, Albert. CONTRADICTORY CHARACTERS: AN INTERPRETATION OF THE MODERN THEATRE. New York: E.P. Dutton, 1973.

Provocative reassessments of major modern texts, focusing on the internal conflicts of characters.

Bigsby, C.W.E. CONFRONTATION AND COMMITMENT: A STUDY OF CONTEMPORARY AMERICAN DRAMA, 1959-1966. Columbia: University of Missouri Press, 1968.

Billington, Michael. "London Avant Garde Who? What? Where?" P&P, 17 (June 1970), 20-21.

Brief, but useful, survey of the English experimental theatre which, Billington argues, began with the 1963 Brook-Marowitz group at the Royal Shakespeare Company.

______. THE MODERN ACTOR. London: Hamish Hamilton, 1973.

A rambling survey of English acting schools, agents, casting, the acting of Olivier, the subsidized companies, and acting theory.

Bladel, Roderick. WALTER KERR: AN ANALYSIS OF HIS CRITICISM. Metuchen, N.J.: Scarecrow Press, 1976.

An admiring analysis of Kerr's aesthetic.

Blau, Herbert. "Language and Structure in Poetic Drama." MODERN LANGUAGE QUARTERLY, 18 (March 1957), 27-34.

Early Blau in an Aristotelian praise of language as civilizer of drama.

______. THE IMPOSSIBLE THEATRE: A MANIFESTO. New York: Macmillan, 1964.

An often irritating book that was at least partially responsible for Blau and his colleague Jules Irving's (brief) tenure at Lincoln Center. The book is a hodge-podge of admirably radical discontent with commercial theatre and a history of the San Francisco Actor's Workshop. The style is determinedly trendy.

Booker, Christopher. THE NEOPHILIACS. London: William Collins, 1969.

This is an often pretentious survey of the "nightmare" changes in English life since 1956, all from a conservative viewpoint. The focus is on the press, the arts, and political trends. The book is weakest when working out a scrappy schemata of cultural fantasies, for instance finding Pinter's plays devoted to "pure fantasy." It is best used as a chatty survey of popular cultural trends.

Bradbrook, M.C. ENGLISH DRAMATIC FORM: A HISTORY OF ITS DEVELOPMENT. London: Chatto and Windus, 1965.

Pages 179-99 constitute a generally unsympathetic account of the comtemporary English and American stage.

Brecht, Stephan. "Peter Schumann's Bread and Puppet Theatre." TDR, 14 (1970), 44-90.

A well-illustrated montage, with a listing of productions.

Brockett, Oscar G. PERSPECTIVES ON CONTEMPORARY THEATRE. Baton Rouge: Louisiana State University Press, 1971.

Six essays, originally lectures, discuss conflicting views of sexuality in the theatre, changing conceptions of plot and structure, and Brechtian versus Wagnerian theories of audience involvement. The essays are quite interesting, and they are addressed to the nonspecialist; some superfluous notes have been added.

Brook, Peter. "The Influence of Gordon Craig in Theory and Practice." DRAMA, n.s. 37 (Summer 1955), 33-36.

Craig's influence is felt virtually everywhere in theatre, and has eliminated fussy historicism from the stage. Brook notes Craig's impractical optimism about stage lighting and the elimination of the actor.

______. "America Cries Havoc, But Cuba Dances." SUNDAY TIMES (London), 12 February 1961, p. 24.

The Cuban character remains the same after the Castro Revolution.

______. "Oh, For Empty Seats!" In THE ENCORE READER: A CHRONICLE OF THE NEW DRAMA. Ed. Charles Marowitz, Tom Milne, and Owen Hale. London: Methuen, 1965, pp. 68-74.

"Through the easy passage of the artist to big commercial success, we have lost the 'avant-garde.'"

______. "Finding Shakespeare on Film." TDR, 11 (Fall 1966), 117-21.

Most film techniques do not get enough theatrical substance onto the film itself; Brook is intrigued by the multiscreen approach of the Johnson's Wax exhibit at the New York World's Fair. Film must free itself from consistency.

______. THE EMPTY SPACE. New York: Atheneum, 1968.

This is an eloquent major statement from England's leading director of this period. He describes four types of theatre: the deadly, the holy, the rough, and the immediate. The deadly is the boring commercial stage; the holy is the theatre that attempts to make the invisible visible, as in the work of Merce Cunningham, Samuel Beckett, Antonin Artaud, and Jerzy Grotowski; the rough is popular and earthy, as in Shakespeare and Brecht; the immediate involves the actor and the disciplined search for a character.

Brown, Helen, and Jane Seitz. "With the Bread and Puppet Theatre: An Interview with Peter Schumann." TDR, 12 (Winter 1968), 62-73.

Interview with the group's leader, illustrated with three scenarios.

Brown, John Russell. EFFECTIVE THEATRE: STUDY WITH DOCUMENTATION. London: Heinemann, 1969.

This interesting guidebook is in two parts: the first is an intelligent introduction to such topics as texts, audiences, stages, acting, design, and production; the second consists of documents illustrating these topics.

______. THEATRE LANGUAGE: A STUDY OF ARDEN, OSBORNE, PINTER, AND WESKER. London: Alan Lane, 1972.

Studies the texts of four English authors of similar historical and social backgrounds who have written plays over at least ten years. The emphasis is on how each controls the stage through language, tempo, space, and gesture.

______. "The Subtle Perils of Subsidy." TQ, 3 (July-September 1973), 33-39.

Risk, not security, has stimulated the great theatre of the past, and the subsidized theatres have little time or money for the risks involved in truly experimental theatre.

______, ed. MODERN BRITISH DRAMATISTS: A COLLECTION OF CRITICAL ESSAYS. Englewood Cliffs, N.J.: Prentice-Hall, 1968.

A collection of essays, useful for the classroom, concentrating on John Arden, John Osborne, Harold Pinter, and Arnold Wesker. The introduction and first three essays provide a broad context for what follows.

Brown, John Russell, and Bernard Harris, eds. AMERICAN THEATRE. London: Edward Arnold, 1967.

Ten commissioned essays, five by Englishmen and five by Americans, each prefaced by informative biographical and bibliographical notes. The analyses are largely literary; of particular interest are the essays by Katherine Worth and Morris Freedman on, respectively, poetic drama and the myth of success.

Brustein, Robert. SEASONS OF DISCONTENT: DRAMATIC OPINIONS 1959-1965. New York: Simon and Schuster, 1965.

Provocative, opinionated reviews and essays, largely from THE NEW REPUBLIC. Brustein lambasts conventional theatre fare and is very sympathetic to the burgeoning avant-garde. He later became dean of Yale's School of Drama, and one of the most influential men of American theatre.

______. THE THIRD THEATRE. New York: Knopf, 1969.

This collection of reviews and essays evaluates the theatre of the mid-sixties and finds it undisciplined, excessive, and immature. The volume also contains essays on such topics as the horror film and Madison Avenue.

_____. REVOLUTION AS THEATRE: NOTES ON THE NEW RADICAL STYLE. New York: Liveright, 1971.

Essays and articles on "theatricalized revolution--revolution for the hell of it." He views, critically, the Black Panthers at Yale and the Becks at the Theatre for Ideas.

_____. THE CULTURE WATCH: ESSAYS ON THEATRE AND SOCIETY, 1969-1974. New York: Knopf, 1975.

Brustein repeats his repudiations of both cultural conservatism and spurious radicalism.

Bryden, Ronald. "Trapped by Her Own Success." OBSERVER, 9 April 1967, p. 11.

Profile of Joan Littlewood.

Budel, Oscar. "Contemporary Theater of Aesthetic Distance." PMLA, 76 (June 1961), 277-91.

This scholarly and suggestive essay places Brecht's attempts to eliminate empathy in the larger context of the movement against illusion, typical of much theatre since Strindberg.

Burns, Elizabeth. THEATRICALITY: A STUDY OF CONVENTION IN THE THEATRE AND IN SOCIAL LIFE. London: Longmans, 1972.

A primarily sociological examination of several varieties of theatrical convention, Burns's study shows a good grasp of theatre history and an occasional weakness for jargon. It is an example of the many redefinitions of the stage from nonliterary perspectives that emerged in the late 1960s.

Chaikin, Joseph. THE PRESENCE OF THE ACTOR. New York: Atheneum, 1972.

Bringing together many previously published interviews and articles, Chaikin presents his theory of acting. As the central force behind the Open Theater, and a skilled actor himself, Chaikin is the most widely admired director-teacher now practicing in America. His book is eloquent and useful.

Clark, Brian. GROUP THEATRE. New York: Theatre Arts, 1971.

Advice, seemingly directed toward British university students, for creating group performances. While emphasizing the practical, the book's tone is that of the newly converted. His definition of group theatre, including as it does Sophocles, Shakespeare, and Brecht, is far too broad.

Clurman, Harold. ON DIRECTING. New York: Macmillan, 1972.

Half a discursive survey of Clurman's opinions of techniques of directing, and half a director's notes for some of his own productions, most notably THE AUTUMN GARDEN, A TOUCH OF THE POET, INCIDENT AT VICHY, and LONG DAY'S JOURNEY INTO NIGHT, this work is a charming introduction to directorial methodology. Using anecdote and his own practice, Clurman takes the reader from script selection through final rehearsals. He restates his appreciation of Konstantin Stanislavski, with a few general sideswipes at "new" theatre techniques.

_____. THE DIVINE PASTIME: THEATRE ESSAYS. New York: Macmillan, 1974.

These essays and reviews, from 1946 to 1971, are always sound and sensible, with an eye to the practical, but occasionally a trifle prosy.

Cohn, Ruby. "Book Review." MD, 11 (September 1968), 214-17.

A review of Eric Bentley's THE THEATRE OF COMMITMENT (1967) occasions a survey of Bentley's writings and an assessment of his contribution to modern theatre studies.

_____. CURRENTS IN CONTEMPORARY DRAMA. Bloomington: University of Indiana Press, 1969.

A stitching together of intelligent essays, encompassing post-war English, American, French, and German drama in rapid, often transitionless, survey fashion. Different chapters treat such topics as the "dialogue of cruelty," the hero in myth and history, and "the role and the real." This latter essay takes up where Lionel Abel left off (see above).

_____. DIALOGUE IN AMERICAN DRAMA. Bloomington: Indiana University Press, 1971.

Consists of essays focusing on the language in the plays of O'Neill, Miller, Williams, and Albee. The chapters on the plays written by novelists and poets are especially useful.

Cole, Toby, ed. PLAYWRIGHTS ON PLAYWRIGHTING: THE MEANING AND THE MAKING OF MODERN DRAMA FROM IBSEN TO IONESCO. Introd. John Gassner. New York: Hill and Wang, 1960.

In two parts: the first contains credos and manifestos; the second contains playwrights talking about their works and work processes. This, and the two collections following, are valuable sources.

Cole, Toby, and Helen Krich Chinoy, eds. DIRECTORS ON DIRECTING: A SOURCE BOOK OF THE MODERN THEATRE. With an illustrated history of directing by Helen Krich Chinoy. Indianapolis, Ind.: Bobbs-Merrill, 1963.

A revised edition of the 1953 DIRECTING THE PLAY, the volume's emphasis is on the European innovators of the early part of this century.

_____. ACTORS IN ACTING: THE THEORIES, TECHNIQUES, AND PRACTICES OF THE GREAT ACTORS OF ALL TIMES AS TOLD IN THEIR OWN WORDS. Rev. ed. New York: Crown, 1970.

Counsell, John PLAY DIRECTION: A PRACTICAL VIEWPOINT. Foreword by Sir Bernard Miles. New York: St. Martin's Press, 1973.

Brief, rather old-fashioned advice from a veteran English director about such things as rehearsal schedules and getting along with actors.

Croyden, Margaret. LUNATICS, LOVERS AND POETS: THE CONTEMPORARY EXPERIMENTAL THEATRE. New York: McGraw-Hill, 1974.

An informative critical account of the major forces of the contemporary theatrical avant-garde: the Living Theatre, Jerzy Grotowski, The Open Theatre, Peter Brook, and Happenings. The book begins with four chapters summarizing the influence of the Romantics, the surrealists, the Russians, and Antonin Artaud. The book also deals perceptively with the links between the new theatre and the changing cultural politics of the 1960s.

Davis, R.G. THE SAN FRANCISCO MIME TROUPE: THE FIRST TEN YEARS. San Francisco: Ramparts Press, 1975.

The founder of the group narrates its history, problems, and commitments.

Dennis, Nigel. DRAMATIC ESSAYS. London: Weidenfeld and Nicolson, 1962.

Discursive, dyspeptic, often witty essays from ENCOUNTER embody Dennis's preference for "illusory representation," or transformation of reality, rather than mere reproduction of reality.

Devine, George. "The Right to Fail." TWENTIETH CENTURY, 169 (February 1961), 128-32.

Devine, the artistic director of the English Stage Company, ruminates about the role of the director, and his hopes for his theatre. This dialogue with Richard Findlater captures Devine's nonprogrammatic enthusiasm for the stage.

______. "The Birth of the English Stage Company." PROMPT, 1 (Summer 1962), 6-12.

A discussion of the company's background is followed by a useful financial analysis of their first six seasons.

Donoghue, Denis. THE THIRD VOICE: MODERN BRITISH AND AMERICAN VERSE DRAMA. Princeton, N.J.: Princeton University Press, 1959.

Using Aristotle as reinterpreted by Francis Fergusson and Kenneth Burke, this is the standard exposition and defense of modern verse drama. After considering some of the many failures of verse drama in the nineteenth century, Donoghue examines in "new" critical fashion the plays of Yeats, W.H. Auden, T.S. Eliot (in six chapters), Christopher Fry, Ezra Pound, Richard Eberhardt, and Archibald Macleish.

Downer, Alan S. THE AMERICAN THEATER TODAY. New York: Basic Books, 1967.

A collection of brief essays, originally broadcast over the Voice of America.

Elsom, John. THEATRE OUTSIDE LONDON. London: Macmillan, 1971.

With a history of the modern English repertory movement, this is a valuable assessment of the role of the touring companies, local repertory theatres, and the stages they use. It also includes a sixty-page "Alphabet of Reps."

______. EROTIC THEATRE. Introd. John Trevelyan. New York: Taplinger, 1974.

An exceptionally thoughtful and provocative study of the sexual standards and implications of contemporary theatre, illuminatingly compared with the standards of the 1890s.

Esslin, Martin. REFLECTIONS: ESSAYS ON MODERN THEATRE. Garden City, N.Y.: Doubleday, 1969.

A collection notable for two essays on Brecht, "Brecht in 1969" and "Brecht and the English Theatre," which, respectively, update Esslin's 1959 critical biography of Brecht and review Brechtian productions and influences on the English stage. The English edition, called BRIEF CHRONICLES (1970), contains five additional essays on Bond, Pinter, and mass media and the drama.

______. THE THEATRE OF THE ABSURD. Rev. and updated ed. Woodstock, N.Y.: Overlook Press, 1973.

First published in 1961, and in hardcover for the first time in this edition, Esslin's study is probably the most widely read critical study of the 1960s. It introduced Beckett and Ionesco to many and popularized the sub-genre it described. A well-written and scholarly study.

Farber, Donald C. FROM OPTION TO OPENING: A GUIDE FOR THE OFF-BROADWAY PRODUCER. 2nd rev. ed. New York: DBS Publications, 1970.

Practical advice to the writer and producer, with typical option contracts and budgets, rendered out of date by the blooming of Off-Off-Broadway and Actor's Equity's control of Off Broadway. It should be supplemented by the 1970 Equity agreement with the League of Off Broadway Theatres and the Equity Showcase Code for Off-Off-Broadway productions, both of which, as of this writing, are in the process of revision and renegotiation.

Fergusson, Francis. "Beyond the Close Embrace: Speculations on the American Stage." In THE ANCHOR REVIEW, ed. Melvin J. Lasky. Garden City, N.Y.: Doubleday, 1955, pp. 189-203.

Some mildly skeptical remarks about the Off Broadway renaissance and the need to get beyond "the close embrace" of realism.

Ferlita, Ernest. THE THEATRE OF PILGRIMAGE. New York: Sheed and Ward, 1971.

Untheatrical, unpersuasive, theological essays on Eliot, Williams, and others, which argue that only the Judeo-Christian tradition has a theatre that features linear time, a search for meaning, and an open, hopeful future.

Feynman, Alberta E. "The Fetal Quality of 'Character' in Plays of the Absurd." MD, 9 (May 1966), 18-25.

The absurd theatre depends on fetal characters who lack coherent, fully human qualities. Eliminate incoherence and the plays become less opaque, less absurd.

Findlater, Richard. BANNED! A REVIEW OF THEATRICAL CENSORSHIP IN BRITAIN. London: MacGibbon & Kee, 1967.

Splendid, invaluable history of the censorship of the British stage, marred only by its missing what one hopes is the last act: the book was published just prior to the legal end of the Lord Chamberlain's power to censor.

______. "The Playwright and His Money." TQ, 2 (October-December 1972), 44-56.

This extremely informative study of the financial rewards of playwriting since Shakespeare concludes that there is persistent potential wealth for playwrights.

Flannery, James W. "Portrait of a Theatre in Its Community: The Royal Shakespeare Company of London." ETJ, 19 (October 1967), 382-91.

An observer at the Peter Hall production of Gogol's THE GOVERNMENT INSPECTOR.

Fox, John. "The Welfare State and The Cosmic Circus." TQ, 2 (October-December 1972), 3-17.

Profile of two different English "fringe" theatre groups, with a chronology, by the director of The Welfare State, one of the two groups.

Gardner, Rufus Hallette. THE SPLINTERED STAGE: THE DECLINE OF THE AMERICAN THEATER. New York: Macmillan, 1965.

A relentlessly conventional look at the American stage by a Christian journalist from Baltimore. His treatment of WHO'S AFRAID OF VIRGINIA WOOLF is typical: "a regurgitative projection of all that is despicable in man." He also presents a lengthy denunciation of Freud's influence on the drama.

Gascoigne, Bamber. "All That Glisters." SPECTATOR, 7 December 1962, p. 895.

A bracingly negative review of Tyrone Guthrie's modernized version of THE ALCHEMIST (1962).

Gassner, John. THE THEATRE IN OUR TIMES: A SURVEY OF THE MEN, MATERIALS AND MOVEMENTS IN THE MODERN THEATRE. New York: Crown, 1954.

A substantial collection of essays and reviews, valuable for its cumulative good sense and scholarly perspective.

______. DIRECTIONS IN MODERN THEATRE AND DRAMA. New York: Holt, Rinehart and Winston, 1965.

This is an expanded version of Gassner's FORM AND IDEA IN MODERN THEATRE (1956). Following historical sequence, the book is a collection of essays by Gassner and others, detailing the many modes of experimentation the theatre has seen since the heyday of realism. This is a conventional study, with sound critical material but very few surprises.

Gatting, Charles, Jr. "Artaud and the Participatory Drama of the New Generation." ETJ, 20 (December 1968), 485-91.

A breathless recitation of Artaud's influence on Off-Off-Broadway.

Gilman, Richard. THE CONFUSION OF REALMS. New York: Random House, 1970.

Fourteen essays ranging across the current cultural scene, from the most persuasive drama critic of the time. Of particular interest are his views of MACBIRD, the Living Theatre, and the differences between stage and film.

_____. COMMON AND UNCOMMON MASKS: WRITINGS ON THEATRE 1961-1970. New York: Random House, 1971.

Gilman is a sensitive, unobtrusive stylist whose intelligence and erudition have enabled him to make the transition from reviewer to critic.

_____. THE MAKING OF MODERN DRAMA: A STUDY OF BUCHNER, IBSEN, STRINDBERG, CHEKHOV, PIRANDELLO, BRECHT, BECKETT, HANDKE. New York: Farrar, Straus and Giroux, 1974.

Intelligent interpretive essays on eight modern dramatists, focusing on the aesthetic shaping of the drama unique to each writer.

Goffman, Erving. THE PRESENTATION OF SELF IN EVERDAY LIFE. Garden City, N.Y.: Doubleday, 1959.

This sociology text has been widely used to demonstrate the general applicability of the concept of performance. The text is an expanded version of a monograph published at the Social Science Research Centre at the University of Edinburgh in 1956.

Golden, Joseph. THE DEATH OF TINKER BELL: THE AMERICAN THEATRE IN THE 20TH CENTURY. Syracuse, N.Y.: Syracuse University Press, 1967.

Rather abstract strictures on the lack of an affirmative American drama.

Goldman, William. THE SEASON: A CANDID LOOK AT BROADWAY. New York: Harcourt, Brace and World, 1969.

A frank, argumentative, caustic autopsy of the 1967-68 Broadway season. Goldman's critical judgments--for example, that Pinter has only snob appeal--are less valuable than his exuberant journalistic account of Broadway's multiple lunacies during one season.

Goodlad, J.S.R. A SOCIOLOGY OF POPULAR DRAMA. London: Heinemann, 1971.

Primarily about television.

Gorelik, Moredecai. "The Absurd Absurdists." NEW YORK TIMES, 6 August 1967, Sec. 2, pp. 1, 3.

A distinguished theatre historian argues that the absurdist vision is merely private and dramatically simplistic. Martin Esslin responded two weeks later in the same section.

Gottfried, Martin. A THEATRE DIVIDED: THE POST-WAR AMERICAN STAGE. Boston: Little, Brown, 1967.

Emphatically a book with a thesis: that the American stage is divisible into a left wing (liberal, uncommercial, and unprofessional) and a right wing (conservative, commercial, and professional) and that these two equally valuable wings of the stage are out of touch with each other.

Gottlieb, Saul. "The Living Theatre in Exile: MYSTERIES, FRANKENSTEIN." TDR, 10 (Summer 1966), 137-52.

A brief account of the travels of the Living Theatre after its tax troubles in New York is accompanied by summaries of two of the works developed abroad.

______. "Awkwardness is Not a Bad Thing: An Interview with Sydney Walter and Marlow Hotchkiss of the Firehouse Theatre of Minneapolis." TDR, 14 (Fall 1969), 121-27.

Interview concerning one of the most experimental of the American regional theatres.

Greenberger, Howard. THE OFF-BROADWAY EXPERIENCE. Englewood Cliffs, N.J.: Prentice-Hall, 1971.

A brief history of Off Broadway going back to the Washington Square Players prefaces a collection of interviews with a producer, director, actor, actress, designer, and others, most of whom no longer work in Off Broadway theatre.

Greenfeld, Josh. "La Mama Experimental Theatre Club, 1967." In EFFECTIVE THEATRE: A STUDY WITH DOCUMENTATION. Ed. John Russell Brown. London: Heinemann, 1969, pp. 163-68.

This 1967 article from the NEW YORK TIMES MAGAZINE graphically describes the theatre's physical and financial situation in mid-1967.

Grotowski, Jerzy. TOWARDS A POOR THEATRE. Several translators, with a preface by Peter Brook. New York: Simon and Schuster, 1968.

A collection of fourteen essays, speeches, reports, and interviews by and about Grotowski and his Polish Laboratory Theatre, this is an exceptionally influential volume. Crucial to his theories is the belief that the theatre must redevote itself to its peculiar essence, the actor-audience relationship, and cease attempting to imitate television and film.

______. "Holiday." Trans. B. Taborski. TQ, 3 (April-June 1973), 19-24.

Based on a shorthand version of a conference at New York University in December 1970. Grotowski talks about the meaning of human actions in and out of theatre and about his relationship to Stanislavski. The article concludes with a checklist of Grotowski's work.

Guthrie, Tyrone. IN VARIOUS DIRECTIONS: A VIEW OF THEATRE. London: Collier-Macmillan; New York: Macmillan, 1965.

A collection of undated essays, introductions, and portraits, with illustrations of some of his productions.

Hainaux, Rene, comp. STAGE DESIGN THROUGHOUT THE WORLD SINCE 1950. Foreword by Paul-Louis Mignon. New York: Theatre Arts Books, 1964.

Text and illustration collected by the national centers of the International Theatre Institute, chosen and presented by Rene Hainaux, with the technical advice of Yves-Bonnat.

______. STAGE DESIGN THROUGHOUT THE WORLD SINCE 1960. New York: Theatre Arts Books, 1973.

Hall, Peter. "The Director and the Permanent Company." In THEATRE AT WORK. Ed. Charles Marowitz and Simon Trussler. London: Methuen, 1967, pp. 148-59.

In an interview with Charles Marowitz, the former director of the Royal Shakespeare Company describes his working methods, with examples from his Shakespeare and Pinter productions.

______. "Is the Beginning the Word?" TQ, 2 (July-September 1972), 5-11.

In this condensed version of a lecture at the Institute of the Contemporary Arts, Hall argues that the essence of theatre is not the word but something almost unanalyzable: performance, unique and communicative.

Hammond, Jonathan. "A Potted History of the Fringe." TQ, 3 (October-December 1973), 37-46.

A valuable history of the English Fringe theatres that gets bogged down trying to list everyone's work. It includes a chronological survey of events and groups influential in the development of the Fringe.

Hardwick, Elizabeth. "The Disaster at Lincoln Center." NYRB, 2 April 1964, pp. 1-3.

A denunciation of the first season of the Lincoln Center repertory company that claims its failure and that of the American theatre in general is due to the theatre's general inability to view drama as a branch of literature.

Harrap, John. "University Theatre USA: Success and Failure." TQ, 3 (April-June 1973), 67-78.

A thoughtful survey of the drama programs at large American universities and their relationship to the professional theatre.

Hartley, Anthony. "Contemporary Arts." SPECTATOR, 21 September 1956, p. 383.

An estimate of the Berliner Ensemble's influential London visit.

Hayes, Richard. "Plays and Publishers." PROMPT, no. 9 (1967), 7-9.

Three of the leading English publishers of new plays respond to a questionaire about the size of editions, whether they publish unsolicited manuscripts or manuscripts of unperformed plays, and whether play publication is for profit or prestige; the consensus is that the answer is profit.

Hayman, Ronald. JOHN GIELGUD. New York: Random House, 1971.

An easygoing straightforward biography without much psychological analysis. The volume includes a valuable chronological table of Gielgud's roles and productions.

______. "Subsidy: Its Effects on Policy and People at the National Theatre and RSC." TQ, 2 (April-June 1972), 63-71.

This extremely informative article details the significant changes in the English theatre made by the development of the National Theatre led by Sir Laurence Olivier and the Royal Shakespeare Company led by Peter Hall. Subjects considered are casting, repertory, the differences between the two companies, the threat they pose to the commercial theatre, and, above all, the problems of money.

______. "The Royal Court 1956-1972." DRAMA, n.s. 105 (Summer 1972), 45-53.

Surveys the English Stage Company's work, emphasizing its role as a theatre for new playwrights.

______. PLAYBACK. London: Davis-Poynter, 1973.

Ten interviews and essays, six of which appeared in shortened versions in the London TIMES, with such contemporary theatre figures as Peter Brook, David Storey, Paul Scofield, Laurence Olivier, John Gielgud, and Noel Coward.

______. PLAYBACK 2: ESSAYS, INTERVIEWS. London: Davis-Poynter, 1973.

Arthur Miller, Peter Cook and Dudley Moore, Alec Guinness, Peter Nichols, Arnold Wesker and John Dexter, Michael Hodern, Maggie Smith and Robert Stephens, and David Mercer are interviewed.

______. THE SET-UP: AN ANATOMY OF THE ENGLISH THEATRE TODAY. London: Eyre and Methuen, 1973.

With chapters on the two subsidized companies (National Theatre and Royal Shakespeare Company), the Royal Court, unions, agents, and actor training, this admirably factual and low-key study gives an accurate picture of the practical realities of the contemporary English stage.

Haynes, Jim. "The Traverse--Edinburgh." PROMPT, no. 6 (1965), 32-33.

The director of the Traverse theatre discusses the group's beginnings.

Hays, H.R. "Transcending Naturalism." MD, 5 (May 1962), 27-36.

A casual survey of the varying responses to naturalism among the new British dramatists.

Heilman, Robert Bechtold. THE ICEMAN, THE ARSONIST, AND THE TROUBLED AGENT: TRAGEDY AND MELODRAMA ON THE MODERN STAGE. Seattle: University of Washington Press, 1973.

This book applies the principles of the author's TRAGEDY AND MELODRAMA (1968) to the modern stage, especially to modern versions of traditional genres, with his definition and defense of melodrama of particular interest.

Hennessy, Brendan. "London's Theatre of the Fringe." G, 4, no. 16, pp. 110-22.

A guide to the club-fringe theatres, giving background details, stage dimensions, finances, repertory, memberships, and plans for ten such organizations.

Hinchcliffe, Arnold P. BRITISH THEATRE 1950-1970. Oxford: Basil Blackwell, 1974.

For a detailed review see Malcolm Page's analysis in the December 1975 issue of MD (vol. 18, pp. 409-11).

Howard, Richard. ALONE WITH AMERICA: ESSAYS ON THE ART OF POETRY IN THE UNITED STATES SINCE 1950. New York: Atheneum, 1971.

Valuable for its treatments of the many poet-playwrights.

Hughes, Catherine. PLAYS, POLITICS AND POLEMICS. New York: Drama Book Specialists, 1973.

Thin treatment of an excellent subject: the contemporary political stage.

Jackson, Esther M. "American Theatre in the Sixties: The Drama of Internal Crisis." PL, 48 (Summer 1973), 236-49.

The Living Theatre, following the surrealists, developed a theatrical style expressive of the crisis of consciousness of the West in the twentieth century.

Jones, D.A.N. "Silent Censorship in Britain." TQ, 1 (January-March 1971), 22-28.

A mild attack upon the power and conventionality of British commercial producers.

Jones, David E., ed. "A Symposium to Mark the Opening of the Tyrone Guthrie Repertory Theatre." DS, 3 (May 1963), 69-116.

Ten articles about Tyrone Guthrie and his repertory theatre.

Joseph, Stephen. NEW THEATRE FORMS. New York: Theatre Arts Books, 1968.

Brief, amply illustrated, readable survey of three major nonproscenium stage forms: center or round, thrust, and end stages.

Kaplan, Donald M. "Homosexuality and the American Theatre: A Psychoanalytic Comment." TDR, 9 (Spring 1965), 25-55.

A turgid study of the links between the actor and the homosexual, filled with some astonishing generalities about both.

______. "On Grotowski." TDR, 14 (Winter 1970), 197-99.

Jerzy Grotowski, Kaplan asserts, is a Skinnerian neobehaviorist whose obsession with the physical half of a performance diminishes his understanding of the mental aspect of the theatre.

Kaprow, Allen. "Self-Service: A Happening." TDR, 12 (Spring 1968), 160-64.

Scenario for a "happening" that was performed in the summer of 1967. It is prefaced by an interview with Richard Schechner in which both defend "happenings."

Kaufmann, Stanley. "Drama on the TIMES: Experience and Observations." NEW AMERICAN REVIEW, 1 (September 1967), 30-49.

Kaufmann reflects on his eight-month tenure as drama reviewer for the NEW YORK TIMES. He provides provocative insights into the many aspects of the relationship between the newspaper critic and the American theatre, going far beyond the usual cliches about the reviewers' power to determine a play's fate.

_____. PERSONS OF THE DRAMA: THEATER CRITICISM AND COMMENT. New York: Harper and Row, 1976.

Thoughtful, unregenerately intellectual and erudite, Kaufmann surveys the late 1960s and early 1970s in this collection of reviews and essays. Particularly valuable are his essays on the history of repertory, on homosexuality in the theatre, and on the career of Joseph Papp.

Kennedy, Andrew K. SIX DRAMATISTS IN SEARCH OF A LANGUAGE: STUDIES IN DRAMATIC LANGUAGE. Cambridge, Engl.: Cambridge University Press, 1975.

This scholarly study examines the various strategies adopted by Shaw, Eliot, Beckett, Pinter, Osborne, and Arden to deal with the crisis of theatre language implicit in the widespread rejection of purely naturalistic drama. Kennedy's approach is through linguistic and textual analysis; his introduction is an excellent treatment of the general problems of language in the modern theatre. The study includes internal documentation and a fine bibliography.

Kermode, Frank. "Lear at Lincoln Center." NYRB, 25 June 1964, pp. 4-5.

While acknowledging the imagination and intelligence of the 1964 Brook-Scofield production of KING LEAR, Kermode is critical of the "provincialism" of Brook's "directorial wantoness" in meddling with the text.

Kerr, Walter. HOW NOT TO WRITE A PLAY. New York: Simon and Schuster, 1955.

The post-Ibsen theatre of ideas has, because of its too predictable social earnestness, become dangerously unpopular.

______. PIECES AT EIGHT. New York: Simon and Schuster, 1957.

Essays on miscellaneous theatre themes.

______. THE THEATER IN SPITE OF ITSELF. New York: Simon and Schuster, 1963.

Kerr is eminently readable and vividly descriptive of the performance he is reviewing. He is, however, instinctively antagonistic toward both intellectual and avant-garde theatre. Perhaps as a result of these antagonisms, he was, from the mid-1950s through the end of the 1960s, the most popular American theatre reviewer.

______. TRAGEDY AND COMEDY. New York: Simon and Schuster, 1967.

Essays in definition.

______. THIRTY PLAYS HATH NOVEMBER: PAIN AND PLEASURE IN THE CONTEMPORARY THEATER. New York: Simon and Schuster, 1969.

More collected reviews.

______. GOD ON THE GYMNASIUM FLOOR AND OTHER THEATRICAL ADVENTURES. New York: Simon and Schuster, 1971.

More reviews, along with a lengthy essay on Harold Pinter, which was also published separately by Columbia University Press in 1967.

Kirby, E.T., ed. TOTAL THEATRE: A CRITICAL ANTHOLOGY. New York: E.P. Dutton, 1969.

An excellent collection of primary and scholarly secondary sources on the theme of theatre as Gesamtkunstwerk. It includes essays by and about Adolph Appia, Richard Wagner, Filippo Marinetti and the Futurists, the Oriental stage, Vsevolod Meyerhold, Gordon Craig, and other authors and subjects. The book provides a valuable background for an understanding of the various nonrepresentational and antiliterary movements in contemporary theatre.

Kirby, Michael. "The Uses of Film in the New Theatre." TDR, 11 (Fall 1966), 49-61.

A description, with illustrations, of multi-media experimentation in the theatres and such places as the 1964 New York World's Fair. This entire issue of TDR is devoted to the relationship between the stage and film.

Kitchin, Laurence. MID-CENTURY DRAMA. 2nd rev. ed. London: Faber and Faber, 1962.

Focusing on the purported decline of classical English acting, this is a quirky survey of the English stage during the late 1950s. Kitchin refers to Artaud's theories as "advocated in the heyday of Fascism by an insane author." The second half of the volume is a series of interviews from the London TIMES.

______. DRAMA IN THE SIXTIES: FORM AND INTERPRETATION. London: Faber and Faber, 1966.

A collection of short radio lectures and essays unified in part by the argument that contemporary drama is of two major kinds: epic, largely influenced by Brecht; and compressionistic, best illustrated by Beckett and THE BRIG (1963).

Knapp, Bettina. ANTONIN ARTAUD: MAN OF VISION. New York: David Lewis, 1969.

Overwritten and overly enthusiastic; see the Winter 1971, volume 1 issue of DIACRITICS, pages 21-26 for Eric Sellin's detailed analysis.

Kostelanetz, Richard. "With the Force of a Plague." PROMPT, no. 7 (1966), 22-26.

On the Living Theatre productions of THE BRIG (1963) and THE CONNECTION (1959), emphasizing the creative contribution of the director.

______. THE THEATRE OF MIXED MEANS: AN INTRODUCTION TO HAPPENINGS, KINETIC ENVIRONMENTS, AND OTHER MIXED-MEANS PERFORMANCES. New York: Dial Press, 1968.

Nine lengthy interviews with the creators of various forms of mixed-media theatre (John Cage, Allan Kaprow, Claes Oldenberg) prefaced by three chapters and an introduction giving a background primarily based in art history.

Laban, Frederick. THE MASTERY OF MOVEMENT ON THE STAGE. Rev. ed. London: Macdonald and Evans, 1960.

Laban's theories of movement and its notation, called choreutics, have given a new emphasis to the actor's physical presence on the stage.

Lahr, John. UP AGAINST THE FOURTH WALL: ESSAYS ON MODERN THEATER. New York: Grove Press, 1970.

Lively reviews from ER, marked by great enthusiasm for experimental theatre.

_____. ASTONISH ME: ADVENTURES IN CONTEMPORARY THEATER. New York: Viking, 1973.

Lahr, as usual, relates the theatre to current political and cultural trends far more than any other contemporary reviewer.

Lahr, John, and Jonathan Price. LIFE-SHOW: HOW TO SEE THEATER IN LIFE AND LIFE IN THEATER. Designed by Stephanie Tevonian. New York: Viking, 1973.

Extremely discursive essays, interspersed with a wide variety of illustrations, on the basic elements of theater and how they are connected to life, the self, and society.

Lambert, J.W. DRAMA IN BRITAIN 1964-1973. London: Longmans, 1974.

Brief, lively survey.

Lewis, Allan. AMERICAN PLAYS AND PLAYWRIGHTS OF THE CONTEMPORARY THEATRE. Rev. ed. New York: Crown, 1970.

This stodgy survey is best typified by its assessment of Martha in WHO'S AFRAID OF VIRGINIA WOOLF as "contemptible," "depraved," and "disgusting."

Lewis, Robert. "Emotional Memory." TDR, 6 (June 1962), 54-60.

A clear statement of the Method technique of acting.

Little, Stuart W. ENTER JOSEPH PAPP: IN SEARCH OF A NEW AMERICAN THEATRE. New York: Coward, McCann and Geoghegan, 1974.

An uncritical biography of the most powerful producer in the current American theatre.

Little, Stuart W., and Arthur Cantor. THE PLAYMAKERS. New York: W.W. Norton, 1970.

A chatty, informal look at the life of Broadway producers, directors, press agents, critics, and actors.

Littlewood, Joan. "Plays for the People." WORLD THEATRE, 8 (Winter 1959-60), 283-90.

A plea for a popular theatre with social purpose.

Littlewood, Joan, and Cedric Price. "The Fun Palace." TDR, 12 (Spring 1968), 127-34.

Plans and programs for an ambitious "laboratory of pleasure," sponsored by Buckminster Fuller, Joan Littlewood and others. The plans were finally abandoned, but they are a combination of technology, environmental theatre, and sheer fantasy.

Lumley, Frederick. NEW TRENDS IN 20TH CENTURY DRAMA: A SURVEY SINCE IBSEN AND SHAW. 4th rev. ed. New York: Oxford University Press, 1972.

A relatively sophisticated survey of dramatic literature, which sees its emphasis as verbal and intellectual, not physical or theatrical.

McCarthy, Mary. MARY McCARTHY'S THEATRE CHRONICLES 1937-1962. New York: Noonday, 1963.

This collection of essays and reviews includes several already published in her SIGHTS AND SPECTACLES (1956), as well as later material. McCarthy's views are those of a none-too-frequent visitor to the theatre, but they are expressed with enviable authority. Her attack upon Kenneth Tynan's CURTAINS (1961) is particularly effective.

MacColl, Ewan. "Grass Roots of Theatre Workshop." TQ, 3 (January-March 1973), 58-68.

MacColl recounts the agitprop activities of Joan Littlewood and himself in the 1930s that were the basis of much of the Theatre Workshop's later efforts.

McCrindle, Joseph F.M., ed. BEHIND THE SCENES: THEATER AND FILM INTERVIEWS FROM THE TRANSATLANTIC REVIEW. Introd. Jean-Claude Van Itallie. New York: Holt, Rinehart and Winston, 1971.

A collection of consistently well-informed interviews; those with Ellen Stewart of La Mama, Kenneth Tynan, and Joan Littlewood are particularly notable.

McNeely, Jerry C. "Atkinson in Immediate Retrospect." ETJ, 13 (1961), 250-58.

An evaluation of Brooks Atkinson who, during most of his lengthy tenure as drama critic for the NEW YORK TIMES, was the most influential American newspaper critic. In the late 1950s that honor began to pass to Walter Kerr.

Malina, Judith. THE ENORMOUS DESPAIR. New York: Random House, 1972.

An allusive, fragmentary diary of the Living Theatre's American tour from 31 Aug. 1968 to 3 April 1969. The book is filled with accounts of meetings with old friends and conflicts over revolutionary tactics, but there are no analyses of performances or the philosophy related to them.

Malina, Judith, and Julian Beck. PARADISE NOW: COLLECTIVE CREATION OF THE LIVING THEATRE, WRITTEN DOWN BY JUDITH MALINA AND JULIAN BECK. Photos by Gianfranco Mantegna. New York: Random House, 1971.

This is the play that was the thematic center of the Living Theatre's return to America. It is a voyage to nonviolent anarchist revolution on wings of occult erudition. Its tone is perhaps best captured in the description of the play's first "Flashout": "Whenever this happens in the play, the actor by the force of his art approaches a transcendent moment in which he is released from all the hangups of the present situation." The book is a record of a major theatrical event.

Malpede, Karen, ed. THREE WORKS BY THE OPEN THEATER. New York: Drama Book Specialists, 1974.

This handsome volume contains the script for TERMINAL, and dialogue for THE MUTATION SHOW and NIGHTWALK, and a lavish portfolio of photographs that are at least as revelatory of the company's work as the texts they surround. The book also includes Alex Gildzen's fine bibliography.

Mandel, Oscar. "Reactionary Notes on the Experimental Theatre." MR, 11 (Winter 1970), 101-16.

Curmudgeonly remarks on thrust staging, theatre as ritual, nudity, and literacy in the theatre.

Mander, John. THE WRITER AND COMMITMENT. London: Secker and Warburg, 1961.

A provocative survey of British left literature from Auden through Orwell, to Osborne and Wesker, with a brief look at Miller's DEATH OF A SALESMAN (1949). Mander's distinction between Socialist and working-class literature is of considerable value.

Mander, Raymond, and Joe Mitchenson. THE THEATRE OF LONDON. Illus. Timothy Birdsell. London: Rupert Hart-Davis, 1961.

A history of fifty-seven London theatres, their ownerships, and the plays produced there, this is an absolutely invaluable and, to anyone interested in British theatre history, utterly charming book.

Marowitz, Charles. "If We Protest Fakery." VV, 4 January 1956, p. 7.

The Off Broadway theatre is threatened by the vapid goodwill of reviewers refusing to apply mature critical standards to the new theatre.

______. "Ionesco Rides Again." VV, 31 July 1957, p. 7.

Ionesco is "the only genuine tragedian the modern theatre has produced."

______. "Artaud at Rodez." TQ, 2 (April-June 1972), 58-62.

A detailed, sympathetic portrait of Artaud's last years, when he was in and out of psychiatric hospitals. Marowitz sees Artaud's incarceration, his sufferings, and the indifference of society as the grotesquely logical climax of Artaud's precarious career as genius and madman.

______. CONFESSIONS OF A COUNTERFEIT CRITIC. London: Methuen, 1972.

Critical collection.

Marowitz, Charles, Tom Milne, and Owen Hale, eds. THE ENCORE READER: A CHRONICLE OF THE NEW DRAMA. Foreword by Richard Findlater. London: Methuen, 1965.

An indispensible collection of essays and reviews from ENCORE, the most provocative of English theatre periodicals. The collection is in five sections: (1) "Murmurs from Abroad"; (2) "Rumbles of Discontent"; (3) "The Good Years"; (4) "Continental Influence"; and (5) "Harbingers of Failure." This often partisan volume provides the most readable, if not the most dispassionate conspectus of the English stage, 1956-1963, with a "London Diary" of significant openings during this period. For a more jaundiced view of the periodical's political and social biases, see Robert Brustein's "The English Stage," in his THE THIRD THEATRE, above.

Marowitz, Charles, and Simon Trussler, eds. THEATRE AT WORK: PLAYWRIGHTS AND PRODUCTIONS IN THE MODERN BRITISH THEATRE. London: Methuen, 1967.

The volume's first half consists of interviews with John Whiting, John Arden, Robert Bolt, Arnold Wesker, and Harold Pinter. The second features six reports on specific productions, most notably the Brook KING LEAR and the 1964 Theatre of Cruelty season of the Royal Shakespeare Company. The interviews and the production reports are on consistently high level, with useful introductory material for each item, and its provenance.

Maschler, Tom, ed. DECLARATION. London: MacGibbon & Kee, 1957.

This collection of credos by Doris Lessing, Colin Wilson, John Osborne, John Wain, Kenneth Tynan, Bill Hopkins, Lindsy Anderson, and Stuart Holroyd is a good sampling of the intellectual ferment in England in the fifties.

Mayer, Martin. BRICKS, MORTAR AND THE PERFORMING ARTS. New York: Twentieth Century Fund, 1970.

A ninety-nine page survey of the economics of performing arts centers.

Mee, Charles L., Jr. "Off-Broadway: A Limited Engagement." TDR, 10 (Autumn 1968), 78-87.

This interview with Off Broadway producer Judith R. Marcheal details some of the financial difficulties that were soon to create Off-Off-Broadway.

Moore, Sonia. TRAINING AN ACTOR: THE STANISLAVSKI SYSTEM IN CLASS. New York: Viking, 1968.

These twenty-four classes, prepared from tapes, concentrate on the first two of the four years needed to assimilate the Stanislavski system, "the only concrete professional acting technique."

Munk, Erica, ed. STANISLAVSKI AND AMERICA. New York: Hill and Wang, 1966.

A splendid collection of pieces from the two 1964 Stanislavski issues of TRD (vol. 9, nos. 1 and 2).

Nardin, James T. "The Renaissance of American Drama." MD, 1 (September 1958), 116-24.

Television's phenomenal popularity will provide a new impetus to the drama and may soon give birth to a drama of the stature of OTHELLO.

Neff, Renfreu. THE LIVING THEATRE: USA. Photographs by Gianfranco Mantegna. Indianapolis: Bobbs-Merrill, 1970.

An often awkward travelogue of the 1968-69 American tour of the Living Theatre, with some interesting details about varying audience responses to the group's apocalyptic politics.

Novick, Julius. BEYOND BROADWAY: THE QUEST FOR PERMANENT THEATRES. 2nd ed. New York: Hill and Wang, 1969.

An excellent survey of the resident professional companies around the United States that provides the best picture of the "repertory" movement in the late sixties.

Oliver, William I. "The Censor in the Ivy." TDR, 15 (Fall 1970), 31-55.

Censorship, both political and sexual, in university theatre is described and decried.

Pasoli, Robert. "The New Playwrights' Scene of the Sixties." TDR, 13 (Fall 1968), 150-62.

Experimental Off-Off-Broadway is largely a myth; most playwrights see it as only a stepping stone to a Broadway success. The article contains a valuable chart of twenty-three OOB playhouses, with financial, advertising, and physical data.

______. A BOOK ON THE OPEN THEATRE. Indianapolis: Bobbs-Merrill, 1970.

A sympathetic description of Joseph Chaikin's Open Theatre, its history, internal dynamics, exercises, performances, and philosophy.

Poggi, Jack. THEATRE IN AMERICA: THE IMPACT OF ECONOMIC FORCES: 1870-1967. Ithaca, N.Y.: Cornell University Press, 1968.

Poland, Albert, and Bruce Mailman, eds. THE OFF OFF BROADWAY BOOK: THE PLAYS, PEOPLE, THEATRE. Indianapolis: Bobbs-Merrill, 1972.

In addition to the texts of thirty-seven plays, this useful collection includes three bibliographies and a unique listing of productions at seventeen of the more important Off-Off-Broadway theatres.

Prior, Allan. "The Role of the Television Dramatist." TQ, 1 (January-March 1971), 10-14.

Optimistic views on television drama from the author of over twenty original television plays. He contrasts the continuing success of the British product with the disasterous collapse of American television writing after the industry left New York.

Pronko, Leonard Cabell. THEATER EAST AND WEST: PERSPECTIVES TOWARD A TOTAL THEATER. Berkeley: University of California Press, 1967.

A valuable study of the theatre of the East--Bali, China, and Japan--in themselves and as a source of enrichment for the Western stage.

Rahv, Philip. "With It." NYRB, 4 June 1970, pp. 57-59.

An attack on Richard Gilman's THE CONFUSION OF REALMS, above, particularly the political writing, for "incorrigible trendiness."

Reiss, Alvin H. "Who Builds Theatres and Why?" TDR, 12 (Spring 1968), 75-92.

Using the Lincoln Center complex as a model, Reiss examines the vagaries of the planning and financing behind hundreds of cultural centers developed in the sixties.

Rogoff, Gordon. "Richard's Himself Again." TRD, 11 (Winter 1966), 29-40.

A survey of English theatre from 1956 to 1966, seeing at its center the figure of Sir Laurence Olivier, actor and director.

Roose-Evans, James. EXPERIMENTAL THEATER FROM STANISLAVSKI TO TODAY. Rev. ed. New York: Universe Books, 1973.

A slender, well-illustrated volume that is particularly strong on the theatrical impact of such figures as Martha Graham and Alwin Nikolais.

Rossi, Alfred. MINNEAPOLIS REHEARSALS: TYRONE GUTHRIE DIRECTS HAMLET. Berkeley: University of California Press, 1970.

An account of the 1963 HAMLET starring George Grizzard at the Tyrone Guthrie Theatre in Minneapolis, with the promptscript, photographs, and reviews.

Rowell, Kenneth. STAGE DESIGN. London: Studio Vista, 1968.

A brief and somewhat vague history of international stage design in this century and an assessment of contemporary trends. It also includes a glossary of technical terms in both English and American usage.

Rundall, Jeremy. "New Sap for the Withered Tree." TDR, 11 (Winter 1966), 132-37.

A too-brief survey of the English provincial theatres that argues a rural renaissance beginning in 1956 similar to the one effected at the Royal Court.

Sainer, Arthur. THE RADICAL THEATRE NOTEBOOK. New York: Avon, 1975.

This collection of scripts, dialogues, and notes from several ensemble performing groups is largely uncritical, but its very lack of selection results in an intriguing cross-section of groups, some talented, some not. No index.

Saint-Denis, Michael. THEATRE: THE REDISCOVERY OF STYLE. London: Heinemann, 1960.

Five lectures by the distinguished director on style, realism, and theatre education.

Schechner, Richard. PUBLIC DOMAIN: ESSAYS ON THE THEATRE. New York: Bobbs-Merrill, 1969.

These essays and editorials, written while Schechner was editor of TDR during the 1960s, are a good sampling of his most influential writing. His stance is polemical, antiliterary, but intellectual, with an emphasis on theories of performance.

______. ENVIRONMENTAL THEATER. New York: Hawthorne, 1973.

Essays on theatre designs that change to suit the appropriate relationship between a given play and its audience.

______, ed. DIONYSUS IN 69/THE PERFORMANCE GROUP. New York: Farrar, Straus and Giroux, 1970.

Text, photographs, and commentary blend to give a vivid impression of Schechner's attempt to put his theories into practice.

Schevill, James, ed. BREAK OUT!: IN SEARCH OF NEW THEATRICAL ENVIRONMENTS. Chicago: Swallow, 1973.

A splendid though somewhat eccentric anthology of playlets and critical writings on aspects of contemporary theatre, interspersed with extensive commentary by Schevill.

Schmidt, Sandra, comp. "Regional Theatre: Some Statistics." TDR, 10 (Autumn 1965), 50-61.

This valuable compilation of such data as seating capacity, type of stage, number and percentage of Equity actors, budget and deficit, and salaries is a useful companion to Novick's book (see above).

Schneider, Alan. "The Director as Dogsbody." In THEATRE 4: THE AMERICAN THEATRE 1970-1971. Ed. Martha Wordsworth Coigney. New York: International Theatre Institute, 1971.

Reminiscences by the director of Albee and Beckett.

Selden, Samuel. THEATRE DOUBLE GAME. Chapel Hill: University of North Carolina Press, 1969.

An academic analysis of the relationship between play and playgoer.

Seymour, Alan. "The Play-Reader, the Playwright, and His Petty Humiliations." TQ, 3 (October-December 1973), 25-35.

Anecdotal recounting of the problems of a playwright-playreader.

Shank, Theodore. THE ART OF DRAMATIC ART. Foreword by Martin Esslin. Belmont, Calif.: Dickenson Publishing, 1969.

An aesthetic for the drama that rather abstractly emphasizes the uniqueness of every performance and the necessity of dramatic illusion. Shank also challenges the common assumption that drama is a fusion of many arts.

Sherek, Henry. NOT IN FRONT OF THE CHILDREN. London: Heinemann, 1959.

Memoirs of the producer of T.S. Eliot's last three plays.

Simon, John. ACID TEST. Intro. Dwight MacDonald. New York: Stein and Day, 1963.

Reviews of film, books, poetry, fine arts, criticism, and theatre. Three New York theatre seasons, fall 1960 to fall 1962, are summarized with intelligence and indignation. Simon's often intrusive erudition is at its best in a demolition of George Steiner's THE DEATH OF TRAGEDY.

_____. UNEASY STAGES: A CHRONICLE OF THE NEW YORK THEATER, 1963-1973. New York: Random House, 1975.

Simon's reviews, mostly of conventional Broadway fare, are intelligent, acidulous, and feature a diction often sesquipedalian.

Smith, A.C.H. ORGHAST AT PERSEPOLIS. New York: Viking, 1973.

Although outside the chronological limits of this guide, this book is a first-hand account of what was in many ways the climax to a decade of international theatre experiments: Peter Brook's ORGHAST at the 1971 Shiraz Festival in Iran.

Smith, Michael. "The Good Scene: Off Off-Broadway." TDR, 10 (Summer 1966), 159-76.

A survey of the origins and main exponents of the OOB stage: Cafe Cino, La Mama, the Open Theatre, the Judson's Poet's Theatre, and Theatre Genesis.

_____. THEATRE TRIP. Introd. Judith Malina and Julian Beck. Indianapolis: Bobbs-Merrill, 1969.

Rambling travel diary, with articles and interviews, of a journey to Europe, focusing on the Living Theatre in exile from New York in the fall of 1966.

Sontag, Susan. AGAINST INTERPRETATION, AND OTHER ESSAYS. New York: Farrar, Straus and Giroux, 1966.

This extremely influential collection includes essay-reviews on such works as AFTER THE FALL, THE DEPUTY, MARAT/SADE, and Abel's METATHEATRE.

_____. "Theatre and Film." In her STYLES OF RADICAL WILL. New York: Farrar, Straus and Giroux, 1969, pp. 99-122.

Written primarily from a cinematic perspective, this essay explores both the theatre's initial influence on film and the growing dominance of film over theatre in popular culture. Whether film and theatre should be rigorously purified of each other or should be fused is an unresolved question for Sontag. The book, with only one of its essays about theatre, is dedicated to director Joseph Chaikin.

Spanos, William V. THE CHRISTIAN TRADITION IN MODERN BRITISH VERSE DRAMA: THE POETICS OF SACRAMENTAL TIME. Foreword by E. Martin Browne. New Brunswick, N.J.: Rutgers University Press, 1967.

Argues that British verse drama was a response to the same cultural phenomena that led to Beckett and the Theatre of the Absurd. The verse dramatists were all "seeking to reintegrate the dissociated sensibility . . . of modern life" by a sacramental aesthetic based on the Christian Incarnation of the Son of God as a man.

Spolin, Viola. IMPROVISATION FOR THE THEATER: A HANDBOOK OF TEACHING AND DIRECTING TECHNIQUES. Evanston, Ill.: Northwestern University Press, 1963.

Despite some occasional verbal infelicities, this is an important collection of exercises and techniques for actors by one of America's most important teachers of acting. Spolin's theatre games have been particularly influential for those interested in alternatives to the method.

Spurling, Hilary. "Angry Middle Age." SPECTATOR, 15 April 1966, p. 467.

Suggests that the English Stage Company at the Royal Court has become, after ten years, the "establishment" it once so gleefully attacked.

______. "Tynan's Progress." SPECTATOR, 7 October 1966, pp. 451-52.

A positive assessment of Tynan's first three years as literary advisor to the National Theatre.

Stein, Karen F. "Metaphysical Silence in Absurd Drama." MD, 13 (February 1971), 423-31.

A survey of the dramatic uses and philosophical implications of silence in the works of Beckett, Pinter, Ionesco, and Vian.

Stynan, J.L. THE ELEMENTS OF DRAMA. Cambridge, Engl.: Cambridge University Press, 1960.

This admirable guide emphasizes the play itself and its reality in front of an audience. The clarity and force of Stynan's work enhanced by the evident good sense of the textual analyses are used to illustrate the various facets of the drama.

______. "Television Drama." In CONTEMPORARY THEATRE. Eds. John Russell Brown and Bernard Harris. London: Edward Arnold, 1962, pp. 184-204.

Intelligent survey of the technical limitations and assets of television, with analyses of the work of Paddy Chayefsky and Alun Owen.

______. THE DARK COMEDY: THE DEVELOPMENT OF MODERN COMIC TRAGEDY. 2nd ed. Cambridge, Engl.: Cambridge University Press, 1968.

Persuasively rejecting preconceptions about what tragedy or comedy must be, Stynan seeks to define the characteristic tone of modern drama in general through a history and analyses of plays from Euripedes to Pinter.

Suvin, Darko. "Eric Bentley: The Hero as Theatre Critic." MR, 9 (Spring 1968), 350-58.

An interesting political interpretation of Bentley's work since 1954.

______. "Reflections on Happenings." TDR, 14 (Spring 1970), 125-44.

Finds debased Rousseauism attempting allegorization in "happenings," which, nevertheless, have forced a serious rethinking of theatrical form.

Taylor, John Russell. THE PENGUIN DICTIONARY OF THE THEATRE. Harmondsworth, Engl.: Penguin, 1966.

______. THE RISE AND FALL OF THE WELL-MADE PLAY. New York: Hill and Wang, 1967.

Chapters on Coward and Rattigan are part of a study of the well-made play that shows a refreshing respect for popular playmaking.

______. ANGER AND AFTER: A GUIDE TO THE NEW BRITISH DRAMA. Rev. ed. London: Methuen, 1968.

First published in 1962, and known in its American printings as THE ANGRY THEATRE: NEW BRITISH DRAMA (1969), this volume has served as an introduction to the subject for innumerable American students. Renewed acquaintance only confirms the soundness of Taylor's critical judgment; a considerable flaw is the large number of plot summaries.

______. THE SECOND WAVE: BRITISH DRAMA FOR THE SIXTIES. London: Methuen, 1971.

An invaluable survey of the post-Osborne English stage. Its chief limitation is the predominance of plot summary over critical analysis.

Taylor, Karen Malpede. PEOPLE'S THEATRE IN AMERIKA. Preface by John Howard Lawson. New York: Drama Book Specialists, 1972.

The title is typical of this tendentiously political reading of American theatre since the thirties. Pinter is alluded to as "the most expertly bourgeois playwright of our time." It is unfortunate that the book is structured as it is because it contains some excellent documents and manifestos.

Trewin, J.C. DRAMATISTS OF TODAY. London: Staples Press, 1953.

A genial introduction to the dramatic world that Osborne's generation changed forever.

______. PETER BROOK. London: Macdonald, 1972.

A biography of the provocative director.

Tutaev, David. "The Theatre of the Absurd . . . How Absurd?" G, 1, no. 2 (1963), pp. 68-70.

Argues the theatrical limitations of the theatre of the Absurd and its lack of influence on the physical and spatial character of the proscenium stage.

Tynan, Kenneth. HE THAT PLAYS THE KING: A VIEW OF THE THEATRE. Introductory letter by Orson Welles. London and New York: Longmans, Green, 1950.

Precocious essays and reviews.

______. "Apathy." OBSERVER, 31 October 1954, p. 6.

A denunciation of the "Loamshire" style of stately country house drama that dominated the post-war English stage.

______. "Theatre and Living." In DECLARATION. Ed. Tom Maschler. London: MacGibbon & Kee, 1957, pp. 107-29.

Tynan defends the drama of social change, and deplores the sexual timidity of the English stage and the joylessness of Socialist literature.

_____. "Above the Crowd." OBSERVER, 10 May 1959, p. 21.

Reviewing Mary McCarthy's collection, SIGHTS AND SPECTACLES (see above), Tynan, after praising her as a detector of phoniness, criticizes her reliance on naturalism as a norm, and suggests that she is too much an elitist to be comfortable in the crowd of a mass audience. Be sure to see McCarthy's review of Tynan's collection, CURTAINS, in her CHRONICLES, above.

_____. CURTAINS: SELECTIONS FROM THE DRAMA CRITICISM AND RELATED WRITINGS. New York: Atheneum, 1961.

A valuable collection of witty, acerbic reviews, and some show business essays of less interest. As a reviewer, Tynan became the spokesman for the new, young dramatists who followed on the heels of Osborne.

_____. "Olivier: The Actor and the Man." P&P, 13 (August 1966), 47-49, 230-34.

Tynan, then literary advisor to the National Theatre, gives a day-by-day account of Olivier's interpretation of OTHELLO.

_____. "Laurence Olivier Interviewed by Kenneth Tynan." TDR, 11 (Winter 1966), 71-111.

A fascinating, well-illustrated portrait of England's leading theatrical personality.

_____. TYNAN RIGHT & LEFT: PLAYS, FILMS, PEOPLE, PLACES AND EVENTS. New York: Atheneum, 1967.

_____. OH! CALCUTTA!: AN ENTERTAINMENT WITH MUSIC DEVISED BY KENNETH TYNAN, DIRECTED BY JACQUES LEVY. New York: Grove Press, 1969.

An erotic revue with contributions from Samuel Beckett, Jules Feiffer, John Lennon, Sam Shepard, and Tynan himself.

Vaughan, Stuart. A POSSIBLE THEATRE: THE EXPERIENCES OF A PIONEER DIRECTOR IN AMERICA'S RESIDENT THEATRE. New York: McGraw-Hill, 1969.

The early days of Joseph Papp's Shakespeare Festival, from the Lower East Side Amphitheatre to Central Park, and then on with Vaughan's own career with the Phoenix Theatre and the Seattle Repertory Company.

Vidal, Gore. ROCKING THE BOAT. Boston: Little, Brown, 1962.

A wide-ranging collection of essays, one of which, "Love Love Love," is a denunciation of America's favorite theatrical panacea.

Vinson, James, ed. CONTEMPORARY DRAMATISTS. London: St. James; New York: St. Martin's, 1973.

By a considerable margin this is the single most valuable research tool available for the study of this period. Limited only by its treatment of living playwrights, and thus excluding such figures as Joe Orton and T.S. Eliot, Vinson's work should be known to every serious student of contemporary British and American drama for its bibliographies, its performance histories, and its brief critical essays.

Wager, Walter, ed. THE PLAYWRIGHTS SPEAK. Introd. by Harold Clurman. New York: Delacorte, 1967.

Interviews with Albee, Miller, Arden, Inge, and others from a variety of sources. Each interview is preceded by an informative introduction.

Wardle, Irving. "London's Subsidized Companies." TDR, 11 (Winter 1966), 105-19.

Brief review of the activities of the National Theatre and the Royal Shakespeare Company, illustrated and accompanied by charts listing the productions and directors of the two companies.

Weales, Gerald. RELIGION IN MODERN ENGLISH DRAMA. Philadelphia: University of Pennsylvania Press, 1961.

An excellent, extremely well-researched survey of religious theatre in England since Henry Arthur Jones, and its two main sources--the church and the commercial stage. Formerly a dissertation, it treats Christopher Fry, James Bridie, T.S. Eliot, Ronald Duncan, Anne Ridler, and a host of obscure ecclesiastical authors.

______. THE JUMPING-OFF PLACE: AMERICAN DRAMA IN THE 1960'S. New York: Macmillan, 1969.

A continuation of the same author's AMERICAN DRAMA SINCE WORLD WAR II (1962), this volume's title is taken from KING LEAR and expresses its author's scepticism about the newness of the new drama. Weales has a scholarly interest in texts and order of composition.

Wellwarth, George E. THE THEATER OF PROTEST AND PARADOX: DEVELOPMENTS IN THE AVANT-GARDE DRAMA. New York: New York University Press, 1964.

A grumpily disapproving view of post-1950 drama.

Williams, Raymond. THE LONG REVOLUTION. Rev. ed. New York: Harper and Row, 1966.

The sixth chapter of part two, "The Social History of Dramatic Form," traces the correlation between the theatre and social change.

______. DRAMA IN PERFORMANCE. Rev. ed. London: C.A. Watts and Co., 1968.

Analyzes the changing historical relationship between text and performance of selected plays and one film.

______. DRAMA FROM IBSEN TO BRECHT. New York: Oxford University Press, 1969.

A thorough revision of his DRAMA FROM IBSEN TO ELIOT (1952), this is a magisterial, difficult survey of Western drama since Ibsen. Contemporary playwrights are treated in brief examinations of particular plays. In his conclusion, Williams analyzes the varying "structures of feeling" which underlie the still-continuing evolution of naturalism.

Worth, Katharine J. REVOLUTIONS IN MODERN ENGLISH DRAMA. London: G. Bell and Sons, 1973.

This thoughtful thematic study of the continuity and transformations of realistic style in English drama since 1918 emphasizes such post-1956 dramatists as Bond, Arden, Pinter, and Osborne.

Zeigler, Joseph Wesley. REGIONAL THEATRE: THE REVOLUTIONARY STAGE. Minneapolis: University of Minnesota Press, 1972.

An interesting administrative and institutional history of American regional theatres since 1950; artistic judgments are few and sometimes erratic.

# PLAYS AND PLAYWRIGHTS

In this portion of the book, following each playwright's name and dates, you will find a chronological listing of plays published between 1950 to 1975. That is then followed by a listing of the author's collaborations, collections, whatever bibliographical material exists, and then a selected list of nondramatic works. Following that is an annotated list, in alphabetical order, of essays, reviews, and books written about the playwright in question. When there is more than one entry from a critic, his or her entries are in chronological order. It should be noted also that the Irish playwrights Samuel Beckett and Brendan Behan are included on the grounds of merit and influence.

# LIONEL ABEL (1910- )

THE DEATH OF ODYSSEUS. In PLAYBOOK: FIVE PLAYS FOR A NEW THEATRE. Ed. James Laughlin. Norfolk, Conn.: New Directions, 1956.

THE PRETENDER. PR, 26 (Fall 1959), 535-51.

Act one of a two-act play.

THE POETRY RECITAL. TR, 2 (Winter 1959-60), 138-42.

ABSOLOM. In ARTISTS' THEATRE: FOUR PLAYS. Ed. Herbert Machiz. New York: Grove Press, 1960.

## SELECTED NONDRAMATIC WRITING

METATHEATRE: A NEW VIEW OF DRAMATIC FORM. New York: Hill and Wang, 1963.

See entry in part 1 of the Selected Secondary Source Reading Lists, above.

## CRITICISM

Anonymous. "And It Won the Prize." VV, 20 June 1956, pp. 14, 17.

Profile of Abel as the first playwright to win an Obie Award, for ABSOLOM.

Bellow, Saul. "Pleasures and Pains of Playgoing." PR, 21 (May-June 1954), 312-17.

A brief review of THE DEATH OF ODYSSEUS is part of Bellow's survey of some then recent theatre experiences.

Gassner, John. DRAMATIC SOUNDINGS: EVALUATIONS AND RETRACTIONS CULLED FROM 30 YEARS OF DRAMATIC CRITICISM. Introd. and posthumous editing by Glenn Loney. New York: Crown, 1968, pp. 489-90.

Brief, negative review of THE PRETENDER.

Marowitz, Charles. "Theatre: ABSOLOM." VV, 23 May 1956, p. 6.

Asserts that, despite Abel's real talent, his play is too diffuse, without a skeletal structure to support its many ideas.

Mottram, Eric. "The New American Wave." EN, 11 (January-February 1964), 32-35.

# PAUL ABLEMAN (1927- )

TESTS. London: Methuen, 1966.
Fourteen very short plays.

GREEN JULIA. New York: Grove Press, 1966.
His most noted play.

BLUE COMEDY. London: Methuen, 1968.
Two one-act plays: MADLY IN LOVE and HANK'S NIGHT.

## SELECTED NONDRAMATIC WRITING

AS NEAR AS I CAN GET. London: N.S. Spearman, 1962.

I HEAR VOICES. Paris: Olympia, 1967.
One of the Traveller's Companion Series.

VAC. London: Gollancz, 1968.

THE TWILIGHT OF THE VILP. London: Gollancz, 1969.

THE MOUTH AND ORAL SEX. London: Running Man Press, 1970.
Reprinted as THE SENSUOUS MOUTH. New York: Ace, 1972.

## DANNIE ABSE (1928- )

FIRE IN HEAVEN. London: Hutchinson, 1956.

This verse play has been revised, in prose, under the name IN THE CAGE, in THREE QUESTOR PLAYS, below.

THE ECCENTRIC. London: Evans Bros., 1961.

GONE. G, 1, 1 (1963), 70-83.

Also in THREE QUESTOR PLAYS (see next item).

THREE QUESTOR PLAYS. London: Scorpion, 1967.

Includes HOUSE OF COWARDS, GONE, and IN THE CAGE.

THE COURTING OF ESSIE GLASS. JEWISH QUARTERLY (London), 1972.

THE DOGS OF PAVLOV. London: Vallentine Mitchell, 1973.

Includes responses by S. Milgram to the play and to the author's accompanying essay, and a bibliography.

### SELECTED NONDRAMATIC WRITING

SOME CORNER OF AN ENGLISH FIELD. London: Hutchinson, 1956.

Novel.

TENANTS OF THE HOUSE: POEMS 1951-1956. London: Hutchinson, 1957.

SELECTED POEMS. London: Hutchinson; New York: Oxford, 1970.

## CRITICISM

Elsom, John. "Dannie Abse." In CONTEMPORARY DRAMATISTS. Ed. James Vinson. London: St. James; New York: St. Martin's, 1973, pp. 14-16.

Good introduction, plus this volume's usual fine bibliography.

# RODNEY ACKLAND (1908- )

BEFORE THE PARTY. London: Samuel French, 1950.

Adaptation of Somerset Maugham's short story (1931) of the same title.

A DEAD SECRET. P&P, 4 (September 1957), 22-32; 5 (November 1957), 22-28.

## COLLABORATION WITH JOHN VARI

FAREWELL, FAREWELL EUGENE. London: Samuel French, 1960.

## NONDRAMATIC WRITING

THE CELLULOID MISTRESS; OR, THE CUSTARD PIE OF DR. CALIGARI. With Elspeth Grant. London: Wingate, 1954.

Autobiography.

## CRITICISM

Spurling, John. "Rodney Ackland." In CONTEMPORARY DRAMATISTS. Ed. James Vinson. London: St. James; New York: St. Martin's, 1973, pp. 18-20.

Good, brief introduction.

# EDWARD ALBEE (1928- )

THE ZOO STORY (A PLAY IN ONE SCENE--1958). ER, 4 (March-April 1960), 28-52.

With the dedication "For William Flanagan."

THE ZOO STORY: THE DEATH OF BESSIE SMITH; THE SANDBOX. New York: Coward-McCann, 1960.

Introduced by the author.

THE AMERICAN DREAM: A COMEDY (1959-1960). MADEMOISELLE, November 1960, pp. 86-89 ff.

THE AMERICAN DREAM. New York: Coward-McCann, 1961.

FAM AND YAM: AN IMAGINARY INTERVIEW. HARPERS BAZAAR, September 1960, pp. 264 ff.

FAM AND YAM. New York: Dramatists Play Service, 1961.

WHO'S AFRAID OF VIRGINIA WOOLF? New York: Atheneum, 1962.

THE PLAY, THE BALLAD OF THE SAD CAFE. Boston: Houghton Mifflin, 1963.

Carson McCullers' novella adapted to the stage.

TINY ALICE. New York: Atheneum, 1965.

MALCOLM. New York: Atheneum, 1966.

Adapted by Edward Albee from the novel by James Purdy.

A DELICATE BALANCE. New York: Atheneum, 1966.

EVERYTHING IN THE GARDEN. New York: Atheneum, 1968.

A free adaptation of the play of the same title by Giles Cooper (1963).

BOX AND QUOTATIONS FROM CHAIRMAN MAO TSE-TUNG: TWO INTER-RELATED PLAYS. New York: Atheneum, 1969.

ALL OVER. New York: Atheneum, 1971.

SEASCAPE. New York: Atheneum, 1975.

## BIBLIOGRAPHY

Amacher, Richard E., and Margaret Rule. EDWARD ALBEE AT HOME AND ABROAD: A BIBLIOGRAPHY. New York: AMS Press, 1973.

Best full-length bibliography for both primary and secondary sources.

Kolin, Philip C. "A Classified Edward Albee Checklist." SERIF, 6 (September 1969), 16-32.

______. "A Supplementary Edward Albee Checklist." SERIF, 10 (Spring 1973), 28-39.

Kolin's is the best primary source bibliography; the supplement includes two extremely early poems by Albee from 1945 and 1946.

Rule, Margaret. "An Edward Albee Bibliography." TCL, 14 (April 1968), 35-45.

Superseded by the above items.

Salem, James M., ed. A GUIDE TO CRITICAL REVIEWS. Part 1: AMERICAN DRAMA, 1909-1969. 2nd ed. Metuchen, N.J.: Scarecrow Press, 1973.

A listing of reviews, pp. 9-15.

## SELECTED NONDRAMATIC WRITING

"Novel Beginning." ES, July 1963, pp. 59-60.

Excerpt from a novel combining dialogue and stream of consciousness.

"Towards a Theatre of Cruelty." TIMES LITERARY SUPPLEMENT, 27 February 1964, p. 166.

Albee asserts that THE AMERICAN DREAM is meant to be offensive.

THREE PLAYS BY NOEL COWARD. New York: Dell, 1965.

Introduction by Albee.

"Which Theatre is the Absurd One?" In DIRECTIONS IN MODERN THEATRE AND DRAMA. Ed. John Gassner. New York: Holt, Rinehart and Winston, 1965, pp. 329-36.

"Who is James Purdy?" NEW YORK TIMES, 9 January 1966, sec. 2, pp. 1, 3.

Comments on the art of adaptation.

"Remarks on TINY ALICE." In THE PLAYWRIGHTS SPEAK. Ed. Walter Wager. New York: Delacorte Press, 1967, pp. 34-35.

A more complete text of this significant response to the critics is to be found in the Lincoln Center Library of the Performing Arts.

## CRITICISM

Adler, Thomas P. "Albee's WHO'S AFRAID OF VIRGINIA WOOLF: A Long Night's Journey into Day." ETJ, 25 (March 1973), 66-70.

Nick and Honey are saved by George and Martha.

Amacher, Richard E. EDWARD ALBEE. New York: Twayne, 1969.

Without a background of stage history and lacking the backup of newspaper and periodical criticism, this is an often trite attempt to apply Aristotelian principles to Albee's plays.

Baxandall, Lee. "The Theatre of Edward Albee." TDR, 9 (Summer 1965), 1-40. Also in MODERN AMERICAN THEATER: A COLLECTION OF CRITICAL ESSAYS. Ed. Alvin B. Kernan. Englewood Cliffs, N.J.: Prentice-Hall, 1967, pp. 80-98.

The sterile family as symbolic of contemporary America is Albee's basic subject. The only escape is transcendence, be it an imaginary child, or masturbatory ecstacy. This perceptive essay argues that Albee's greatest success is as a satirist, but that his focus on the family limits his range.

Bigsby, C.W.E. "WHO'S AFRAID OF VIRGINIA WOOLF: Edward Albee's Mortality Play." JOURNAL OF AMERICAN STUDIES, 1 (October 1967), 251-68.

The play is an affirmation of the need to face reality and an attack, similar to that in O'Neill's THE ICEMAN COMETH (1946), upon the illusions that perpetuate the American dream.

______. "Curiouser and Curiouser: A Study of Edward Albee's TINY ALICE." MD, 10 (December 1967), 258-66.

______. "Edward Albee's Georgia Ballad." TCL, 14 (April 1968), 35-44.

THE BALLAD OF THE SAD CAFE does no service to Albee's reputation or the particular virtues of Carson McCullers's novella.

______. ALBEE. Edinburgh: Oliver and Boyd, 1969.

Brief handbook.

______, ed. EDWARD ALBEE: A COLLECTION OF CRITICAL ESSAYS. Englewood Cliffs, N.J.: Prenctice-Hall, 1975. Hereafter cited as ALBEE, ed. Bigsby.

A disappointing collection, with too many reviews and chapters from books and a surprising number of entries from the editor.

Brustein, Robert. "Listening to the Past." In his SEASONS OF DISCONTENT: DRAMATIC OPINIONS 1959-1965. New York: Simon and Schuster, 1965, pp. 26-29.

THE ZOO STORY, despite some strong writing, is flawed by the conventional assumption of the "beat" ideology that the psychotic and the invert are somehow holy.

______. "Albee's Allegory of Innocence." In his THE THIRD THEATRE. New York: Knopf, 1969, pp. 79-82.

MALCOLM is "Albee's most deeply homosexual work. As Albee gets closer and closer to his true subjects . . . he tends to get more abstract and incoherent."

______. "Albee Decorates an Old House." In his THE THIRD THEATRE. New York: Knopf, 1969, pp. 83-86.

A DELICATE BALANCE "suffers from a borrowed style and a hollow center."

______. "Albee at the Crossroads." In his THE THIRD THEATRE. New York: Knopf, 1969, pp. 87-90.

On EVERYTHING IN THE GARDEN.

Campbell, Mary Elizabeth. "The Tempters in Albee's TINY ALICE." MD, 13 (May 1970), 22-33.

TINY ALICE is a spiritual allegory, with the butler, Miss Alice, and the lawyer representing, respectively, the temptations of the world, the flesh, and the devil.

Chiaromonte, Nicolo. "Albee Damned." NYRB, 1 (Winter 1963), 16.

Condemns Albee's inability to end a play. The son in VIRGINIA WOOLF is an attempt to create symbolic meaning and a dramatic action where none exist.

Coe, Richard N. "Beyond Absurdity: Albee's Awareness of Audience in TINY ALICE." MD, 18 (December 1975), 371-83.

While TINY ALICE portrays absurdist themes on its story level, its style is "parabolic realism."

Cohn, Ruby. "Albee's Box and Ours." MD, 14 (September 1971), 137-43.

An explication of BOX and CHAIRMAN MAO, primarily in musical terms, arguing that while the voices never blend, they do affect our perception of the nature of art and mortality.

_____. DIALOGUE IN AMERICAN DRAMA. Bloomington: Indiana University Press, 1971, pp. 130-69.

Davison, Richard Allan. "Albee's TINY ALICE: A Note of Re-Examination." MD, 11 (May 1968), 54-60.

TINY ALICE is a good, if not overwhelming, treatment of contemporary themes. Albee's stage sense and his "reinforcement of the verbal with the visual" are his play's greatest virtues.

Debusscher, Gilbert. EDWARD ALBEE: TRADITION AND RENEWAL. Trans. Anne W. Williams. Brussels: American Studies Center, 1967.

The first full-length study of Albee's works.

"Edward Albee Interviewed by Digby Diehl." In BEHIND THE SCENES: THEATER AND FILM INTERVIEWS FROM THE TRANSATLANTIC REVIEW. Ed. Joseph F.M. McCrindle, introd. Jean-Claude van Itallie. New York: Holt, Rinehart and Winston, 1971, pp. 223-42.

This interview was given in 1963, while Albee was adapting BALLAD.

Dozier, Richard J. "Adultery and Disappointment in WHO'S AFRAID OF VIRGINIA WOOLF." MD, 11 (February 1969), 432-36.

The third act of VIRGINIA WOOLF draws a disappointingly optimistic conclusion from what had seemed a no-holds-barred, serious conflict over the breakdown of George and Martha's entire life.

Dukore, Bernard F. "Tiny Albee." DS, 5 (Spring 1966), 60-66.

TINY ALICE is claptrap and Albee is the Pinero of the Absurd.

Falk, Eugene H. "NO EXIT and WHO'S AFRAID OF VIRGINIA WOOLF: A Thematic Comparison." SP, 67 (July 1970), 406-17.

In both plays the central characters continually and painfully remind each other of their inauthenticity; in both the characters are trapped in these relationships.

Flanagan, William. "Albee in the Village." NEW YORK HERALD TRIBUNE, 27 October 1963, p. 27.

Albee's former roommate, a composer, comments on the musical qualities of the early plays and reminisces about Albee's early years in the city.

Flasch, Joy. "Games People Play in WHO'S AFRAID OF VIRGINIA WOOLF." MD, 10 (December 1967), 280-88.

VIRGINIA WOOLF interpreted through the terminology of Dr. Eric Berne's GAMES PEOPLE PLAY (1964).

Hardwick, Elizabeth. "Straight Play." NYRB, 7 (20 October 1966), 4-5.

Thoughts on Walter Kerr's position at the TIMES preface a review of A DELICATE BALANCE that finds the play a genteel, suburban bore.

Holtan, Orley. "WHO'S AFRAID OF VIRGINIA WOOLF and the Patterns of History." ETJ, 25 (March 1973), 46-52.

An ingenious reading of VIRGINIA WOOLF as an allegory of the American experience.

Hopkins, Anthony. "Conventional Albee: BOX and CHAIRMAN MAO." MD, 16 (September 1973), 141-47.

For all of their formal innovations, BOX and CHAIRMAN MAO continue themes present throughout Albee's work.

Kingsley, Lawrence. "Reality and Illusion: Continuity of a Theme in Albee." ETJ, 25 (March 1973), 71-79.

The conflict between reality and illusion traced through some of Albee's major plays.

Lahr, John. "The Adaptable Mr. Albee." In his UP AGAINST THE FOURTH WALL: ESSAYS ON MODERN THEATRE. New York: Grove Press, 1970, pp. 18-34.

An attack upon Albee's version of EVERYTHING IN THE GARDEN.

Lyons, Charles R. "Two Projections of the Isolation of the Human Soul: Brecht's IM DICKICT DER STAEDTE and Albee's THE ZOO STORY." DS, 4 (Summer 1965), 121-38.

Interesting parallels between Garga-Shlink and Peter-Jerry.

______. "Some Variations of KINDERMORD as Dramatic Archetype." COMPARATIVE DRAMA, 1 (Spring 1967), 56-71.

VIRGINIA WOOLF and ENDGAME are analyzed with plays by Shakespeare, Racine, Ibsen, Pirandello and others, as part of a pattern in which, unsurprisingly, the death of a child, real or imaginary, signals a crucial, often purgative, event in the life of the protagonist.

Mandanis, Alice. "Symbol and Substance in TINY ALICE." MD, 12 (May 1969), 92-98.

Following Albee's press conference reading of his play, Mandanis finds the theatrical surface of the play too thin to bear the weight of the subject Albee confronts.

Markus, Thomas B. "TINY ALICE and Tragic Catharsis." ETJ, 17 (October 1965), 225-33.

Defends Albee and claims that TINY ALICE is a true tragedy, the first in "hundreds of years."

Meyer, Ruth. "Language: Truth and Illusion in WHO'S AFRAID OF VIRGINIA WOOLF." ETJ, 20 (March 1968), 60-69.

Albee's language creates a series of ambiguities which makes the "illusory" son as real as anything else in the play.

Nelson, Gerald. "Edward Albee and His Well-Made Plays." TQ, no. 5 (1966), 182-88.

Albee is prone to explaining what his plays are about, rather than allowing his characters and their actions to explain themselves.

Nilan, Mary M. "Albee's THE ZOO STORY: Alienated Man and the Nature of Love." MD, 16 (June 1973), 55-59.

Jerry's perverted attempt at making Peter love him, or at least remember him, is seen as perhaps the best that modern alienated man can expect.

Otten, Terry. "Ibsen and Albee's Spurious Children." COMPARATIVE DRAMA, 2 (Summer 1968), 83-93.

In both VIRGINIA WOOLF and LITTLE EYOLF, along with many other similarities, the death of a child marks the end of illusion and a tentative new beginning.

Paolucci, Anne. FROM TENSION TO TONIC: THE PLAYS OF EDWARD ALBEE. Carbondale: Southern Illinois University Press, 1972.

The most interesting full-length study.

Roth, Philip. "The Play That Dare Not Speak Its Name." NYRB, 4 (25 February 1965), 4.

The notorious denunciation of TINY ALICE as a "homosexual daydream" disguised as a passion play. See also the exchange of letters in the volume 4, April 1965 issue of this periodical (pp. 37-38).

Rutenberg, Michael E. EDWARD ALBEE: PLAYWRIGHT IN PROTEST. New York: DBS Publications, 1969.

Sees Albee as part of the social protest of the sixties, with CHAIRMAN MAO a plea for recognition of mainland China. The book concludes with two interviews with Albee.

Samuels, Charles Thomas. "The Theatre of Edward Albee." MR, 6 (Autumn-Winter 1964), 187-201.

Albee has only the gift of invective; otherwise he is inept and pretentious, his plays filled with feeble characterization and cheap satire: "By borrowing from Europe the latest geegaws of the avant-garde, Albee has made possible the continued stink of sensationalism and sentimentality that has wafted from every Broadway theater since the beginning of World War II." For more in a similar vein, on the son in VIRGINIA WOOLF, see Carol D. Hill's letter in the volume 6, Spring-Summer 1965 issue of the same periodical (pp. 649-50).

Schechner, Richard. "Who's Afraid of Edward Albee?" TDR, 7 (Spring 1963), 7-10. Also in ALBEE, ed. Bigsby, pp. 62-65.

VIRGINIA WOOLF is "Bad theater, bad literature, bad taste . . . . VIRGINIA WOOLF is a ludicrous play; but the joke is on us." See the response by Alan Schneider immediately following Schechner's piece in both the TDR and in Bigsby's collection.

_____. "Reality is Not Enough: An Interview with Alan Schneider." TDR, 9 (Spring 1965), 118-52. Also in ALBEE, ed. Bigsby, pp. 69-75.

Informative interview about the rehearsals for the first production of VIRGINIA WOOLF.

Spielberg, Peter. "The Albatross in Albee's Zoo." CE, 27 (April 1966), 562-65.

Jerry is the Ancient Mariner; Peter is the Wedding Guest; the dog is the Albatross.

Taylor, Marion A. "Edward Albee and August Strindberg: Some Parallels between THE DANCE OF DEATH and WHO'S AFRAID OF VIRGINIA WOOLF?" PAPERS ON ENGLISH LANGUAGE AND LITERATURE, 1 (Winter 1965), 59-71.

Trilling, Diana. "The Riddle of Albee's WHO'S AFRAID OF VIRGINIA WOOLF." In her CLAREMONT ESSAYS. New York: Harcourt, Brace, 1964, pp. 203-27. Also a shorter version in ALBEE, ed. Bigsby, pp. 80-88.

VIRGINIA WOOLF provides an easy comfort by depicting the failings of our presumed superiors.

Valgemae, Mardi. "Albee's Great God Alice." MD, 10 (December 1967), 267-73.

Traces the resemblance between TINY ALICE and O'Neill's expressionistic dramas.

von Szeliski, John J. "A Rare BALANCE." TCL, 16 (April 1970), 123-30.

A DELICATE BALANCE, despite negative reviews, is Albee's finest play, a realistic study of the terror of mortality.

Way, Brian. "Albee and the Absurd: THE AMERICAN DREAM and THE ZOO STORY." In AMERICAN THEATRE. Ed. John Russell Brown and Bernard Harris. London: Edward Arnold, 1967, pp. 188-207. Also in ALBEE, ed. Bigsby, pp. 26-44.

Comparing the two early Albee successes with plays by Ionesco, Way finds that Albee avoids the philosophical implications of absurdity and confines himself to the purely satiric and parodistic.

White, James E. "An Early Play by Edward Albee." AL, 42 (March 1970), 98-99.

SCHISM, a product of Albee's days at Choate, is similar in theme to TINY ALICE.

Willeford, William. "The Mouse in the Model." MD, 12 (September 1969), 135-45.

The enigmatic figure of Miss Alice and the mouse-deity are seen to contain an astonishing number of literary and mythic echoes.

Witherington, Paul. "Language of Movement in Albee's THE DEATH OF BESSIE SMITH." TCL, 13 (July 1967), 84-88.

Imagery of action and inaction unifies the play thematically.

Zimbardo, Rose. "Symbolism and Naturalism in Edward Albee's THE ZOO STORY." TCL, 8 (April 1962), 10-17. Also in ALBEE, ed. Bigsby, pp. 45-53.

Jerry is Christ, Peter is St. Peter, and THE ZOO STORY follows the pattern of Christ's sacrificial death.

# WILLIAM ALFRED (1922- )

AGAMEMNON. BO, no. 11 (1953), 249-353.

AGAMEMNON. New York: Knopf, 1954.

HOGAN'S GOAT. New York: Farrar, Straus and Giroux, 1966.

## BIBLIOGRAPHY

Salem, James M., ed. A GUIDE TO CRITICAL REVIEWS. Part I: AMERICAN DRAMA, 1909-1969. 2nd ed. Metuchen, N.J.: Scarecrow Press, 1973.

A listing of reviews, pp. 15-16.

## CRITICISM

Barbour, Thomas. "Marginalia for a Myth." HR, 7 (Winter 1955), 607-09.

AGAMEMNON succeeds in many ways: the verse, the use of details, and the characterization are all quite fine. But the play itself lacks development and true profundity.

# WOODY ALLEN (1935- )

DON'T DRINK THE WATER. New York: Random House, 1967.

DEATH KNOCKS. NEW YORKER, 44 (27 July 1968), 31-33

PLAY IT AGAIN, SAM. New York: Random House, 1969.

DEATH: A COMEDY IN ONE ACT. New York: Samuel French, 1975.

GOD: A COMEDY IN ONE ACT. New York: Samuel French, 1975.

## BIBLIOGRAPHY

Salem, James M., ed. A GUIDE TO CRITICAL REVIEWS. Part 1: AMERICAN DRAMA, 1909-1969. 2nd ed. Metuchen, N.J.: Scarecrow Press, 1973.

A listing of reviews, page 17.

## SELECTED NONDRAMATIC WRITING

Albert, Marvin H. WHAT'S NEW PUSSY CAT. London: Mayflower, 1965.

A novel adapted from Allen's screenplay, which is available, but only in French, in L'AVANT-SCENE DES CINEMA, 59 (May 1966), 1-56.

## CRITICISM

Lahr, John. "Neil Simon and Woody Allen: Images of Impotence." In his ASTONISH ME: ADVENTURES IN CONTEMPORARY THEATER. New York: Viking, 1973, pp. 120-36.

Allen, like Simon, depicts the "castration of capitalism."

Lax, Eric. ON BEING FUNNY: WOODY ALLEN AND COMEDY. New York: Charterhouse, 1975.

A collection of anecdotes mixed with some biographical material, but no critical approach.

# MAXWELL ANDERSON (1888-1959)

LOST IN THE STARS. New York: William Sloane Associates, 1950.

Anderson's book for the Kurt Weill musical based on Alan Paton's 1948 novel CRY, THE BELOVED COUNTRY.

BAREFOOT IN ATHENS. New York: William Sloane Associates, 1951.

THE BAD SEED. New York: Dodd, Mead, 1955.

A dramatization of William March's novel of the same name.

THE DAY THE MONEY STOPPED. New York: Lincoln Center Library of the Performing Arts, 1958.

Typescript, from the novel of the same name by Brendan Gill.

THE GOLDEN SIX. New York: Lincoln Center Library of the Performing Arts, 1962.

Microfilm of typescript.

## BIBLIOGRAPHY

Avery, Laurence G., comp. A CATALOGUE OF THE MAXWELL ANDERSON COLLECTION AT THE UNIVERSITY OF TEXAS. Austin: University of Texas, 1968.

A manuscript bibliography that describes, among much else, eight unpublished playscripts from the 1950s.

Cox, Martha. MAXWELL ANDERSON BIBLIOGRAPHY. Charlottesville: University of Virginia Bibliographical Society, 1958.

Gilbert, Vedder M. "The Career of Maxwell Anderson: A Check List of Books and Periodicals." MD, 2 (February 1960), 386-94.

Omits book for LOST IN THE STARS, and the manuscript for THE DAY THE MONEY STOPPED.

Salem, James M., ed. A GUIDE TO CRITICAL REVIEWS. Part 1: AMERICAN DRAMA, 1909-1969. 2nd ed. Metuchen, N.J.: Scarecrow Press, 1973.

A listing, by production, of reviews, pp. 18-30.

## SELECTED NONDRAMATIC WRITING

"WHITE DESERT to BAD SEED." TA, 39 (March 1955), 28-29, 93.

## CRITICISM

Bailey, Mabel D. MAXWELL ANDERSON: THE PLAYWRIGHT AS PROPHET. New York: Abelard-Schuman, 1957.

Knepler, Henry. "Maxwell Anderson: A Historical Parallel." QUEEN'S QUARTERLY, 64 (1957), 250-63.

Lee, Henry. "Maxwell Anderson's Impact on the Theatre." NORTH DAKOTA QUARTERLY, 25 (Spring 1957), 49-52.

Nathan, George Jean. "Lost in the Stars." In his THEATRE BOOK OF THE YEAR, 1949-1950: A RECORD AND AN INTERPRETATION. New York: Knopf, 1950, pp. 72-76.

A review of LOST IN THE STARS.

______. "Maxwell Anderson." In his THEATRE IN THE FIFTIES. New York: Knopf, 1953, pp. 40-42.

A review of BAREFOOT IN ATHENS.

# ROBERT ANDERSON (1917- )

TEA AND SYMPATHY. New York: Random House, 1953.

On the title page of a 1948 typescript in the Lincoln Center Library of the Performing Arts, Robert Anderson wrote, "This was a version of TEA AND SYMPATHY written in 1948, but not produced. I later 'crossed' it with a short story I wrote in 1946, called 'Katharina and pity and love and I,' and that together with some new material became the 1952 version of TEA AND SYMPATHY, as produced in 1953."

ALL SUMMER LONG. New York: Samuel French, 1955.

Adapted from the novel A WREATH AND A CURSE by Donald Wetzel.

ALL SUMMER LONG. TA, 39 (August 1955), 35-63.

SILENT NIGHT, LONELY NIGHT. New York: Random House, 1960.

THE DAYS BETWEEN. New York: Random House, 1965.

THE DAYS BETWEEN. Revised and rewritten. London: Samuel French, 1968.

YOU KNOW I CAN'T HEAR YOU WHEN THE WATER'S RUNNING. New York: Random House, 1967.

Consists of four one-act plays: THE SHOCK OF RECOGNITION, THE FOOTSTEPS OF DOVES, I'LL BE HOME FOR CHRISTMAS, and I'M HERBERT.

I NEVER SANG FOR MY FATHER. New York: Random House, 1968.

I NEVER SANG FOR MY FATHER. New York: New American Library, 1970.

A screenplay based on Anderson's play, with an introduction by Robert Anderson and notes by Gilbert Cates.

SOLITAIRE AND DOUBLE SOLITAIRE. New York: Random House, 1972.

Two short plays.

## BIBLIOGRAPHY

Salem, James M., ed. A GUIDE TO CRITICAL REVIEWS. Part 1: AMERICAN DRAMA. 1909-1969. 2nd ed. Metuchen, N.J.: Scarecrow Press, 1973, pp. 31-33.

A listing of the reviews of the New York productions.

## SELECTED NONDRAMATIC WRITING

"Comment." In CONTEMPORARY DRAMATISTS. Ed. James Vinson. London: St. James; New York: St. Martin's, 1973, pp. 32-33.

This description of his own work begins with a disavowal of any attempt at analysis. He has read a thesis on his plays and wishes he had not.

## CRITICISM

Bentley, Eric. "Folklore on Forty-Seventh Street." In his THE DRAMATIC EVENT: AN AMERICAN CHRONICLE. New York: Horizon, 1954, pp. 149-53.

On TEA AND SYMPATHY: "The formula for such a work is Daring as Calculated Caution. Or: Audacity, Audacity, But Not Too Much Audacity."

Gassner, John. THEATRE AT THE CROSSROADS: PLAYS AND PLAYWRIGHTS OF THE MID-CENTURY AMERICAN STAGE. New York: Holt, Rinehart and Winston, 1960, pp. 288-93.

Weales, Gerald. "The New Pineros." In his AMERICAN DRAMA SINCE WORLD WAR II. New York: Harcourt, Brace, 1962, pp. 40-56.

Wooton, Carl. "THE COUNTRY WIFE and Contemporary Wife: A World Apart." DS, 2 (February 1963), 333-43.

Contrasts TEA AND SYMPATHY, among others, with Wycherley's THE COUNTRY WIFE (1675).

## JOHN ANTROBUS (1933- )

YOU'LL COME TO LOVE YOUR SPERM TEST. P&P, 12 (February 1965), 24-30 ff or (March 1965), 27-32 ff.

YOU'LL COME TO LOVE YOUR SPERM TEST. NEW WRITERS 4: PLAYS AND HAPPENINGS. London: Calder and Boyars, 1967.

TRIXIE AND BABA. London: Calder and Boyars, 1969.

WHY BOURNEMOUTH? AND OTHER PLAYS. London: Calder and Boyars, 1970.

Also includes THE MISSING LINKS and AN APPLE A DAY, both teleplays.

CAPTAIN OATES' LEFT SOCK. London: Samuel French, 1974.

### COLLABORATION WITH SPIKE MULLIGAN

THE BED-SITTING ROOM. London: Jack Hobbs, 1970.

### CRITICISM

O'Shea, Kevin. "A Tale From the Mermaid." NTM, 4 (April-June 1963), 11-13.

How THE BED-SITTING ROOM was created.

# JANE ARDEN

THE PARTY. London: Samuel French, 1958.

VAGINA REX AND THE GAS OVEN. London: Calder and Boyars, 1971.

## CRITICISM

Baker, Roger. "Jane Arden." In CONTEMPORARY DRAMATISTS. Ed. James Vinson. London: St. James; New York: St. Martin's, 1973, pp. 42-43.

# JOHN ARDEN (1930-  )

SERJEANT MUSGRAVE'S DANCE: AN UNHISTORICAL PARABLE. London: Methuen, 1960.

LIVE LIKE PIGS. In NEW ENGLISH DRAMATISTS, no. 2. Ed. Elliott Martin Browne. Harmondsworth, Engl.: Penguin, 1961.

THE WORKHOUSE DONKEY: A VULGAR MELO-DRAMA. P&P, 10 (August 1963), 18-29: (September 1963), 19-32.

THE WORKHOUSE DONKEY: A VULGAR MELO-DRAMA. London: Methuen, 1964.

THE BUSINESS OF GOOD GOVERNMENT: A CHRISTMAS PLAY. London: Methuen, 1963.

THREE PLAYS: THE WATERS OF BABYLON, LIVE LIKE PIGS, THE HAPPY HAVEN. Harmondsworth, Engl.: Penguin, 1964.

> This is the only published version of THE WATERS OF BABYLON. For THE HAPPY HAVEN, see Collaborations, below.

IRONHAND, ADAPTED BY JOHN ARDEN FROM GOETHE'S "GOETZ VON BERLICHINGEN." London: Methuen, 1965.

ARMSTRONG'S LAST GOODNIGHT: AN EXERCISE IN DIPLOMACY. London: Methuen, 1965.

LEFT-HANDED LIBERTY: A PLAY ABOUT MAGNA CARTA. London: Methuen, 1965.

> With an appendix providing an alternative for Act Two, Scene Four.

SOLDIER, SOLDIER, AND OTHER PLAYS. London: Methuen, 1967.

Includes four plays: SOLDIER, SOLDIER; WET FISH; WHEN IS A DOOR NOT A DOOR?; and, in collaboration with Margaretta D'Arcy, FRIDAY'S HIDING.

THE TRUE HISTORY OF SQUIRE JONATHAN AND HIS UNFORTUNATE TREASURE. P&P, 15 (August 1968), 60-64.

TWO AUTOBIOGRAPHICAL PLAYS: THE TRUE HISTORY OF SQUIRE JONATHAN AND HIS UNFORTUNATE TREASURE, AND THE BAGMAN, OR, THE IMPROMPTU OF MUSWELL HILL. London: Methuen, 1971.

## COLLABORATIONS WITH MARGARETTA D'ARCY

THE HAPPY HAVEN. In NEW ENGLISH DRAMATISTS, no. 4. Ed. Elliott Martin Browne. Harmondsworth, Engl.: Penguin, 1962.

THE HAPPY HAVEN. In THREE PLAYS: THE WATERS OF BABYLON, LIVE LIKE PIGS, THE HAPPY HAVEN. Harmondsworth, Engl.: Penguin, 1964.

ARS LONGA, VITA BREVIS. EN, 11 (March-April 1964), 13-20.

ARS LONGA. In EIGHT PLAYS. 2 vols. Ed. Malcolm Stuart Fellows. London: Cassell, 1965.

A collection of plays by various authors, issued in two volumes, with ARS LONGA, VITA BREVIS in the first; also issued in eight parts, with ARS LONGA, VITA BREVIS as the second part.

FRIDAY'S HIDING. In Arden's SOLDIER, SOLDIER, AND OTHER PLAYS. London: Methuen, 1967.

THE HERO RISES UP: A MELODRAMA. London: Methuen, 1969.

THE BALLYGOMBEEN BEQUEST: AN ANGLO-IRISH MELODRAMA. SCRIPTS, 9 (September 1972), 4-50.

THS ISLAND OF THE MIGHTY: A PLAY ON A TRADITIONAL BRITISH THEME IN THREE PARTS. London: Methuen, 1974.

## BIBLIOGRAPHY

Page, Malcolm, comp. "Theatre Checklist No. 7: John Arden." TF, 2, no. 3 (1975), 2-13.

A major contribution to contemporary theatre scholarship.

## SELECTED NONDRAMATIC WRITING

"The Reps and New Plays--A Writer's Viewpoint." NTM, 1 (January 1960), 23-26.

Repertory theatres provide a balance to the London stage, and may prove fertile ground for more poetic, less naturalistic dramatic writing.

"Telling a True Tale." In THE ENCORE READER. Ed. Charles Marowitz, Tom Milne, and Owen Hale. London: Methuen, 1965, pp. 125-29.

Reprinted from the May-June 1960, issue of ENCORE; Arden argues that the use of the ballad tradition can enable social criticism in the theatre to "have a weight and an impact derived from something more than contemporary documentary facility."

"Book Review: THE CARETAKER." NTM, 1 (July 1960), 29-30.

Pinter is a new kind of realist, neither an Ibsenite, nor a symbolist. His orchestrated verbal patterns alone convey a great deal.

"Verse in the Theatre." NTM, 2 (April 1961), 12-17.

Argues for a mixed drama using both prose and verse, shifting from the low intensity of prose to the fuller, beyond the surface, meanings of verse. He also defends the merit of ballads as poetry and music.

"The Difficulty of Getting Things Done Properly." In EFFECTIVE THEATRE. Ed. John Russell Brown. London: Methuen, 1969, pp. 146-48.

Reprinted from THE GUARDIAN of 16 May 1964, where it is titled, "Tatty Theatre."

"Building a Play: An Interview." In THE NEW BRITISH DRAMA. Ed. Henry Popkin. New York: Grove Press, 1964, pp. 581-606.

For the rather complicated provenance of this and the following article, see Malcolm Page's splendid bibliography, above; on Arden's background as an architect, the origins of his early plays, and his use of verse.

"Who's for a Revolution?: Two Interviews." TDR, 11 (Winter 1966), 41-53.

Discusses the origins of ARMSTRONG'S LAST GOODNIGHT; LEFT-HANDED LIBERTY; ARS LONGA, VITA BREVIS; and Arden's Kerbymoorside venture in community art.

"A BOND HONORED." TIMES (London), 11 June 1966, p. 11.

On the Osborne adaptation.

CHILDREN OF ALBION. Ed. Michael Horowitz. Harmondsworth, Engl.: Penguin, 1969, pp. 14-20.

Four poems by Arden.

## CRITICISM

Blindheim, Joan Tindale. "John Arden's Use of the Stage." MD, 11 (December 1960), 306-16.

A play-by-play survey, examining Arden's stage directions and visual effects.

Brandt, G.W. "Realism and Parables (from Brecht to Arden)." In CONTEMPORARY THEATRE. Ed. John Russell Brown and Bernard Harris. London: Edward Arnold, 1962, pp. 32-55.

Defends SERJEANT MUSGRAVE as an effective parable, while tracing, from Brecht through O'Casey, Auden, and others, the elusive nature of the parable play.

Brown, John Russell. "Artificial Theatre." In his THEATRE LANGUAGE. London: Allen Lane Penguin Press, 1972, pp. 190-234.

Traces Arden's varied theatre effects, arguing that Arden sees theatre as an exuberant surrogate for life, "as a means of discovery in its own terms not as a stimulus for debate or platform for verbal affirmation."

Corrigan, Robert. "The Theatre of John Arden." In his THE THEATRE IN SEARCH OF A FIX. New York: Delacorte, 1973, pp. 316-24.

Unlike most of his generation of playwrights, who were more interested in a reform of style than in political reform, Arden is a social playwright. His vision is of a community at odds with itself.

Day, Paul W. "Individual and Society in the Early Plays of John Arden." MD, 18 (September 1975), 239-49.

Arden's first three plays depict, beneath the music hall structure and other surface features, a conflict between the individual and the highly equivocal power of society.

Gilman, Richard. "Arden's Unsteady Ground." In his COMMON AND UNCOMMON MASKS: WRITINGS ON THEATRE 1961-1970. New York: Random House, 1971, pp. 116-29. Rpt. in MODERN BRITISH DRAMATISTS: A COLLECTION OF CRITICAL ESSAYS. Ed. John Russell Brown. Englewood Cliffs, N.J.: Prentice-Hall, 1968, pp. 104-16.

Arden's stance hovers between political concern and aesthetic independence.

Hunt, Albert. "Arden's Stagecraft." EN, no. 12 (1965), 9-12.

Arden is an anti-illusionist, a Brechtian; his plays illustrate the dangers of identification. Like the preceding entry, a much-reprinted essay.

Jordan, Robert John. "Serjeant Musgrave's Problem." MD, 13 (May 1970), 54-62.

Arden's treatment of what is essentially a problem play is confused and contradictory, leaving the ideals of pacificism and radical action unsynthesized.

Kennedy, Andrew K. "Arden." In his SIX DRAMATISTS IN SEARCH OF A LANGUAGE. Cambridge, Engl.: Cambridge University Press, 1975, pp. 213-29.

Arden's use of the ballad and archaic language has not made for inner complexity; only when there is full interplay of languages, as in SERJEANT MUSGRAVE'S DANCE and ARMSTRONG'S LAST GOODNIGHT, does Arden break out of the isolation of a specialized language.

Kitchen, Laurence. "Arden." In his DRAMA IN THE SIXTIES: FORMAL INTERPRETATION. London: Faber and Faber, 1967, pp. 85-89.

On ARMSTRONG'S LAST GOODNIGHT, epic theatre, and Arden's university education.

Messenger, Ann P. "John Arden's Essential Vision: Tragical-Historical-Political." QJS, 58 (October 1972), 307-12.

Arden's plays are political-historical tragedies, despite the theme of the individual in conflict with society.

Milne, Tom. "The Hidden Face of Violence." In THE ENCORE READER: A CHRONICLE OF THE NEW DRAMA. Ed. Charles Marowitz, Tom Milne, and

Owen Hale. London: Methuen, 1965, pp. 115-24. Also in MODERN BRITISH DRAMATISTS: A COLLECTION OF CRITICAL ESSAYS. Ed. John Russell Brown. Englewood Cliffs, N.J.: Prentice-Hall, 1968, pp. 38-46.

SERJEANT MUSGRAVE'S DANCE, Pinter's THE BIRTHDAY PARTY, and John Whiting's SAINT'S DAY "share a common theme: the nature of violence."

O'Casey, Sean. "The Blind Primaqueera." In his BEASTS AND BENEDICTIONS. London: Macmillan, 1967, pp. 63-76.

On MUSGRAVE.

O'Connell, Mary B. "Ritual Elements in John Arden's SERJEANT MUSGRAVE'S DANCE. MD, 13 (February 1971), 356-59.

The mummer's play of PLOUGH MONDAY is the basis for MUSGRAVE, its plot and characterization.

Page, Malcolm. "The Motives of Pacifists: John Arden's SERJEANT MUSGRAVE'S DANCE." DS, 6 (Spring-Summer 1967), 66-73.

Defends Arden's willingness to see both sides of an issue. Arden supports pacifism, but finds Musgrave unable to face the violence that underlies his belief in nonviolence.

______. "Some Sources of Arden's SERJEANT MUSGRAVE'S DANCE." MODERNA SPRAK, 67, no. 4 (1973), 332-41.

Page, Malcolm, and Virginia Evans. "Approaches to John Arden's SQUIRE JONATHAN." MD, 13 (February 1971), 360-65.

A wide variety of textual readings are offered for Arden's fairy tale-erotic fantasy.

Skloot, Robert. "Spreading the Word: The Meaning of Musgrave's Logic." ETJ, 27 (May 1975), 208-19.

A production of MUSGRAVE should shift the stress from the social context of the play to the individual's problems of self-understanding and enlightenment.

Stitt, Ken. "Arden's History Plays." PROMPT, no. 12 (1968), 5-7.

Taylor, John Russell. "John Arden." In his ANGER AND AFTER: A GUIDE TO THE NEW BRITISH DRAMA. Rev. ed. London: Methuen, 1968, pp. 85-105.

Balanced, attractive survey and summary; the Arden section from the first edition (1962), as Malcolm Page points out in his bibliography, above, is reprinted in MODERN BRITISH DRAMATISTS: A COLLECTION OF CRITICAL ESSAYS. Ed. John Russell Brown. Englewood Cliffs, N.J.: Prentice-Hall, 1968, pp. 83-97.

Trussler, Simon. "Political Progress of a Paralyzed Liberal: The Community Dramas of John Arden." TDR, 11 (Summer 1969), 181-91.

On the background and staging of THE HERO RISES UP and HAROLD MUGGINS IS A MARTYR; Trussler argues that, despite their continuity with Arden's style, these plays were self-defeating experiments that Arden should put behind him.

Watson, Ian. "Kirbymoorside '63, with a Footnote by John Arden." EN, 10 (November-December 1963), 17-21.

Brief description of the Ardens' thirty evenings of free entertainment.

Worth, Katherine J. "New Forms of Melodrama and Epic Theatre." In her REVOLUTIONS IN MODERN ENGLISH DRAMA. London: G. Bell, 1973, pp. 126-33.

Discusses Arden's use of the popular English tradition--ballads and melodrama--to break the bonds of Ibsenite realism.

# ROBERT ARDREY (1908- )

SING ME NO LULLABY. New York: Dramatists Play Service, 1955.

SHADOW OF HEROES. London: Collins, 1958.

PLAYS OF THREE DECADES: THUNDER ROCK, 1939; JEB, 1946; SHADOW OF HEROES, 1958. With a preface by the author. London: Collins, 1968.

## BIBLIOGRAPHY

Salem, James M., ed. A GUIDE TO CRITICAL REVIEWS. Part 1: AMERICAN DRAMA, 1909-1969. 2nd ed. Metuchen, N.J.: Scarecrow Press, 1973.

See pages 36-38.

## SELECTED NONDRAMATIC WRITING

AFRICAN GENESIS: A PERSONAL INVESTIGATION INTO THE ANIMAL ORIGINS AND NATURE OF MAN. Illus. Berdine Ardrey. London: Collins, 1961.

THE TERRITORIAL IMPERATIVE: A PERSONAL INQUIRY INTO THE ANIMAL ORIGINS OF PROPERTY AND NATIONS. Illus. Berdine Ardrey. London: Collins, 1967.

THE SOCIAL CONTRACT: A PERSONAL INQUIRY INTO THE EVOLUTIONARY SOURCES OF ORDER AND DISORDER. Illus. Berdine Ardrey. London: Collins, 1970.

## CRITICISM

Tynan, Kenneth. TYNAN RIGHT AND LEFT: PLAYS, FILMS, PEOPLE, PLACES

AND EVENTS. New York: Atheneum, 1967, pp. 7-9.
Review of SHADOW OF HEROES.

## JOHN ASHBERY (1927- )

THE HEROES. In THE ARTISTS' THEATRE: FOUR PLAYS. Ed. Herbert Machiz. New York: Grove Press, 1960.

### CRITICISM

Howard, Richard. "John Ashbery." In his ALONE WITH AMERICA: ESSAYS ON THE ART OF POETRY IN THE UNITED STATES SINCE 1950. New York: Atheneum, 1971, pp. 18-37.

> Finds in THE HEROES speeches which reveal Ashbery's poetic principles.

## WYSTAN HUGH AUDEN (1907-1973)

THE PLAY OF DANIEL. Ed. W.H. Auden and Noah Greenberg. New York: Oxford University Press, 1959.

Auden wrote the narration.

THE CAUCASIAN CHALK CIRCLE. In BERTOLT BRECHT PLAYS. Vol. 1. Trans. James and Tania Stern with W.H. Auden. London: Methuen, 1961.

Act V of this Brecht translation had appeared in THE KENYON REVIEW in 1946.

### COLLABORATIONS WITH CHESTER KALLMAN

THE RAKE'S PROGRESS: OPERA IN THREE ACTS, A FABLE BY W.H. AUDEN AND CHESTER KALLMAN. London: Boosey and Hawkes, 1951.

The libretto for Stravinski's music.

DELIA, OR A MASQUE OF NIGHT. BO, no. 12 (1953), 164-210.

THE MAGIC FLUTE: AN OPERA IN TWO ACTS. New York: Random House, 1956.

Translation of the Schikaneder and Giesecke libretto.

DON GIOVANNI. New York: G. Schirmer, 1961.

Translation of the da Ponte libretto.

ELEGY FOR YOUNG LOVERS: OPERA IN THREE ACTS. Mainz, Germany: Schott, 1961.

Libretto for Hans Werner Henze's opera.

THE SEVEN DEADLY SINS OF THE LOWER MIDDLE CLASS. TDR, 6 (September 1961), 123-29.

Brecht translation.

THE KNIGHTS OF THE ROUND TABLE. In THE INFERNAL MACHINE AND OTHER PLAYS. New York: New Directions, 1963.

Adaptation of Cocteau's LES CHEVALIERS DE LA TABLE ROUNDE.

THE BASSARIDS: OPERA SERIA WITH INTERMEZZO IN ONE ACT. New York: Schott Music Co., 1966.

Libretto for Hans Werner Henze's opera, based on the BACCHAE of Euripides.

## BIBLIOGRAPHY

Bloomfield, B.C., and Edward Mendelsohn. W.H. AUDEN: A BIBLIOGRAPHY 1924-1969. 2nd ed. Charlottesville: Bibliographical Society of the University of Virginia, 1972.

Lists the works with reviews; pp. 354-58 list criticism of Auden's dramatic works.

## CRITICISM

Fuller, John. A READER'S GUIDE TO W.H. AUDEN. New York: Farrar, Straus and Giroux, 1970.

Kerman, Joseph. OPERA AS DRAMA. New York: Knopf, 1956, pp. 234-49.

Substantial consideration of THE RAKE'S PROGRESS.

______. "Auden's MAGIC FLUTE." HR, 10 (Summer 1957), 309-16.

The success of Auden's praiseworthy translation-adaptation is mitigated by the musical consequences of his rearrangements.

McFadden, George. "THE RAKE'S PROGRESS: A Note on the Libretto." HR, 8 (Spring 1955), 105-12.

Defends THE RAKE'S PROGRESS libretto partially in terms of Auden's interest in Kierkegaard. See also Herbert Weinstodk's letter in the next issue of this journal.

Spears, Monroe K. "Operas, Criticism, and Rites of Homage." In his THE POETRY OF W.H. AUDEN: THE DISENCHANTED ISLAND. New York: Oxford University Press, 1963, pp. 262-239.

Detailed critical analysis of the later stage works, with some interesting notes on Kallman's contribution, an excellent chronology, and copious bibliographical material in the notes.

______. "Auden and Dionysus." SHENANDOAH, 18 (1967), 85-95.

On THE BASSARIDS and its source, the BACCHAE.

Weales, Gerald. RELIGION IN MODERN ENGLISH DRAMA. Philadelphia: University of Pennsylvania, 1961.

On THE RAKE'S PROGRESS as a Christian morality play and a fairy tale, pages 224-25.

# GEORGE AXELROD (1922- )

THE SEVEN YEAR ITCH: A ROMANTIC COMEDY. New York: Random House, 1955.

THE SEVEN YEAR ITCH: A ROMANTIC COMEDY. Rev. ed. New York: Dramatists Play Service, 1956.

WILL SUCCESS SPOIL ROCK HUNTER? New York: Random House, 1956.

GOODBYE CHARLIE. New York: Samuel French, 1961.

THE MANCHURIAN CANDIDATE. In THE CINEMA OF JOHN FRANKENHEIMER. By Gerald Pratley. London: A. Zwemmer; New York: A.S. Barnes, 1969, pp. 94-96.

Brief excerpts from Axelrod's screenplay from Richard Condon's novel.

## BIBLIOGRAPHY

Salem, James M., ed. A GUIDE TO CRITICAL REVIEWS. Part 1: AMERICAN DRAMA, 1909-1969. 2nd ed. Metuchen, N.J.: Scarecrow Press, 1973.

A listing of reviews, pages 39-40.

## SELECTED NONDRAMATIC WRITING

BLACKMAILER. New York: Fawcett, 1952; London: Gold Medal, 1959.

Novel.

## CRITICISM

Kerr, Walter. THE THEATER IN SPITE OF ITSELF. New York: Simon and Schuster, 1963, pp. 265-68.

Charts the decline of Axelrod's writing, from THE SEVEN YEAR ITCH to GOODBYE CHARLIE.

Wooton, Carl. "THE COUNTRY WIFE and Contemporary Comedy: A World Apart." DS, 2 (February 1963), 333-43.

Contrasts THE SEVEN YEAR ITCH, among others, with THE COUNTRY WIFE (1675) of Wycherley.

# ALAN AYCKBOURN (1939- )

RELATIVELY SPEAKING. London: Evans Brothers, 1968.

ERNIE'S INCREDIBLE ILLUCINATIONS. In PLAYBILL ONE. Ed. Alan Durband. London: Hutchinson, 1969.

COUNTDOWN. In MIXED DOUBLES: AN ENTERTAINMENT ON MARRIAGE. London: Methuen, 1970.

One of several one-act plays.

HOW THE OTHER HALF LOVES. London: Evans Brothers, 1972.

TIME AND TIME AGAIN. New York: Samuel French, 1973.

ABSURD PERSON SINGULAR. Garden City, N.Y.: Doubleday, 1974.

CONFUSIONS: FIVE INTERLINKED ONE-ACT PLAYS. London: Margaret Ramsey, 1974.

ABSENT FRIENDS. London: Samuel French, 1975.

THE NORMAN CONQUESTS: A TRILOGY OF PLAYS. London: Chatto and Windus, 1975.

Consists of TABLE MANNERS, LIVING TOGETHER, and ROUND AND ROUND THE GARDEN. Each play has been published by Samuel French in separate acting editions.

## CRITICISM

Taylor, John Russell. "Three Farceurs: Alan Ayckbourn, David Cregan, Simon

Gray." In his THE SECOND WAVE. London: Methuen, 1971, pp. 156-62.

Plot summaries and the then unsurprising assessment that Ayckbourn is a light comedian without pretentions.

# ENID BAGNOLD (1889-1981)

THE CHALK GARDEN. London: Heinemann, 1956.

THE CHINESE PRIME MINISTER. New York: Random House, 1964.

CALL ME JACKY. In PLAYS OF THE YEAR, 67-68. Vol. 34. Ed. J.C. Trewin. London: Elek Books, 1968.

THE LAST JOKE. In her FOUR PLAYS. London: Heinemann, 1970.

## COLLECTIONS

TWO PLAYS. London: Heinemann, 1951.

Two early plays, LOTTE DUNDASS and POOR JUDAS.

FOUR PLAYS. London: Heinemann, 1970.

THE CHALK GARDEN, THE LAST JOKE, THE CHINESE PRIME MINISTER, and CALL ME JACKY.

## SELECTED NONDRAMATIC WRITING

ENID BAGNOLD'S AUTOBIOGRAPHY (FROM 1899). London: Heinemann, 1969.

## BIBLIOGRAPHY

Salem, James M., ed. A GUIDE TO CRITICAL REVIEWS. Part 3: BRITISH AND CONTINENTAL DRAMA FROM IBSEN TO PINTER. Metuchen, N.J.: Scarecrow Press, 1968, pp. 21-22.

List of reviews for New York productions of her plays.

## CRITICISM

Maltack, Cynthia S. "Metaphor and Dramatic Structure in THE CHALK GARDEN." QJS, 59 (October 1973), 304-11.

The chalk garden is a recurring, unifying metaphor throughout the play. Maltack notes that several changes and cuts from the first edition were made in the text in FOUR PLAYS.

Osborne, John. "They Call It Cricket." In DECLARATION. Ed. Tom Maschler. London: MacGibbon & Kee, 1957, p. 68.

Describes THE CHALK GARDEN as "that doddering apotheosis of the English theatrical decadence of the last thirty years."

Tynan, Kenneth. CURTAINS: SELECTIONS FROM THE DRAMA: CRITICISM AND RELATED WRITINGS. London: Longmans, 1961.

THE CHALK GARDEN "may well be the finest artificial comedy to have flowed from an English (as opposed to an Irish) pen since the death of Congreve." See pages 127-28.

Weales, Gerald. "The Madrigal in the Garden." TDR, 3 (December 1958), 42-50.

A sensitive assessment of the language and use of theatrical metaphor in THE CHALK GARDEN; Weales also finds humor in the play.

# DJUNA BARNES (1892- )

THE ANTIPHON. London: Faber and Faber, 1958.

## COLLECTIONS

SELECTED WORKS: SPILLWAY, THE ANTIPHON, NIGHTWOOD. New York: Farrar, Straus and Cudahy, 1962.

## BIBLIOGRAPHY

Hipkiss, Robert A. "Djuna Barnes (1892- )--A Bibliography." TCL, 14 (October 1968), 161-63.

Primary and secondary sources, lightly annotated.

## CRITICISM

Abel, Lionel. "Bad by North and South." In his METATHEATRE: A NEW VIEW OF DRAMATIC FORM. New York: Hill and Wang, 1963, pp. 116-21.

A scathing review of THE ANTIPHON and MacLeish's J.B.

Eberhart, Richard. "Outer and Inner Verse Drama." VIRGINIA QUARTERLY REVIEW, 34 (Autumn 1958), 618-23.

On ANTIPHON and MacLeish's J.B.

A FESTSCHRIFT FOR DJUNA BARNES ON HER 80TH BIRTHDAY. OCCASIONAL PAPERS FROM KENT STATE UNIVERSITY PRESS, No. 9. Kent, Ohio: Kent University Press, 1972.

Contributors include Joseph Chaikin, Lawrence Durrell, and Richard Eberhart.

Gerstenberger, Donna. "Three Verse Playwrights and the American Fifties." In MODERN AMERICAN DRAMA: ESSAYS IN CRITICISM. Ed. William E. Taylor. DeLand, Fla.: Everett-Edwards, 1968, pp. 117-28.

Treats THE ANTIPHON, MacLeish's J.B., and Eberhart's VISIONARY FARMS.

Nemerov, Howard. "THE ANTIPHON." NORTHWEST REVIEW, 1 (Summer 1958), 88-91.

Ponsot, Marie. "Careful Sorrow and Observed Compline." POETRY, 95 (October 1959), 47-50.

Review of THE ANTIPHON.

Scott, James B. DJUNA BARNES. Boston: Twayne, 1976.

Chapter seven is devoted to THE ANTIPHON, which Scott finds "the culmination of the tendencies, techniques, and knowledge that extend back to the beginnings of Miss Barnes's writing career." The volume has a slim bibliography.

Williamson, Alan. "The Divided Image: The Quest for Identity in the Works of Djuna Barnes." CRITIQUE: STUDIES IN MODERN FICTION, 7, no. 1 (1964), 58-74.

Discusses THE ANTIPHON and NIGHTWOOD.

## PETER BARNES (1931- )

THE RULING CLASS: A BAROQUE COMEDY. Introd. by Harold Hobson. London: Heinemann, 1969.

LEONARDO'S LAST SUPPER, AND NOONDAY DEMONS. London: Heinemann, 1970.

LULU: A SEX TRAGEDY. London: Heinemann, 1971.

> Adaptation of Frank Wedekind's plays (EARTH SPIRIT and PANDORA'S BOX), as translated by Charlotte Beck, with an introduction by Martin Esslin.

THE BEWITCHED. London: Heinemann, 1974.

### CRITICISM

"Peter Barnes Interviewed by Brendan Hennessy." TR, 37-38 (Autumn and Winter 1970-71), 118-24.

> On language, cinema, and religion in THE RULING CLASS and the two short plays.

Taylor, John Russell. "The Dark Fantastic." In his THE SECOND WAVE. London: Methuen, 1971, pp. 206-08.

> Brief summaries.

Worth, Katharine J. "Forms of Freedom and Mystery: Beneath the Subtext." In his REVOLUTIONS IN MODERN ENGLISH DRAMA. London: G. Bell, 1973, pp. 156-60.

> On THE RULING CLASS'S mixture of farce and "painful private material."

# PHILIP BARRY (1896-1949)

SECOND THRESHOLD. With revisions and a preface by Robert E. Sherwood. New York: Harper, 1951.

Posthumous.

## COLLECTIONS

STATES OF GRACE: EIGHT PLAYS BY PHILIP BARRY. Ed. and with biographical essay by Brendan Gill. New York: Harcourt Brace Jovanovich, 1975.

The biographical essay, "The Dark Advantage," an expanded version of a NEW YORKER profile, is an excellent, sympathetic introduction to Barry and his career. The collected plays are pre-1950.

## BIBLIOGRAPHY

Salem, James M., ed. A GUIDE TO CRITICAL REVIEWS. Part 1: AMERICAN DRAMA, 1909-1969. 2nd ed. Metuchen, N.J.: Scarecrow Press, 1973.

List of reviews of SECOND THRESHOLD, p. 48.

## CRITICISM

Clurman, Harold. "From Lorca Down." NR, 124 (5 February 1951), 22-23.

Review of SECOND THRESHOLD.

Lavery, Emmet. "The World of Philip Barry." DC, 3 (November 1960), 98-107.

Meserve, Walter J. "Philip Barry: A Dramatist's Search." MD, 13 (May 1970), 93-99.

SECOND THRESHOLD is a culmination of Barry's search for a philosophical drama.

Rappolo, J.P. PHILIP BARRY. New York: Twayne, 1965.

Sievers, Wieder D. FREUD ON BROADWAY. New York: Hermitage House, 1955.

On SECOND THRESHOLD, pages 208-11.

## SAMUEL BECKETT (1906- )

EN ATTENDANT GODOT. Paris: Editions de Minuit, 1952. Trans. the author as WAITING FOR GODOT, A TRAGICOMEDY IN TWO ACTS. New York: Grove Press, 1954; London: Faber and Faber, 1956.

FIN DE PARTIE, SUIVI DE ACTE SANS PAROLES. Paris: Editions de Minuit, 1957. Trans. the author as ENDGAME, A PLAY IN ONE ACT, FOLLOWED BY ACT WITHOUT WORDS, A MIME FOR ONE PLAYER. New York: Grove Press; London: Faber and Faber, 1958.

> The American edition omits the note that by contract ACT WITHOUT WORDS must be performed with the music of Beckett's cousin, John Beckett.

ALL THAT FALL. New York: Grove Press, 1957.

ALL THAT FALL: A PLAY FOR RADIO. London: Faber and Faber, 1957.

KRAPP'S LAST TAPE. ER, 2 (Summer 1958), 13-24.

KRAPP'S LAST TAPE AND EMBERS. London: Faber and Faber, 1959.

KRAPP'S LAST TAPE AND OTHER DRAMATIC PIECES. New York: Grove Press, 1960.

> Includes ALL THAT FALL, EMBERS, and ACT WITHOUT WORDS I and ACT WITHOUT WORDS II.

ACT WITHOUT WORDS II: A MIME FOR TWO PLAYERS. NEW DEPARTURES (South Hinksey, Engl.), 1 (Summer 1959), 89-90.

ACT WITHOUT WORDS II: A MIME FOR TWO PLAYERS. In his KRAPP'S LAST TAPE AND OTHER DRAMATIC PIECES. New York: Grove Press, 1960.

ACT WITHOUT WORDS II: A MIME FOR TWO PLAYERS. In EH JOE AND OTHER WRITINGS. London: Faber and Faber, 1967.

ACT WITHOUT WORDS II, according to Raymond Federman and John Fletcher's authoritative SAMUEL BECKETT: HIS WORKS AND CRITICS: AN ESSAY IN BIBLIOGRAPHY, was written in French in 1956. The original French text was first published in Germany, with Beckett's English translation and a German translation, in 1963 in DRAMATISCHE DICHTUNGEN I. Frankfurt: Suhrkamp Verlag, 1963.

EMBERS: A PLAY FOR RADIO. ER, 3 (November-December 1959), 28-41.

EMBERS: A PLAY FOR RADIO. In his KRAPP'S LAST TAPE AND EMBERS. London: Faber and Faber, 1959.

EMBERS: A PLAY FOR RADIO. In his KRAPP'S LAST TAPE AND OTHER DRAMATIC PIECES. New York: Grove Press, 1960.

HAPPY DAYS. New York: Grove Press, 1961.

WORDS AND MUSIC: A RADIO PLAY. ER, 6 (November-December 1962), 34-43.

WORDS AND MUSIC: A RADIO PLAY. In his PLAY AND TWO SHORT PIECES FOR RADIO. London: Faber and Faber, 1964.

Includes CASCANDO, as well as PLAY and WORDS AND MUSIC.

CASCANDO. Paris: Editions de Minuit, 1963. Trans. the author as CASCANDO: A RADIO PIECE FOR MUSIC AND VOICE. In his PLAY AND TWO SHORT PIECES FOR RADIO. London: Faber and Faber, 1964.

CASCANDO. In his CASCANDO AND OTHER SHORT DRAMATIC PIECES. New York: Grove Press, 1968.

Includes WORDS AND MUSIC, EH JOE, PLAY, and COME AND GO.

PLAY: A STAGE PLAY. In his PLAY AND TWO SHORT PLAYS FOR RADIO. London: Faber and Faber, 1964.

Beckett provides some interesting notes on the placement of the urns, the repeats, and his suggestions on the use of lights.

EH JOE AND OTHER WRITINGS. London: Faber and Faber, 1967.

Includes EH JOE, ACT WITHOUT WORDS II, and FILM.

COME AND GO: DRAMATICULE. London: Faber and Faber, 1967.

COME AND GO: DRAMATICULE. In his CASCANDO AND OTHER SHORT PIECES. New York: Grove Press, 1968.

"For John Calder."

FILM. In his EH JOE AND OTHER WRITINGS. London: Faber and Faber, 1967.

FILM. New York: Grove Press, 1969.

The complete scenario, with illustrations, production shots, and an essay on directing FILM by Alan Schneider.

BREATH. In OH! CALCUTTA! AN ENTERTAINMENT WITH MUSIC. New York: Grove Press, 1969.

Beckett's is the unidentified opening scene in the nude review OH! CALCUTTA! devised by Kenneth Tynan (see above).

BREATH. G, 4, no. 16 (1970), pp. 6-9.

Beckett's OH! CALCUTTA! contribution minus the changes (Tynan's ?) in the stage directions which added nude bodies to the rubbish pile. John Calder's introductory note explains the changes and Beckett's reaction.

BREATH AND OTHER SHORTS. London: Faber and Faber, 1971.

Includes COME AND GO, ACTS WITHOUT WORDS I AND II, and the fiction, FROM AN ABANDONED WORK.

NOT I. London: Faber and Faber, 1973.

## BIBLIOGRAPHY

Federman, Raymond, and John Fletcher. SAMUEL BECKETT: HIS WORKS AND HIS CRITICS. AN ESSAY IN BIBLIOGRAPHY. Berkeley: University of California Press, 1970.

An indispensable guide for the student of Beckett, this is among the very best scholarly bibliographies.

## SELECTED NONDRAMATIC WRITING

MOLLOY. Paris: Editions de Minuit, 1951. Trans. the author and Patrick

Bowles. Paris: Olympia Press; New York: Grove Press, 1955; London: John Calder, 1959.

MALONE MEURT. Paris: Editions de Minuit, 1951. Trans. the author as MALONE DIES. New York: Grove Press, 1956.

L'INNOMMABLE. Paris: Editions de Minuit, 1953. Trans. the author as THE UNNAMABLE. New York: Grove Press, 1958.

WATT. Paris: Olympia Press, 1953; New York: Grove Press, 1959; London: John Calder, 1963.

NOUVELLES ET TEXTES POUR RIEN. Paris: Editions de Minuit, 1955. Trans. the author as STORIES AND TEXTS FOR NOTHING. New York: Grove Press, 1967.

FROM AN ABANDONED WORK. TRINITY NEWS, A DUBLIN UNIVERSITY WEEKLY, 3 (7 June 1956), 4.

FROM AN ABANDONED WORK. ER, 1, no. 3 (1957), 83-91.

FROM AN ABANDONED WORK. London: Faber and Faber, 1958.

> According to Federman and Fletcher, who cite Beckett as their source, "the fragment results from an attempt to return to fiction in English, in 1954 or 1955. Asked why it ends abruptly, he has replied 'there was no more to be said.'"

MERCIER ET CAMIER. Paris: Editions de Minuit, 1970. Trans. the author as MERCIER AND CAMIER. New York: Grove Press, 1975.

"Letters on ENDGAME." VV, 19 March 1958, pp. 8, 15. Also in THE VILLAGE VOICE READER: A MIXED BAG FROM THE GREENWICH VILLAGE NEWSPAPER. Eds. Daniel Wolf and Edwin Fancher. New York: Grove Press, 1963, pp. 166-69.

> Extracts from Beckett's letters to Alan Schneider tracing the origins of ENDGAME, described by Beckett as "more inhuman" than GODOT. Beckett worries that the translation from French to English will involve more loss than was the case with GODOT. He also writes of his refusal to explain his plays to journalists: "My work is made of fundamental sounds (no joke intended), made as fully as possible, and I accept responsibility for nothing else. If people want to have headaches among the overtones, let them."

COMMENT C'EST. Paris: Editions de Minuit, 1961. Trans. the author as

HOW IT IS. New York: Grove Press; London: John Calder, 1964.

POEMS IN ENGLISH. London: John Calder, 1961; New York: Grove Press, 1964.

IMAGINATION MORTE IMAGINEZ. Paris: Editions de Minuit, 1965. Trans. the author as IMAGINATION DEAD IMAGINE. London: Calder and Boyars, 1965.

NO'S KNIFE: SELECTED SHORTER PROSE, 1945-1966. London: Calder and Boyars, 1967.

Includes STORIES AND TEXTS FOR NOTHING, FROM AN ABANDONED WORK, IMAGINATION DEAD IMAGINE, ENOUGH, and PING.

## CRITICISM

Abel, Lionel. METATHEATRE: A NEW VIEW OF DRAMATIC FORM. New York: Hill and Wang, 1963.

A curious essay claiming that ENDGAME is theatre à clef, with James Joyce as Hamm and Beckett as Clov, see pages 134-40.

Admussen, Richard L. "The Manuscripts of Beckett's PLAY." MD, 16 (June 1973), 23-27.

Alpaugh, David J. "Negative Definition in Samuel Beckett's HAPPY DAY'S." TCL, 11 (January 1966), 202-10.

HAPPY DAYS shows not what is, but what is not. This is done by Beckett's various uses of the "old style," as Winnie calls it.

______. "The Symbolic Structure of Samuel Beckett's ALL THAT FALL." MD, 9 (December 1966), 324-32.

Physical movement, culminating in the child's death, provides the central despairing metaphor of ALL THAT FALL.

______. "EMBERS and the Sea: Beckettian Intimations of Immortality." MD, 16 (December 1973), 317-28.

A surprising comparison of EMBERS and Wordsworth's ode on immortality.

Alvarez, A. BECKETT. London: Fontana, 1973.

Brief, chronological survey.

Anderson, Irmgard Zeyss. "Beckett's 'Tabernacle' in FIN DE PARTIE." ROMANCE NOTES, 14 (Spring 1973), 417-20.

Hamm's house is similar to a Jewish temple, as described in EXODUS: chapters 25-28.

Atkins, Anselm. "Lucky's Speech in Beckett's WAITING FOR GODOT: A Punctuated Sense-Line Arrangement." ETJ, 19 (December 1967), 426-32.

An explication of Lucky's speech, explaining it as an argument for absurdity.

Avigal, Shoshana. "Beckett's PLAY: The Circular Line of Existence." MD, 18 (September 1975), 251-58.

Barnard, G.C. SAMUEL BECKETT: A NEW APPROACH. A STUDY OF THE NOVELS AND PLAYS. New York: Dodd, Mead, 1970.

This is a psychological reading, arguing that Beckett's plays and novels are unified by their continued depiction of schizophrenia.

Beausang, Michael. "Myth and Tragi-Comedy in Beckett's HAPPY DAYS." In FROM AN ANCIENT TO A MODERN THEATRE. Ed. R.G. Collins. Winnipeg: University of Manitoba, 1972, pp. 117-35.

Winnie, Willie, and the fertility god Tammuz.

BECKETT AT SIXTY: A FESTSCHRIFT. London: Calder and Boyars, 1967.

Includes, among other interesting material, a letter from Harold Pinter about Beckett.

Bedient, Calvin. "Beckett and the Drama of Gravity." SR, 78 (January-March 1970), 143-55.

Images of inertia, entrapment, and gravitation unify the disparate world of the Beckett plays.

Berlin, Normand. "Beckett and Shakespeare." FRENCH REVIEW, 40 (April 1967), 647-51.

Disputes Kott's theory of an absurdist KING LEAR, in SHAKESPEARE, OUR CONTEMPORARY (1964), by contrasting the play with Beckett's approach to the absurd.

Bermel, Albert. "Hero and Heroine as Topographical Features." In his CONTRADICTORY CHARACTERS: AN INTERPRETATION OF MODERN THEATRE. New York: E.P. Dutton, 1973, pp. 159-84.

On the often antagonistic dialog between the paired protagonists of KRAPP'S LAST TAPE and HAPPY DAYS. In the case of KRAPP'S LAST TAPE the dialog is between the old and the young Krapp.

Brater, Enoch. "The 'Absurd' Actor in the Theatre of Samuel Beckett." ETJ, 27 (May 1975), 197-207.

A look at the dilemmas of performing Beckett.

Brooks, Curtis M. "Mythic Pattern in WAITING FOR GODOT." MD, 9 (December 1966), 292-99.

Vegetation myths and myths of the "regeneration of time," provide a partial key to GODOT.

Brown, John Russell. "Mr. Beckett's Shakespeare." CQ, 5 (Winter 1963), 310-26.

"Mr. Beckett can recognize traditional symbols . . . nevertheless his dramatis personae are actuated by forces not represented by those symbols."

Chase, N.C. "Images of Man: LE MALENTENDU and EN ATTENDANT GODOT." WS, 7 (Autumn 1966), 295-302.

Beckett's and Camus' plays, while sharing several absurdist premises, present opposing images of man: irrational and rational, respectively.

Chevigny, Bell Gale, ed. TWENTIETH CENTURY INTERPRETATIONS OF ENDGAME. Englewood Cliffs, N.J.: Prentice-Hall, 1969.

Cleveland, Louise O. "Trials in the Soundscape: The Radio Plays of Samuel Beckett." MD, 11 (December 1968), 267-82.

Beckett's radio plays, in the manner unique to the medium, are attempts to do what the stage plays do with physical presence: explore confrontations with an "indeterminant world."

Coe, Richard N. BECKETT. Edinburgh: Oliver and Boyd, 1964.

The plays are treated intelligently but quite abstractly in one of the book's six chapters. There are some typographical errors in the American edition, titled SAMUEL BECKETT (New York: Grove Press, 1969).

Cohen, Robert S. "Parallels and the Possibility of Influence Between Simone Weil's WAITING FOR GOD and Samuel Beckett's WAITING FOR GODOT." MD, 6 (February 1964), 425-36.

Finds Weil's work, first published posthumously in Paris in 1950, as a source for Beckett's treatment of alienation and, less certainly, a clue to the identity of Godot.

Cohn, Ruby. "Samuel Beckett Self-Translator." PMLA, 76 (December 1961), 613-21.

This is a splendidly detailed comparison of Beckett in French and Beckett in English. GODOT in French is more colloquial, in English bleaker and less comic. In its original French ENDGAME is larger, including details about the small boy Clov glimpses near the play's conclusion.

______. "Play and Player in the Plays of Samuel Beckett." YALE FRENCH STUDIES, 29 (Spring-Summer 1962), 43-48.

______. SAMUEL BECKETT: THE COMIC GAMUT. New Brunswick, N.J.: Rutgers University, 1962.

A survey of Beckett's comic techniques and styles. The last four chapters deal, in whole or in part, with the dramas. Pages 209-10 give a summary of Beckett's first play, ELEUTHERIA, as yet unpublished. An appendix contains WHOROSCOPE, TEXT, OAFTISH, and a translation of Watt's "Anti-Language." There is also a valuable chronology of Beckett's works to 1961, and a bibliography of secondary sources.

______. "The Absurdly Absurd: Avatars of Godot." COMPARATIVE LITERATURE STUDIES, 2, no. 2 (1965), 233-40.

Distinguishes between absurd form and absurd content, and then compares WAITING FOR GODOT with Pinter's THE DUMB WAITER.

______. "The Beginning of ENDGAME." MD, 9 (December 1966), 319-23.

A comparison of the early two-act French version of ENDGAME, with the finished one-act version.

______. "THEATRUM MUNDI and Contemporary Theater." COMPARATIVE DRAMA, 1 (Spring 1967), 28-35.

______. "Beckett and Shakespeare." MD, 15 (December 1972), 223-30.

Charts Beckett's use of Shakespeare, especially in ENDGAME and HAPPY DAYS, with some remarkable allusions and thematic similarities.

______. BACK TO BECKETT. Princeton, N.J.: Princeton University Press, 1973.

Even without footnotes or index, this is a splendid study, full of new, useful information, from one of the most respected of all Beckett scholars.

______, ed. PERSPECTIVE, 11 (Autumn 1959), entire issue.

Beckett issue.

______, ed. MD, 9 (December 1966), entire issue.

A Beckett issue containing, among others, six essays on GODOT.

______, ed. CASEBOOK ON WAITING FOR GODOT. New York: Grove Press, 1967.

In two parts, called Impact and Interpretation, this is the best collection of reviews and essays on GODOT.

______, ed. SAMUEL BECKETT: A COLLECTION OF CRITICISM. New York: McGraw-Hill, 1975.

A fine collection of eleven essays, all especially written for this volume. Of particular interest are the essays by Yasunari Takahashi, Alec Reid, Hersh Zeifman, and Elin Diamond, along with a useful chronology and introduction by the ubiquitous and invaluable editor.

Dennis, Nigel. "Original Sin and Dog Biscuits." NYRB, 16 (8 April 1971), 21-23.

After comparing it to THE THREE SISTERS, Dennis finds GODOT, despite its beautiful vision, "a badly flawed play," in which Lucky and Pozzo are completely extraneous. He suggests that they are padding, added to make the play produceable. ENDGAME, though less beautiful, has a more pleasing aesthetic form.

Driver, Tom F. "Beckett by the Madelaine." COLUMBIA UNIVERSITY FORUM, 4 (Spring 1961), 21-25.

Interview with Beckett.

Duckworth, Colin. "The Making of GODOT." THEATRE RESEARCH, 7, no. 3 (1966), 123-45. Also in CASEBOOK ON WAITING FOR GODOT. Ed. Ruby Cohn. New York: Grove Press, 1967, pp. 89-100.

This striking comparison of the manuscript of GODOT with Beckett's MERCIER ET CAMIER (1970) reveals the numerous alterations made prior to the play's publication and its debt to the novel. The evidence of these alterations runs counter to the many fanciful interpretations of the play. A revised and expanded version of this valuable essay is the introduction to Duckworth's edition of the French text of the play, published by Harrup in London in 1966.

Dukore, Bernard F. "Gogo, Didi, and the Absent Godot." DS, 1 (February 1962), 301-07.

Vladimir as the Id and Estragon as the Ego.

______. "KRAPP'S LAST TAPE as Tragicomedy." MD, 15 (March 1973), 351-54.

From the numerous puns in its title to its basic style, KRAPP'S LAST TAPE plays the comic and the tragic against each other.

Eastman, Richard M. "The Strategy of Samuel Beckett's ENDGAME." MD, 2 (May 1959), 36-44.

Beckett does not write allegory; he refuses to give his audience acceptable abstractions to explain his plays. The audience is thus forced to experience the kind of alienation the play depicts.

______. "Samuel Beckett and HAPPY DAYS." MD, 6 (February 1964), 417-24.

Beckett is a poet of entropy, but in HAPPY DAYS he comes his closest to comedy.

Esslin, Martin. "Godot and His Children: The Theatre of Samuel Beckett and Harold Pinter." In EXPERIMENTAL DRAMA. Ed. William A. Armstrong. London: G. Bell and Sons, 1963, pp. 128-46. Also in MODERN BRITISH DRAMATISTS: A COLLECTION OF CRITICAL ESSAYS. Ed. John Russell Brown. Englewood Cliffs, N.J.: Prentice-Hall, 1968, pp. 58-70.

______, ed. SAMUEL BECKETT: A COLLECTION OF CRITICAL ESSAYS. Englewood Cliffs, N.J.: Prentice-Hall, 1965.

Fletcher, John. "Action and Play in Beckett's Theater." MD, 9 (December 1966), 242-50.

Gestures derived from the circus, vaudeville, and mime, all have a crucial role in Beckett's plays.

______. SAMUEL BECKETT'S ART. London: Chatto and Windus, 1967.

[Fraser, G.S.] "They Also Serve." TIMES LITERARY SUPPLEMENT, 10 February 1956, p. 84.

Originally published anonymously, this famous article suggests a Christian interpretation of WAITING FOR GODOT: "The tree on the stage . . . obviously stands for both the Tree of Knowledge of Good and Evil . . . and for the Cross."

Friedman, Melvin J. "Crritic!" MD, 9 (December 1966), 300-308.

A good-natured bibliographical journey through the thickets of the GODOT controversy.

_____, ed. SAMUEL BECKETT NOW: CRITICAL APPROACHES TO HIS NOVELS, POETRY AND PLAYS. Chicago: University of Chicago Press, 1970.

Frisch, Jack E. "ENDGAME: A Play as Poem." DS, 3 (October 1963), 257-63.

A reading of ENDGAME focusing on the relationships and rhythms between words and silence.

Gilman, Richard. "Beckett." In his THE MAKING OF MODERN DRAMA: A STUDY OF BUCHNER, IBSEN, STRINDBERG, CHEKHOV, PIRANDELLO, BRECHT, BECKETT, HANDKE. New York: Farrar, Straus and Giroux, 1974, pp. 234-66.

Gilman emphasizes Beckett's creation of a world without conventional social and philosophical connections, a world of pure ontology that must be accepted on its own terms.

Hampton, Charles C., Jr. "Samuel Beckett's FILM." MD, 11 (December 1968), 299-305.

FILM ironically uses Berkeley's "esse est percipi" to demonstrate self-destruction through self-perception.

Hassan, Ihab. THE LITERATURE OF SILENCE: HENRY MILLER AND SAMUEL BECKETT. New York: Knopf, 1967.

Hesla, David H. THE SHAPE OF CHAOS: AN INTERPRETATION OF THE ART OF SAMUEL BECKETT. Minneapolis: University of Minnesota Press, 1971.

The one chapter on the plays is, like the rest of this volume, primarily devoted to expounding Beckett's philosophic premises, and their parallels in the history of philosophy.

Hubert, Renee Riese. "Beckett's PLAY Between Poetry and Performance." MD, 9 (December 1966), 339-46.

After comparing it with Sartre's NO EXIT, Hubert sees PLAY as culmination and prototype of Beckett's art, hovering between play and poetry, life and death.

Iser, Wolfgang. "Samuel Beckett's Dramatic Language." MD,9 (December 1966), 251-59.

The disjunction between language and action gives Beckett's plays their unique shock effect.

Kennedy, Andrew K. SIX DRAMATISTS IN SEARCH OF A LANGUAGE. Cambridge, Engl.: Cambridge University Press, 1975.

The idea of the failure of language is, for Beckett, a myth for creation. In the plays, various kinds of decayed language become part of the action and are renewed, but this strategy, with so many styles pre-empted, now seems exhausted.

Kenner, Hugh. SAMUEL BECKETT: A CRITICAL STUDY. 2nd ed. Berkeley: University of California Press, 1968.

This magisterial, if often elliptical, survey of Beckett's work is very strong on Beckett's philosophical roots in Descartes, and in the mystery of irrational numbers. Kenner is positively eloquent on that quintessential Beckettian vehicle, the bicycle.

______. A READER'S GUIDE TO SAMUEL BECKETT. New York: Farrar, Straus and Giroux, 1973.

This superlative introduction to Beckett is arranged largely in chronological order, with chapters devoted to specific works or groupings of works, beginning with GODOT. The volume is written in simpler fashion than Kenner's earlier, thematically organized, critical study of Beckett.

Kern, Edith. "Drama Stripped for Inaction: Beckett's GODOT." YALE FRENCH STUDIES, 14 (Winter 1954-55), 41-47.

______. "Beckett and the Spirit of the Commedia dell'Arte." MD, 9 (December 1966), 260-67.

Beckett's plays, especially GODOT, are filled with the self-conscious, physical theatricality typical of the Commedia.

Kott, Jan. "A Note on Beckett's Realism." Trans. Boleslaw Taborski. TDR, 10 (Spring 1966), 156-59.

Kott compares HAPPY DAYS with the behavior of elderly patients in hospitals and finds that in the play, as in all Beckett's work, there is a correspondence between the realistically conceived details and the generalized human situation.

Lowenkron, David Henry. "A Case for 'The Tragicall Historie of Hamm.'" ARIZONA QUARTERLY, 30 (Autumn 1974), 254-63.

Lyons, Charles R. "Some Variations of KINDERMORD as Dramatic Archetype." COMPARATIVE DRAMA, 1 (Spring 1967), 56-71.

ENDGAME and Albee's WHO'S AFRAID OF VIRGINIA WOOLF? are each analyzed, along with plays by Shakespeare, Racine, Ibsen,

Pirandello, and others, as part of a pattern in which the death of a child, real or imaginary, signals a crucial, often purgative, event in the life of the protagonist.

______. "Some Analogies Between the Epic Brecht and the Absurdist Beckett." COMPARATIVE DRAMA, 1 (Winter 1967-68), 297-304.

Both Brecht and Beckett have broken away from Aristotelian time sense, both oppose any identification of performance and reality, and for both, in MOTHER COURAGE and HAPPY DAYS, the assertion of the power of the individual is a deeply ambiguous act.

______. "Beckett's Major Plays and the Trilogy." COMPARATIVE DRAMA, 5 (Winter 1971-72), 254-68.

Compares and contrasts the later trilogy of novels, MOLLOY, MALONE MEURT, and L'INNOMMABLE, with the major plays.

McCoy, Charles. "WAITING FOR GODOT: A Biblical Approach." FLORIDA REVIEW, 2 (Spring 1958), 63-72.

Mailer, Norman. "The Hip and the Square." VV, 2 May 1956, p. 5.

Without having read or seen the play, Mailer claims that GODOT is a "poem to impotence."

______. "A Public Notice by Norman Mailer." VV, 9 May 1956, p. 12.

Mailer retracts his previous week's analysis of GODOT, having now both read and seen the play. He praises it as a work of art, speculating that Lucky might be Godot, that Beckett believes in a finite, fleshy God, and that most of Beckett's admirers are snobs. This item is often erroneously dated as of May 7.

Mercier, Vivian. "Samuel Beckett and the Sheela-na-gig." KR, 23 (Spring 1961), 298-324.

Irish comedy, with its macabre sexuality, is an integral part of Irish literature down to Beckett. This theme is expanded upon in the following entry.

______. THE IRISH COMIC TRADITION. Oxford: Oxford University Press, 1962.

Murphy, Vincent J. "Being and Perception: Beckett's FILM." MD, 18 (March 1975), 43-48.

Too facile an identification of FILM with its Berkeleian epigraph blurs Beckett's true achievement.

Oberg, Arthur K. KRAPP'S LAST TAPE and the Proustian Vision." MD, 9 (December 1966), 333-38.

KRAPP'S LAST TAPE begins as a parody of Proust and ends as a unique expression of sexual futility.

Reid, Alec. "Beckett and the Drama of Unknowing." DS, 2 (October 1962), 130-38.

Beckett has been over allegorized. His plays actually give artistic form to the experience of nonknowing.

_____. ALL I CAN MANAGE, MORE THAN I COULD: AN APPROACH TO THE PLAYS OF SAMUEL BECKETT. Rev. ed. New York: Grove Press, 1971.

Originally published in 1968 by Dolmen Press of Dublin.

Schechner, Richard. "Reality if Not Enough: An Interview with Alan Schneider." TDR, 9 (Spring 1965), 118-52.

Beckett's American director recalls PLAY and FILM, as well as Albee's WHO'S AFRAID OF VIRGINIA WOOLF.

_____. "There's Lots of Time in GODOT." MD, 9 (December 1966), 268-76.

The rhythm of GODOT is that of "habit interrupted by memory, memory obliterated by games." Schechner sees the play as a varied series of strategies by the two protagonists to avoid awareness.

Schoell, Konrad. "The Chain and the Circle: A Structural Comparison of WAITING FOR GODOT and ENDGAME." MD, 11 (May 1968), 48-54.

All of Beckett's plays fall into two temporal and structural categories: the linear and the closed, the chain and the circle. GODOT is open-ended, having neither beginning nor end. ENDGAME begins after an unspecified catastrophe and moves toward ultimate entrophy.

Simpson, Alan. BECKETT AND BEHAN AND A THEATRE IN DUBLIN. London: Routledge and Kegan Paul, 1962.

On the first Irish production of GODOT, and a defense of "Irish" interpretations of the play.

Szanto, George H. "Samuel Beckett: Dramatic Possibilities." MR, 15 (Autumn 1974), 735-61.

Beckett's is an empty theatre filled with cultural junk, on which critics and audiences seek to impose a meaning. The argument ranges over contemporary culture and concludes that Beckett's plays are paradigms for a future revolutionary culture deeply influenced by technological availability.

Todd, Robert E. "Proust and Redemption in WAITING FOR GODOT." MD, 10 (September 1967), 175-81.

The distinction between hope and desire, drawn from Proust and Beckett's early monograph on Proust (1931), provides a Christian context for the interpretation of Godot's identity.

Trousdale, Marion. "Dramatic Form: The Example of GODOT." MD, 11 (May 1968), 1-9.

In GODOT, Beckett dispenses with traditional surface action and focuses on the act of playing itself, creating a uniquely abstract and metaphoric drama.

Weales, Gerald. "The Language of ENDGAME." TDR, 6 (June 1962), 107-17.

An effective defense of the play.

Webb, Eugene. THE PLAYS OF SAMUEL BECKETT. Seattle: University of Washington Press, 1972.

As in his earlier SAMUEL BECKETT: A STUDY OF HIS NOVELS (1970), Webb's emphasis is philosophical; theatrical and artistic questions are all but ignored.

Zilliacus, Clas. "Three Times GODOT: Beckett, Brecht, Bulatovic." COMPARATIVE DRAMA, 4 (Spring 1970), 3-17.

Fascinating examination of Brecht's unpublished revision of GODOT, as well as Bulatovic's 1966 sequel to Beckett.

______. "Samuel Beckett's EMBERS: 'A Matter of Fundamental Sounds.'" MD, 13 (September 1970), 216-25.

Treats the BBC production, its unique properties as a radio play, and Beckett's refusal to allow stage performances.

# BRENDAN BEHAN (1923-1964)

THE QUARE FELLOW: A COMEDY-DRAMA. London: Methuen, 1956.

THE BIG HOUSE, IRISH WRITING, 37 (Autumn 1957), 17-34.

A one-act play commissioned by BBC Radio.

THE BIG HOUSE. ER, 5 (September-October 1961), 40-63.

AN GIALL. Baile Atha, Ire.: An Chomhairle Naisiunta Dramaiochta, n.d.

The play upon which THE HOSTAGE is based, not yet translated into English.

THE HOSTAGE. London: Methuen, 1958.

THE HOSTAGE. 3rd ed. rev. London: Methuen, 1962.

"MOVING OUT" AND "A GARDEN PARTY": TWO PLAYS. Introd. by Michael O'hAodala and ed. Robert Hogan. Dixon, Calif.: Proscenium Press, 1967.

Two radio plays from the fifties.

RICHARD'S CORK LEG. Ed. and introd. Alan Simpson. London: Methuen, 1973.

Redaction of rough drafts left by Behan.

## BIBLIOGRAPHY

Salem, James M., ed. A GUIDE TO CRITICAL REVIEWS. Part 3: BRITISH AND CONTINENTAL DRAMA FROM IBSEN TO PINTER. Metuchen, N.J.: Scarecrow Press, 1968.

A list of the reviews of the New York productions, pages 34-35.

## SELECTED NONDRAMATIC WRITING

BORSTAL BOY. London: Hutchinson, 1958.

Autobiography. See also CONFESSIONS, below.

BRENDAN BEHAN'S ISLAND: AN IRISH SKETCH-BOOK. Illus. Paul Hogarth. London: Hutchinson, 1962.

Brief, descriptive essays.

HOLD YOUR HOUR AND HAVE ANOTHER. Illus. Beatrice Behan. London: Hutchinson, 1963.

Articles from the Irish press, 1954-56.

SCARPER. Garden City: Doubleday, 1964.

Mystery novel.

CONFESSIONS OF AN IRISH REBEL. London: Hutchinson, 1965.

The second part of the autobiography, compiled from tapes by Rae Jeffs.

## CRITICISM

Armstrong, William A. "The Irish Point of View: The Plays of Sean O'Casey, Brendan Behan, and Thomas Murray." In EXPERIMENTAL DRAMA. Ed. William A. Armstrong. London: G. Bell, 1963, pp. 79-102.

Behan, Beatrice, with Des Hickey and Gus Smith. MY LIFE WITH BRENDAN. Los Angeles: Nash Publications, 1974.

His wife's reminiscences.

Behan, Dominic. MY BROTHER BRENDAN. New York: Simon and Schuster, 1966.

Boyle, Ted. BRENDAN BEHAN. New York: Twayne, 1969.

DeBurca, Seamus. "The Essential Brendan Behan." MD, 8 (February 1966), 374-81.

Gerdes, Peter R. THE MAJOR WORKS OF BRENDAN BEHAN. Bern, Switzerland: Herbert Lang, 1973.

A published dissertation.

Murphy, Brian. "Brendan Behan at Theatre Workshop: Storyteller into Playwright." PROMPT, no. 5 (1964), 4-6.

An actor from the original Theatre Workshop productions of THE QUARE FELLOW and THE HOSTAGE reminisces about Behan's contribution to the company and the relationship between Behan's script and the final performing version of each play.

O'Connor, Ulick. BRENDAN BEHAN. London: Hamilton, 1970.

Porter, Raymond. BRENDAN BEHAN. New York: Columbia University Press, 1973.

Brief, informative pamphlet.

Simpson, Alan. BECKETT AND BEHAN AND A THEATRE IN DUBLIN. London: Routledge and Kegan Paul, 1962.

The producer of the first production of THE QUARE FELLOW recollects his experiences with Behan. The book vividly describes the Dublin theatrical scene.

Sullivan, Kevin. "Last Playboy of the Western World." NATION, 15 March 1965, pp. 283-87.

Obituary tribute.

Wall, Richard. "AN GIALL and THE HOSTAGE Compared." MD, 18 (June 1975), 165-72.

An important study asserting that THE HOSTAGE is vulgarized from its Irish original.

Wickstrom, Gordon M. "The Heroic Dimension in Brendan Behan's THE HOSTAGE." ETJ, 22 (December 1970), 406-11.

The hostage's death and revival are seen as mythic affirmation.

# S[AMUEL] N[ATHANIEL] BEHRMAN (1893-1973)

LET ME HEAR THE MELODY! Rev. ed. New York: 1951.

Typescript, Lincoln Center Library of the Performing Arts.

THE FOREIGN LANGUAGE. New York: n.p., 1951.

Typescript of an early version of JANE, Lincoln Center Library of the Performing Arts. The play is based on the short story "Jane" by W. Somerset Maugham.

JANE. New York: Random House, 1952.

I KNOW MY LOVE. New York: Samuel French, 1952.

Adapted from AUPRES DE MA BLONDE by Marcel Achard.

THE COLD WIND AND THE WARM. New York: Random House, 1959.

Suggested by his NEW YORKER series and his book THE WORCESTER ACCOUNT.

LORD PENGO. New York: Random House, 1963.

Suggested by his NEW YORKER series, "The Days of Duveen."

BUT FOR WHOM CHARLIE. New York: Random House, 1964.

One of the early theatrical catastrophes at the Lincoln Center Theatre, New York City.

## COLLABORATION

FANNY. New York: Random House, 1955.

Behrman and director Joshua Logan collaborated on the libretto.

Based on the trilogy by Marcel Pagnol; music and lyrics by Harold Rome.

## COLLECTIONS

4 PLAYS: THE SECOND MAN, BIOGRAPHY, RAIN FROM HEAVEN, END OF SUMMER. New York: Random House, 1955.

Earlier plays reprinted.

## BIBLIOGRAPHY

Salem, James M., ed. A GUIDE TO CRITICAL REVIEWS. Part 1: AMERICAN DRAMA, 1909-1969. 2nd ed. Metuchen, N.J.: Scarecrow Press, 1973, pp. 52-60.

A listing of reviews.

## SELECTED NONDRAMATIC WRITING

DUVEEN. Illus. Saul Steinberg. New York: Random House, 1952.

Based on NEW YORKER series, and the basis for LORD PENGO.

THE WORCESTER ACCOUNT. New York: Random House, 1954.

Early reminiscences.

PORTRAIT OF MAX: AN INTIMATE MEMOIR OF SIR MAX BEERBOHM. New York: Random House, 1960.

The English edition (London: H. Hamilton, 1960), is titled CONVERSATIONS WITH MAX.

THE SUSPENDED DRAWING ROOM. New York: Stein and Day, 1965.

Brief, biographical portraits.

THE BURNING GLASS. Boston: Little, Brown, 1968.

Novel.

PEOPLE IN A DIARY: A MEMOIR. Boston: Little, Brown, 1972.

Published as TRIBULATIONS AND LAUGHTER: A MEMOIR (London: H. Hamilton, 1972).

## CRITICISM

Asher, Don. THE EMINENT YACHTSMAN AND THE WHOREHOUSE PIANO PLAYER. New York: Coward, McCann and Geoghegan, 1973.

An account of his father's relationship with Behrman, the relationship behind Behrman's THE COLD WIND AND THE WARM.

Brown, John Mason. STILL SEEING THINGS. New York: McGraw-Hill, 1950.

Review of I KNOW MY LOVE, pages 127-31.

Reed, Kenneth T. S.N. BEHRMAN. Boston: Twayne, 1975.

Pages 80-89 focus on the late plays.

Simon, John. "S.N. Behrman: A Dialogue with John Simon." THEATRE: THE ANNUAL OF THE REPERTORY THEATRE OF LINCOLN CENTER, 1, no. 1 (1964), 35-47.

## SAUL BELLOW (1915-  )

THE WRECKER. NEW WORLD WRITING, no. 6 (1954), 271-87.

"Scenes from HUMANITIS--A FARCE." PR, 29 (Summer 1962), 327-49.

Scenes from an early version of THE LAST ANALYSIS, described as "scheduled for Broadway production by Robert Stevens this Fall."

THE WEN. ES, January 1965, pp. 72-74, 111.

THE WEN. In TRAVERSE PLAYS. Ed. Jim Haynes. Harmondsworth, Engl.: Penguin, 1967.

ORANGE SOUFFLE. ES, October 1965, pp. 131 ff.

ORANGE SOUFFLE. In TRAVERSE PLAYS. Ed. Jim Haynes. Harmondsworth: Engl.: Penguin, 1967.

THE LAST ANALYSIS. New York: Viking Press, 1965.

THE LAST ANALYSIS. In BROADWAY'S BEAUTIFUL LOSERS. Ed. Marilyn Stasio. New York: Delacorte, 1972.

Discusses, most sympathetically, the reasons for the play's failure.

### BIBLIOGRAPHY

Salem, James M., ed. A GUIDE TO CRITICAL REVIEWS. Part 1: AMERICAN DRAMA, 1909-1969. 2nd ed. Metuchen, N.J.: Scarecrow Press, 1973.

A listing of American reviews, pages 63-64.

Sokoloff, B.A., and Mark E. Posner, eds. SAUL BELLOW: A COMPREHENSIVE

BIBLIOGRAPHY. Folcroft, Pa.: Folcroft Press, 1971.

Fiction only.

## SELECTED NONDRAMATIC WRITING

"Pleasures and Pains of Playgoing." PR, 21 (May-June 1954), 312-17.

Miscellaneous reviews, prefaced by his claim that he goes to the theatre, not for ideas, but "to be diverted, delighted, awed, and in search of opportunities to laugh and to cry." T.S. Eliot's THE CONFIDENTIAL CLERK bores him.

For Bellow's novels, see Sololoff and Posner in the bibliography section above.

## CRITICISM

Bigsby, C.W.E. CONFRONTATION AND COMMITMENT. Columbia: University of Missouri Press, 1968, pp. 93-99.

Discusses THE LAST ANALYSIS.

Brustein, Robert. "Saul Bellow on the Dragstrip." In his SEASONS OF DISCONTENT: DRAMATIC OPINIONS 1959-1965. New York: Simon and Schuster, 1965, pp. 172-75.

THE LAST ANALYSIS is a bravura writing performance, subverted by disasterous casting and inept direction. The play's flaw is a lack of focus, but it deserved better than Broadway has given it.

Clayton, John Jacob. SAUL BELLOW: IN DEFENCE OF MAN. Bloomington: Indiana University Press, 1968.

Dutton, Robert R. SAUL BELLOW. New York: Twayne, 1971.

Malin, Irving, ed. SAUL BELLOW AND THE CRITICS. London: London University Press; New York: New York University Press, 1967.

Only the novels.

Phillips, Louis. "The Novelist as Playwright: Baldwin, McCullers, and Bellow." In MODERN AMERICAN DRAMA: ESSAYS IN CRITICISM. Ed. William E. Taylor. DeLand, Fla.: Everett-Edwards, 1968, pp. 145-62.

Rovit, Earl H., ed. SAUL BELLOW: A COLLECTION OF CRITICAL ESSAYS. Englewood Cliffs, N.J.: Prentice-Hall, 1975.

Scott, Nathan A. THREE AMERICAN MORALISTS: MAILER, BELLOW, TRILLING. South Bend, Ind.: University of Notre Dame Press, 1973.

Simon, John. UNEASY STAGES. New York: Random House, 1975, pp. 59-61.

THE LAST ANALYSIS is a provocative comedy betrayed by an inept production.

## ALAN BENNETT (1934- )

FORTY YEARS ON. London: Faber and Faber, 1969.

GETTING ON. London: Faber and Faber, 1972.

HABEAS CORPUS. London: Faber and Faber, 1973.

### COLLABORATION WITH PETER COOK, JONATHAN MILLER, DUDLEY MOORE

BEYOND THE FRINGE. London: Souvenir Press, 1962.

### CRITICISM

Kendle, Burton. "Alan Bennett." In CONTEMPORARY DRAMATISTS. Ed. James Vinson. London: St. James; New York: St. Martin's Press, 1973, pp. 90-93.

# BARRY BERMANGE (1933- )

NATHAN AND TABILETH, OLDENBERG. London: Methuen, 1967.

Two plays.

NO QUARTER. In NEW ENGLISH DRAMATISTS 12. Harmondsworth, Engl.: Penguin, 1968.

NO QUARTER, AND THE INTERVIEW. London: Methuen, 1969.

Also includes INVASION: A SCENARIO, as well as an introduction by Donald McWhinnie.

SCENES FROM FAMILY LIFE. In COLLECTION: LITERATURE FOR THE SEVENTIES. Ed. Nancy Shingler Massinger. Boston: Heath, 1972.

## CRITICISM

Burton, Peter. "Barry Bermange Interviewed by Peter Burton." TR, 36 (Summer 1970), 126-39.

Elsom, John. "Barry Bermange." In CONTEMPORARY DRAMATISTS. Ed. James Vinson. London: St. James; New York: St. Martin's, 1973, pp. 94-95.

# KENNETH BERNARD (1930- )

MACKO'S: A VEGETARIAN FANTASY. MR, 10 (Summer 1969), 557-69.

NIGHT CLUB AND OTHER PLAYS. Intro. by Michael Feingold. New York: Winter House, 1971.

Includes THE MOKE-EATER, THE LOVERS, MARY JANE, THE MONKEYS OF THE ORGAN GRINDER, and THE GIANTS IN THE EARTH.

GOODBYE DAN BAILEY. DRAMA AND THEATRE, 9 (Spring 1971), 179-98.

THE UNKNOWN CHINAMAN. In PLAYWRIGHTS FOR TOMORROW: A COLLECTION OF PLAYS. Vol. 10. Ed. Arthur H. Ballet. Minneapolis: University of Minnesota Press, 1971.

## SELECTED NONDRAMATIC WRITING

THE MALDIVE CHRONICLES, A NOVEL. Drawing by Norman Morris. MINNESOTA REVIEW, 10, no. 2 (1970), 5-86.

## CRITICISM

Feingold, Michael. "Introduction." NIGHT CLUB AND OTHER PLAYS. New York: Winter House, 1971, pp. 1-6.

______. "Kenneth Bernard." In CONTEMPORARY DRAMATISTS. Ed. James Vinson. London: St. James; New York: St. Martin's, 1973, pp. 96-98.

# BRIDGET BOLAND (1913- )

THE RETURN. London: Samuel French, 1954.

TEMPLE FOLLY. London: Evans Bros., 1958.

THE PRISONER. In PLAYS OF THE YEAR 10. Ed. J.C. Trewin. London: Elek, 1954.

THE PRISONER. New York: Dramatists Play Service, 1956.

GORDON. In PLAYS OF THE YEAR 25. Ed. J.C. Trewin. London: Elek Books, 1963.

THE ZODIAC IN THE ESTABLISHMENT. London: Evans Bros., 1963.

## CRITICISM

Hayman, Ronald. "Bridget Boland." In CONTEMPORARY DRAMATISTS. Ed. James Vinson. London: St. James; New York: St. Martin's, 1973, pp. 101-02.

Williamson, Audrey. CONTEMPORARY THEATRE, 1953-56. London: Rockliff, 1956.

Review of THE PRISONER, pages 39-41.

# ROBERT BOLT (1924- )

FLOWERING CHERRY. London: Heinemann, 1959.

A MAN FOR ALL SEASONS. London: Heinemann, 1961.
Frequently reprinted, international stage success, later a film.

THE TIGER AND THE HORSE. London: Heinemann, 1961.

GENTLE JACK. London: Samuel French, 1964.

GENTLE JACK. Introd. the author. New York: Random House, 1965.

THE THWARTING OF BARON BELLIGREW. London: Heinemann, 1966.

DR. ZHIVAGO. London: Harvill Press, 1966.
The screenplay based on the novel by Boris Pasternak.

VIVAT! VIVAT REGINA! London: Heinemann, 1971.

## COLLECTIONS

THREE PLAYS. London: Heinemann, 1963.
FLOWERING CHERRY, A MAN FOR ALL SEASONS, and THE TIGER AND THE HORSE.

## BIBLIOGRAPHY

Salem, James M., ed. A GUIDE TO CRITICAL REVIEWS. Part 3: BRITISH AND CONTINENTAL DRAMA FROM IBSEN TO PINTER. Metuchen, N.J.: Scarecrow Press, 1968.

A list of reviews for American productions of FLOWERING CHERRY and A MAN FOR ALL SEASONS, page 42.

## SELECTED NONDRAMATIC WRITING

"Mr. Coward had the Last of the Wine." SUNDAY TIMES (London), 29 January 1961, p. 25.

In his response to Coward's three articles in the SUNDAY TIMES, Bolt defends the political character of much contemporary theatre and the search for new theatrical forms and styles.

"Theatre in the Sixties." NTM, 2 (July 1961), 8-10.

A much abbreviated text of a speech. Bolt, after a brief discussion of the H Bomb, expresses his doubts about both the Christian interpretation of life and the newer belief that nothing much matters.

## CRITICISM

Atkins, Anselm. "Robert Bolt: Self, Shadow, and the Theater of Recognition." MD, 10 (September 1967), 182-88.

Both More and the Common Man share a redeeming concern with the self.

Dennis, Nigel. "Down Among the Dead Men." In his DRAMATIC ESSAYS. London: Weidenfeld and Nicolson, 1962, pp. 85-92.

A MAN FOR ALL SEASONS merely pretends to be about the Tudor age; its costumes mask twentieth-century characters who lack zest and stature.

Hayman, Ronald. "Like a Woman They Keep Going Back To." DRAMA, n.s. 98 (Autumn 1970), 57-66.

Bolt, like John Mortimer, Peter Shaffer, and John Bowen, is very reluctant to abandon conventional West End naturalism.

McElrath, Joseph R., Jr. "The Metaphoric Structure of A MAN FOR ALL SEASONS." MD, 14 (May 1971), 84-92.

Land and water imagery.

Marowitz, Charles. "Some Conventional Words: An Interview with Robert Bolt." TDR, 11 (Winter 1966), 138-40.

Milne, Tom, and Clive Goodwin. "Interview with Tom Milne and Clive Goodwin." In THEATRE AT WORK. Ed. Charles Marowitz and Simon Trussler. London: Methuen, 1967, pp. 58-77.

Originally published in 1961, with additional questions in 1966 from Simon Trussler, the interview focuses on Bolt's writing methods, nuclear war, Brecht, his film writing, and late plays.

Perceval, Michael. "An Interview with Robert Bolt." CRITIC, 24, no. 3 (1965), 14-23.

On the film of DR. ZHIVAGO.

Tynan, Kenneth. "A MAN FOR ALL SEASONS." In his TYNAN LEFT AND RIGHT. New York: Atheneum, 1967, pp. 26-32.

Tynan's review and an exchange between Bolt and Tynan on the differences between Brecht's GALILEO and Bolt's A MAN FOR ALL SEASONS. Tynan's major question is why More's beliefs are of such little importance to Bolt's play.

## EDWARD BOND (1934- )

SAVED. P&P, 13 (January 1966), 29-44 ff.

SAVED. London: Methuen, 1966.

NARROW ROAD TO THE DEEP NORTH. London: Methuen, 1968.

EARLY MORNING. London: Calder and Boyars, 1968.

THE POPE'S WEDDING. P&P, 16 (April 1969).

PASSION. P&P, 18 (June 1971), 66-69.
Written on behalf of the Campaign for Nuclear Disarmament.

THE POPE'S WEDDING AND OTHER PLAYS. London: Methuen, 1971.
Includes MR. DOG, THE KING WITH GOLDEN EYES, SHARPEVILLE SEQUENCE, and BLACK MASS.

LEAR. London: Methuen, 1972.

THE SEA. London: Eyre Methuen, 1973.

BINGO: SCENES OF MONEY AND DEATH; PASSION. London: Eyre Methuen, 1974.

### SELECTED NONDRAMATIC WRITING

"Millstones Round the Playwright's Neck: An Author's View of Critics." P&P, 13 (April 1966).

The impact of the critics is particularly malign on new plays and playwrights.

"Drama and the Dialectics of Violence." TQ, 2 (January-March 1972), 4-14.

Extremely informative interview about, among other things, Bond's childhood, and its influence on his work, violence and modern technology, and the titles of his plays.

"Letter to the Editors." TQ, 2 (April-June 1972), 105.

Persuasively attacks Arthur Arnold's review of his work, in the previous issue, as full of misstatements. See Criticism, below.

## CRITICISM

Arnold, Arthur. "Lines of Development in Bond's Plays." TQ, 2 (January-March 1972), 15-19.

Finds a gradual sublimation of violence and a growing mastery of form, if not content. See Bond's response, cited in his nondramatic writings, above.

Babula, William. "Scene Thirteen of Bond's SAVED." MD, 15 (September 1972), 147-49.

SAVED's last scene has some meagre signs of hope, of "clutching at straws."

Barth, Adolf K.H. "The Agressive 'Theatrum Mundi' of Edward Bond: NARROW ROAD TO THE DEEP NORTH." MD, 18 (June 1975), 189-200.

"Drama in Court--Act One." P&P, 13 (May 1966), 66-67.

Partial report on the Lord Chamberlain's suit against the Royal Court Theatre for its production of SAVED.

Durbach, Errol. "Herod in the Welfare State: KINDERMORD in the Plays of Edward Bond." ETJ, 27 (December 1975), 480-87.

The murder of children as a social metaphor.

Esslin, Martin. "Edward Bond's Three Plays." In his BRIEF CHRONICLES. London: Temple Smith, 1970, pp. 174-80.

Recycled reviews.

Findlater, Richard. BANNED! London: MacGibbon & Kee, 1967.

On the stage history of SAVED, pages 171-74.

Olivier, Sir Laurence. "The Tragic Theme." P&P, 13 (January 1966), 28.

Reprint of letter to the OBSERVER, defending SAVED.

Taylor, John Russell. "Edward Bond." In his THE SECOND WAVE. London: Methuen, 1971, pp. 77-93.

The key scene in SAVED, the killing of the baby, does not mesh with the rest of the play, particularly if presented realistically. Bond's plays, with growing mastery, each depict the survival of something uncorrupted amid universal Oedipal destructiveness.

Worth, Katherine J. "Edward Bond." In her REVOLUTIONS IN MODERN ENGLISH DRAMA. London: G. Bell, 1973, pp. 168-87.

"Moral passion is certainly a great driving force behind his writing. He is very close in some ways to the moralist playwrights in the Shavian tradition, to Osborne and even to Shaw himself."

Worthen, John. "Endings and Beginnings: Edward Bond and the Shock of Recognition." ETJ, 27 (December 1975), 466-79.

How Bond's audience is led to realize that the violence in his plays is similar to the violence in their own lives.

# JOHN BOWEN (1924- )

THE ESSAY PRIZE, WITH A HOLIDAY ABROAD, AND THE CANDIDATE: PLAYS FOR TELEVISION. London: Faber and Faber, 1962.

I LOVE YOU, MRS. PATTERSON. London: Evans Bros., 1964.

AFTER THE RAIN. London: Faber and Faber, 1967.

LITTLE BOXES: TWO PLAYS. London: Methuen, 1968.

THE COFFEE LACE and TREVOR.

THE FALL AND REDEMPTION OF MAN. London: Faber and Faber, 1968.

Title page notes "Selected, Arranged and Rendered into Modern English from the Chester, Coventry, Lincoln, Norwich, Wakefield and York Mystery Plays."

THE DISORDERLY WOMEN. London: Methuen, 1968.

Based on the BACCHAE of Euripides.

THE CORSICAN BROTHERS: A PLAY WITH MUSIC IN TWO ACTS. London: Methuen, 1970.

Based on the novela by Alexandre Dumas; lyrics by John Holmstrom and John Bowen.

SILVER WEDDING. In MIXED DOUBLES. London: Methuen, 1970.

THE WAITING ROOM. London: Samuel French, 1970.

AFTER THE RAIN. Rev. version. London: Faber and Faber, 1972.

Adaptations of his own novel.

ROBIN REDBREAST. In THE TELEVISION DRAMATIST. Ed. Robert Muller. London: Paul Elek, 1973, pp. 149-240.

HEIL CAESAR! London: British Broadcasting Corporation, 1974.

Based on Shakespeare's JULIUS CAESAR.

## SELECTED NONDRAMATIC WRITING

THE TRUTH WILL NOT HELP US: EMBROIDERY ON AN HISTORICAL THEME. London: Chatto and Windus, 1956.

AFTER THE RAIN. London: Faber and Faber, 1958.

THE CENTRE OF THE GREEN. London: Faber and Faber, 1959.

STORYBOARD. London: Faber and Faber, 1960.

"Accepting the Illusion." TWENTIETH CENTURY, 169 (February 1961), 153-65.

Defends the realistic style in drama, attacks its critics, especially Peter Brook, and argues the uses of television for the novice dramatist.

THE BIRDCAGE. London: Faber and Faber, 1962.

A WORLD ELSEWHERE. London: Faber and Faber, 1966.

## CRITICISM

Hayman, Ronald. "Like a Woman They Keep Going Back To." DRAMA, n.s. 98 (Autumn 1970), 57-66.

Bowen, like Bolt, John Mortimer, and Peter Shaffer, has found it difficult to go beyond conventional West End naturalism.

# JANE BOWLES (1917-1973)

IN THE SUMMER HOUSE. New York: Random House, 1954.

A QUARRELING PAIR. ART AND LITERATURE, 2 (Summer 1964), 65-69.

AT THE JUMPING BEAN. In FEMININE WILES. Introd. Tennessee Williams. Santa Barbara, Calif.: Black Sparrow Press, 1976.

"A Scene from a play Jane Bowles was writing in Ceylon in 1955."

## COLLECTIONS

COLLECTED WORKS. New York: Farrar, Straus and Giroux, 1966. Introd. Truman Capote.

## BIBLIOGRAPHY

Salem, James M., ed. A GUIDE TO CRITICAL REVIEWS. Part 1: AMERICAN DRAMA, 1909-1969. 2nd ed. Metuchen, N.J.: Scarecrow Press, 1973.

A listing of reviews, pages 73-74.

## CRITICISM

Bentley, Eric. "The Ill-Made Play." In his THE DRAMATIC EVENT: AN AMERICAN CHRONICLE. New York: Horizon, 1954, pp. 176-81.

Although IN THE SUMMER HOUSE is derivative, Bowles' talent keeps us interested.

# HOWARD BRENTON (1942- )

REVENGE. London: Methuen, 1970.

CHRISTIE IN LOVE, AND OTHER PLAYS. London: Methuen, 1970.

Also contains HEADS and THE EDUCATION OF SKINNY SPEW.

PLAYS FOR PUBLIC PLACES. London: Eyre Methuen, 1972.

Consists of GUM AND GOO, WESLEY, and SCOTT OF THE ANTARTIC; OR, WHAT GOD DIDN'T SEE.

MAGNIFICENCE. London: Eyre Methuen, 1973.

THE CHURCHILL PLAY: AS IT WILL BE PERFORMED IN THE WINTER OF 1984 BY THE INTERNS OF CHURCHILL CAMP SOMEWHERE IN ENGLAND. London: Eyre Methuen, 1974.

## COLLABORATIONS

LAY BY. P&P, 19 (November 1971), 65-75.

One-act play written in collaboration with Brian Clark, Trevor Griffiths, David Hare, Steven Poliakoff, Hugh Stoddart, and Snoo Wilson.

LAY BY. London: Calder and Boyars, 1972.

BRASSNECK. London: Eyre Methuen, 1973.

In collaboration with David Hare.

## BIBLIOGRAPHY

Mitchell, Tony, comp. "Theatre Checklist No. 5: Howard Brenton." TF, 2 (1975), 1-9.

## CRITICISM

Ansorge, Peter. "The Theatre is a Dusty Place." P&P, 19 (February 1972), 14-18.

Interview with Brenton on his background and his work with the Portable Theatre.

Taylor, John Russell. "The Dark Fantastic." In his THE SECOND WAVE. London: Methuen, 1971, pp. 217-19.

Brief description of Brenton's stripped-down, minimal style.

# JAMES BRIDIE (OSBORNE HENRY MAVOR) (1888-1951)

MR. GILLIE. London: Constable, 1950.

In memory of John Brandane, W.G. Fry, and H.K. Ayliff.

THE QUEEN'S COMEDY: A HEROIC FRAGMENT. London: Constable, 1950.

DR. ANGELUS. London: Constable, 1950.

THE BAIKIE CHARIVARI; OR, THE SEVEN PROPHETS, A MIRACLE PLAY. With a Preface by Walter Elliot. London: Constable, 1953.

This and the next item were published posthumously.

MEETING AT NIGHT. Introd. J.B. Priestley. London: Constable, 1956.

## CRITICISM

Bannister, Winifred. JAMES BRIDIE AND HIS THEATRE: A STUDY OF JAMES BRIDIE'S PERSONALITY, HIS STAGE PLAYS AND HIS WORK FOR THE FOUNDATION OF A SCOTTISH NATIONAL THEATRE. London: Rockliff, 1955.

Luyben, Helen L. "Bridie's Last Play." MD, 5 (February 1963), 400-414.

Bridie's medium is the comic fantasia and, in THE BAIKIE CHARIVARI, his theme is religious: temptation and moral choice.

______. "The Dramatic Method of James Bridie." ETJ, 15 (1963), 332-42.

______. JAMES BRIDIE: CLOWN AND PHILOSOPHER. Philadelphia: University of Pennsylvania Press, 1965.

Mardon, Ernest G. THE CONFLICT BETWEEN THE INDIVIDUAL AND SOCIETY

IN THE PLAYS OF JAMES BRIDIE. Glasgow: Maclellan, 1972.

Trewin, J.C. "The Good-Natured Man." In his DRAMATISTS OF TODAY. London and New York: Staples Press, 1953, pp. 91-101.

Chatty survey of Bridie's works.

Weales, Gerald. RELIGION IN MODERN ENGLISH DRAMA. Philadelphia: University of Pennsylvania Press, 1961, pp. 79-90.

Treats Bridie's religious plays, THE BAIKIE CHARIVARI and THE QUEEN'S COMEDY among them.

## BRIGID BROPHY (1929- )

THE WASTE DISPOSAL UNIT. LONDON MAGAZINE, 4 (April 1964), 35-58.

Radio play.

THE BURGLAR. London: Jonathan Cape, 1968.

### SELECTED NONDRAMATIC WRITING

HACKENFELLER'S APE. London: Hart-Davis, 1953.

Novel.

MOZART THE DRAMATIST: A NEW VIEW OF MOZART, HIS OPERAS AND HIS AGE. London: Faber and Faber, 1964.

DON'T NEVER FORGET: COLLECTED VIEWS AND REVIEWS. London: Jonathan Cape, 1966.

### COLLABORATION WITH MICHAEL LEVEY AND CHARLES OSBORNE

FIFTY WORKS OF ENGLISH AND AMERICAN LITERATURE WE COULD DO WITHOUT. London: Rapp and Carroll, 1967.

Brief and delightfully dyspeptic essays.

# KENNETH H. BROWN (1936-  )

THE BRIG. TDR, 8 (Spring 1964), 222-59.

Brown's text.

THE BRIG: A CONCEPT FOR THEATRE OR FILM. With an essay on the Living Theatre by Julian Beck, and director's notes by Judith Malina. New York: Hill and Wang, 1965.

The acting version used by the Living Theatre.

THE HAPPY BAR. New York: H. Matson, 1967.

A typescript at the Lincoln Center Library of the Performing Arts.

BLAKE'S DESIGN. In BEST SHORT PLAYS, 1969. Ed. Stanley Richards. Philadelphia: Chilton Books, 1969.

NIGHTLIGHT. New York: Samuel French, 1973.

## SELECTED NONDRAMATIC WRITING

"For Julian and Judith--June, 1963." YT, 1 (Spring 1968), 69.

A poem.

## CRITICISM

Bigsby, C.W.E. "The Violent Image: The Significance of Kenneth Brown's THE BRIG." WS, 8 (Summer 1967), 421-30.

THE BRIG realizes Artaud's vision of dramatic communication on levels more fundamental than language.

Brustein, Robert. "A Harrowing Night in the Brig." In his SEASONS OF DISCONTENT: DRAMATIC OPINIONS 1959-1965. New York: Simon and Schuster, 1965, pp. 79-82.

Daily reviewers seem more concerned about the audience's feelings than the full implications of THE BRIG. The play succeeds by monotonously presenting the prison's horrors without conventional dramatic incident.

Brown, Kent R. "Kenneth H. Brown: The Career of an Accidental Playwright." PL, 46 (August-September), 276-79.

Whatever happened to Kenneth H. Brown?

Jackson, Esther M. "American Theatre in the Sixties: The Drama of Internal Crisis." PL, 48 (Summer 1973), 236-49.

THE BRIG is an example of the Living Theatre's extension of the theatre into the unconscious.

Rogoff, Gordon. "THE BRIG." In THE ENCORE READER: A CHRONICLE OF THE NEW DRAMA. Ed. Charles Marowitz, Tom Milne, and Owen Hale. London: Methuen, 1965, pp. 267-74.

A review of the Beck-Malina-Living Theatre collaboration with Brown, "a triumph of craft, a craft which has finally revealed itself, not through talk and training, but through the logical rhythms of action."

Schechner, Richard. "Interview with Kenneth Brown." TDR, 8 (Spring 1964), 212-19.

Brown's interpretation of THE BRIG and the work process with the Living Theatre.

# WYNARD BROWNE (1911- )

DARK SUMMER. London: Evans Bros., 1950.

THE HOLLY AND THE IVY. In PLAYS OF THE YEAR 3. Ed. J.C. Trewin. London: Paul Elek, 1950.

THE HOLLY AND THE IVY. London: Evans Bros., 1951.

The prototypical vicarage play.

QUESTION OF FACT. London: Evans Bros., 1955.

THE RING OF TRUTH. P&P, 7 (January 1960), 27-32; (February 1960), 27-32.

THE RING OF TRUTH. London: Evans Bros., 1960.

THE HOLLY AND THE IVY. London: Evans Bros., 1967.

## SELECTED NONDRAMATIC WRITING

"The Mystery of Comedy." DRAMA, n.s. 53 (Summer 1959), 31-33.

## CRITICISM

Trewin, J.C. "Up-and-Coming." In his DRAMATISTS OF TODAY. London and New York: Staples Press, 1953, pp. 197-200.

## DAVID CAMPTON (1924- )

GOING HOME. Manchester, Engl.: Abel Haywood, 1951.

HONEYMOON EXPRESS. Manchester, Engl.: Abel Haywood, 1951.

CHANGE PARTNERS. Manchester, Engl.: Abel Haywood, 1951.

SUNSHINE ON THE RIGHTEOUS. London: Rylee, 1952.

THE LABORATORY: A FARCE IN ONE ACT. London: J. Garnet Miller, 1955.

DOCTOR ALEXANDER. Leicester, Engl.: Campton, 1956.

CUCKOO SONG. Leicester, Engl.: Campton, 1956.

THE LUNATIC VIEW: A COMEDY OF MENACE. Leicester, Engl.: Studio Theatre, 1960.

> Also contains A SMELL OF BURNING, THEN. . . . MEMENTO MORI, and GETTING AND SPENDING.

LITTLE BROTHER, LITTLE SISTER. Leicester, Engl.: Campton, 1960.

MUTATIS MUTANDIS: A COMEDY OF MENACE. Leicester, Engl.: Campton, 1960.

FOUR MINUTE WARNING. Leicester, Engl.: Campton, 1960.

> Consists of LITTLE BROTHER, LITTLE SISTER, MUTATIS MUTANDIS, SOLIDER FROM THE WARS RETURNING: A GROTESQUE COMEDY IN ONE ACT, and AT SEA.

FUNERAL DANCE: A PLAY FOR WOMEN. London: J. Garnet Miller, 1962.

FUNERAL DANCE: A PLAY FOR WOMEN. In SIX ONE-ACT COMEDIES FOR WOMEN. London: J. Garnet Miller, 1964.

ON STAGE: CONTAINING SEVENTEEN SKETCHES AND ONE MONOLOGUE. London: J. Garnet Miller, 1964.

ROSES ROUND THE DOOR, AND OTHER COMEDIES. London: J. Garnet Miller, 1967.

Also includes THE CACTUS GARDEN and PASSPORT TO FLORENCE.

DON'T WAIT FOR ME. In WORTH A HEARING: A COLLECTION OF RADIO PLAYS. Ed. Alfred Bradley. Glasgow: Blackie, 1967.

MORE SKETCHES. Leicester, Engl.: Campton, 1967.

LADIES NIGHT: FOUR PLAYS FOR WOMEN. London: J. Garnet Miller, 1967.

Includes TWO LEAVES AND A STALK, INCIDENT, SILENCE ON THE BATTLEFIELD, and THE MANIPULATOR.

THE RIGHT PLACE. In PLAYBILL ONE. Ed. Alan Durband. London: Hutchinson, 1969.

LAUGHTER AND FEAR: NINE ONE ACT PLAYS. Ed. Michael Marland, with a personal note by David Campton. Glasgow: Blackie, 1969.

Contains INCIDENT, THEN. . . . MEMENTO MORI, THE END OF THE PICNIC, THE LABORATORY, A POINT OF VIEW, SOLDIER FROM THE WARS RETURNING, MUTATIS MUTANDIS, and WHERE HAVE ALL THE GHOSTS GONE?

ON STAGE AGAIN: CONTAINING FOURTEEN SKETCHES AND TWO MONOLOGUES. London: J. Garnet Miller, 1969.

RESTING PLACE. In MIXED DOUBLES. London: Methuen, 1970.

From ON STAGE AGAIN.

ANGEL UNWILLING. Leicester, Engl.: Campton, 1972.

THE LIFE AND DEATH OF ALMOST EVERYBODY. New York: Dramatists Play Service, 1972.

JONAH. London: J. Garnet Miller, 1972.

THE CAGEBIRDS. Leicester, Engl.: Campton, 1972.

US AND THEM. In THE SIXTH WINDMILL BOOK OF ONE-ACT PLAYS. London: Heinemann, 1972.

COME BACK TOMORROW. Leicester, Engl.: Campton, 1972.

IN COMMITTEE. Leicester, Engl.: Campton, 1972.

FRANKENSTEIN: THE GIFT OF FIRE. London: J. Garnet Miller, 1973.

Adaptation of the Mary Shelley novel (1818).

USHER. London: J. Garnet Miller, 1973.

Adaptation of Poe's "The Fall of the House of Usher" (1839).

SPLIT DOWN THE MIDDLE. London: J. Garnet Miller, 1973.

NOW AND THEN. London: J. Garnet Miller, 1973.

CARMILLA. London: J. Garnet Miller, 1973.

Adaptation of Sheridan Le Fanu's short story (1872).

TIME SNEEZE. Foreword by Geoffrey Hodson. London: Eyre Methuen, 1974.

## SELECTED NONDRAMATIC WRITING

"Why Do You Write Plays, Mr. Campton." NTM, 10 (Summer 1970), 16-20.

An interview on his career, the influence of Stephen Joseph, and pantomime.

## CRITICISM

Taylor, John Russell. "David Campton." In his ANGER AND AFTER: A GUIDE TO THE NEW BRITISH DRAMA. Rev. ed. Harmondsworth, Engl.: Penguin, 1963, pp. 162-69.

Taylor says that for Campton the menace is clear enough: "it is the Bomb."

Wardle, Irving. "Comedy of Menace." In THE ENCORE READER: A CHRONI-

CLE OF THE NEW DRAMA. Ed. Charles Marowitz, Tom Milne, and Owen Hale. London: Methuen, 1965, pp. 86-91.

Campton is "the only writer I know of who has adapted Joyce's verbal techniques for the theatre."

## DENIS CANAAN (DENNIS PULLEIN-THOMPSON) (1919-  )

CAPTAIN CARVALLO: A TRADITIONAL COMEDY IN THREE ACTS. London: Samuel French, 1951.

COLOMBE. London: Methuen, 1952.

Canaan's version of Anouilh's COLOMBE (1950).

MISERY ME! A COMEDY OF WOE. London: Samuel French, 1956.

YOU AND YOUR WIFE. London: Samuel French, 1956.

WHO'S YOUR FATHER? London: Samuel French, 1959.

U S: THE BOOK OF ROYAL SHAKESPEARE THEATRE PRODUCTION/U S/VIET-NAM/U S/EXPERIMENT/POLITICS/FULL TEXT/REHEARSALS/REACTIONS/SOURCES/ BY PETER BROOK/DENIS CANAAN/ALBERT HUNT/SALLY JACOBS/MICHAEL KUSTOW/ADRIAN MITCHELL/RICHARD PEASLEE/DO IT YOURSELF. Introd. Peter Brook. London: Calder and Boyars, 1968.

Canaan's script for Brook's experimental, improvisational production, featuring pictures, rehearsal notes, and lengthy excerpts from the critics' reactions. This production, aside from its politics and controversial reception, was notable for the rehearsal visits of Jerzy Grotowski and Joseph Chaikin.

TELL ME LIES: THE BOOK OF ROYAL SHAKESPEARE THEATRE PRODUCTION. . . . Indianapolis: Bobbs-Merrill, 1968.

The English text of US retitled, with editorial and design credits added to the title page.

### CRITICISM

Spurling, Hilary. "Mr. Brook's Lemon." SPECTATOR, 21 October 1966, p. 517.

A full-throated denunciation of Peter Brook's production of US as hypocritical exhibitionism; the same review praises a production of THE ODD COUPLE.

Taylor, John Russell. In his ANGER AND AFTER: A GUIDE TO THE NEW BRITISH DRAMA. Rev. ed. Harmondsworth, Engl.: Penguin, 1963, pp. 22-23.

Williamson, Audrey. In her CONTEMPORARY THEATRE, 1953-1956. London: Rockliff, 1956, pp. 44-46.

Review of MISERY ME.

## TRUMAN CAPOTE (1924- )

THE GRASS HARP. New York: Random House, 1952.

BEAT THE DEVIL. London: Romulius Films, 1953.

Edited version of the shooting of the film, directed by John Huston, available at the Lincoln Center Library of the Performing Arts.

HOUSE OF FLOWERS. New York: Random House, 1968.

Capote's book for Harold Arlen's music.

### BIBLIOGRAPHY

Salem, James M., ed. A GUIDE TO CRITICAL REVIEWS. Part 1: AMERICAN DRAMA, 1909-1969. 2nd ed. Metuchen, N.J.: Scarecrow Press, 1973, pp. 77-78.

### SELECTED NONDRAMATIC WRITING

THE GRASS HARP. New York: Random House, 1951.

The novelistic source for the play.

BREAKFAST AT TIFFANY'S: A SHORT NOVEL AND THREE SHORT STORIES. New York: Random House, 1958.

IN COLD BLOOD. A TRUE ACCOUNT OF A MULTIPLE MURDER AND ITS CONSEQUENCES. New York: Random House, 1966.

First appeared in THE NEW YORKER in a slightly different form.

## COLLABORATION

TRILOGY: AN EXPERIMENT IN MULTIMEDIA. Introd. John M. Culkin. New York· Macmillan, 1969.

Filmscripts by Eleanor Perry and Capote, with the Capote short stories they are based on, plus reminiscences and notes by Capote, Eleanor Perry, and Frank Perry.

## CRITICISM

Bentley, Eric. "Pity His Simplicity." In his THE DRAMATIC EVENT: AN AMERICAN CHRONICLE. New York: Horizon, 1954, pp. 20-24.

THE GRASS HARP is a sentimental combination of the trite and the ridiculous.

Drutman, Irving. "Capote: End of the Affair." NEW YORK TIMES, 20 November 1966, sec. 2, p. 3.

On why Capote no longer writes for the stage.

Gassner, John. "Points of Return: THE GRASS HARP: Capote vs. Saroyan." In his THEATRE AT THE CROSSROADS: PLAYS AND PLAYWRIGHTS OF THE MID-CENTURY AMERICAN STAGE. New York: Holt, Rinehart and Winston, 1960, pp. 149-51.

Nance, William L. THE WORLDS OF TRUMAN CAPOTE. New York: Stein and Day, 1970.

Sympathetic study written after the great success of IN COLD BLOOD. Brief treatment of the plays.

## LEWIS JOHN CARLINO (1932- )

THE BRICK AND THE ROSE: A COLLAGE FOR VOICES. New York: Dramatists Play Service, 1959.

USED CAR SALE. New York: Dramatists Play Service, 1959.

JUNK YARD. New York: Dramatists Play Service, 1959.

MR. FLANNERY'S OCEAN; OBJECTIVE CASE: TWO SHORT PLAYS. New York: Dramatists Play Service, 1961.

TWO SHORT PLAYS: HIGH SIGN; SARAH AND THE SAX. New York: Dramatists Play Service, 1962.

TELEMACHUS: A COLLAGE FOR SOUNDS AND VOICES IN TWO ACTS. New York: Dramatists Play Service, 1963.

CAGES: SNOWANGEL, EPIPHANY: TWO ONE-ACT PLAYS. New York: Random House, 1963.

TELEMACHUS CLAY: A COLLAGE FOR VOICES. New York: Random House, 1964.

DOUBLETALK. New York: Random House, 1964.

Contains THE DIRTY OLD MAN and SARAH AND THE SAX.

TELEMACHUS CLAY: A COLLAGE FOR VOICES. Rev. ed. New York: Dramatists Play Service, 1967.

THE EXERCISE. New York: Dramatists Play Service, 1968.

## SELECTED NONDRAMATIC WRITING

"Seconds." Rev. N.p., 1965.

Mimeographed typescript of the screenplay of David Ely's novel, available at the Metropolitan Bibliographic Centre of the Toronto Public Library.

## CRITICISM

Gottfried, Martin. "Lewis John Carlino." In CONTEMPORARY DRAMATISTS. Ed. James Vinson. London: St. James; New York: St. Martin's, 1973, pp. 139-40.

# DAVID CAUTE (1936-  )

THE CONFRONTATION: A TRILOGY. London: Andre Deutsch, 1970.

Includes the play, THE DEMONSTRATION, as well as a novel, THE OCCUPATION, and an essay, "The Illusion."

## CRITICISM

Taylor, John Russell. "The Legacy of Realism." In his THE SECOND WAVE. London: Methuen, 1971, pp. 202-04.

Brief summaries.

## MARY CHASE (1907- )

MRS. McTHING. Illus. Madeleine Gekiere and Helen Sewell. New York: Oxford University Press, 1952.

Next to HARVEY (1944), her most successful play.

BERNADINE. Illus. William Sharp. New York: Oxford University Press, 1952.

THE PRIZE PLAY: A SKIT. New York: Dramatists Play Service, 1961.

MIDGIE PURVIS. New York: Dramatists Play Service, 1963.

THE DOG SITTERS. New York: Dramatists Play Service, 1963.

MICKEY. New York: Dramatists Play Service, 1969.

Based on her 1958 children's novel, LORETTA MASON BOTTS.

COCKTAILS WITH MIMI. New York: Dramatists Play Service, 1974.

### BIBLIOGRAPHY

Salem, James M., ed. A GUIDE TO CRITICAL REVIEWS. Part 1: AMERICAN DRAMA, 1909-1969. 2nd ed. Metuchen, N.J.: Scarecrow Press, 1973, pp. 78-81.

A listing of reviews.

### CRITICISM

Nathan, George Jean. THEATRE IN THE FIFTIES. New York: Knopf, 1953, pp. 59-65.

# PADDY CHAYEFSKY (1923-1981)

TELEVISION PLAYS. New York: Simon and Schuster, 1955.

THE BACHELOR PARTY, THE BIG DEAL, HOLIDAY SONG, MARTY, THE MOTHER, and PINTER'S MEASURE.

MIDDLE OF THE NIGHT: A LOVE STORY. New York: Random House, 1957.

THE BACHELOR PARTY: A SCREENPLAY. New York: New American Library, 1957.

THE GODDESS: A SCREENPLAY. New York: Simon and Schuster, 1958.

THE TENTH MAN. New York: Random House, 1960.

GIDEON. ES, December 1961, pp. 215-30 ff.

GIDEON. New York: Random House, 1962.

THE PASSION OF JOSEF D. New York: Random House, 1964.

THE LATENT HETEROSEXUAL. New York: Random House, 1967.

## BIBLIOGRAPHY

Salem, James M., ed. A GUIDE TO CRITICAL REVIEWS. Part 1: AMERICAN DRAMA, 1909-1969. 2nd ed. Metuchen, N.J.: Scarecrow Press, 1973.

See pages 81-83.

## CRITICISM

Brustein, Robert. "Dr. Chayefsky's Panacea." In his SEASONS OF DISCONTENT: DRAMATIC OPINIONS 1959-1965. New York: Simon and Schuster, 1965, pp. 94-97.

> In THE TENTH MAN, Chayefsky asserts the redeeming power of love, confusing love and religion, and throwing in a few self-serving miracles to prove his point.

______. "The Mahomet of Middle Seriousness." In his SEASONS OF DISCONTENT: DRAMATIC OPINIONS 1959-1965. New York: Simon and Schuster, 1965, pp. 122-25.

> GIDEON is a "lumpish mediocrity," perfectly calculated to appeal to the middle-class mind.

Sayre, Nora, and Robert B. Silvers. "An Interview with Paddy Chayefsky." HORIZON, 3 (September 1960), 50-56.

> Valuable interview about how Chayefsky came to do television work, his working methods, THE TENTH MAN, and his feelings about his early writing.

Styan, J.L. "Television Drama." In CONTEMPORARY THEATRE. Ed. John Russell Brown and Bernard Harris. London: Edward Arnold, 1962, pp. 184-204.

> A balanced assessment of Chayefsky's contribution to the television medium is part of a general survey of television and a playwright's place in it.

## AGATHA CHRISTIE (MARY CLARISSA MILLER) (1890-1978)

THE HOLLOW. London: Samuel French, 1952.

Based on her 1946 novel with the same title.

THE MOUSETRAP. London: Samuel French, 1954.

Adapted from her short story, "Three Blind Mice," this is the longest running play in the history of the English stage; it failed in the United States.

WITNESS FOR THE PROSECUTION. London: Samuel French, 1954.

This, her other great stage success, is based on the 1948 story.

SPIDER'S WEB. London: Samuel French, 1956.

THE UNEXPECTED GUEST. London: Samuel French, 1958.

VERDICT. London: Samuel French, 1958.

GO BACK FOR MURDER. London: Samuel French, 1960.

Adapted from the FIVE LITTLE PIGS (in the United States, MURDER IN RETROSPECT), 1942.

AFTERNOON AT THE SEASIDE. London: Samuel French, 1963.

With THE PATIENT and THE RATS, produced as RULE OF THREE.

THE PATIENT. London: Samuel French, 1963.

THE RATS. London: Samuel French, 1963.

## COLLABORATION

MURDER AT THE VICARAGE. London: Samuel French, 1950.

Based on the 1930 novel, and dramatized by Moie Charles and Barbara Toy.

TOWARDS ZERO. London: Samuel French; New York: Dramatists Play Service, 1957.

Based on the 1944 novel, and adapted by Agatha Christie and Gerald Verner.

## BIBLIOGRAPHY

Salem, James M., ed. A GUIDE TO CRITICAL REVIEWS. Part 3: BRITISH AND CONTINENTAL DRAMA FROM IBSEN TO PINTER. Metuchen, N.J.: Scarecrow Press, 1968.

List of reviews for the American production of WITNESS FOR THE PROSECUTION, page 69.

## SELECTED NONDRAMATIC WRITING

Despite the inevitable waning of her powers--Christie's first novel having been published in 1920--her many novels of the fifties and early sixties are heartily recommended to all lovers of traditional detective fiction.

## CRITICISM

Ramsey, Gordon C. AGATHA CHRISTIE: MISTRESS OF MYSTERY. New York: Dodd, Mead, 1967.

Brief, without an index, but with several appendixes on the various adaptations, collaborations, and title changes affecting the Christie corpus.

Shorter, Eric. "Quite a Nice Run." DRAMA, n.s. 112 (Spring 1974), pp. 51-53.

On THE MOUSE TRAP, its theatre, its acting, and its incredible longevity.

Thurber, James. "Is There a Killer in the House?" OBSERVER, 9 July 1955, p. 10.

Inimitable remarks on mystery plays and THE MOUSETRAP, then in its third year.

Tynan, Kenneth. "Open Secret." OBSERVER, 19 December 1954, p. 13.

A few unkind words about that bizarre English convention, the mystery play, and Christie's SPIDER'S WEB.

# STEWART CONN (1936- )

FANCY SEEING YOU, THEN. In PLAYBILL II. Ed. Alan Durband. London: Hutchinson, 1969.

THE KING. In NEW ENGLISH DRAMATISTS 14. Harmondsworth, Engl.: Penguin, 1970.

THE BURNING. London: Calder and Boyars, 1972.

IN TRANSIT. New York: Breakthrough Press, 1972.

## CRITICISM

Hammond, Jonathan. "Stewart Conn." In CONTEMPORARY DRAMATISTS. Ed. James Vinson. London: St. James; New York: St. Martin's, 1973, pp. 163-64.

## GILES COOPER (1918-1966)

EVERYTHING IN THE GARDEN. In NEW ENGLISH DRAMATISTS 7. Ed. Elliott Martin Browne. Harmondsworth, Engl.: Penguin, 1963.

EVERYTHING IN THE GARDEN. London: Evans Bros., 1963.

For a rather broad dramatic adaptation of this play which uses the same title, see Albee, above.

THE LADY OF THE CAMELIAS. New York: Hart Stenographic Bureau, 1963.

Typescript, available at the Lincoln Center Library of the Performing Arts in New York City, for the short-lived Susan Strasberg vehicle which was adapted from Alexandre Dumas Fils by Giles Cooper and Franco Zeffirelli.

OUT OF THE CROCODILE. In PLAYS OF THE YEAR 17. Ed. J.C. Trewin. London: Elek Books, 1963.

OUT OF THE CROCODILE. London: Evans Bros., 1964.

SIX PLAYS FOR RADIO. London: British Broadcasting Corporation, 1966.

BEFORE MONDAY; THE DISAGREEABLE OYSTER; MATHRY BEACON; UNDER THE LOOFAH TREE; UNMAN, WITTERING AND ZIGO; and WITHOUT THE GRAIL.

HAPPY FAMILY. In NEW ENGLISH DRAMATISTS 11. Harmondsworth, Engl.: Penguin, 1967.

THE OBJECT. In NEW ENGLISH DRAMATISTS: RADIO PLAYS 12. Harmondsworth, Engl.: Penguin, 1968.

UNMAN, WITTERING AND ZIGO. London: Macmillan, 1971.

Slightly modified version of the radio play, with stage directions.

## BIBLIOGRAPHY

Cleveland, Louise, comp. "Theatre Checklist No. 4: Giles Cooper." TF, 4 (November-January 1975), 3-14.

An excellent compilation.

## SELECTED NONDRAMATIC WRITING

"Author's Note." In his OUT OF THE CROCODILE. London: Evans Bros., 1963.

THE OTHER MAN. A Novel Based on his Play for Television. London: Panther, 1964.

Cooper's own adaptation of his teleplay.

"The Long House." RADIO TIMES, 8 July 1965, p. 12.

Notes on the unpublished radio play, at time of broadcast.

"Note." In his SIX PLAYS FOR RADIO. London: British Broadcasting Corporation, 1966.

## CRITICISM

Gascoigne, Bamber. "A Weeded Garden." SPECTATOR, 25 May 1962, p. 684.

Compares the two endings of EVERYTHING IN THE GARDEN.

McWhinnie, Donald. "Introduction." GILES COOPER: SIX PLAYS FOR RADIO. London British Broadcasting Co., 1966, pp. 7-13.

# GREGORY CORSO (1930- )

IN THIS HUNG-UP AGE. ENCOUNTER, 18 (January 1962), 83-92.

IN THIS HUNG-UP AGE. In NEW DIRECTIONS IN PROSE AND POETRY. Ed. James Laughlin. Philadelphia: Lippincott, 1964.

STANDING ON A STREETCORNER: A LITTLE PLAY. ER, 6 (March-April 1962), 63-78.

## SELECTED NONDRAMATIC WRITING

NEW AMERICAN POETRY. Ed. Donald M. Allen. New York: Grove Press; London: Evergreen Books Ltd., 1960.

> Corso's section in this landmark collection represents a good sampling of his work.

## CRITICISM

Howard, Richard. "Gregory Corso." In his ALONE WITH AMERICA: ESSAYS ON THE ART OF POETRY IN THE UNITED STATES SINCE 1950. New York: Atheneum, 1971, pp. 57-64.

## NOEL COWARD (1899-1973)

BRIEF ENCOUNTER. In THREE BRITISH SCREENPLAYS. Ed. Rogert Manvil. London: Methuen, 1950.

Adaptation of STILL LIFE from TONIGHT AT 8:30.

RELATIVE VALUES: A LIGHT COMEDY IN THREE ACTS. London: Heinemann, 1952.

QUADRILLE· A ROMANTIC COMEDY IN THREE ACTS. London: Heinemann, 1952.

AFTER THE BALL. London: William Chappell, 1954.

Coward's lyrics for the adaptation, called an operetta, of Oscar Wilde's LADY WINDEMERE'S FAN (1893).

SOUTH SEA BUBBLE. London: Heinemann, 1956.

NUDE WITH VIOLIN: A LIGHT COMEDY IN THREE ACTS. P&P, 4 (December 1956), 23-32; (January 1957), 23-30.

NUDE WITH VIOLIN: A LIGHT COMEDY IN THREE ACTS. London: Heinemann, 1957.

FALLEN ANGELS. Rev. and rewritten. New York: Samuel French, 1958.

Reworking of the 1925 comedy.

LOOK AFTER LULU! London: Heinemann, 1959.

Based on OCCUPE-TOI D'AMELIE (1908) by Georges Feydeau.

WAITING IN THE WINGS. London: Heinemann, 1960.

SAIL AWAY. New York: n.p., 1961.

Typescript for the libretto of the 1961 musical, available at the Lincoln Center Library of the Peforming Arts.

SUITE IN THREE KEYS: A SONG AT TWILIGHT, SHADOWS OF THE EVENING, COME INTO THE GARDEN, MAUDE. London: Heinemann, 1966.

## COLLECTIONS

PLAY PARADE. Vols. 5-6. London: Heinemann, 1958, 1962.

These two volumes contain, along with earlier works, RELATIVE VALUES, QUADRILLE, SOUTH SEA BUBBLE, NUDE WITH VIOLIN, WAITING IN THE WINGS, and ACE OF CLUBS. Volume 6 contains only the published text of the 1952 ACE OF CLUBS.

## BIBLIOGRAPHY

Salem, James M., ed. A GUIDE TO CRITICAL REVIEWS. Part 3: BRITISH AND CONTINENTAL DRAMA FROM IBSEN TO PINTER. Metuchen, N.J.: Scarecrow Press, 1968.

Lists reviews of American productions, pp. 73-80.

## SELECTED NONDRAMATIC WRITING

FUTURE INDEFINITE. London: Heinemann, 1954.

This second volume of autobiography is the one relevant to our period.

POMP AND CIRCUMSTANCE. London: Heinemann, 1960.

Novel.

"These Old-Fashioned Revolutionaries." SUNDAY TIMES (London), 15 January 1961, p. 23.

For all of their trivial vulgarity, their obsession with a fast disappearing proletariat, the "New Movement" writers fail by boring and generally disregarding their audience. This is the first of a controversial three-part series of articles. See also the following two entries.

"The Scratch-and-Mumble School." SUNDAY TIMES (London), 22 January 1961, p. 23.

The "small grey plays" of the modern playwright do not demand enough of actors; the "common man" is best in small doses and is too easy for a skilled performer. The Method only legitimizes the actor's arrogant disregard for technique and all other acting styles.

"A Warning to Critics." SUNDAY TIMES (London), 29 January 1961, pp. 24-25.

If critics knew more, they would be either actors or authors. Today critics not only favor "dustbin drama," they have oversold it to the disservice of both the artists and the theatre itself.

THE COLLECTED SHORT STORIES. London: Heinemann, 1963.

THE LYRICS OF NOEL COWARD. London: Heinemann, 1965.

BON VOYAGE AND OTHER STORIES. London: Heinemann, 1967.

NOT YET THE DODO AND OTHER VERSES. London: Heinemann, 1967.

## CRITICISM

Levin, Milton. NOEL COWARD. New York: Twayne, 1968.

Thin, rather conventional analyses; Levin treats the plays by types, with some good words for the English popular theatre that was at the root of Coward's conception of the stage.

Mander, Raymond, and Joe Mitchenson. THEATRICAL COMPANION TO COWARD. London: Rockliff, 1957.

Indispensable.

Marchant, William. THE PRIVILEGE OF HIS COMPANY: NOEL COWARD REMEMBERED. Indianapolis: Bobbs-Merrill, 1975.

Affectionate, anecdotal reminiscence, dating from 1950 onwards. It is of particular interest for Coward's lengthy strictures on the Actor's Studio and for the depiction of the fortunes of SAIL AWAY.

Mazzocco, Robert. "Whipped Cream." NYRB, 14 March 1968, pp. 29-31.

An appreciation of Coward's career on the American publication of SUITE IN THREE KEYS.

Morley, Sheridan. A TALENT TO AMUSE: A BIOGRAPHY OF NOEL COWARD. Garden City, N.Y.: Doubleday, 1969.

Except for the predictable sexual reticence, this is a careful, detailed biography.

Taylor, John Russell. "Noel Coward." In his THE RISE AND FALL OF THE WELL-MADE PLAY. New York: Hill and Wang, 1967, pp. 124-45.

Excellent treatment of Coward's evolution within and outside the tradition of the well-made play.

## DAVID CREGAN (1931- )

TRANSCENDING, AND THE DANCERS. London: Methuen, 1967.

THREE MEN FOR COLVERTON. London: Methuen, 1967.

THE HOUSES BY THE GREEN. London: Methuen, 1969.

ARTHUR. In PLAYBILL I. Ed. Alan Durband. London: Hutchinson, 1969.

MINIATURES. London: Methuen, 1970.

Revised after its 1965 production at the Royal Court.

HOW WE HELD THE SQUARE: A PLAY FOR CHILDREN. London: Eyre Methuen, 1972.

THE LAND OF PSALMS AND OTHER PLAYS. London: Eyre Methuen, 1973.

Also includes LIEBESTRAUM, GEORGE REBORN, THE PROBLEM, JACK IN THE BOX, and IF YOU DON'T LAUGH YOU CRY.

### SELECTED NONDRAMATIC WRITING

"New Voice at the Court." PROMPT, 8 (Autumn 1966), 6-8.

Cregan deplores the division between entertaining and discursive drama, and then turns to an explanation of THREE MEN FOR COLVERTON.

RONALD ROSSITER. London: Hutchinson, 1969.

## CRITICISM

Taylor, John Russell. "Three Farceurs: Alan Ayckbourn, David Cregan, Simon Gray." In his THE SECOND WAVE. London: Methuen, 1971, pp. 162-69.

Cregan is observed with the patterns of human behavior, making him the author of painful farces.

# BEVERLEY CROSS (1931- )

ONE MORE RIVER. London: Hart-Davis, 1958.

THE SINGING DOLPHIN AND THE THREE CAVALIERS: TWO PLAYS FOR CHILDREN. London· Hart-Davis, 1960.

STRIP THE WILLOW. London: Evans Bros., 1961.

THE MINES OF SULPHER. Music by Richard Rodney Bennett. In PLAYS OF THE YEAR 30. Ed. J.C. Trewin. London: Elek Books, 1965.

BOEING-BOEING. By Marc Camoletti. Trans. Beverly Cross. London: Evans Bros., 1967.

THE CRICKETS SING. In PLAYBILL I. Ed. Alan Durband. London: Hutchinson, 1969.

THE CRICKETS SING. London: Hutchinson, 1970.

VICTORY. London: Universal Editions, 1970.

Adaptation of Joseph Conrad's novel (1915), with music by Richard Rodney Bennett.

THE RISING OF THE MOON: AN OPERA IN THREE ACTS. London: Boosey and Hawkes, 1971.

Music by Nicholas Maw.

CATHARINE HOWARD. In THE SIX WIVES OF HENRY VIII. Ed. J.C. Trewin. London: Elek Books, 1972.

CATHARINE HOWARD. Rev. ed. London: Samuel French, 1973.

Stage adaptation of the television episode.

## SELECTED NONDRAMATIC WRITING

MARS IN CAPRICORN: AN ADVENTURE AND AN EXPERIENCE. London: Hart-Davis, 1955.

Novel.

THE NIGHTWALKERS. London: Hart-Davis, 1956.

# MART CROWLEY (1935- )

THE BOYS IN THE BAND. New York: Farrar, Straus and Giroux, 1968.

A BREEZE FROM THE GULF. New York: Farrar, Straus and Giroux, 1974.

## BIBLIOGRAPHY

Salem, James M., ed. A GUIDE TO CRITICAL REVIEWS. Part 1: AMERICAN DRAMA, 1909-1969. 2nd ed. Metuchen, N.J.: Scarecrow Press, 1973.

Listing of reviews, page 111.

# SHELAGH DELANEY (1939- )

A TASTE OF HONEY. London: Methuen, 1959.

"Originally published January 22, 1959 and reprinted with minor corrections in 1959."

THE LION IN LOVE. London: Methuen, 1961.

## BIBLIOGRAPHY

Salem, James M., ed. A GUIDE TO CRITICAL REVIEWS. Part 3: BRITISH AND CONTINENTAL DRAMA FROM IBSEN TO PINTER. Metuchen, N.J.: Scarecrow Press, 1968.

List of reviews of American productions, pages 82-83.

## SELECTED NONDRAMATIC WRITING

SWEETLY SINGS THE DONKEY. London: Methuen, 1964.

Short stories.

## CRITICISM

Ippolito G.J. "The New Dramatists, I: Shelagh Delaney." DS, 1 (May 1961), 86-91.

Despite her realistic, nonpolitical style, A TASTE OF HONEY is full of the symbols typical of contemporary drama. Her work is favorably compared with that of Jean Genet, John Osborne, and Peter Shaffer.

Oberg, Arthur K. "A TASTE OF HONEY and the Popular Play." WS, 7 (Summer 1966), 160-67.

The very style that made A TASTE OF HONEY a popular success--music-hall patter, detachment, humor--prevents the play from fully realizing its true, serious nature.

Stitt, Ken. "The Lioness Lies Low." PROMPT, 1 (Summer 1962), 37.

Argues that THE LION IN LOVE is superior to A TASTE OF HONEY.

Taylor, John Russell. "Shelagh Delaney." In his ANGER AND AFTER: A GUIDE TO THE NEW BRITISH DRAMA. Rev. ed. Harmondsworth, Engl.: Penguin, 1963, pp. 111-21.

"Her future remains the big question-mark in the English theatrical scene."

# HENRY DENKER (1912- )

A FAR COUNTRY. New York: Random House, 1961.

A pseudo-psychological study of Freud, typical of serious Broadway fare of the period.

A CASE OF LIBEL. New York: Random House, 1964.

WHAT DID WE DO WRONG. London: Samuel French, 1967.

## COLLABORATION WITH RALPH BERKEY

TIME LIMIT! New York: Samuel French, 1956.

Earlier unpublished typescript versions, then called VALOR WILL WEEP and BREAKING POINT, are available at the Lincoln Center Library of the Performing Arts.

## BIBLIOGRAPHY

Salem, James M., ed. A GUIDE TO CRITICAL REVIEWS. Part 1: AMERICAN DRAMA, 1909-1969. 2nd ed. Metuchen, N.J.: Scarecrow Press, 1973.

See pages 126-28.

# NIGEL DENNIS (1912- )

TWO PLAYS AND A PREFACE: CARDS OF IDENTITY AND THE MAKING OF MOO. London: Weidenfeld and Nicolson, 1958.

AUGUST FOR THE PEOPLE. P&P, 9 (November 1961), 25-33; (December 1961), 25-32.

AUGUST FOR THE PEOPLE. London: Samuel French, 1962.

## SELECTED NONDRAMATIC WRITING

CARDS OF IDENTITY. London: Weidenfeld and Nicolson, 1955.

The novel on which the play is based.

DRAMATIC ESSAYS. London: Weidenfeld and Nicolson, 1962.

JONATHAN SWIFT: A SHORT CHARACTER. New York: Macmillan, 1964.

A HOUSE IN ORDER. London: Weidenfeld and Nicolson, 1966.

EXOTICS: POEMS OF THE MEDITERRANEAN AND MIDDLE EAST. London: Weidenfeld and Nicolson, 1970.

## CRITICISM

Wardle, Irving. "Comedy of Menace." In THE ENCORE READER: A CHRONICLE OF THE NEW DRAMA. Ed. Charles Marowitz, Tom Milne, and Owen Hale. London: Methuen, 1965, pp. 86-91.

Dennis is "the arch-abstractionist; his plays . . . are parables that invite you to gaze at a naked theme through the transparancies of plot and character."

Wellwarth, George. THE THEATRE OF PROTEST AND PARADOX. New York: New York University Press, 1964, pp. 261-67.

Dennis's plays "constitute the best that the English theatre has produced since the death of Shaw."

# KEITH DEWHURST (1931- )

RAFFERTY'S CHANT. In PLAYS OF THE YEAR 33. Ed. J.C. Trewin. London: Elek Books, 1967.

RUNNING MULLIGAN. In Z CARS: FOUR SCRIPTS FROM THE TELEVISION SERIES. Ed. Michael Marland. London: Longmans, 1968.

THE LAST BUS. In SCENE SCRIPTS. Ed. Michael Marland. London: Longmans, 1972.

## CRITICISM

Simmons, Judith Cooke. "Keith Dewhurst." In CONTEMPORARY DRAMATISTS. Ed. James Vinson. London: St. James; New York: St. Martin's, 1973, pp. 200-201.

# CHARLES DIZENZO (1938- )

THE DRAPES COME. New York: Dramatists Play Service, 1966.

AN EVENING FOR MELIN FINCH. New York: Dramatists Play Service, 1968.

A GREAT CAREER. New York: Dramatists Play Service, 1968.

BIG MOTHER AND OTHER PLAYS. New York: Grove Press, 1970.
Includes AN EVENING FOR MERLIN FINCH and THE LAST STRAW.

THE DRAPES COME. In OFF BROADWAY PLAYS I. Harmondsworth, Engl.: Penguin, 1970.

AN EVENING FOR MERLIN FINCH. In OFF BROADWAY PLAYS I. Harmondsworth, Engl.: Penguin, 1970.

THE LAST STRAW, AND SOCIABILITY: TWO SHORT PLAYS. New York: Dramatists Play Service, 1970.

## CRITICISM

Carragher, Bernard. "Charles Dizenzo." In CONTEMPORARY DRAMATISTS. Ed. James Vinson. London: St. James; New York: St. Martin's, 1973, pp. 203-04.

> "Dizenzo's playwrighting is always startlingly inventive and for the most part consistently amusing."

# J[AMES] P[ATRICK] DONLEAVY (1926-  )

THE GINGER MAN, A PLAY. New York: Random House, 1961.

This title also contains an introduction, "What They Did in Dublin," by Donleavy.

FAIRY TALES OF NEW YORK. Harmondsworth, Engl.: Penguin, 1961.

WHAT THEY DID IN DUBLIN, WITH THE GINGER MAN, A PLAY. London: MacGibbon & Kee, 1962.

Same text, different title for Donleavy's adaptation of his novel.

A SINGULAR MAN. London: Bodley Head, 1965.

THE INTERVIEW. In THEATRE TODAY. Ed. David Thompson. London: Longmans, 1965.

Donleavy's least known work, apparently unproduced.

## COLLECTIONS

THE PLAYS OF J.P. DONLEAVY. New York: Delacorte, 1972.

With a preface, "What They Did in Dublin," by Donleavy and photographs of the productions. The volume contains THE GINGER MAN, FAIRY TALES OF NEW YORK, A SINGULAR MAN, and the only published version of the play form of THE SADDEST SUMMER OF SAMUEL S.

## SELECTED NONDRAMATIC WRITING

THE GINGER MAN. Paris: Olympia Press, 1955.

A SINGULAR MAN. Boston: Little, Brown, 1963.

The novel adapted into the 1965 play.

THE GINGER MAN. Complete Ed. New York: Delacorte, 1965.

THE SADDEST SUMMER OF SAMUEL S. New York: Delacorte, 1966.

The novel adapted into the play in his collected PLAYS.

## CRITICISM

Elsom, John. "J.P. Donleavy." In CONTEMPORARY DRAMATISTS. Ed. James Vinson. London: St. James; New York: St. Martin's, 1973, pp. 205-06.

"Although as a dramatist, he may not yet have lived up to the promise of FAIRY TALES OF NEW YORK, he remains one of the most potentially exciting dramatists in the West."

Moore, John Rees. "Hard Times and the Noble Savage: J.P. Donleavy's A SINGULAR MAN." HC, 1 (February 1964), 1-11.

FAIRY TALES OF NEW YORK is "a step toward" A SINGULAR MAN.

# ROSALYN DREXLER (1926- )

THE LINE OF LEAST EXISTENCE, AND OTHER PLAYS. New York: Random House, 1967.

With an introduction by Richard Gilman, the volume also includes HOME MOVIES; THE INVESTIGATION; HOT BUTTERED ROLL; SOFTLY, AND CONSIDER THE NEARNESS; and THE BED WAS FULL.

SKYWRITING. In COLLISION COURSE. Ed. Edward Parone. New York: Random House, 1968.

## SELECTED NONDRAMATIC WRITING

I AM THE BEAUTIFUL STRANGER. New York: Grossman, 1965.

Novel.

## CRITICISM

Sainer, Arthur. "Rosalyn Drexler." In CONTEMPORARY DRAMATISTS. Ed. James Vinson. London: St. James; New York: St. Martin's, 1973, pp. 207-09.

# MARTIN DUBERMAN (1930- )

IN WHITE AMERICA: A DOCUMENTARY. Boston: Houghton Mifflin, 1964.

METAPHORS. In COLLISION COURSE. Ed. Edward Parone. New York: Random House, 1968.

HISTORY. ER, 13 (April 1969), 49-55.

THE MEMORY BANK. New York: Dial, 1970.

Consists of THE RECORDER and THE ELECTRIC MAP.

MALE ARMOR. New York: E.P. Dutton, 1975.

Consists of PAYMENTS, ELAGABULUS, and the one-act plays, THE RECORDER, GUTTMAN ORDINARY SCALE, THE ELECTRIC MAP, THE COLONIAL DUDES, and METAPHORS.

## BIBLIOGRAPHY

Salem, James M., ed. A GUIDE TO CRITICAL REVIEWS. Part 1: AMERICAN DRAMA, 1909-1969. 2nd ed. Metuchen, N.J.: Scarecrow Press, 1973, pp. 130-31.

## SELECTED NONDRAMATIC WRITING

THE UNCOMPLETED PAST. New York: Random House, 1969.

Essays.

## CRITICISM

Markus, Thomas B. "Martin Duberman." In CONTEMPORARY DRAMATISTS. Ed. James Vinson. London: St. James; New York: St. Martin's, 1973, pp. 210-12.

# MAUREEN DUFFY (1933- )

RITES. In NEW SHORT PLAYS 2. London: Methuen, 1969.

RITES. P&P, 17 (October 1969), 57-66.

A variation on the BACCHAE.

## SELECTED NONDRAMATIC WRITING

THE MICROCOSM. London: Hutchinson, 1966.

Novel.

THE PARADOX PLAYERS. London: Hutchinson, 1967.

LYRICS FOR THE DOG HOUR: POEMS. London: Hutchinson, 1968.

## CRITICISM

Barber, Dulan. "Maureen Duffy Talking to Dulan Barber." TR, 45 (Spring 1973), 5-16.

On her novels, homosexuality, and politics.

# RONALD DUNCAN (1914- )

STRATTON. London: Faber and Faber, 1950.

OUR LADY'S TUMBLER. London: Faber and Faber, 1951.

DON JUAN. London: Faber and Faber, 1954.

THE DEATH OF SATAN. London: Faber and Faber, 1955.

> Duncan was one of the founders of the English Stage Company. THE DEATH OF SATAN and DON JUAN formed the double bill that followed Osborne's LOOK BACK IN ANGER into the Royal Court Theatre during the company's first season there.

THE APOLLO OF BELLAC. London: Samuel French, 1958.

> Abridged version of the Jean Giradoux play (1942).

ABELARD AND HELOISE: A CORRESPONDENCE FOR THE STAGE IN TWO ACTS. London: Faber and Faber, 1961.

SAINT SPIV. London: Dobson, 1961.

THE CATALYST. London: Rebel Press, 1964.

K-M<br>
O-B-A-F-G : A PLAY IN ONE ACT FOR STEREOPHONIC SOUND. London:<br>
S R-N<br>
Rebel Press, 1964.

THE TROJAN WOMEN. London: Hamish Hamilton, 1967.

> English version adapted by Duncan from Jean-Paul Sartre.

THE GIFT. G, no. 3 (1968), 93-110.

## COLLECTIONS

COLLECTED PLAYS. London: Hart-Davis, 1971.

THIS WAY TO THE TOMB, ST. SPIV, THE REHEARSAL, OUR LADY'S TUMBLER, THE SEVEN DEADLY VIRTUES, O-B-A-F-G, and THE GIFT.

## SELECTED NONDRAMATIC WRITING

SELECTED WRITINGS OF MAHATMA GANDHI. Selected and Introd. Ronald Duncan. London: Faber and Faber, 1951.

"Murder by the Management." OBSERVER, 29 March 1953, p. 10.

Duncan decries the conservatism, the expense, the predominance of revivals, and the lack of poetry on the English stage. His article should be read for his motives for starting the English Stage Company.

ALL MEN ARE ISLANDS: AN AUTOBIOGRAPHY. London: Hart-Davis, 1964.

DEVON AND CORNWALL. London: Batsford, 1966.

Representative of Duncan's many writings on the English countryside.

HOW TO MAKE ENEMIES. London: Hart-Davis, 1968.

A second volume of autobiography.

UNPOPULAR POEMS. London: Hart-Davis, 1969.

## CRITICISM

Hauter, Max Walter. RONALD DUNCAN: THE METAPHYSICAL CONTEXT OF HIS PLAYS. London: Rebel Press, 1969.

Wahl, William B. A LONE WOLF HOWLING: THE THEMATIC CONTENT OF RONALD DUNCAN'S PLAYS. Salzburg, Austria: University of Salzburg, 1973.

Weales, Gerald. RELIGION IN MODERN ENGLISH DRAMA. Philadelphia: University of Pennsylvania, 1961, pp. 233-39.

Treats Duncan's religious plays, largely pre-1950.

# LAWRENCE DURRELL (1912- )

SAPPHO: A PLAY IN VERSE. London: Faber and Faber, 1950.

ACTE; OR, THE PRISONER OF TIME. S, 1 (December 1961), 48-55 ff.

With an "Author's Note," explaining his intentions.

AN IRISH FAUSTUS: A MORALITY IN NINE SCENES. London: Faber and Faber, 1963.

ACTE: OR, THE PRISONER OF TIME. London: Faber and Faber, 1965.

ULYSSES COME BACK. London: Turrett Books, 1970.

"Outline Sketch of a musical based on the last three love-affairs of Ulysses the Greek adventurer of mythology, adaptated rather light heartedly from Homer; 99 copies only issued on June 1970, numbered and signed by the author."

## BIBLIOGRAPHY

Alan G. Thomas has a fine bibliography in G.S. Fraser's LAWRENCE DURRELL: A STUDY. Rev. ed. London: Faber and Faber, 1973, pages 177-233.

## CRITICISM

Cole, Douglas. "Faust and Anti-Faust in Modern Drama." DS, 5 (Spring 1966), 49-52.

MacClintock, Lander. "Durrell's Plays." In THE WORLD OF LAWRENCE DURRELL. Ed. Harry T. Moore. Carbondale: Southern Illinois University Press, pp. 66-86.

Weigel, John A. LAWRENCE DURRELL. New York: Twayne, 1966.
Chapter 9 treats the plays as literature, not theatre.

# CHARLES DYER (1928- )

WANTED, ONE BODY! A FARCICAL THRILLER. London: English Theatre Guild, 1961.

TIME, MURDERER, PLEASE. London: English Theatre Guild, 1962.

RATTLE OF A SIMPLE MAN. London: Samuel French, 1963.

STAIRCASE. Harmondsworth, Engl.: Penguin, 1966.

A HOT GODLY WIND. In SECOND PLAYBILL 3. Ed. Alan Durband. London: Hutchinson, 1972.

MOTHER ADAM. London: Davis Poynter, 1972.

## BIBLIOGRAPHY

Salem, James M., ed. A GUIDE TO CRITICAL REVIEWS. Part 3: BRITISH AND CONTINENTAL DRAMA FROM IBSEN TO PINTER. Metuchen, N.J.: Scarecrow Press, 1968.

List of American reviews of RATTLE OF A SIMPLE MAN, page 90.

## SELECTED NONDRAMATIC WRITING

RATTLE OF A SIMPLE MAN. London: Elek Books, 1964.

Novel.

CHARLIE ALWAYS TOLD HARRY ALMOST EVERYTHING. London: W.H. Allen, 1969.

Despite the dates of publication, the two novels, RATTLE and

CHARLIE, are the bases for the plays, RATTLE OF A SIMPLE MAN and STAIRCASE.

STAIRCASE; OR, CHARLIE ALWAYS TOLD HARRY ALMOST EVERYTHING. New York: Doubleday, 1969.

American retitling of CHARLIE.

## CRITICISM

Hobson, Harold. "Charles Dyer." In CONTEMPORARY DRAMATISTS. Ed. James Vinson. London: St. James; New York: St. Martin's, 1973, pp. 227-29.

"We clothe our inadequacies. This is what Charles Dyer's plays are all about."

Orton, Joe. "Joe Orton Interviewed by Giles Gordon." In BEHIND THE SCENES: THEATER AND FILM INTERVIEWS FROM THE TRANSATLANTIC REVIEW. Ed. Joseph F.M. McCrindle, introd. Jean-Claude van Itallie. New York: Holt, Rinehart and Winston, 1971, pp. 116-24.

Orton and Gordon discuss, among other things, the reaction to STAIRCASE.

## RICHARD EBERHART (1904- )

THE APPARITION. P, 77 (March 1951), 311-21.

VISIONARY FARMS. NWW, no. 3 (1953), 63-97.

PREAMBLE II. SR, 62 (Winter 1954), 84-99.

With a note by Eberhart explaining the origins of this and others of his plays.

A DIALOGUE. DISCOVERY, no. 6 (1955), 77-86.

Retitled as PREAMBLE I in COLLECTED VERSE PLAYS, below.

VISIONARY FARMS. QRL, 8 (1955), 169-75.

A final scene, XV, not completed in time for publication in 1951, is to be found here.

DEVILS AND ANGELS. TDR, 6 (June 1962), 15-32.

THE MAD MUSICIAN. TDR, 6 (June 1962), 33-53.

THE BRIDE OF MANTUA. No imprint.

An adaptation from Lope de Vega (1619) available at the Library of the College of William and Mary, Williamsburg, Virginia.

### COLLECTIONS

COLLECTED VERSE PLAYS. Chapel Hill: University of North Carolina Press, 1962.

Dedicated to the Poets' Theatre of Cambridge, Mass., with an introduction by Eberhart, and notes on first publication and production, this volume contains the first publication of TRIPTYCH, as well as reprinting PREAMBLE I, PREAMBLE II, THE APPARITION, VISIONARY FARMS (with changes in the last scene and other places), DEVILS AND ANGELS, and THE MAD MUSICIAN.

## SELECTED NONDRAMATIC WRITING

"Outer and Inner Verse Drama." VIRGINIA QUARTERLY REVIEW, 34 (Autumn 1958), 618-23.

An analysis of Djuna Barnes's THE ANTIPHON.

"Tragedy as Limitation: Comedy as Control and Resolution." TDR, 6 (June 1962), 3-14.

Eberhart discusses his intentions in VISIONARY FARMS.

## CRITICISM

Donoghue, Denis. THE THIRD VOICE: MODERN BRITISH AND AMERICAN VERSE DRAMA. Princeton, N.J.: Princeton University Press, 1959, pp. 194-95, 223-35.

On THE APPARITION and VISIONARY FARMS.

______. "An Interview with Richard Eberhart." SH, 15 (Summer 1964), 7-29.

Engel, Bernard Francis. RICHARD EBERHART. New York: Twayne, 1971.

Pages 97-112 detail how the plays illustrate the development of the poet.

Gerstenberger, Donna. "Three Verse Playwrights and the American Fifties." In MODERN AMERICAN DRAMA: ESSAYS IN CRITICISM. Ed. William E. Taylor. Deland, Fla.: Everett-Edwards, 1968, pp. 117-28.

Treats Barnes's THE ANTIPHON, MacLeish's J.B., and Eberhart's VISIONARY FARMS.

Roache, Joel. RICHARD EBERHART: THE PROGRESS OF AN AMERICAN POET. New York: Oxford University Press, 1971.

Excellent critical biography, extremely detailed up to 1961.

# T[HOMAS] S[TEARNS] ELIOT (1888-1965)

THE COCKTAIL PARTY: A COMEDY. London: Faber and Faber, 1950.

THE COCKTAIL PARTY: A COMEDY. 4th impression, rev. London: Faber and Faber, 1950.

> Eliot's note: "In addition to some minor corrections, certain alterations in Act III, based on the experience of the play's production, were made in the fourth impression of the text." The revisions, largely deletions, were incorporated into COLLECTED PLAYS.

THE CONFIDENTIAL CLERK. London: Faber and Faber, 1954.

THE ELDER STATESMAN. London: Faber and Faber, 1959.

## COLLABORATION WITH GEORGE HOELLERING

THE FILM OF MURDER IN THE CATHEDRAL. London: Faber and Faber, 1952.

> The screenplay is substantially different from the text of the original play (1935). Prefaces by Eliot and Hoellering explain and detail the cinematic reasons for the changes, notably in the opening of the film and in the treatment of the Four Knights. Eliot seems to have been most cooperative in carrying out the emendations and additions suggested by Hoellering, the film's director.

## COLLECTIONS

COLLECTED PLAYS. London: Faber and Faber, 1962.

> Omits THE ROCK and SWEENEY AGONISTES, and uses the revised text of THE COCKTAIL PARTY.

## BIBLIOGRAPHY

Gallup, Donald, ed. T.S. ELIOT: A BIBLIOGRAPHY. Rev. and expanded ed. New York: Harcourt, Brace and World, 1970.

Exemplary.

Martin, Mildred, ed. A HALF-CENTURY OF ELIOT CRITICISM: AN ANNOTATED BIBLIOGRAPHY OF BOOKS AND ARTICLES IN ENGLISH, 1916-1965. Lewisburg, Pa.: Bucknell University Press, 1972.

Salem, James M., ed. A GUIDE TO CRITICAL REVIEWS. Part 1: AMERICAN DRAMA, 1909-1969. 2nd ed. Metuchen, N.J.: Scarecrow Press, 1973.

A listing of American reviews, pages 134-37.

## SELECTED NONDRAMATIC WRITING

ON POETRY AND POETS. London: Faber and Faber, 1957.

Contains the important lectures, "Poetry and Drama" and "The Three Voices of Poetry," in which Eliot discusses the aims and nature of poetic drama, in general, and his own plays, in particular.

## CRITICISM

Arrowsmith, William. "English Verse Drama (II): THE COCKTAIL PARTY." HR, 3 (Autumn 1950), 411-30.

The first part of the essay discusses Eliot's subtle attempts to revitalize the remnants of Christian belief in his dramatized society. The second part argues that the Chamberlaynes are given a less than rich Christian life, and that none of the characters have the "wholeness of the whole man."

______. "Transfiguration in Eliot and Euripides." SR, 63 (Summer 1955), 421-42.

Eliot and Euripides both depict a double reality. Euripides' conventional world is at least as intensely realized as his moments of transfiguration, while Eliot has no respect for the world he means to transfigure, and thus defeats his own purpose.

Bellow, Saul. "Pleasures and Pains of Playgoing." PR, 21 (May-June 1954), 312-17.

On, in part, the aridity of THE CONFIDENTIAL CLERK.

Bergonzi, Bernard. T.S. ELIOT. New York: Macmillan, 1972.

This brief, well-written, critical biography is particularly strong on cultural history, but lamentably brief on the late plays.

Browne, E. Martin. THE MAKING OF T.S. ELIOT'S PLAYS. Cambridge, Engl.: Cambridge University Press, 1969.

The original director of all of Eliot's plays, and a moving force in the postwar revival of English poetic drama, describes the creation of each of the plays. He includes lengthy excerpts from various drafts of the plays, notes, and correspondence to and from Eliot discussing suggested changes in the text and staging. Despite Browne's reluctance to criticize his friend, his book is an invaluable documentation of the step-by-step evolution of Eliot's plays. Browne also provides a list of manuscripts, typescripts, and printed copies of the plays and their present locations.

Carnell, Corbin S. "Creation's Lonely Flesh: T.S. Eliot and Christopher Fry on the Life of the Senses." MD, 6 (September 1963), 141-49.

Contrasts Eliot's and Fry's views about the senses, characterizing those views, respectively, as the way of rejection and the way of affirmation.

Coghill, Nevill. T.S. ELIOT'S <u>THE COCKTAIL PARTY</u>. London: Faber and Faber, 1974.

The text, with copious notes and commentary.

Donoghue, Denis. THE THIRD VOICE: MODERN BRITISH AND AMERICAN VERSE DRAMA. Princeton, N.J.: Princeton University Press, 1959, pp. 138-79.

THE CONFIDENTIAL CLERK is Eliot's first fully consistent verse drama, with none of the lapses of his earlier efforts. And, just as THE CONFIDENTIAL CLERK is a revision of THE COCKTAIL PARTY, THE ELDER STATESMAN is a response to THE FAMILY REUNION.

Fleming, Rudd. "THE ELDER STATESMAN and Eliot's Programme for the Metier of Poetry." WS, 2 (Winter 1961), 54-64.

While each of Eliot's plays is in some fashion related to past literature, THE ELDER STATESMAN marks the climax of his creative relationship to literary tradition.

Gardener, Helen. "The Comedies of T.S. Eliot." SR, 74 (Winter 1966), 153-75.

This magisterial lecture defends the vitality of drawing-room comedy, and Eliot's decision in each of his last three plays to work within that genre.

Harding, D.W. "Progression of Theme in Eliot's Modern Plays." KR, 18 (Summer 1956), 337-60.

The modern plays "deal with human loneliness" from several aspects, as characters work away from the mother and toward the father and a vocation.

Heilman, Robert B. "ALCESTIS and THE COCKTAIL PARTY." CL, 5 (Spring 1953), 105-16.

Examines what otherwise might seem to be only a minimal relationship between the two plays.

Jones, D.E. THE PLAYS OF T.S. ELIOT. Toronto: University of Toronto Press, 1960.

The first full-length study of the plays; each of the three late plays receives a well-documented chapter, emphasizing the play in the context of Eliot's other writings. Includes a fine bibliography.

Kennedy, Andrew K. "Eliot." In his SIX DRAMATISTS IN SEARCH OF A LANGUAGE. Cambridge, Engl.: Cambridge University Press, 1975, pp. 87-129.

Traces Eliot's evolving theoretical and practical concern with theatre language. In the last three plays Eliot uses naturalistic chatter as foreground noise, and then makes the transition to revelatory, confessional dialogues. But at the crucial religious moments his characters evade full expression of their inner states.

Knieger, Bernard. "The Dramatic Achievement of T.S. Eliot." MD, 3 (February 1961), 387-92.

Aside from MURDER IN THE CATHEDRAL, Eliot's plays fail to express theatrically their internal, spiritual action.

Mitchell, John D. "Applied Psychoanalysis in the Drama." AMERICAN IMAGO, 14 (Fall 1957), 263-80.

THE CONFIDENTIAL CLERK illustrates how a play can reflect both an author's wish-fulfillment fantasy and also an audience's cultural beliefs.

Pryce-Jones, David. "Towards the Cocktail Party." In AGE OF AUSTERITY: 1945-1951. Ed. Michael Sissons and Philip French. London: Hodder and Stoughton, 1963, pp. 216-39.

An interesting survey of the postwar English literary scene that finds some remarkable similarities between the attitudes of Eliot and the popular Tory novelist Angela Thirkell.

Schwartz, Edward. "Eliot's COCKTAIL PARTY and the New Humanism." PHILOLOGICAL QUARTERLY, 32 (January 1953), 58-68.

The influence of Irving Babbitt is still a considerable force in THE COCKTAIL PARTY.

Sena, Vinod. "The Ambivalence of THE COCKTAIL PARTY." MD, 14 (February 1972), 392-404.

THE COCKTAIL PARTY's complications are largely over by the end of the first act. Eliot resorts to surprise and the manipulations of the Guardians to save the play, but at great cost to its spiritual meanings.

Smith, Carol H. T.S. ELIOT'S DRAMATIC THEORY AND PRACTICE: FROM SWEENEY AGONISTES TO THE ELDER STATESMAN. Princeton, N.J.: Princeton University Press, 1963.

Eliot's search for religious, artistic, and social order led him to the theatre. In THE CONFIDENTIAL CLERK he uses the very arbitrariness of farce to convey spiritual meaning, while in THE ELDER STATESMAN there is a greater fusion of dramatic surface and symbolic meaning.

Smith, Grover, Jr. "The Ghosts in T.S. Eliot's THE ELDER STATESMAN." NOTES AND QUERIES, 205 (June 1962), 233-35.

Like most of Eliot's plays, THE ELDER STATESMAN features ghosts, in this case, Gomez and Mrs. Carghill.

______. T.S. ELIOT'S POETRY AND PLAYS: A STUDY IN SOURCES AND MEANING. 2nd ed. Chicago: Chicago University Press, 1974.

Stynan, J.L. THE ELEMENTS OF DRAMA. Cambridge, Engl.: Cambridge University Press, 1960, pp. 275-84.

THE COCKTAIL PARTY "sets itself the impossible task of persuading us both at the rational level of social comedy and at the emotional level of tragedy."

Thurber, James. "WHAT Cocktail Party?" NEW YORKER, 1 April 1950, pp. 26-29.

"Ever since the distinguished Mr. T.S. Eliot's widely discussed play came to town, I have been cornered at parties by women, and men, who seem intent on making me say what I think THE

COCKTAIL PARTY means, so they can cry, 'Great God, how naive!'"

Williams, Raymond. DRAMA FROM IBSEN TO BRECHT. New York: Oxford University Press, 1968, pp. 188-98.

THE COCKTAIL PARTY is a "theatrical compromise"; THE CONFIDENTIAL CLERK is a "parody of a play"; THE ELDER STATESMAN is the epilogue to Eliot's tragic loss of a true dramatic voice.

Wimsatt, William K., Jr. "Eliot's Comedy." SR, 58 (October-December 1950), 666-78.

THE COCKTAIL PARTY "is perhaps the best morality play in English since EVERYMAN and the only comical-morality."

Worth, Katharine J. "Eliot and the Living Theatre." In ELIOT IN PERSPECTIVE: A SYMPOSIUM. Ed. Graham Martin. London: Macmillan, 1970.

Primarily about the early plays, especially SWEENEY AGONISTES, the essay imaginatively compares Eliot's work with Pinter, Beckett, and Coward.

______. "T.S. Eliot." In her REVOLUTIONS IN MODERN ENGLISH DRAMA. London: G. Bell, 1973, pp. 55-66.

On Eliot's anticipations of Pinter.

# STANLEY EVELING (1925-   )

THE BALACHITES, AND THE STRANGE CASE OF MARTIN RICHTER. London: Calder and Boyars, 1970.

The latter play is Eveling's most political work.

THE LUNATIC, THE SECRET SPORTSMAN, AND THE WOMAN NEXT DOOR, AND VIBRATIONS. London: Calder and Boyars, 1970.

Two plays.

COME AND BE KILLED, AND DEAR JANET ROSENBERG, DEAR MR. KOONING. London: Calder and Boyars, 1971.

Includes a third play, JAKEY FAT BOY.

OH STARLINGS. P&P, 18 (March 1971), 76-79.

SWEET ALICE. P&P, 18 (March 1971), 79-85.

## CRITICISM

Spurling, John. "Stanley Eveling." In CONTEMPORARY DRAMATISTS. Ed. James Vinson. London: St. James; New York: St. Martin's, 1973, pp. 235-36.

# CLIVE EXTON (1930- )

NO FIXED ABODE. In SIX GRANADA PLAYS. London: Faber and Faber, 1960.

HAVE YOU ANY DIRTY WASHING, MOTHER DEAR? P&P, 16 (May 1969), 35-50.

HAVE YOU ANY DIRTY WASHING, MOTHER DEAR? In PLAYS OF THE YEAR 37. Ed. J.C. Trewin. London: Elek Books, 1970.

## CRITICISM

Taylor, John Russell. "Clive Exton." In his ANGER AND AFTER: A GUIDE TO THE NEW BRITISH DRAMA. Rev. ed. Harmondsworth, Engl.: Penguin, 1963, pp. 222-35.

> NO FIXED ABODE, like nearly all of Exton's plays, focuses on "the desperate need of man in modern society to feel he belongs, the endless search for a context, a hierarchy, a fixed standard."

## TOM EYEN (1940- )

THE WHITE WHORE AND THE BIT PLAYER. In NEW AMERICAN PLAYS. Vol. 2. Ed. William M. Hoffman. New York: Hill and Wang, 1968.

SARAH B. DIVINE! AND OTHER PLAYS. New York: Winter House, 1971.

Includes the trilogy, THREE SISTERS FROM SPRINGFIELD, ILLINOIS: I. WHY HANNAH'S SKIRT WON'T STAY DOWN, II. WHO KILLED MY BALD SISTER SOPHIE?, III. WHAT'S MAKING GILDA SO GRAY? Also includes ARETHA IN THE ICE PALACE, THE KAMA SUTRA: AN ORGANIC HAPPENING, MY NEXT HUSBAND WILL BE A BEAUTY, THE DEATH OF OFF-BROADWAY: A STREET PLAY, THE WHITE WHORE AND THE BIT PLAYER, and GRAND TENEMENT/NOVEMBER 22ND. Despite publication date, these plays date from the mid to late sixties. They have, however, undergone substantial revision from the acting versions.

WHY HANNAH'S SKIRT WON'T STAY DOWN. New York: Samuel French, 1971.

WOMEN BEHIND BARS. New York: Samuel French, 1975.

### CRITICISM

Ansorge, Peter. "The Dirtiest Author in Town?" P&P, 18 (June 1971), 14-16.

Interview with Eyen on the Living Theatre, nudity, and the dangers of success.

Valgemae, Mardi. "Expressionism and the New American Drama." TCL, 17 (October 1971), 227-34.

THE WHITE WHORE AND THE BIT PLAYER is an example of the subjective dislocation used by young American dramatists.

# WILLIAM FAULKNER (1897-1962)

REQUIEM FOR A NUN. New York: Random House, 1959.

A play from the novel adapted to the stage by Ruth Ford and Faulkner. See also Izard below.

## BIBLIOGRAPHY

Salem, James M., ed. A GUIDE TO CRITICAL REVIEWS. Part 1: AMERICAN DRAMA, 1909-1969. 2nd ed. Metuchen, N.J.: Scarecrow Press, 1973.

List of reviews, page 139.

## CRITICISM

Bree, Germaine. CAMUS. Rev. ed. New York: Harcourt, Brace and World, 1964, pp. 162-65.

On Camus's adaptation of REQUIEM FOR A NUN.

Izard, Barbara, and Clara Hieronymus. REQUIEM FOR A NUN: ON STAGE AND OFF. Nashville, Tenn.: Aurora Publishers, 1970.

Provides a stage history, while tracing the play's complicated, collaborative provenance, primarily through interviews.

O'Connor, William Van. "Faulkner on Broadway." KR, 21 (Spring 1959), 334-36.

REQUIEM FOR A NUN unsuccessfully mixes two fictional worlds, and Faulkner permits himself to indulge in a kind of writing he formerly avoided.

Tynan, Kenneth. CURTAINS: SELECTIONS FROM THE DRAMA CRITICISM AND RELATED WRITINGS. New York: Atheneum, 1961.

Extremely negative reviews of the English and American stagings of REQUIEM. See pages 276-78, 299-301.

# JULES FEIFFER (1929- )

CRAWLING ARNOLD. HORIZON, 4 (November 1961), 49-56.

CRAWLING ARNOLD. New York: Dramatists Play Service, 1963.

LITTLE MURDERS. New York: Random House, 1968.

THE UNEXPURGATED MEMOIRS OF BERNARD MERGENDEILER. In COLLISION COURSE. Ed. Edward Parone. New York: Random House, 1968.

GOD BLESS. P&P, 16 (January 1969), 35-50.

DICK AND JANE. RAMPARTS, 8 (August 1969), 23-26.

FEIFFER'S PEOPLE: SKETCHES AND OBSERVATIONS. New York: Dramatists Play Service, 1969.

DICK AND JANE. In OH! CALCUTTA! AN ENTERTAINMENT WITH MUSIC. New York: Grove Press, 1970.

THE WHITE HOUSE MURDER CASE; DICK AND JANE. New York: Grove Press, 1970.

CARNAL KNOWLEDGE: A SCREENPLAY. New York: Farrar, Straus and Giroux, 1971.

## CRITICISM

Hughes, Catharine. PLAYS, POLITICS, AND POLEMICS. New York: Drama Book Specialists, 1973, pp. 3-15.

Lahr, John. "Jules Feiffer: Satire as Subversion." In his UP AGAINST THE FOURTH WALL: ESSAYS ON MODERN THEATER. New York: Grove Press, 1970, pp. 78-94.

A tribute to Feiffer's power as a satirist of American culture.

______. "Jules Feiffer Interviewed by John Lahr." In BEHIND THE SCENES: THEATER AND FILM INTERVIEWS FROM THE TRANSATLANTIC REVIEW. Ed. Joseph F.M. McCrindle, introd. Jean-Claude van Itallie. New York: Holt, Rinehart and Winston, 1971, pp. 19-30.

On satire, politics, and GOD BLESS.

______. "Jules Feiffer and Sam Shepard: Spectacles of Disintegration." In his ASTONISH ME: ADVENTURES IN CONTEMPORARY THEATER. New York: Viking, 1973, pp. 102-19.

THE WHITE HOUSE MURDER CASE satirizes the political dishonesty of the Vietnam War.

# LAWRENCE FERLINGHETTI (1919- )

SPURT OF BLOOD. ER, 7 (January-February 1963), 62-66.

Translation of Antonin Artaud's play (1925).

UNFAIR ARGUMENTS WITH EXISTENCE: SEVEN PLAYS FOR A NEW THEATRE. New York: New Directions, 1963.

Includes, along with a brief "Note on the Plays," THE SOLDIERS OF NO COUNTRY, THREE THOUSAND RED ANTS, THE ALLIGATION, THE VICTIMS OF AMNESIA, MOTHERLODE, THE CUSTOMS COLLECTOR IN BAGGY PANTS, THE NOSE OF SISYPHUS.

SERVANTS OF THE PEOPLE. In NEW DIRECTIONS EIGHTEEN. Ed. James Laughlin. Philadelphia: Lippincott, 1964.

ROUTINES. New York: New Directions, 1964.

Twelve short pieces, including SERVANTS OF THE PEOPLE, and a brief note.

## HORTON FOOTE (1916- )

THE CHASE. New York: Dramatists Play Service, 1952.

Later adapted into a novel (1956), then made into a film (1966).

THE TRIP TO BOUNTIFUL. New York: Dramatists Play Service, 1954.

THE TRAVELING LADY. New York: Dramatists Play Service, 1955.

With a foreword by Stark Young.

A YOUNG LADY OF PROPERTY: SIX SHORT PLAYS. New York: Dramatists Play Service, 1955.

The title play, and DANCERS, JOHN TURNER DAVIS, THE DEATH OF THE OLD MAN, THE OLD BEGINNING, and THE OIL WELL.

HARRISON, TEXAS: EIGHT TELEVISION PLAYS. New York: Harcourt, Brace and World, 1956.

The first four plays from A YOUNG LADY OF PROPERTY, plus EXPECTANT RELATIONS, THE MIDNIGHT CALLER, TEARS OF MY SISTER, and THE TRIP TO BOUNTIFUL.

THE FLIGHT. In TELEVISION PLAYS FOR WRITERS. Ed. A.S. Burack. Boston: the author, 1957.

THE MIDNIGHT CALLER. Rev. ed. New York: Dramatists Play Service, 1959.

The stage adaptation of the novel.

MAMIE BORDEN. New York: n.p., n.d.

Typescript promptbook written in the 1950s at the Lincoln Center Library of the Performing Arts.

STORM FEAR. Hollywood: Alert Agency, n.d.

Television script written in the 1950s at the Lincoln Center Library of the Performing Arts.

THREE PLAYS: OLD MAN, TOMORROW (ADAPTED FROM STORIES BY WILLIAM FAULKNER), AND ROOTS IN A PARCHED GROUND. New York: Harcourt, Brace and World, 1962.

Television plays for Playhouse 90.

ROOTS IN A PARCHED GROUND. Rev. ed. New York: Dramatists Play Service, 1962.

Adapted to the stage, with a foreword by Stark Young.

TOMORROW. Rev. ed. New York: Dramatists Play Service, 1963.

A play adapted from a story by William Faulkner.

THE SCREENPLAY OF TO KILL A MOCKINGBIRD. New York: Harcourt, Brace and World, 1964.

## CRITICISM

Becker, William. "The New American Play." HR, 6 (Winter 1954), 578-88.

Deals in part with THE TRIP TO BOUNTIFUL as an example of a mood play that never truly exists as drama.

Bentley, Eric. "New Playwright, New Actress." In his THE DRAMATIC EVENT: AN AMERICAN CHRONICLE. New York: Horizon, 1954, pp. 163-66.

On THE TRIP TO BOUNTIFUL and the Neurotic Woman as a character type.

## MARIA IRENE FORNES (1930- )

LA VIDUA. In CUATRO AUTORES CUBANOS. Havana: Casa de los Americas, 1961.

PROMENADE. In THE BOLD NEW WOMAN. New York: Fawcett, 1966.

The one-act version; see Collection, below, for full-length version.

THE SUCCESSFUL LIFE OF THREE: A SKIT FOR VAUDEVILLE. In PLAYWRIGHTS FOR TOMORROW: A COLLECTION OF PLAYS. Vol. 2. Ed. Arthur H. Ballet. Minneapolis: University of Minnesota Press, 1966.

TANGO PALACE. In PLAYWRIGHTS FOR TOMORROW: A COLLECTION OF PLAYS. Vol. 2. Ed. Arthur H. Ballet. Minneapolis: University of Minnesota Press, 1966.

DR. KHEAL. YT, 1 (Winter 1968), 32-40.

DR. KHEAL. In THE BEST OF OFF-OFF BROADWAY. Ed. Michael Smith. New York: E.P. Dutton, 1969.

### COLLECTIONS

PROMENADE AND OTHER PLAYS. New York: Winter House, 1971.

In addition to the title play (in its full length version), and DR. KHEAL, THE SUCCESSFUL LIFE OF THREE, and TANGO PALACE, this volume includes A VIETNAMESE WEDDING, THE RED BURNING LIGHT OF DR. MISSION XQ3, and MOLLY'S DREAM, all performed during the mid and late sixties; with an introduction by Richard Gilman.

## CRITICISM

Lopate, Philip. "Cue the Giant Maraschino." HERALD (New York), 23 January 1972, p. 23.

# JAMES FORSYTH (1913-  )

EMMANUEL: A NATIVITY PLAY. London: Heinemann, 1952; New York: Theatre Arts, 1963.

THREE PLAYS: THE OTHER HEART, HELOISE, ADELAISE. Introd. by Tyrone Guthrie. London: Heinemann, 1956.

THE ROAD TO EMMAUS: A PLAY FOR EASTERTIDE. Foreword by Michael Berry. London: Heinemann, 1958.

BRAND. London: Heinemann, 1960.

An Ibsen adaptation, introduced by Tyrone Guthrie.

DEAR WORMWOOD. Chicago: Dramatic Publishing Co., 1961.

Based on C.S. Lewis' THE SCREWTAPE LETTERS.

TROG. N.p.: n.p., 1964.

Typescript at the library of Florida State University, Talahassee.

CYRANO DE BERGERAC. Chicago: Dramatic Publishing Co., 1968.

An adaptation of the play by Edmond Rostand.

## CRITICISM

Roose-Evans, James. "James Forsyth." In CONTEMPORARY DRAMATISTS. Ed. James Vinson. London: St. James; New York: St. Martin's, 1973, pp. 252-53.

"James Forsyth belongs to that great tradition of bardic poets, who sang the exploits and epics of heroes."

## PAUL FOSTER (1931- )

MINNIE THE WHORE; THE BIRTHDAY PARTY. Caracas, Venezuela: Zodiaco, 1962.

THE RECLUSE. New York: n.p., 1963.

Typescript at the Lincoln Center Library of the Performing Arts.

BALLS. New York: n.p., 1964.

Typescript at the Lincoln Center Library of the Performing Arts.

HURRAH FOR THE BRIDGE. Bogata, Colombia: Canal Ramirez, 1965.

BALLS. In EIGHT PLAYS FROM OFF-OFF BROADWAY. Eds. Nick Orzel and Michael Smith. Indianapolis: Bobbs-Merrill, 1966.

TOM PAINE. London: Calder and Boyars, 1967.

TOM PAINE: A PLAY IN TWO PARTS. New York: Grove Press, 1968.

HELMSKRINGA! OR, THE STONED ANGELS. London: Calder and Boyars, 1970.

THE MADONNA IN THE ORCHARD. New York: Breakthrough Press, 1971.

ELIZABETH I. London: Samuel French, 1972.

ELIZABETH I AND OTHER PLAYS. London: Calder and Boyars, 1972.

Also includes SATYRICON and THE MADONNA IN THE ORCHARD.

SATYRICON. In THE OFF-OFF BROADWAY BOOK. Ed. Bruce Mailman and Albert Poland. Indianapolis: Bobbs, Merrill, 1972.

## COLLECTIONS

BALLS AND OTHER PLAYS. London: Calder and Boyars, 1967.

Includes THE RECLUSE, HURRAH FOR THE BRIDGE, and THE HESSIAN CORPORAL.

## BIBLIOGRAPHY

Salem, James M., ed. A GUIDE TO CRITICAL REVIEWS. Part 1: AMERICAN DRAMA, 1909-1969. 2nd ed. Metuchen, N.J.: Scarecrow Press, 1973.

See pages 152-53.

# MICHAEL FRAYN (1933- )

THE TWO OF US: FOUR ONE-ACT PLAYS FOR TWO PLAYERS. London: Fontana, 1970.

Consists of BLACK AND SILVER, CHINAMEN, MR. FOOT, and THE NEW QUIXOTE.

## CRITICISM

Jones, Mervyn. "Michael Frayn." In CONTEMPORARY DRAMATISTS. Ed. James Vinson. London: St. James; New York: St. Martin's, 1973, pp. 261-63.

"Michael Frayn is a serious funny writer."

# BRUCE JAY FRIEDMAN (1930-  )

SCUBA DUBA: A TENSE COMEDY. New York: Simon and Schuster, 1968.

THE CAR LOVER. ES, June 1968, p. 120.

PARDON ME, SIR, BUT IS MY EYE HURTING YOUR ELBOW? New York: Bernard Geis, 1968.

Unproduced screenplay by Friedman and eleven other screenwriters.

STEAMBATH. New York: Knopf, 1971.

## BIBLIOGRAPHY

Salem, James M., ed. A GUIDE TO CRITICAL REVIEWS. Part 1: AMERICAN DRAMA, 1909-1969. 2nd ed. Metuchen, N.J.: Scarecrow Press, 1973.

See pages 155-56.

## CRITICISM

Gilman, Richard. "Anatomy of a Hit." NR, 157 (October 28, 1967), 31-33.

______. "Who Needs Critics?" NR, 158 (February 17, 1968), 25-26.

Unsympathetic reviews of SCUBA DUBA.

Schultz, Max F. BRUCE JAY FRIEDMAN. New York: Twayne, 1974.

Finds SCUBA DUBA capable of compelling a reassessment "of our deepest responses to alien races."

# TERENCE FRISBY (1932- )

THE SUBTOPIANS. London: Samuel French, 1964.

THERE'S A GIRL IN MY SOUP. P&P, 13 (September 1966), 31-46 ff.

THERE'S A GIRL IN MY SOUP. London: Samuel French, 1968.

THERE'S A GIRL IN MY SOUP. London: W.H. Allen, 1970.

This is a novel by Raymond Hitchcock based on Frisby's screenplay.

THE BANDWAGON. London: Samuel French, 1973.

## CRITICISM

Raynor, Henry. "Terence Frisby." In CONTEMPORARY DRAMATISTS. Ed. James Vinson. London: St. James; New York: St. Martin's, 1973, pp. 270-71.

Interesting for a summary of the BBC's conflict with Frisby over the airing of THE BANDWAGON, and its subsequent transfer to the stage.

Taylor, John Russell. "More Playwrights in the Provinces." In his ANGER AND AFTER: A GUIDE TO THE NEW BRITISH DRAMA. Rev. ed. Harmondsworth, Engl.: Penguin, 1963, pp. 189-90.

Praise for THE SUBTOPIANS as nondoctrinaire.

## CHRISTOPHER FRY (1907- )

THE LADY'S NOT FOR BURNING. 2nd ed. London: Oxford University Press, 1950.

RING ROUND THE MOON: A CHARADE WITH MUSIC. Trans. Christopher Fry, with a preface by Peter Brook. London: Oxford University Press, 1950.

A translation of Jean Anouilh's L'INVITATION AU CHATEAU (1947).

VENUS OBSERVED. London: Oxford University Press, 1950.

A SLEEP OF PRISONERS. London: Oxford University Press, 1951.

THE FIRSTBORN. 2nd ed. London: Oxford University Press, 1952.

For a third edition see COLLECTION, below.

THE DARK IS LIGHT ENOUGH: A WINTER COMEDY. London: Oxford University Press, 1954.

THE LARK. Trans. Christopher Fry. London: Methuen, 1955.

A translation of Jean Anouilh's L'ALOUETTE (1952).

THE TIGER AT THE GATES. Trans. Christopher Fry. London: Methuen, 1955.

A translation of Jean Giradoux's LA GUERRE DE TROIE N'AURA PAS LIEU (1935).

DUEL OF ANGELS. Trans. Christopher Fry. London: Methuen, 1958.

A translation of Jean Giradoux's POUR LUCRECE (1944).

CURTMANTLE. London: Oxford University Press, 1961.

CURTMANTLE. 2nd ed. London: Oxford University Press, 1965.

With a note explaining the revisions.

PEER GYNT. Trans. Christopher Fry. London: Oxford University Press, 1970.

Translation of the 1867 Ibsen play.

A YARD OF SUN: A SUMMER COMEDY. London: Oxford University Press, 1970.

## COLLABORATION WITH JONATHAN GRIFFIN

THE BIBLE: ORIGINAL SCREENPLAY. New York: Pocket Books, 1966.

## COLLECTIONS

THREE PLAYS. London: Oxford University Press, 1960.

THE FIRSTBORN, in its third edition; THOR, WITH ANGELS; and A SLEEP OF PRISONERS.

## BIBLIOGRAPHY

Salem, James M., ed. A GUIDE TO CRITICAL REVIEWS. Part 3: BRITISH AND CONTINENTAL DRAMA FROM IBSEN TO PINTER. Metuchen, N.J.: Scarecrow Press, 1968.

List of reviews of New York productions, pages 98-101.

Scheer, Bernice L., and Eugene G. Prater, eds. "A Bibliography on Christopher Fry." TDR, 4 (March 1960), 88-98.

## SELECTED NONDRAMATIC WRITING

"Comedy." TDR, 4 (March 1960), 77-79.

Major statement on comedy, derived in part from his last meeting with Charles Williams.

"Talking of Henry." TWENTIETH CENTURY, 169 (February 1961), 185-90.

On CURTMANTLE.

## CRITICISM

Arrowsmith, William. "Notes on English Verse Drama: Christopher Fry." HR, 3 (Summer 1950), 203-16.

T.S. Eliot's plays having prepared the way, Fry and all other verse dramatists must face up to competition with the commercial stage and not hide behind poetic trappings. Fry, whose language has been much misunderstood, uses it as his true subject: the conflict between prose and poetry. But this conflict is too easy; it lacks a moral base and is essentially undramatic.

Becker, William. "Some French Plays in Translation." HR, 9 (Summer 1956), 277-88.

Most Broadway versions of foreign plays huddle somewhere between translation and adaptation. Fry's TIGER AT THE GATES, as a textual comparison proves, is the finest Giradoux translation yet. His version of THE LARK, remarkable as it was, was only a fine translation of a poor play, while Lillian Hellman's 1955 adaptation remade Anouilh's play into an American success.

Browne, E. Martin. "Henry II as Hero: Christopher Fry's New Play CURTMANTLE." DS, 2 (June 1962), 63-71.

Fry's portrait of Henry II is remarkably faithful to the historical Henry and is a most successful dramatic biography.

Bullough, Geoffry. "Christopher Fry and the 'Revolt' Against Eliot." In EXPERIMENTAL DRAMA. Ed. Walter A. Armstrong. London: G. Bell, 1963, pp. 56-78.

Donoghue, Denis. THE THIRD VOICE: MODERN BRITISH AND AMERICAN VERSE DRAMA. Princeton, N.J.: Princeton University Press, 1959.

A dismissive survey of Fry's work that concludes with an unflattering comparison with William Inge. See pages 180-92.

Ferguson, John. "THE BOY WITH A CART." MD, 8 (December 1965), 284-92.

THE BOY WITH A CART is an unsophisticated pastoral and should not be overburdened with critical exegesis.

Greene, Anne. "Fry's Cosmic Vision." MD, 4 (February 1962), 355-64.

Each of Fry's plays revolves around paradoxes concerning the relationship between divinity and humanity.

Knepler, Henry W. "THE LARK: Translation vs. Adaptation: A Case History." MD, 1 (May 1968), 15-28.

Lillian Hellman's 1955 adaptation is superior to Fry's translation because she is conscious of the differences between French and American theatrical expectations. This detailed comparison focuses on Fry's toning down of Anouilh's language and Hellman's change of Anouilh's flashback.

Louis, Dolores Gros. "Tragedy in Christopher Fry and Shakespeare: A Comparison of CURTMANTLE and RICHARD II." COLLEGE LANGUAGE ASSOCIATION JOURNAL, 9 (December 1965), 151-58.

Mandel, O. "Theme in the Drama of Christopher Fry." ETUDES ANGLAISES, 10 (October-December 1957), 335-49.

Fry's theme is that of a Bergsonian life-force perpetuating itself through love, while opposing the death impulse. Mandel denies the theories of Arrowsmith and Spears that the major opposition in Fry's plays is between those poetically aware and those prosaically unaware of life's mystery. An analysis of each play in terms of Fry's "master theme" then follows.

Marowitz, Charles. "Christopher Fry Directs." VV, 2 October 1957, pp. 8, 10.

Brief description of Fry the director.

Roy, Emil. "Imagery in the Comedies of Christopher Fry." MD, 7 (May 1964), 79-88.

This useful essay argues that Fry's imagery is not mere verbal icing, but an integral part of the thematic development.

______. "Archetypal Patterns in Fry." COMPARATIVE DRAMA, 1 (Summer 1967), 93-104.

Traces numerous themes in Fry's plays, often using Northrop Frye's terminologies. Two of the many themes cited are fathers blocking sons and the obsessive use of fire at dramatic moments.

Spanos, William V. "Christopher Fry's A SLEEP OF PRISONERS: The Choreography of Comedy." MD, 8 (May 1965), 58-72.

More than his seasonal comedies, A SLEEP OF PRISONERS reflects Fry's sacramental view of comedy, a view in large measure derived from Charles Williams.

Spears, Monroe K. "Christopher Fry and the Redemption of Joy." P, 78 (April 1951), 23-43.

Spender, Stephen. "Christopher Fry." SPECTATOR, 24 March 1950, pp. 364-65.

Although optimistic about the future of verse drama, Spender finds Fry's verse bloodless and his plays hopelessly compromised between seriousness and frivolity.

Stanford, Derek. "Comedy and Tragedy in Christopher Fry." MD, 2 (May 1959), 3-7.

Fry's plays, comic as they are, have as a religious core the struggle between life and death, and a nonrational appreciation of an immanent deity.

Stynan, J.L. ELEMENTS OF DRAMA. Cambridge, Engl.: Cambridge University Press, 1960, pp. 39-45, 263-67.

On Fry's verse in A SLEEP OF PRISONERS; on the curious lightness of THE LADY'S NOT FOR BURNING.

Weales, Gerald. RELIGION IN MODERN ENGLISH DRAMA. Philadelphia: University of Pennsylvania Press, 1961.

Sympathetic treatment of Fry's religious plays, with some interesting points about Fry's revisions of THE FIRSTBORN. See pages 206-24.

Wiersma, Stanley M. "Spring and the Apocalypse, Law and Prophets: A Reading of Christopher Fry's THE LADY'S NOT FOR BURNING." MD, 13 (February 1971), 432-47.

The play is, paradoxically, a spring comedy, a merry play about death, judgment, the apocalypse, and love.

# FRANK GAGLIANO (1931- )

THE CITY SCENE. New York: Samuel French, 1966.

Consists of PARADISE GARDENS EAST and CONERICO WAS HERE TO STAY.

FATHER UXBRIDGE WANTS TO MARRY. New York: n.p., 1967.

Typescript at the Lincoln Center Library of the Performing Arts.

NIGHT OF THE DUNCE. New York: Dramatists Play Service, 1967.

FATHER UXBRIDGE WANTS TO MARRY. New York: Grove Press, 1968.

THE HIDE-AND-SEEK ODYSSEY OF MADELAINE GIMPLE. New York: Dramatists Play Service, 1970.

BIG SUR: A PLAY IN ONE ACT. New York: Dramatists Play Service, 1971.

## SELECTED NONDRAMATIC WRITING

"Comment." In CONTEMPORARY DRAMATISTS. Ed. James Vinson. London: St. James; New York: St. Martin's, 1973, pp. 279-80.

An explanation of his techniques and an evaluation of his own work, particularly FATHER UXBRIDGE WANTS TO MARRY. See also A. Richard Sogliuzzo's critical commentary on the succeeding three pages.

# HERB GARDNER (1934- )

A THOUSAND CLOWNS. New York: Random House, 1962.

A THOUSAND CLOWNS. New York: F. Coe, 1964.

Screenplay, with revisions, available at the Lincoln Center Library of the Performing Arts.

WHO IS HARRY KELLERMAN AND WHY IS HE SAYING THOSE TERRIBLE THINGS ABOUT ME? New York: Signet, 1967.

Screenplay.

THE GOODBYE PEOPLE. New York: Farrar, Straus and Giroux, 1974.

## BIBLIOGRAPHY

Salem, James M., ed. A GUIDE TO CRITICAL REVIEWS. Part 1: AMERICAN DRAMA, 1909-1969. 2nd ed. Metuchen, N.J.: Scarecrow Press, 1973.

List of reviews, pages 159-60.

## BARBARA GARSON (c. 1940- )

MACBIRD. Berkeley, Calif.: Grassy Knoll Press, 1966.

MACBIRD. RA, 5 (December 1966), 26-38.

Excerpts from the first half.

MACBIRD. New York: Grove Press, 1967.

The Grove Press edition includes a foreword outlining the more than usually complicated textual evolution of the play.

### CRITICISM

Abel, Lionel. "Much Ado." PR, 34 (Winter 1967), 110-14.

Atchity, Kenneth. "Barbara Garson's MACBIRD: Revolt, Revolution and Responsibility." MOTIVE, 27 (February 1967), 16-21.

Brustein, Robert. "All Hail, MacBird." In his THE THIRD THEATRE. New York: Knopf, 1969, pp. 55-59.

Praises Garson's liberating audacity.

Gilman, Richard. "MACBIRD and Its Audience." In his THE CONFUSION OF REALMS. New York: Random House, 1969, pp. 234-47.

MACBIRD is based on a shoddy, irresponsible nihilism, and is, beyond cavil, appallingly written. One may attack Lyndon Johnson and the Vietnam war without descending to Mrs. Garson's level.

Macdonald, Dwight. "Birds of America." NYRB, 1 December 1966, pp. 12-14.

Despite its faults, MACBIRD is anarchically funny and filled with "faultless bad taste."

# JACK GELBER (1932-  )

THE CONNECTION. New York: Grove Press, 1957.

The apparently improvised play, produced by the Living Theatre, with an introduction by Kenneth Tynan.

THE APPLE. New York: Grove Press, 1961.

SQUARE IN THE EYE. New York: Grove Press, 1964.

THE CUBAN THING. New York: Grove Press, 1969.

SLEEP. New York: Hill and Wang, 1972.

## BIBLIOGRAPHY

Salem, James M., ed. A GUIDE TO CRITICAL REVIEWS. Part 1: AMERICAN DRAMA, 1909-1969. 2nd ed. Metuchen, N.J.: Scarecrow Press, 1973.

List of reviews, pages 161-62.

## SELECTED NONDRAMATIC WRITING

ON ICE. New York: Macmillan, 1964.

## CRITICISM

Abel, Lionel. METATHEATRE: A NEW VIEW OF DRAMATIC FORM. New York: Hill and Wang, 1963.

THE CONNECTION is valuable because it epitomizes the aimlessness, the search for a high, typical of modern life; includes a review of THE APPLE (see pp. 122-27, 128-34).

Brook, Peter. "From Zero to the Infinite: A Letter." In THE ENCORE READER: A CHRONICLE OF THE NEW DRAMA. Ed. Charles Marowitz, Tom Milne, and Owen Hale. London: Methuen, 1965, pp. 245-51.

> "THE CONNECTION proves to me that the development of the tradition of naturalism will be towards an ever greater focus on the person or the people, and an increasing ability to dispense with such props to our interest as story and dialogue."

Brustein, Robert. "Junk and Jazz." In his SEASONS OF DISCONTENT: DRAMATIC OPINIONS 1959-1965. New York: Simon and Schuster, 1965, pp. 23-26.

> In his first review for NR, Brustein finds THE CONNECTION an honest and brilliant theatrical event, evading traditional dramatic expectations.

Dukore, Bernard F. "The New Dramatists, 5: Jack Gelber." DS, 2 (October 1962), 146-57.

> A vivid description of the Living Theatre's amplification of the text of THE CONNECTION and a detailed exegesis of THE APPLE.

Eskin, Stanley G. "Theatricality in the Avant-Garde Drama: A Reconsideration of a Theme in the Light of THE BALCONY and THE CONNECTION." MD, 7 (September 1964), 213-22.

> Self-conscious theatricality, or plays within plays, appeals to the modern playwright as a means of questioning the "reality" of modern life. Gelber, however, uses it to make his play more, not less, realistic.

Jeffrey, David K. "Genet and Gelber: Studies in Addiction." MD, 11 (September 1968), 151-56.

> Both Genet's THE BALCONY (1956) and THE CONNECTION create shifting, multileveled realities that pit the inauthentic against the spontaneous.

Kostelanetz, Richard. "THE CONNECTION: Heroin as Existential Choice." TEQ, 5 (Winter 1962), 159-62.

Tallmer, Jerry. "THE APPLE at the Living Theatre, N.Y." EN, 9 (March-April 1962), 47.

> An extraordinary rave for THE APPLE.

# WILLIAM GIBSON (1914- )

THE RUBY. New York: Ricordi, 1955.

Gibson's libretto is based on Lord Dunsany's one-act play, A NIGHT AT AN INN (1916), and was written under the pseudonym of William Mass.

THE MIRACLE WORKER: A PLAY FOR TELEVISION. New York: Knopf, 1957.

THE SEESAW LOG: A CHRONICLE OF THE STAGE PRODUCTION WITH THE TEXT OF TWO FOR THE SEESAW. New York: Alfred Knopf, 1959.

This is a witty, exhausting story of a novelist's experiences in the "collaborative gluepot of the theater." It is less a sociological document of Broadway life of the fifties than an account of the conflict between a literary sensibility and the irredeemably impure demands of the stage. The text is neither the original script nor the final playing script--typical of Gibson's dilemma.

DINNY AND THE WITCHES, AND THE MIRACLE WORKER. New York: Atheneum, 1960.

DINNY AND THE WITCHES: A FROLIC ON GRAVE MATTERS. New York: Dramatists Play Service, 1961.

A CRY OF PLAYERS. New York: Atheneum, 1969.

AMERICAN PRIMITIVE: THE WORDS OF JOHN AND ABAGAIL ADAMS PUT INTO A SEQUENCE FOR THE THEATRE. New York: Atheneum, 1972.

With an addenda in rhyme; first performed as JOHN AND ABAGAIL.

## COLLABORATION WITH CLIFFORD ODETS

GOLDEN BOY. New York: Atheneum, 1965.

The book of a musical by Clifford Odets and William Gibson with lyrics by Lee Adams and music by Charles Strouse.

## BIBLIOGRAPHY

Salem, James M., ed. A GUIDE TO CRITICAL REVIEWS. Part 1: AMERICAN DRAMA, 1909-1969. 2nd ed. Metuchen, N.J.: Scarecrow Press, 1973.

See pages 163-64.

## SELECTED NONDRAMATIC WRITING

THE COBWEB. New York: Knopf, 1954.

Novel, later made into a film (1955).

A MASS FOR THE DEAD. New York: Atheneum, 1968.

## CRITICISM

Trilling, Lionel. "All Aboard the Seesaw." TDR, 4 (May 1960), 16-20.

Reviewing THE SEESAW LOG, Trilling compares the rigors of publication with those of production. He also argues that the comparative weight of the roles of Gittel and Jerry is indicative of contemporary taste.

# PETER GILL (1939-  )

FREE TRICK WEATHER. TR, 11 (Winter 1962), 60-74.

The first two scenes.

THE SLEEPER'S DEN. P&P, 17 (January 1970), 68-78.

OVER GARDENS OUT. P&P, 17 (January 1970), 62-68.

THE SLEEPER'S DEN AND OVER GARDENS OUT. London: Calder and Boyars, 1970.

## SELECTED NONDRAMATIC WRITING

DROPS IN THE OCEAN: THE WORK OF OXFAM 1960-1970. London: Macdonald and Co., 1970.

## CRITICISM

Marcus, Frank. "Peter Gill." In CONTEMPORARY DRAMATISTS. Ed. James Vinson. London: St. James; New York: St. Martin's, 1973, pp. 289-90.

# FRANK GILROY (1925- )

A MATTER OF PRIDE. In BEST TELEVISION PLAYS 1957. Ed. Florence Britton. New York: Ballantine, 1957.

WHO'LL SAVE THE PLOWBOY? New York: Random House, 1962.

A production typescript is also available at the Lincoln Center Library of the Performing Arts.

ABOUT THOSE ROSES; OR, HOW NOT TO DO A PLAY AND SUCCEED, AND THE TEXT OF THE SUBJECT WAS ROSES. New York: Random House, 1965.

THAT SUMMER, THAT FALL; AND FAR ROCKAWAY. New York: Random House, 1967.

THE ONLY GAME IN TOWN. New York: Random House, 1968.

A MATTER OF PRIDE. New York: Samuel French, 1970.

An adaptation of the story, "The Blue Serge Suit," by John Langdon (1957).

PRESENT TENSE: FOUR PLAYS. New York: Samuel French, 1973.

## BIBLIOGRAPHY

Salem, James M., ed. A GUIDE TO CRITICAL REVIEWS. Part 1: AMERICAN DRAMA, 1909-1969. 2nd ed. Metuchen, N.J.: Scarecrow Press, 1973.

See pages 167-68.

## SELECTED NONDRAMATIC WRITING

LITTLE EGO. New York: Simon and Schuster, 1970.

Juvenile, in collaboration with Ruth G. Gilroy.

PRIVATE. New York: Harcourt Brace Jovanovich, 1970.

Novel.

## CRITICISM

Simon, John. UNEASY STAGES. New York: Random House, 1975.

Brief survey of Gilroy's plays, arguing that PLOUGHBOY is his best, because it is the most spare, see pages 416-18.

# WILLIAM GOLDING (1911- )

THE BRASS BUTTERFLY. London: Faber and Faber, 1958.

THE BRASS BUTTERFLY. In THE GENIUS OF THE LATER ENGLISH THEATER. Ed. Sylvan Barnet et al. New York: Mentor, 1962.

Based on his novella ENVOY EXTRAORDINARY.

## BIBLIOGRAPHY

Biles, Jack I., ed. "A William Golding Checklist." TCL, 17 (April 1971), 107-21.

Primary and secondary sources, unannotated.

## CRITICISM

Baker, James R. WILLIAM GOLDING: A CRITICAL STUDY. New York: St. Martin's Press, 1965.

Dick, Bernard F. WILLIAM GOLDING. New York: Twayne, 1967.

Particularly strong on Golding's classical sources.

Kinkead-Weekes, Mark, and Ian Gregor. WILLIAM GOLDING: A CRITICAL STUDY. London: Faber and Faber, 1967.

Oldsey, Bernard S., and Stanley Weintraub. "Ambassadors at Large: Other Writings." In their THE ART OF WILLIAM GOLDING. New York: Harcourt, Brace and World, 1965, pp. 149-58.

Discussion of THE BRASS BUTTERFLY and ENVOY EXTRAORDINARY; there is a 1968 edition of this book published by Indiana University Press which I have not seen.

# JAMES GOLDMAN (1927-  )

THE LION IN WINTER. New York: Random House, 1966; London: Samuel French, 1970.

THE LION IN WINTER. New York: Dell, 1968.

Screenplay.

THEY MIGHT BE GIANTS. New York: Lancer, 1970.

Screenplay based on an unpublished 1961 play.

FOLLIES: A MUSICAL. New York: Random House, 1971.

Music and lyrics by Stephen Sondheim.

## COLLABORATION WITH WILLIAM GOLDMAN

BLOOD, SWEAT AND STANLEY POOLE. New York: Dramatists Play Service, 1962.

## BIBLIOGRAPHY

Salem, James M., ed. A GUIDE TO CRITICAL REVIEWS. Part 1: AMERICAN DRAMA, 1909-1969. 2nd ed. Metuchen, N.J.: Scarecrow Press, 1973.

A listing of reviews, pages 173-74.

## SELECTED NONDRAMATIC WRITING

WALDORF. New York: Random House, 1965.

Novel.

# PAUL GOODMAN (1911-1972)

THEORY OF TRAGEDY. QRL, 5, no. 4 (1950), 318-38.

ABRAHAM AND ISAAC. CR (Mass.), November 1955.

THE CAVE AT MACHPELAH. COMMENTARY, 25 (June 1958), 512-17.

FAUSTINA: RITUAL TRAGEDY. QRL, 11, nos. 2-3 (1961), 69-116.

THREE PLAYS: THE YOUNG DISCIPLE, FAUSTINA, JONAH. New York: Random House, 1965.

Goodman's preface articulates many of his ideas about theater.

THE BIRTHDAY. In THEATRE EXPERIMENT. Ed. Michael Benedikt. New York: Doubleday, 1967.

TRAGEDY AND COMEDY: FOUR CUBIST PLAYS. Los Angeles: Black Sparrow, 1970.

Consists of STRUCTURE OF TRAGEDY, AFTER AESCHYLUS; STRUCTURE OF TRAGEDY, AFTER SOPHOCLES; STRUCTURE OF PATHOS, AFTER EURIPEDES; LITTLE HERO, AFTER MOLIERE.

## SELECTED NONDRAMATIC WRITING

CENSORSHIP AND PORNOGRAPHY ON THE STAGE. ARE WRITERS SHIRKING THEIR POLITICAL DUTY?--ASKED BY ANVIL MAGAZINE. New York: Living Theatre, 1959.

Pamphlet.

GROWING UP ABSURD: PROBLEMS OF YOUTH IN AN ORGANIZED SOCIETY. New York: Random House, 1960.

One of the most influential books of the 1960s.

## CRITICISM

Howard, Richard. "Paul Goodman." In his ALONE WITH AMERICA: ESSAYS ON THE ART OF POETRY IN THE UNITED STATES SINCE 1950. New York: Atheneum, 1971, pp. 153-63.

# RONALD GOW (1897- )

ANN VERONICA. In PLAYS OF THE YEAR 1949. Ed. J.C. Trewin. London: Paul Elek, 1950.

ANN VERONICA. London: Samuel French, 1951.

Adaptation of the H.G. Wells's novel (1904).

THE SHERIFF'S KITCHEN. In SEVEN ONE-ACT PLAYS. Ed. A.J. Merson. Harlow, Essex: Longmans, 1953.

THE EDWARDIANS. London: Samuel French, 1960.

From the novel by V. Sackville West (1930).

A BOSTON STORY. London: English Theatre Guild, 1969.

A comedy in three acts based on the novel WATCH AND WARD (1878) by Henry James.

## CRITICISM

Darlington, W.A. "Ronald Gow." In CONTEMPORARY DRAMATISTS. Ed. James Vinson. London: St. James; New York: St. Martin's, 1973, pp. 302-04.

## SIMON GRAY (1936- )

WISE CHILD. P&P, 15 (December 1967), 23-38 ff.

SLEEPING DOG: A PLAY FOR TELEVISION. London: Faber and Faber, 1968.

WISE CHILD. London: Faber and Faber, 1968.

DUTCH UNCLE. London: Faber and Faber, 1969.

BUTLEY. London: Methuen, 1971.

THE IDIOT. London: Methuen, 1971.
Adaptation of the Dostoyevsky novel (1869).

OTHERWISE ENGAGED AND OTHER PLAYS. London: Eyre Methuen, 1975.
Also includes TWO SUNDAYS and PLAINTIFFS AND DEFENDANTS.

### SELECTED NONDRAMATIC WRITING

COLMAIN. London: Faber and Faber, 1963.

SIMPLE PEOPLE. London: Faber and Faber, 1965.

LITTLE PORTIA. London: Faber and Faber, 1968.

A COMEBACK FOR STARK. London: Faber and Faber, 1969.
Under pseudonym of Hamish Reade.

## CRITICISM

Baker, Roger. "Simon Gray." In CONTEMPORARY DRAMATISTS. Ed. James Vinson. London: St. James; New York: St. Martin's, 1973, pp. 307-09.

On role-playing in Gray's works.

Taylor, John Russell. "Three Farceurs: Alan Ayckbourn, David Cregan, Simon Gray." In his THE SECOND WAVE. London: Methuen, 1971, pp. 169-71.

Plot summaries and remarks on Orton's influence on Gray.

# PAUL GREEN (1894- )

PEER GYNT. New York: Samuel French, 1951.

Ibsen adaptation.

THE NO 'COUNT BOY. New York: Samuel French, 1953.

Revision of his 1924 play.

WILDERNESS ROAD: A SYMPHONIC OUTDOOR DRAMA. New York: Samuel French, 1956.

THE FOUNDERS: A SYMPHONIC OUTDOOR DRAMA. New York: Samuel French, 1957.

THE CONFEDERACY: A SYMPHONIC OUTDOOR DRAMA BASED ON THE LIFE OF GEN. ROBERT E. LEE. New York: Samuel French, 1959.

WINGS FOR TO FLY: THREE PLAYS OF NEGRO LIFE, MOSTLY FOR THE EAR BUT ALSO FOR THE EYE. New York: Samuel French, 1959.

Includes THE THIRSTING HEART, FIVE WAGONS, and LAY THIS BODY DOWN; the latter is a revision of his HOT IRON (1926).

THE STEPHEN FOSTER STORY: A SYMPHONIC DRAMA BASED ON THE LIFE AND MUSIC OF THE COMPOSER. New York: Samuel French, 1960.

THE FOUNDERS: THE JAMESTOWN STORY, A SYMPHONIC DRAMA OF AMERICAN HISTORY. N.p., 1963.

Revised version, from November 1963, available at the Lincoln Center Library of the Performing Arts.

THE SHELTERING PLAID: A DRAMA ABOUT FLORA MACDONALD AND THE REVOLUTIONARY WAR IN NORTH CAROLINA. New York: Samuel French, 1965.

CROSS AND SWORD: A SYMPHONIC DRAMA OF THE SPANISH SETTLEMENT OF FLORIDA. New York: Samuel French, 1966.

TEXAS: A SYMPHONIC OUTDOOR DRAMA OF AMERICAN LIFE. New York: Samuel French, 1967.

SING ALL A GREEN WILLOW: A FOLK MORALITY FANTASY, WITH HYMN-TUNES, DUMB SHOW, MASKS, INTERLUDES, FOLK-MUSIC AND DANCE. No imprint.

Post-1960 typescript available at the Lincoln Center Library of the Performing Arts and the University of North Carolina at Chapel Hill Library.

THE HONEYCOMB. New York: Samuel French, 1972.

A revision of his SHROUD MY BODY DOWN (1935).

JOHNNY JOHNSON: THE BIOGRAPHY OF A COMMON MAN. Rev. ed. New York: Samuel French, 1972.

TRUMPET IN THE LAND: A SYMPHONIC DRAMA OF PEACE AND BROTHERHOOD. New York: Samuel French, 1972.

THE COMMON GLORY: A SYMPHONIC DRAMA OF AMERICAN HISTORY. New York: Samuel French, 1975.

A bicentennial edition, revised and rewritten, with music, commentary, folksong, and dance.

## COLLECTIONS

FIVE PLAYS OF THE SOUTH. New York: Hill and Wang, 1963.

Includes IN ABRAHAM'S BOSOM, JOHNNY JOHNSON, HYMN TO THE RISING SUN, WHITE DRESSES, and a revised version of THE HOUSE OF CONNELLY.

## BIBLIOGRAPHY

Salem, James M., ed. A GUIDE TO CRITICAL REVIEWS. Part 1: AMERICAN DRAMA, 1909-1969. 2nd ed. Metuchen, N.J.: Scarecrow Press, 1973.

A listing of reviews, pages 179-84.

## SELECTED NONDRAMATIC WRITING

DRAMATIC HERITAGE. New York: Samuel French, 1953.

Essays and lectures.

"Interpreting America: Conversation on a Train." CAROLINA QUARTERLY, 9 (Summer 1957), 5-13.

"Symphonic Drama: A Narrative of Reminiscence." In TEN TALENTS IN THE AMERICAN THEATRE. Ed. D.H. Stevens. Norman: University of Oklahoma Press, 1957, pp. 224-71.

DRAMA AND THE WEATHER: SOME NOTES AND PAPERS ON LIFE AND THE THEATRE. New York: Samuel French, 1958.

PLOUGH AND FURROW: SOME ESSAYS AND PAPERS ON LIFE AND THE THEATRE. New York: Samuel French, 1963.

HOME TO MY VALLEY. Chapel Hill: University of North Carolina Press, 1970.

Autobiography.

## CRITICISM

Clifford, John. "Paul Green: True American Artist." PL, 48 (Summer 1973), 210-15.

Brief analysis of the structure, settings, characters, and language of Green's symphonic dramas.

Colbath, Arnold. "Outdoor Historical Drama." DRAMA, n.s. 41 (Summer 1956), 22-26.

The script for THE WILDERNESS ROAD is stiff and without imagination, while the production is full of life.

Kenny, Vincent S. PAUL GREEN. New York: Twayne, 1971.

Part 2 treats Green's symphonic drama.

# GRAHAM GREENE (1904-    )

THE LIVING ROOM. London: Heinemann, 1953.

THE POTTING SHED. New York: Viking, 1957.

THE COMPLAISANT LOVER. London: Heinemann, 1959.

CARVING A STATUE. London: Bodley Head, 1964.

THE THIRD MAN. London: Lorrimer, 1968.

Complete screenplay for the 1950 film.

THE RETURN OF A.J. RAFFLES: AN EDWARDIAN COMEDY IN THREE ACTS. London: Bodley Head, 1975.

"Based somewhat loosely on E.W. Hornung's characters in THE AMATEUR CRACKSMAN."

## COLLECTIONS

THREE PLAYS. London: Heinemann, 1961.

THE LIVING ROOM, THE POTTING SHED, and THE COMPLAISANT LOVER.

## BIBLIOGRAPHY

Salem, James M., ed. A GUIDE TO CRITICAL REVIEWS. Part 3: BRITISH AND CONTINENTAL DRAMA FROM IBSEN TO PINTER. Metuchen, N.J.: Scarecrow Press, 1968.

List of reviews of the New York productions, pages 113-15.

Vann, Jerry Don, ed. GRAHAM GREENE: A CHECKLIST OF CRITICISM. Kent, Ohio: Kent State University Press, 1970.

## SELECTED NONDRAMATIC WRITING

THE LOST CHILDHOOD AND OTHER ESSAYS. London: Eyre and Spottiswoode, 1951.

COLLECTED ESSAYS. London: Bodley Head; New York: Viking, 1969.

A SORT OF LIFE. London: Bodley Head; New York: Simon and Schuster, 1971.

Autobiography.

## CRITICISM

Adler, Jacob H. "Graham Greene's Plays: Technique Versus Value." In GRAHAM GREENE: SOME CRITICAL CONSIDERATIONS. Ed. Robert O. Evans. Livingston: University of Kentucky Press, 1963, pp. 219-30.

Alkins, John. GRAHAM GREENE: A BIOGRAPHICAL AND LITERARY STUDY. Rev. ed. London: J. Calder, 1966.

Boyd, John D., S.J. "Earth Imagery in Graham Greene's THE POTTING SHED." MD, 16 (June 1973), 69-80.

The play's pervasive earth imagery adds validity to the play's basic themes.

Codey, Regina. "Notes on Graham Greene's Dramatic Technique." APPROACH, 17 (Fall 1955), 23-27.

On the flaws of THE LIVING ROOM.

Costello, Donald P. "Graham Greene and the Catholic Press." RENASCENCE, 12 (Autumn 1959), 3-28.

On the reception of the novels, not the plays, but of much interest.

Cotterell, Beekman W. "The Second Time Charm: The Theatre of Graham Greene." MODERN FICTION STUDIES, 3 (Autumn 1957), 249-55.

Praise for Greene's success with his second play.

Findlater, Richard. "Graham Greene as Dramatist." TWENTIETH CENTURY, 156 (June 1953), 471-73.

Gassner, John. "Broadway in Review." ETJ, 9 (May 1957), 114-15.

Argues that the mystery plot structure of THE POTTING SHED, as successful as it is, ultimately detracts from the seriousness of the play.

Hortmann, Wilhelm. "Graham Greene: The Burnt-Out Catholic." TCL, 10 (July 1964), 64-76.

THE POTTING SHED marks the end of Greene as rebel Catholic.

Kerr, Walter. THE THEATER IN SPITE OF ITSELF. New York: Simon and Schuster, 1963, pp. 157-60.

Praise for the silence and reticences of THE COMPLAISANT LOVER.

McCarthy, Mary. "Sheep in Wolves Clothing." In her MARY McCARTHY'S THEATRE CHRONICLES 1937-1962. New York: Noonday, 1963, pp. 179-85.

Attacks THE POTTING SHED as tediously chic and as more demonic than Christian; she concludes by comparing it to pornography.

Murphy, John P., S.J. "THE POTTING SHED." RENASCENCE, 12 (Autumn 1959), 43-49.

The miracle is psychologically and theologically false; Greene again has excessive compassion for the sinner, and no interest in the sin.

Pryce-Jones, David. GRAHAM GREENE. Edinburgh: Oliver and Boyd, 1963.

•Robertson, Roderick. "Toward a Definition of Religious Drama." ETJ, 9 (May 1957), 99-105.

Spends seven pages proving that THE LIVING ROOM is indeed a religious drama.

Stratford, Philip. "Graham Greene: Master of Melodrama." TAMARACK REVIEW, 19 (Spring 1961), 67-86.

______. "The Uncomplacent Dramatist: Some Aspects of Graham Greene's Theatre." WS, 2 (1961), 5-19.

Greene's gradual abandonment of tragic and religious themes and his movement toward comedy is paralleled by the changes in his fiction after the World War II. THE COMPLAISANT LOVER repeats in comic form Greene's obsessive interest in individualism, here expressed in practical jokes and a childish, anarchic faith in love.

______. "Unlocking the Potting Shed." KR, 23 (Winter 1962), 129-43.

On Greene's fascination with names, puns, and practical jokes.

Weales, Gerald. RELIGION IN MODERN ENGLISH DRAMA. Philadelphia: University of Pennsylvania Press, 1961, pp. 243-47.

Brief treatment of Greene as a religious playwright; he asserts that the miracle in THE POTTING SHED is just a device.

# WALTER GREENWOOD (1903- )

TOO CLEVER FOR LOVE. London: Samuel French, 1952.

SATURDAY NIGHT AT THE CROWN. London: Samuel French, 1958.

## SELECTED NONDRAMATIC WRITING

THERE WAS A TIME. London: Jonathan Cape, 1967.
Autobiography.

# JOHN GRILLO (1942- )

HELLO, GOODBYE, SEBASTIAN. G, 4, no. 16 (1970), 11-68.

NUMBER THREE. In NEW SHORT PLAYS. London: Eyre Methuen, 1972.

## CRITICISM

Elsom, John. "John Grillo." In CONTEMPORARY DRAMATISTS. Ed. James Vinson. London: St. James; New York: St. Martin's, 1973, pp. 326-27.

Greer, Germaine. "One Kind of Undergraduate Theatre." CR, 29 May 1965, pp. 457-59.

> Greer praises Grillo's avoidance of didacticism, which she considers the worst fault of the contemporary stage, especially the undergraduate stage. She also praises the genuinely theatrical quality of his dialogue in HELLO, GOODBYE, SEBASTIAN, while providing a lengthy descriptive analysis of the play.

# JOHN GUARE (1938- )

SOMETHING I'LL TELL YOU TUESDAY, THE LOVELIEST AFTERNOON OF THE YEAR: TWO PLAYS. New York: Dramatists Play Service, 1968.

COP-OUT, HOME FIRES: TWO PLAYS. New York: Samuel French, 1968.

MUZEEKA. New York: Dramatists Play Service, 1968.

A DAY FOR SURPRISES, AND KISSING SWEET. New York: Dramatists Play Service, 1970.

THE HOUSE OF BLUE LEAVES. New York: Viking, 1972.

## COLLABORATIONS

TAKING OFF. New York: New American Library, 1971.

Screenplay with Milos Forman.

TWO GENTLEMEN OF VERONA. New York: Holt, Rinehart and Winston, 1973.

Adaptation of Shakespeare's play, with Mel Shapiro.

## COLLECTIONS

COP-OUT, MUZEEKA, HOME FIRES: THREE PLAYS. New York: Grove Press, 1969.

## CRITICISM

Markus, Thomas B. "John Guare." In CONTEMPORARY DRAMATISTS. Ed. James Vinson. London: St. James; New York: St. Martin's, 1973, pp. 328-29.

Guare is "the most successful and promising American playwright to forge to the front of the public's attention since Edward Albee."

# OLIVER HAILEY (1932- )

HEY YOU, LIGHT MAN! PL, 38 (October 1961), 15-30.

HEY YOU, LIGHT MAN! In THE YALE SCHOOL OF DRAMA PRESENTS. Ed. John Gassner. New York: E.P. Dutton, 1964.

FIRST ONE ASLEEP, WHISTLE. Frankfurt, Germany: S. Fischer Verlag, 1967.

The Lincoln Center Library of the Performing Arts also has a typescript from the New York production.

ANIMAL. In COLLISION COURSE. Ed. Edward Parone. New York: Random House, 1968.

WHO'S HAPPY NOW? New York: Random House, 1969.

PICTURE, ANIMAL, CRISSCROSS: THREE SHORT PLAYS. New York: Dramatists Play Service, 1970.

FATHER'S DAY. New York: Dramatists Play Service, 1971.

CONTINENTAL DIVIDE. New York: Dramatists Play Service, 1973.

# JOHN HALE (1926- )

BLACK SWAN WINTER. P&P, 16 (July 1969), 35-47 ff.

BLACK SWAN WINTER. In PLAYS OF THE YEAR 37. Ed. J.C. Trewin. London: Elek Books, 1970.

SPITHEAD. In PLAYS OF THE YEAR 38. Ed. J.C. Trewin. London: Elek Books, 1970.

THE LION'S CUB. In ELIZABETH R. London: Elek Books, 1971.

MARY, QUEEN OF SCOTS. New York: New American Library, 1972.

Screenplay.

## SELECTED NONDRAMATIC WRITING

POST-WAR DRAMA: EXTRACTS FROM ELEVEN PLAYS. Ed. John Hale. London: Faber and Faber, 1966.

Includes an introductory note by Hale.

## CRITICISM

Appelbee, Tim. "Playwright and Producer." NTM, 10 (Summer 1970), 25-30.

In this interview, Hale talks of his experiences as a director, particularly of his own work.

# WILLIS HALL (1929- )

FINAL AT FURNELL. London: Evans Bros., 1956.

Radio play.

THE LONG AND THE SHORT AND THE TALL. London: Heinemann, 1959.

POET AND PHEASANT. London: H.F.W. Deane and Sons, 1959.

Radio play adapted to the stage.

THE PLAY OF THE ROYAL ASTROLOGERS. London: Heinemann, 1960.

AIR MAIL FROM CYPRUS. In THE TELEVISION PLAYWRIGHT: TEN PLAYS FOR B.B.C. TELEVISION. Selected by Michael Barry, introd. and notes by Donald Wilson. London: Stephen Joseph, 1960.

A GLIMPSE OF THE SEA: THREE SHORT PLAYS. London: Evans Bros., 1960.

Consists of A GLIMPSE OF THE SEA, LAST DAY IN DREAMLAND, and RETURN TO THE SEA.

THE DAYS BEGINNING: AN EASTER PLAY. London: Heinemann, 1963.

THE GENTLE KNIGHT. Illus. Bob Monkhouse. Glasgow: Blackie, 1966.

A 1957 radio play adapted to the stage.

KIDNAPPED AT CHRISTMAS: A PLAY FOR CHRISTMAS. London: Samuel French, 1975.

## COLLABORATIONS WITH KEITH WATERHOUSE

BILLY LIAR. London: Michael Joseph, 1960.

Adapted from the novel of the same title by Keith Waterhouse (1959).

CELEBRATION. London: Michael Joseph, 1961.

A double bill of THE WEDDING and THE FUNERAL.

ALL THINGS BRIGHT AND BEAUTIFUL. London: Michael Joseph, 1963.

THE SPONGE ROOM, AND SQUAT BETTY. London: Evans Bros., 1963.

Two short plays.

ENGLAND, OUR ENGLAND: A REVUE. London: Evans Bros., 1964.

Book and lyrics by Keith Waterhouse and Willis Hall; music by Dudley Moore.

COME LAUGHING HOME. London: Evans Bros., 1965.

HELP STAMP OUT MARRIAGE. New York: Samuel French, 1966.

Retitling of SAY WHO YOU ARE.

SAY WHO YOU ARE. London: Evans Bros., 1966.

SATURDAY, SUNDAY, MONDAY. London: Heinemann, 1974.

Adaptation of the play by Eduardo de Filippo.

WHO'S WHO? London: Samuel French, 1974.

## SELECTED NONDRAMATIC WRITING

WRITERS' THEATRE. Ed. Keith Waterhouse and Willis Hall. London: Heinemann, 1967.

# DAVID HALLIWELL (1936- )

LITTLE MALCOLM AND HIS STRUGGLE AGAINST THE EUNUCHS. London: Samuel French, 1966.

HAIL SCRAWDYKE! New York: Grove Press, 1967.

American retitling of LITTLE MALCOLM.

LITTLE MALCOLM AND HIS STRUGGLE AGAINST THE EUNUCHS. London: Faber and Faber, 1967.

K.D. DUFFORD HEARS K.D. DUFFORD ASK K.D. DUFFORD HOW K.D. DUFFORD'LL MAKE K.D. DUFFORD. London: Faber and Faber, 1970.

A WHO'S WHO OF FLAPLAND AND OTHER PLAYS. London: Faber and Faber, 1971.

Includes A DISCUSSION and MUCK FROM THREE ANGLES.

## CRITICISM

Spurling, Hilary. "What's Up?" SPECTATOR, 16 September 1966, pp. 351-52.

Praises Halliwell's "verbal tours de force."

Taylor, John Russell. "The Dark Fantastic." In his THE SECOND WAVE. London: Methuen, 1971, pp. 213-17.

Plot summaries, with praise for Halliwell's depiction of the eccentric.

## CHRISTOPHER HAMPTON (1946- )

WHEN DID YOU LAST SEE MY MOTHER? London: Faber and Faber, 1967.

MARYA. A Version by Christopher Hampton. In PLAYS OF THE YEAR 35. Ed. J.C. Trewin. London: Elek Books, 1969.

Adaptation of an Isaac Babel play, as translated by Michael Glenny and Harold Shukman.

TOTAL ECLIPSE. London: Faber and Faber, 1969.

Hampton's treatment, while playwright-in-residence at the Royal Court Theatre, of the Rimbaud-Verlaine relationship.

THE PHILANTHROPIST: A BOURGEOIS COMEDY. London: Faber and Faber, 1970.

UNCLE VANYA. London: Elek Books, 1971.

Adaptation of Chekhov, as translated by Nina Froud.

A DOLL'S HOUSE. New York: Samuel French, 1972.

Ibsen adaptation.

HEDDA GABLER. New York: Samuel French, 1972.

Ibsen adaptation.

DON JUAN. London: Faber and Faber, 1973.

SAVAGES. London: Faber and Faber, 1973.

## SELECTED NONDRAMATIC WRITING

"Christopher Hampton Interviewed by Brian Hennessy." In BEHIND THE SCENES: THEATER AND FILM INTERVIEWS FROM THE TRANSATLANTIC REVIEW. Ed. Joseph F.M. McCrindle, introd. Jean-Claude van Itallie. New York: Holt, Rinehart and Winston, 1971, pp. 44-50.

On TOTAL ECLIPSE.

"On His Early Plays." TQ, 3 (October-December 1973), 62-67.

In this interview with the editors of TQ, Hampton tells of his precocious dramatic debut, the origins of his plays, and discusses at length SAVAGES, his 1973 play for the Royal Court Theatre.

## CRITICISM

Simon, John. In his UNEASY STAGES. New York: Random House, 1975.

THE PHILANTHROPIST is a largely successful critique of goodness. See pages 342-45.

Taylor, John Russell. "The Legacy of Realism." In his THE SECOND WAVE. London: Methuen, 1971, pp. 196-99.

Brief summaries of Hampton's plays.

# JAMES HANLEY (1901- )

SAY NOTHING. In PLAYS OF THE YEAR 27. Ed. J.C. Trewin. London: Elek Books, 1964.

Originally a radio play, it was adapted to the stage, televised, and then adapted into a novel.

THE INNER JOURNEY. Plaistow, Engl.: Black Raven Press; New York: Horizon Press, 1965.

PLAYS ONE. London: Kaye and Ward, 1968.

Consists of THE INNER JOURNEY and A STONE FLOWER.

## SELECTED NONDRAMATIC WRITING

WINTER SONG. London: Phoenix House, 1950.

Novel.

COLLECTED STORIES. London: Macdonald, 1953.

DON QUIXOTE DROWNED. London: Macdonald, 1953.

Essays.

AN END AND A BEGINNING. London: Macdonald, 1958.

With WINTER SONG, above, the fourth and fifth novels of Hanley's series, THE FURYS.

SAY NOTHING. London: Macdonald, 1962.

The novel.

"No Answers." P&P, 10 (January 1963), p. 24.

Introduces SAY NOTHING, the play.

## CRITICISM

Roose-Evans, James. "James Hanley." In CONTEMPORARY DRAMATISTS. Ed. James Vinson. London: St. James; New York: St. Martin's, 1973, pp. 347-49.

Stokes, Edward. THE NOVELS OF JAMES HANLEY. Melbourne: F.W. Cheshire, 1964.

Contains scattered allusions to the plays.

## WILLIAM HANLEY (1931- )

MRS. DALLY HAS A LOVER AND OTHER PLAYS. New York: Dial Press, 1962.

Includes WHISPER INTO MY GOOD EAR and TODAY IS INDEPENDENCE DAY.

SLOW DANCE ON THE KILLING GROUND. New York: Random House, 1964.

FLESH AND BLOOD. New York: Random House, 1968.

Teleplay.

NO ANSWER. In COLLISION COURSE. Ed. Edward Parone. New York: Random House, 1968.

### BIBLIOGRAPHY

Salem, James M., ed. A GUIDE TO CRITICAL REVIEWS. Part 1: AMERICAN DRAMA, 1909-1969. 2nd ed. Metuchen, N.J.: Scarecrow Press, 1973.

List of reviews, pages 186-87.

# DAVID HARE (1947- )

SLAG. P&P, 17 (June 1970), 61-77.

HOW BROPHY MADE GOOD. G, no. 5 (1970), 83-125.

SLAG. London: Faber and Faber, 1971.

THE GREAT EXHIBITION. London: Faber and Faber, 1972.

KNUCKLE. London: Faber and Faber, 1974.

## COLLABORATIONS

LAY BY. P&P, 19 (November 1971), 65-75.

Collaboration with Howard Brenton, Brian Clark, Trevor Griffiths, Steven Poliakoff, Hugh Stoddart, and Snoo Wilson.

LAY BY. London: Calder and Boyars, 1972.

BRASSNECK. London: Eyre Methuen, 1974.

Collaboration with Howard Brenton.

## BIBLIOGRAPHY

Page, Malcolm, and Ria Julian, comps. "Theatre Checklist No. 8: David Hare." TF, 2 (1975), 2-4.

## CRITICISM

Ansorge, Peter. "Humanity and Compassion Don't Count." P&P, 19 (February 1972), 18-20.

An interview with Hare on comedy and the Portable Theatre.

Hammond, Jonathan. "David Hare." In CONTEMPORARY DRAMATISTS. Ed. James Vinson. London: St. James; New York: St. Martin's, 1973, pp. 351-53.

# MOSS HART (1904-1961)

THE CLIMATE OF EDEN. New York: Random House, 1953.

Based on Edward Mittleholzer's novel SHADOWS MOVE OVER THEM (1951).

## BIBLIOGRAPHY

Salem, James M., ed. A GUIDE TO CRITICAL REVIEWS. Part 1: AMERICAN DRAMA, 1909-1969. 2nd ed. Metuchen, N.J.: Scarecrow Press, 1973.

A list of reviews of THE CLIMATE OF EDEN. See pages 189-90.

## SELECTED NONDRAMATIC WRITING

ACT ONE: AN AUTOBIOGRAPHY. New York: Random House, 1959.

## CRITICISM

Sievers, Wieder David. FREUD ON BROADWAY. New York: Hermitage House, 1955.

See pages 296-98.

# MICHAEL HASTINGS (1938- )

DON'T DESTROY ME. London: Nimbus, 1956.

YES, AND AFTER. In NEW ENGLISH DRAMATISTS 4. Ed. Tom Maschler. Harmondsworth, Engl.: Penguin, 1962.

THE SILENCE OF LEE HARVEY OSWALD. Harmondsworth, Engl.: Penguin, 1966.

THREE PLAYS. London: W.H. Allen, 1966.

First publication of THE WORLD'S BABY, as well as reprints of DON'T DESTROY ME and YES, AND AFTER.

## SELECTED NONDRAMATIC WRITING

THE GAME. London: W.H. Allen, 1957.

Novel.

THE FRAUDS. London: W.H. Allen, 1960.

Novel.

LOVE ME LAMBETH AND OTHER POEMS. London: W.H. Allen, 1961.

THE HANDSOMEST YOUNG MAN IN ENGLAND: RUPERT BROOKE: A BIOGRAPHICAL ESSAY. London: Stephen Joseph, 1967.

TUSSY IS ME: A ROMANCE. London: Weidenfeld and Nicolson, 1970.

## JOHN HAWKES (1925- )

THE INNOCENT PARTY: FOUR SHORT PLAYS. New York: New Directions, 1966.

Consists of THE WAX MUSEUM, THE QUESTIONS, THE UNDERTAKER, and THE INNOCENT PARTY, with a preface by Herbert Blau.

### SELECTED NONDRAMATIC WRITING

THE GOOSE ON THE GRAVE AND THE OWL: TWO SHORT NOVELS. New York: New Directions, 1954.

THE LIME TWIG. Introd. Leslie A. Fiedler. New York: New Directions, 1961.

Novel.

SECOND SKIN. New York: New Directions, 1964.

Novel.

THE BEETLE LEG. New York: New Directions, 1951; London: Chatto and Windus, 1967.

Novel.

LUNAR LANDSCAPES: STORIES AND SHORT NOVELS 1949-1963. New York: New Directions, 1969.

### CRITICISM

Busch, Frederick. HAWKES: A GUIDE TO HIS FICTION. Syracuse, N.Y.: Syracuse University Press, 1973.

Chapter 3 treats THE INNOCENT PARTY with summaries and exegeses.

Dennis, Nigel. "Color It Orange." NYRB, 13 July 1967, pp. 6, 8.

Attacks THE INNOCENT PARTY, and Blau's introduction, as full of meaningless, pretentious symbolism.

Kuehl, John Richard. JOHN HAWKES AND THE CRAFT OF CONFLICT. New Brunswick, N.J.: Rutgers University Press, 1975.

# JOSEPH HELLER (1923-  )

WE BOMBED IN NEW HAVEN. New York: Knopf, 1968.

WE BOMBED IN NEW HAVEN. Rev. ed. New York: Dell, 1970.

## BIBLIOGRAPHY

Salem, James M., ed. A GUIDE TO CRITICAL REVIEWS. Part 1: AMERICAN DRAMA, 1909-1969. 2nd ed. Metuchen, N.J.: Scarecrow Press, 1973.

List of reviews of WE BOMBED IN NEW HAVEN. See page 200.

## SELECTED NONDRAMATIC WRITING

CATCH-22. New York: Simon and Schuster, 1961.

An immensely popular novel.

## CRITICISM

Hughes, Catharine. PLAYS, POLITICS AND POLEMICS. New York: Drama Book Specialists, 1973.

See pages 99-106.

Pinsker, Sanford. "Heller's CATCH-22: The Protest of a PUER ETERNIS." CRITIQUE: STUDIES IN MODERN FICTION, 7 (Winter 1964-65), 150-62.

Discusses Heller and the theatre of the absurd, before he wrote his play.

## LILLIAN HELLMAN (1907- )

MONSERRAT. New York: Dramatists Play Service, 1950.

An adaptation from the French play by Emmanuel Robles.

THE AUTUMN GARDEN. Boston: Little, Brown, 1951.

Her Chekhovian play.

THE LARK. New York: Random House, 1956.

Hellman's version of Jean Anouilh's Joan of Arc play, L'ALOUETTE.

CANDIDE: A COMIC OPERETTA BASED ON VOLTAIRE'S SATIRE. New York: Random House, 1957.

Music by Leonard Bernstein, book by Lillian Hellman, lyrics by Richard Wilbur, other lyrics by John LaTouche and Dorothy Parker.

TOYS IN THE ATTIC. New York: Random House, 1960.

MY MOTHER, MY FATHER AND ME. New York: Random House, 1963.

Based on Burt Blechman's novel HOW MUCH?

### COLLECTIONS

SIX PLAYS. New York: Modern Library, 1960.

Only THE AUTUMN GARDEN of the post-1950 plays is included in this expanded edition of the 1942 collection, FOUR PLAYS.

THE COLLECTED PLAYS. Boston: Little, Brown, 1972.

Twelve plays, including each of the six post-1950 plays.

## BIBLIOGRAPHY

Salem, James M., ed. A GUIDE TO CRITICAL REVIEWS. Part 1: AMERICAN DRAMA, 1909-1969. 2nd ed. Metuchen, N.J.: Scarecrow Press, 1973.

A list of reviews, pages 200-206.

## SELECTED NONDRAMATIC WRITING

THE BIG KNOCKOVER: SELECTED STORIES AND SHORT NOVELS. Ed. and introd. Lillian Hellman. New York: Random House, 1966.

Ten short stories and novellas by Dashiell Hammett with a moving introduction.

"Lillian Hellman." In WRITERS AT WORK: THE PARIS REVIEW INTERVIEWS. 3rd series. Introd. Alfred Kazin. New York: Viking, 1967, pp. 115-40.

AN UNFINISHED WOMAN: MEMOIR. Boston: Little, Brown, 1969.

## CRITICISM

Adler, Jacob H. "Professor Moody's Miss Hellman." SOUTHERN LITERARY JOURNAL, 5 (Spring 1973), 131-40.

Essay-review of Richard Moody's critical study of Hellman's plays.

Becker, William. "Some French Plays in Translation." HR, 9 (Summer 1956), 277-88.

Most Broadway versions of foreign plays hover somewhere between translations and adaptations. Christopher Fry's version of THE LARK, remarkable as it was, was only a fine translation of a poor play, while Hellman's adaptation remade Anouilh's play into an American success. (See also section on Christopher Fry.)

Bentley, Eric, ed. THIRTY YEARS OF TREASON: EXCERPTS FROM HEARINGS BEFORE THE HOUSE COMMITTEE ON UN-AMERICAN ACTIVITIES, 1938-1968. New York: Viking, 1971, pp. 532-43.

Excerpts from Hellman's 1952 testimony before HUAC, with passages from her autobiography.

Felheim, Marvin. "THE AUTUMN GARDEN: Mechanics and Dialectics." MD, 3 (September 1960), 191-95.

Expounds on the Chekhovian qualities of Hellman's play.

Knepler, Henry W. "THE LARK: Translation vs. Adaptation: A Case History." MD, 1 (May 1968), 15-28.

Hellman's adaptation is superior to Fry's translation because of her consciousness of the difference between French and American theatrical expectations. The essay focuses on Fry's toning down of Anouilh's language and Hellman's change of Anouilh's flashback technique. (See also section on Christopher Fry.)

Moody, Richard. LILLIAN HELLMAN: PLAYWRIGHT. Indianapolis: Bobbs-Merrill, 1972.

A factual survey of the career, with little critical analysis. See also Jacob Adler, above.

Stern, Richard G. "Lillian Hellman on Her Plays." CONTACT, no. 3 (1959), 113-19.

Tynan, Kenneth. "Theatre." SPECTATOR, 18 April 1952, p. 512.

Suggests that Hellman accepts too glibly the virtue of Monserrat's causes and misses the dramatic possibilities of escape for the hostages.

# F. HUGH HERBERT (1897-1958)

THE MOON IS BLUE. Introd. Ben Hecht. New York: Random House, 1951.

When filmed in 1953, this otherwise innocuous comedy caused a furor because it contained the word "virgin."

A GIRL CAN TELL. New York: Dramatists Play Service, 1954.

## BIBLIOGRAPHY

Salem, James M., ed. A GUIDE TO CRITICAL REVIEWS. Part 1: AMERICAN DRAMA, 1909-1969. 2nd ed. Metuchen, N.J.: Scarecrow Press, 1973.

See pages 203-09.

# JAMES LEO HERLIHY (1927- )

STOP, YOU'RE KILLING ME: THREE SHORT PLAYS. New York: Dramatists Play Service, 1969.

STOP, YOU'RE KILLING ME: THREE SHORT PLAYS. New York: Simon and Schuster, 1970.

Three one-acts: TERRIBLE JIM FITCH; BAD, BAD JO-JO; LAUGHS, ETC.

## COLLABORATION WITH WILLIAM NOBLE

BLUE DENIM. New York: Random House, 1958.

## SELECTED NONDRAMATIC WRITING

THE SLEEP OF BABY FILBERTON AND OTHER STORIES. Illus. Tom Keogh. New York: E.P. Dutton, 1959.

ALL FALL DOWN. New York: Simon and Schuster, 1960.

Novel, later made into a film with a William Inge screenplay.

MIDNIGHT COWBOY. New York: Simon and Schuster, 1965.

Novel, later an extremely popular movie.

A STORY THAT ENDS WITH A SCREAM AND EIGHT OTHERS. New York: Simon and Schuster, 1967.

## CRITICISM

Kendle, Burton. "James Leo Herlihy." In CONTEMPORARY DRAMATISTS. Ed. James Vinson. London: St. James; New York: St. Martin's, 1973, pp. 373-75.

# ROBERT HIVNOR (1916- )

THE TICKLISH ACROBAT. In PLAYBOOK: FIVE PLAYS FOR A NEW THEATRE. Ed. James Laughlin. Norfolk, Connecticut: New Directions, 1956.

THE ASSAULT UPON CHARLES SUMNER. In PLAYS FOR A NEW THEATRE: PLAYBOOK 2. New York: New Directions, 1966.

LOVE RECONCILED TO WAR. In BREAKOUT! IN SEARCH OF NEW THEATRICAL ENVIRONMENTS. Ed. James Schevill. Chicago: Swallow Press, 1973.

## CRITICISM

Barbour, Thomas. "The Stuff of the Theatre." HR, 10 (Spring 1957), 132-40.

This review of PLAYBOOK and, in particular, THE TICKLISH ACROBAT suggests that although very funny the play's focus is vague, allowing a metaphor to do too much work.

Bellow, Saul. "Pleasures and Pains of Playgoing." PR, 21 (May-June 1954), 312-17.

Concludes with a review of THE TICKLISH ACROBAT, finding it enchanting, and Hivnor "the real thing, a writer."

## WILLIAM DOUGLAS HOME (1912- )

MASTER OF ARTS: A FARCICAL COMEDY IN THREE ACTS. London: Samuel French, 1950.

THE THISTLE AND THE ROSE. In PLAYS OF THE YEAR 4. Ed. J.C. Trewin. London: Elek Books, 1951.

THE BAD SAMARITAN. London: Evans Bros., 1954.

THE MANOR OF NORTHSTEAD. London: Samuel French, 1956.

THE RELUCTANT DEBUTANT. London: Evans Bros., 1956.

> Home's most successful play, making the trip from the West End to Broadway to Hollywood.

THE IRON DUCHESS. London: Evans Bros., 1958.

AUNT EDWINA. London: Samuel French, 1960.

THE BAD SOLDIER SMITH. London: Evans Bros., 1962.

THE RELUCTANT PEER. London: Evans Bros., 1965.

A FRIEND INDEED. London: Samuel French, 1966.

THE QUEEN'S HIGHLAND SERVANT. In PLAYS OF THE YEAR 35. Ed. J.C. Trewin. London: Elek Books, 1968.

THE SECRETARY BIRD. London: Samuel French, 1968.

THE BISHOP AND THE ACTRESS. London: Samuel French, 1969.

THE JOCKEY CLUB STAKES. In PLAYS OF THE YEAR 40. Ed. J.C. Trewin. London: Elek Books, 1971.

THE JOCKEY CLUB STAKES. London: Samuel French, 1973.

LLOYD GEORGE KNEW MY FATHER. London: Samuel French, 1973.

## COLLECTIONS

THE PLAYS OF WILLIAM DOUGLAS HOME. London: Heinemann, 1958.

NOW BARABBAS, THE CHILTERN HUNDREDS, THE THISTLE AND THE ROSE, THE BAD SAMARITAN, and THE RELUCTANT DEBUTANT.

## SELECTED NONDRAMATIC WRITING

HALF-TERM REPORT: AN AUTOBIOGRAPHY. London: Longmans, 1954.

## CRITICISM

Tynan, Kenneth. "At the Theatre." OBSERVER, 29 May 1955, p. 6.

Argues that the very success of a play like THE RELUCTANT DEBUTANT limits the horizons of the English theatre.

______. "Home and Colonial." OBSERVER, 17 March 1957, p. 13.

A devastatingly funny summary of THE IRON DUCHESS.

## JOHN HOPKINS (1931- )

TALKING TO A STRANGER: FOUR TELEVISION PLAYS. Harmondsworth, Engl.: Penguin, 1967.

Consists of ANY TIME YOU'RE READY, I'LL SPARKLE; NO SKILL OR SPECIAL KNOWLEDGE IS REQUIRED; GLADLY, MY CROSS-EYED BEAR; and THE INNOCENT MUST SUFFER.

A GAME-LIKE-ONLY A GAME. In CONFLICTING GENERATIONS: FIVE TELEVISION PLAYS. Ed. Michael Marland. London: Longmans, 1968.

A PLACE OF SAFETY. In Z CARS: FOUR SCRIPTS FROM THE TELEVISION SERIES. Ed. Michael Marland. London: Longmans, 1968.

THIS STORY OF YOURS. Harmondsworth, Engl.: Penguin, 1969.

FIND YOUR WAY HOME. Harmondsworth, Engl.: Penguin, 1970.

FIND YOUR WAY HOME. Rev. ed. New York: Samuel French, 1975.

### CRITICISM

"John Hopkins Interviewed by Giles Gordon." In BEHIND THE SCENES: THEATRE AND FILM INTERVIEWS FROM THE TRANSATLANTIC REVIEW. Ed. Joseph F.M. McCrindle, introd. Jean-Claude van Itallie. New York: Holt, Rinehart and Winston, 1971, pp. 31-43.

On writing for television.

Taylor, John Russell. "Three Social Realists: John Hopkins, Alan Plater, Cecil P. Taylor." In his THE SECOND WAVE. London: Methuen, 1971, pp. 172-81.

Traces, with plot summaries, Hopkins' work in television and the stage.

# ISRAEL HOROVITZ (1939- )

FIRST SEASON. New York: Random House, 1968.

Consists of LINE, IT'S CALLED THE SUGAR PLUM, THE INDIAN WANTS THE BRONX, and RATS. The volume begins with Horovitz's thirteen-page explanation of how his four plays all received their first New York production within four months.

MORNING. In MORNING, NOON, AND NIGHT. With Terrence McNally and Leonard Melfi. New York: Random House, 1969.

TREES, AND LEADER: TWO SHORT PLAYS. New York: Dramatists Play Service, 1970.

ACROBATS AND LINE. New York: Dramatists Play Service, 1971.

Two short plays.

THE HONEST TO GOD SCHNOZZOLA. New York: Breakthrough Press, 1971.

CLAIR-OBSCUR. Paris: Gallimard, 1972.

DR. HERO. New York: Dramatists Play Service, 1973.

SHOOTING GALLERY AND PLAY FOR GERMS: TWO SHORT PLAYS. New York: Dramatists Play Service, 1973.

ALFRED THE GREAT. New York: Harper and Row, 1974.

## BIBLIOGRAPHY

Salem, James M., ed. A GUIDE TO CRITICAL REVIEWS. Part 1: AMERI-

CAN DRAMA, 1909-1969. 2nd ed. Metuchen, N.J.: Scarecrow Press, 1973.
List of reviews, pages 212-13.

## CRITICISM

Simon, John. UNEASY STAGES. New York: Random House, 1975.
Praise for MORNING's witty writing. See pages 186-87.

Sogliuzzo, A. Richard. "Israel Horovitz." In CONTEMPORARY DRAMATISTS. Ed. James Vinson. London: St. James; New York: St. Martin's, 1973, pp. 391-93.

"Horovitz is a master craftsman, but his craftsmanship has yet to evolve into complex artistry."

## ROGER HOWARD (1931- )

NEW SHORT PLAYS. London: Methuen, 1968.

Four of the plays in this collection are Howard's: THE CARRYING OF X FROM Z TO Z, DIS, THE LOVE SUICIDES AT HAVERING, and SEVEN STATIONS ON THE ROAD TO EXILE.

SLAUGHTER NIGHT, AND OTHER PLAYS. London: Calder and Boyars, 1971.

Also includes THE MEANING OF THE STATUE, THE TRAVELS OF YI YUK-SA TO THE CAVES AT YENAN, RETURNING TO THE CAPITAL, WRITING ON STONE, KOROTOV'S EGO-THEATRE, REPORT FROM THE CITY OF REDS IN THE YEAR 1970, THE DRUM OF THE STRICT MASTER, THE PLAY OF IRON, EPISODES FROM THE FIGHTING IN THE EAST, and A NEW BESTIARY.

### SELECTED NONDRAMATIC WRITING

FOUR STORIES. London: Mouthpiece, 1964.

With twelve sketches by Tony Astbury.

PRAISE SONGS. London: Mouthpiece, 1966.

THE TECHNIQUE OF THE STRUGGLE MEETING. London: Clandestine, 1968.

"Statement." In CONTEMPORARY DRAMATISTS. Ed. James Vinson. London: St. James; New York: St. Martin's, 1973, pp. 395-96.

Describes the revolutionary character of Howard's intentions and his plays.

## DONALD HOWARTH (1931- )

ALL GOOD CHILDREN. London: Samuel French, 1965.

A LILY IN LITTLE INDIA. London: Samuel French, 1966.

A LILY IN LITTLE INDIA. In NEW ENGLISH DRAMATISTS 9. Introd. Michael Billington. Harmondsworth, Engl.: Penguin, 1966.

SCHOOL PLAY. In PLAYBILL ONE. Ed. Alan Durband. London: Hutchinson, 1969.

THREE MONTHS GONE. P&P, 17 (April 1970), 57-77.

THREE MONTHS GONE. London: Samuel French, 1970.

### CRITICISM

Hayman, Ronald. "Donald Howarth." In CONTEMPORARY DRAMATISTS. Ed. James Vinson. London: St. James; New York: St. Martin's, 1973, pp. 398-99.

> Howarth is "finding his way to an individual and successful compromise between naturalism and freewheeling expressionism by dint of returning again and again to the same themes and the same characters but never to the same style."

# TED HUGHES (1930- )

THE WOUND. In WODWO. London: Faber and Faber, 1967.

SENECA'S OEDIPUS. London: Faber and Faber, 1969.

Adaptation from Seneca.

THE COMING OF THE KINGS AND OTHER PLAYS. London: Faber and Faber, 1970.

Plays for children, including THE TIGER'S BONES; BEAUTY AND THE BEAST; SEAN, THE FOOL, THE DEVIL, AND THE CATS, as well as the title play.

SENECA'S OEDIPUS. Garden City, N.Y.: Doubleday, 1972.

Introduced by Peter Brook.

SEAN, THE FOOL, THE DEVIL, AND THE CATS: A PLAY IN ONE ACT. Chicago: Dramatic Publishing, 1974.

## CRITICISM

Sagar, Keith. TED HUGHES. Harlow, Engl.: Longmans for the British Council, 1972.

Basic, biographical, only fifty pages long; praises the children's plays.

Smith, A.C.H. ORGHAST AT PERSEPOLIS: AN INTERNATIONAL EXPERIMENT IN THEATRE. New York: Viking, 1973.

On ORGHAST, the second Brook-Hughes collaboration, the first was SENECA'S OEDIPUS, above.

# N[ORMAN] C[HARLES] HUNTER (1908-1971)

WATERS OF THE MOON. London: English Theatre Guild, 1951.

ADAM'S APPLE: A VICTORIAN FAIRY TALE IN THREE ACTS. London: English Theatre Guild, 1953.

A DAY BY THE SEA. London: English Theatre Guild, 1954.

A PICTURE OF AUTUMN. London: English Theatre Guild, 1957.

A TOUCH OF THE SUN. London: English Theatre Guild, 1958.

THE TULIP TREE. London: English Theatre Guild, 1963.

THE EXCURSION. London: English Theatre Guild, 1964.

## CRITICISM

Dobree, Bonamy. "Some London Plays." SR, 63 (Autumn 1955), 271-73.
Summary and assessment of A DAY BY THE SEA.

## WILLIAM INGE (1913-1973)

COME BACK, LITTLE SHEBA. New York: Random House, 1950.

TO BOBOLINK, FOR HER SPIRIT. In NEW DIRECTIONS IN PROSE AND POETRY XII. Ed. James Laughlin. New York: New Directions, 1950.

PICNIC: A SUMMER ROMANCE. New York: Random House, 1953.

PICNIC. Rev. as SUMMER BRAVE. In SUMMER BRAVE AND ELEVEN SHORT PLAYS. New York: Random House, 1962.

"The rewritten and final version of the romantic comedy PICNIC."

BUS STOP. New York: Random House, 1955.

An early typescript bears the subtitle, "A Three-Act Romance."

THE DARK AT THE TOP OF THE STAIRS. New York: Random House, 1958.

GLORY IN THE FLOWER. In 24 FAVORITE ONE-ACT PLAYS. Ed. Bennett Cerf and Van H. Cartmell. New York: Doubleday, 1958.

THE MALL. ES, January 1959, pages 75-78.

A LOSS OF ROSES. Foreword by the author. New York: Random House, 1960.

Later transformed into the film THE STRIPPER.

SPLENDOR IN THE GRASS: A SCREENPLAY. New York: Bantam Books, 1961.

Academy Award winning screenplay.

SUMMER BRAVE AND ELEVEN SHORT PLAYS. New York: Random House, 1962.

Includes TO BOBOLINK, FOR HER SPIRIT; A SOCIAL EVENT; THE BOY IN THE BASEMENT; THE TINY CLOSET; MEMORY OF SUMMER; THE RAINY AFTERNOON; THE MALL; AN INCIDENT AT THE STANDISH ARMS; PEOPLE IN WIND; BUS RILEY'S BACK IN TOWN; and THE STRAINS OF TRIUMPH.

NATURAL AFFECTION. New York: Random House, 1963.

WHERE'S DADDY? New York: Random House, 1966.

THE DISPOSAL. In BEST SHORT PLAYS OF THE WORLD THEATRE, 1958-1967. Ed. Stanley Richards. New York: Crown, 1968.

TWO SHORT PLAYS: THE CALL, A MURDER. New York: Dramatists Play Service, 1968.

MIDWESTERN MANIAC. In BEST SHORT PLAYS 1969. Ed. Stanley Richards. Philadelphia: Chilton, 1969.

## COLLECTIONS

FOUR PLAYS. New York: Random House, 1958.

COME BACK, LITTLE SHEBA; PICNIC; BUS STOP; and THE DARK AT THE TOP OF THE STAIRS.

## BIBLIOGRAPHY

Salem, James M., ed. A GUIDE TO CRITICAL REVIEWS. Part 1: AMERICAN DRAMA, 1909-1969. 2nd ed. Metuchen, N.J.: Scarecrow Press, 1973.

List of reviews, pages 228-31. See also Schuman's bibliography (below).

## CRITICISM

Bentley, Eric. "Pathetic Phalluses." In his THE DRAMATIC EVENT: AN AMERICAN CHRONICLE. New York: Horizon, 1954, pp. 103-06.

On PICNIC and Inge's catering to popular tastes for both sentiment and sensationalism.

Brustein, Robert. "The Men-Taming Women of William Inge." In his SEASONS OF DISCONTENT: DRAMATIC OPINIONS 1959-1965. New York: Simon and Schuster, 1965, pp. 83-93.

Inge depicts a severely limited world in which excessively masculine protagonists achieve a rather confining romantic love only by admitting to their flawed, essentially timid natures.

______. "No Loss." In his SEASONS OF DISCONTENT: DRAMATIC OPINIONS 1959-1965. New York: Simon and Schuster, 1965, pp. 97-101.

Inge's decline continues with further repetition of the same thin story in A LOSS OF ROSES. NATURAL AFFECTION is a grotesque disaster.

Diehl, Digby. "William Inge, A Playwright in Transition: A Conversation with Digby Diehl." In BEHIND THE SCENES: THEATRE AND FILM INTERVIEWS FROM THE TRANSATLANTIC REVIEW. Ed. Joseph F.M. McCrindle, introd. Jean-Claude van Itallie. New York: Holt, Rinehart and Winston, 1971, pp. 108-15.

From 1967, on his plays, his films, New York, and fame.

Hamblet, Edwin Joseph. "The North American Outlook of Marcel Dube and William Inge." QUEENS QUARTERLY, 77 (Autumn 1971), 374-87.

Some parallels between PICNIC and Dube's LE TEMP DES LILACS (1958).

Herron, Ima Honaker. "Our Vanishing Towns: Modern Broadway Versions." SOUTHWEST REVIEW, 51 (Summer 1966), 209-20.

Uncritical tracing of Inge's career, ostensibly in terms of small-town America.

Kael, Pauline. "Canned Americana." In her I LOST IT AT THE MOVIES. Boston: Little, Brown, 1965, pp. 136-38.

Scathing review of Inge's unpublished screenplay, ALL FALL DOWN, and of SPLENDOR IN THE GRASS.

Miller, Jordan Y. "William Inge: Last of the Realists?" KANSAS QUARTERLY, 2 (Spring 1970), 17-26.

Schuman, R. Baird. WILLIAM INGE. New York: Twayne, 1965.

This first full-length consideration of Inge's work is only reluctantly critical; with an annotated bibliography.

"William Inge." In THE PLAYWRIGHTS SPEAK. Ed. Walter Wager. New York: Delacorte, 1967, pp. 110-39.

Williams, Tennessee. "The Writing is Honest." NEW YORK TIMES, 16 March 1958, Sec. 2, pp. 1, 3.

Inge's world is one of sincerity and an unashamed realism; Williams also recalls his first meeting with Inge. Reprinted as an introduction to DARK AT THE TOP OF THE STAIRS (Random House, 1958).

Wolfson, Lester M. "Inge, O'Neill, and the Human Condition." SOUTHERN SPEECH JOURNAL, 22 (1957), 221-32.

# ROBINSON JEFFERS (1887-1962)

THE CRETAN WOMAN. In HUNGERFIELD, AND OTHER POEMS. New York: Random House, 1954.

THE CRETAN WOMAN. In FROM THE MODERN REPERTORY. Series 3. Ed. Eric Bentley. Bloomington: Indiana University Press, 1956.

Jeffers' version of the HIPPOLYTUS of Euripides.

## BIBLIOGRAPHY

Salem, James M., ed. A GUIDE TO CRITICAL REVIEWS. Part 1: AMERICAN DRAMA, 1909-1969. 2nd ed. Metuchen, N.J.: Scarecrow Press, 1973.

See page 232.

Vardamis, Alex A. THE CRITICAL REPUTATION OF ROBINSON JEFFERS: A BIBLIOGRAPHICAL STUDY. Hampden, Conn.: Archon Books, 1972.

The fullest listing of the reviews, fully annotated, for THE CRETAN WOMAN, is on pages 146-49 of this splendid study.

## CRITICISM

Brophy, Robert J. ROBINSON JEFFERS: MYTH, RITUAL, AND SYMBOL IN HIS NARRATIVE POEMS. Cleveland: Press of the Case Western Reserve University, 1973.

Carpenter, Frederick. ROBINSON JEFFERS. New York: Twayne, 1962.

Barely alludes to THE CRETAN WOMAN.

Coffin, Arthur B. ROBINSON JEFFERS: POET OF INHUMANISM. Madison: University of Wisconsin Press, 1971.

Brief treatment of THE CRETAN WOMAN, claiming that the play sacrifices "some of the moral tone of the original." See pages 235-40.

# ANN JELLICOE (1927- )

THE SPORT OF MY MAD MOTHER. In THE OBSERVER PLAYS. Preface by Kenneth Tynan. London: Faber and Faber, 1958.

ROSMERSHOLM. Introd. Alrik Gustafson. San Francisco: Chandler Publishing, 1961.

An Ibsen translation.

ROSMERSHOLM. In FOUR MODERN PLAYS. 2nd series. Ed. Henry Popkin. New York: Holt, Rinehart and Winston, 1961.

THE KNACK. London: Encore Publishing, 1962.

Later a movie.

THE SPORT OF MY MAD MOTHER. 2nd ed. London: Faber and Faber, 1964.

With a preface by Jellicoe to the new version.

SHELLEY; OR, THE IDEALIST. London: Faber and Faber, 1966.

With a preface by Jellicoe.

THE RISING GENERATION. In PLAYBILL 2. Ed. Alan Durband. London: Hutchinson, 1969.

THE GIVEAWAY. London: Faber and Faber, 1970.

## SELECTED NONDRAMATIC WRITING

"Question and Answer." NTM, 1 (July 1960), 24-28.

Interview in which Jellicoe disavows the title of "poetic" and asserts the desire to communicate directly without overt address to the intellect or intellectuals.

SOME UNCONSCIOUS INFLUENCES IN THE THEATRE. London: Cambridge University Press, 1967.

Lectures.

## CRITICISM

"Ann Jellicoe Interviewed by Robert Rubens." In BEHIND THE SCENES: THEATRE AND FILM INTERVIEWS FROM THE TRANSATLANTIC REVIEW. Ed. Joseph F.M. McCrindle, introd. Jean-Claude van Itallie. New York: Holt, Rinehart and Winston, 1971, pp. 243-55.

"Interview." P&P, 13 (November 1965), 12, 50.

Interview with Simon Trussler on SHELLEY.

Taylor, John Russell. "Ann Jellicoe." In his ANGER AND AFTER: A GUIDE TO THE NEW BRITISH DRAMA. Rev. ed. Harmondsworth, Engl.: Penguin, 1963, pp. 64-71.

Her work "stands out by virtue of its complete command of theatrical effect."

## LEE KALCHEIM (1938- )

MATCH PLAY. In NEW THEATRE IN AMERICA. Ed. Edward Parone. New York: Dell, 1965.

. . . AND THE BOY WHO CAME TO LEAVE. In PLAYWRIGHTS FOR TOMORROW: A COLLECTION OF PLAYS. Vol. 2. Ed. Arthur H. Ballet. Minneapolis: University of Minnesota, 1966.

AN AUDIBLE SIGH. N.p., 1969.

Typescript at Brown University Library.

### CRITICISM

Ballet, Arthur H. "Lee Kalcheim." In CONTEMPORARY DRAMATISTS. Ed. James Vinson. London: St. James; New York: St. Martin's, 1973, pp. 428-29.

"People trying--desperately, lazily, sadly, hopefully, pathetically, ridiculously--to make contact with other people is what his plays not only are but are about."

# GARSON KANIN (1912- )

THE RAT RACE. New York: Dramatists Play Service, 1950.

DIE FLEDERMAUS. New York: Boosey and Hawkes, 1951.

The Metropolitan Opera version of Johann Strauss's FLEDERMAUS, lyrics by Howard Dietz, text by Garson Kanin.

THE LIVE WIRE. New York: Dramatists Play Service, 1951.

IT SHOULD HAPPEN TO YOU: SCREENPLAY. Hollywood: n.p., 1953.

Shooting script at the Lincoln Center Library of the Performing Arts.

A GIFT OF TIME. New York: Random House, 1962.

Adapted from DEATH OF A MAN by Lael Tucker Wertenbaker.

COME ON STRONG. New York: Dramatists Play Service, 1964.

ADAM'S RIB. New York: Viking, 1972.

Screenplay of the 1949 Hepburn-Tracy film.

## BIBLIOGRAPHY

Salem, James M., ed. A GUIDE TO CRITICAL REVIEWS. Part 1: AMERICAN DRAMA, 1909-1969. 2nd ed. Metuchen, N.J.: Scarecrow Press, 1973.

List of reviews, pages 238-39.

## SELECTED NONDRAMATIC WRITING

DO RE MI. Boston: Little, Brown, 1955.

Novel on which the Phil Silvers musical (1960) was based.

THE RAT RACE. New York: Pocket Books, 1960.

Novel based on the screenplay, itself based on his 1950 play.

REMEMBERING MR. MAUGHAM. New York: Atheneum, 1966.

CAST OF CHARACTERS: STORIES OF BROADWAY AND HOLLYWOOD. New York: Atheneum, 1969.

# GEORGE S. KAUFMAN (1889-1961)

## COLLABORATIONS

FANCY MEETING YOU AGAIN. With Leueen MacGrath. New York: Dramatists Play Service, 1951.

THE SMALL HOURS. With Leueen MacGrath. New York: Dramatists Play Service, 1951.

THE SOLID GOLD CADILLAC. With Howard Teichmann. New York: Random House, 1954.

Kaufman's last hit.

AMICABLE PARTING: A FIFTEEN MINUTE SKETCH. With Leueen MacGrath. New York: Dramatists Play Service, 1957.

A NIGHT AT THE OPERA. New York: Viking, 1972.

The screenplay for the 1935 Marx Brother's film, in collaboration with Morris Ryskind.

## BIBLIOGRAPHY

Salem, James M., ed. A GUIDE TO CRITICAL REVIEWS. Part 1: AMERICAN DRAMA, 1909-1969. 2nd ed. Metuchen, N.J.: Scarecrow Press, 1973.

See pages 242-48.

## CRITICISM

Meredith, Scott. GEORGE S. KAUFMAN AND HIS FRIENDS. Garden City, N.Y.: Doubleday, 1974.

An ungainly volume, made unnecessarily large by canned biographies of Kaufman's friends; Meredith claims that Teichman was not so close to Kaufman as his book, below, suggests.

Teichman, Howard. GEORGE S. KAUFMAN: AN INTIMATE PORTRAIT. New York: Atheneum, 1972.

# SIDNEY KINGSLEY (1906- )

DARKNESS AT NOON. New York: Random House, 1951.

A play based on the novel by Arthur Koestler.

LUNATICS AND LOVERS. In THEATER '55. Ed. John Chapman. New York: Random House, 1955.

Excerpts; a complete typescript is available at the Lincoln Center Library of the Performing Arts.

NIGHT LIFE. New York: Dramatists Play Service, 1966.

## BIBLIOGRAPHY

Salem, James M., ed. A GUIDE TO CRITICAL REVIEWS. Part 1: AMERICAN DRAMA, 1909-1969. 2nd ed. Metuchen, N.J.: Scarecrow Press, 1973.

A list of reviews, pages 260-64.

# KENNETH KOCH (1925- )

BERTHA. ER, 4 (November-December 1960), 42-45.

BERTHA. In BERTHA AND OTHER PLAYS. New York: Grove Press, 1966.

Sixteen neo-Dadaist short plays.

A CHANGE OF HEARTS: PLAYS, FILMS, AND OTHER DRAMATIC WORKS, 1951-1971. New York: Random House, 1973.

Reprints BERTHA AND OTHER PLAYS, along with ten films and five more short whimsies.

## SELECTED NONDRAMATIC WRITING

KO; OR, A SEASON ON EARTH. New York: Grove Press, 1960.

Poems.

WHEN THE SUN TRIES TO GO ON. Los Angeles: Black Sparrow Press, 1969.

Poems.

WISHES, LIES AND DREAMS: TEACHING CHILDREN TO WRITE POETRY. New York: Random House, 1970.

Influential introduction to poetry on the elementary school level.

## CRITICISM

Howard, Richard. "Kenneth Koch." In his ALONE WITH AMERICA: ESSAYS ON THE ART OF POETRY IN THE UNITED STATES SINCE 1950. New York: Atheneum, 1971, pp. 281-91.

## ARTHUR KOPIT (1937- )

TO DWELL IN A PLACE OF STRANGERS. HARVARD ADVOCATE, 142 (Spring 1959), 2-15.

Act one only.

OH, DAD, POOR DAD, MAMA'S HUNG YOU IN THE CLOSET AND I'M FEELING SO SAD: A PSEUDOCLASSICAL TRAGIFARCE IN A BASTARD FRENCH TRADITION. New York: Hill and Wang, 1960.

The collegiate parody of the absurdists.

THE DAY THE WHORES CAME OUT TO PLAY TENNIS, AND OTHER PLAYS. New York: Hill and Wang, 1965.

Includes CHAMBER MUSIC, THE QUESTIONING OF NICK, SING TO ME THROUGH OPEN WINDOWS, THE HERO, THE CONQUEST OF EVEREST, and an introduction by Kopit.

AN INCIDENT IN THE PARK. In PARDON ME, SIR, BUT IS MY EYE HURTING YOUR ELBOW? New York: Bernard Geis, 1968.

Segment of an unproduced film.

THE DAY THE WHORES CAME OUT TO PLAY TENNIS, AND OTHER PLAYS. Rpt. in England as CHAMBER MUSIC AND OTHER PLAYS. London: Methuen, 1969.

INDIANS. New York: Hill and Wang, 1969.

Kopit's most considerable effort, despite its Broadway failure; the 1971 Bantam edition contains an interview between Kopit and John Lahr.

## BIBLIOGRAPHY

Salem, James M., ed. A GUIDE TO CRITICAL REVIEWS. Part 1: AMERICAN DRAMA, 1909-1969. 2nd ed. Metuchen, N.J.: Scarecrow Press, 1973.

List of reviews, pages 269-70.

## CRITICISM

"Arthur Kopit Interviewed by Brian Hennessy." In BEHIND THE SCENES: THEATER AND FILM INTERVIEWS FROM THE TRANSATLANTIC REVIEW. Ed. Joseph F.M. McCrindle, introd. Jean-Claude van Italie. New York: Holt, Rinehart and Winston, 1971, pp. 70-76.

On INDIANS.

Hughes, Catharine. PLAYS, POLITICS AND POLEMICS. New York: Drama Book Specialists, 1973.

On INDIANS, pages 61-66.

Jiji, Vera M. "INDIANS: A Mosaic of Memories and Methodologies." PL, 47 (Summer 1972), 230-36.

Jones, John B. "Impersonation and Authenticity: The Theatre as Metaphor in Kopit's INDIANS." QJS, 59 (December 1973), 443-51.

How structure carries theme, as impersonation and theatricality both convey and are the play's main idea.

Kaufman, Stanley. "INDIANS." In his PERSONS OF THE DRAMA. New York: Harper and Row, 1976, pp. 183-86.

INDIANS is a thin failure; its language is its worst fault.

Lahr, John. "Arthur Kopit's INDIANS: Dramatizing National Amnesia." In his UP AGAINST THE FOURTH WALL: ESSAYS ON MODERN THEATER. New York: Grove Press, 1970, pp. 136-57.

Unreserved praise for the play's political insight into American history. INDIANS is also discussed in "In Search of a New Mythology," in the same volume.

Murch, Anne C. "Genet-Triana-Kopit: Ritual as 'Danse Macabre.'" MD, 15 (March 1973), 369-81.

Kopit's CHAMBER MUSIC, like Genet's THE MAIDS and Triana's THE NIGHT OF THE ASSASSINS, depicts a ritual murder meant to liberate characters from a spiritual bondage.

# BERNARD KOPS (1926- )

THE HAMLET OF STEPNEY GREEN: A (SAD) COMEDY IN THREE ACTS. In NEW ENGLISH DRAMATISTS. Ed. Elliott Martin Browne. Harmondsworth, Engl.: Penguin, 1959.

THE DREAM OF PETER MANN. Introd. Mervyn Jones. Harmondsworth, Engl.: Penguin, 1960.

ENTER SOLLY GOLD. In SATAN, SOCIALITES, AND SOLLY GOLD: THREE PLAYS FROM ENGLAND. New York: Coward-McCann, 1961.

THE BOY WHO WOULDN'T PLAY JESUS: A MODERN MYSTERY PLAY FOR CHILDREN. In EIGHT PLAYS: BOOK I. Ed. Malcolm Stuart Fellows. London: Cassell, 1965.

DAVID, IT IS GETTING DARK. Trans. Edith Zetline. L'AVANT SCENE, 454 (1 August 1970), 7-38.

Only available in a French translation.

## COLLECTIONS

FOUR PLAYS. London: MacGibbon & Kee, 1964.

Consists of reprints of THE HAMLET OF STEPNEY GREEN, and ENTER SOLLY GOLD, along with the first publication of HOME SWEET HONEYCOMB (1962) and LEMMINGS (1963).

## SELECTED NONDRAMATIC WRITING

POEMS. London: Bell and Baker Press, 1955.

POEMS AND SONGS. Lowescroft, Suffolk: Scorpion Press, 1958.

AWAKE FOR MOURNING. London: MacGibbon & Kee, 1958.

Novel.

MOTORBIKE. London: New English Library, 1962.

Novel.

THE WORLD IS A WEDDING. London: MacGibbon & Kee, 1963.

Autobiography.

YES FROM NO-MAN'S LAND. London: MacGibbon & Kee, 1965.

Novel.

THE DISSENT OF DOMINICK SHAPIRO. London: MacGibbon & Kee, 1967.

Novel.

ERICA, I WANT TO READ YOU SOMETHING. Lowescroft, Suffolk: Scorpion Press, 1967.

BY THE WATERS OF WHITECHAPEL. London: Bodley Head, 1969.

Novel.

## CRITICISM

Taylor, John Russell. "Bernard Kops." In his ANGER AND AFTER: A GUIDE TO THE NEW BRITISH DRAMA. Rev. ed. Harmondsworth, Engl.: Penguin, 1963, pp. 152-61.

"Kops is still in many ways a primitive, but in ENTER SOLLY GOLD and HOME SWEET HONEYCOMB he has proved capable of real development without losing any of his essential qualities."

Wellwarth, George. THE THEATRE OF PROTEST AND PARADOX. New York: New York University Press, 1964.

"To Kops reality is one long, manic vaudeville act." See pages 244-48.

## H.M. KOUTOUKAS (1947- )

TIDY PASSIONS; OR, KILL, KALEIDOSCOPE, KILL. In MORE PLAYS FROM OFF OFF BROADWAY. Ed. Michael Smith. Indianapolis: Bobbs-Merrill, 1972.

Here is another instance of an active figure from OOB who had to wait several years before one of his plays was published. In this case there was a delay of seven years between performance and publication.

### CRITICISM

Smith, Michael. "H.M. Koutoukas." In CONTEMPORARY DRAMATISTS. Ed. James Vinson. London: St. James; New York: St. Martin's, 1973, p. 448.

"He is likely to be remembered as one of the most original dramatists of his time."

# NORMAN KRASNA (1909- )

KIND SIR. New York: Dramatists Play Service, 1954.

WHO WAS THAT LADY I SAW YOU WITH? New York: Random House, 1958.

Later a movie (1960).

SUNDAY IN NEW YORK. New York: Random House, 1962.

Later a movie (1963).

LOVE IN E-FLAT. New York: Dramatists Play Service, 1967.

WATCH THE BIRDIE. New York: Dramatists Play Service, 1969.

## BIBLIOGRAPHY

Salem, James M., ed. A GUIDE TO CRITICAL REVIEWS. Part 1: AMERICAN DRAMA, 1909-1969. 2nd ed. Metuchen, N.J.: Scarecrow Press, 1973.

List of reviews, pages 271-74.

# RUTH KRAUSS (1911- )

THE 50,000 DOGWOODS AT VALLEY FORGE. KULCHUR, 3 (Spring 1963), 24.

THE CANTILEVER RAINBOW. Woodcuts by Antonia Frasconi. New York: Pantheon Books, 1965.

THE CANTILEVER RAINBOW. In THEATRE EXPERIMENT. Ed. Michael Benedikt. New York: Doubleday, 1967.

Five theatre poems: four are reprints from THE CANTILEVER RAINBOW, and one, THERE'S A LITTLE AMBIGUITY OVER THERE AMONG THE BLUEBELLS, is first published here.

THERE'S A LITTLE AMBIGUITY OVER THERE AMONG THE BLUEBELLS AND OTHER THEATRE POEMS. New York: Something Else Press, 1968.

This is the best collection of Krauss's work, with most of THE CANTILEVER RAINBOW, plus many other short pieces.

IF ONLY. Eugene, Oreg.: Toad Press, 1969.

First published in THERE'S A LITTLE AMBIGUITY.

UNDER TWENTY. Eugene, Oreg.: Toad Press, 1970.

LOVE AND THE INVENTION OF PUNCTUATION. Lenox, Mass.: Bookstore Press, 1973.

## CRITICISM

Sainer, Arthur. "Ruth Krauss." In CONTEMPORARY DRAMATISTS. Ed. James Vinson. London: St. James; New York: St. Martin's, 1973, pp. 450-51.

# KEVIN LAFFAN (1922- )

ZOO ZOO WIDDERSHINS ZOO. London: Faber and Faber, 1969.

IT'S A TWO-FOOT-SIX-INCHES-ABOVE-THE-GROUND WORLD. London: Faber and Faber, 1970.

## CRITICISM

Taylor, John Russell. "The Legacy of Realism." In his THE SECOND WAVE. London: Methuen, 1971, pp. 194-96.

Brief remarks on Laffan's use of realism, with plot summaries.

# ARTHUR LAURENTS (1918- )

THE BIRD CAGE. New York: Dramatists Play Service, 1950.

THE TIME OF THE CUCKOO. New York: Random House, 1953.

A CLEARING IN THE WOODS. New York: Random House, 1957.

WEST SIDE STORY. New York: Random House, 1958.

A musical based on a conception of Jerome Robbins, with book by Arthur Laurents, lyrics by Stephen Sondheim, and music by Leonard Bernstein.

GYPSY. New York: Random House, 1960.

A musical suggested by the memoirs of Gypsy Rose Lee, with book by Arthur Laurents, lyrics by Stephen Sondheim, and music by Jule Stein.

INVITATION TO A MARCH. New York: Random House, 1961.

ANYONE CAN WHISTLE: A MUSICAL FABLE. New York: Random House, 1965.

Book by Arthur Laurents, music and lyrics by Stephen Sondheim.

DO I HEAR A WALTZ? New York: Random House, 1966.

Book by Arthur Laurents, lyrics by Stephen Sondheim, and music by Richard Rodgers.

Note: In CONTEMPORARY DRAMATISTS, edited by James Vinson (London: St. James; New York: St. Martin's, 1973), it is claimed that Laurents' book for HALLELUJAH, BABY! was published in 1967 by Random House. There is no other record of actual publication.

THE ENCLAVE. New York: Dramatists Play Service, 1974.

## BIBLIOGRAPHY

Salem, James M., ed. A GUIDE TO CRITICAL REVIEWS. Part 1: AMERICAN DRAMA, 1909-1969. 2nd ed. Metuchen, N.J.: Scarecrow Press, 1973.

See pages 278-80.

## CRITICISM

Brustein, Robert. "Broadway Non-Conformism." In his SEASONS OF DISCONTENT: DRAMATIC OPINIONS 1959-1965. New York: Simon and Schuster, 1965, pp. 114-16.

INVITATION TO A MARCH merely appears to be about non-conformity. Instead it is "another horrible chapter in that dismal chronicle of the American bourgeois mind...on our commercial stage."

Cerf, Walter. "Psychoanalysis and the Realistic Drama." JOURNAL OF AESTHETICS AND ART CRITICISM, 16 (March 1958), 330-36.

On A CLEARING IN THE WOODS.

Tallmer, Jerry. "Enter One Playwright, Pursued by Scenery." In THE VILLAGE VOICE READER: A MIXED BAG FROM THE GREENWICH VILLAGE NEWSPAPER. Ed. Daniel Wolf and Edwin Fancher. New York: Grove Press, 1963, pp. 171-73.

In this interview, Laurents discusses Broadway's mishandling of his plays.

# JEROME LAWRENCE ( - )

LIVE SPELLED BACKWARDS. New York: Dramatists Play Service, 1950.

Note: SOMEBODY'S VALENTINE, listed in CONTEMPORARY DRAMATISTS, edited by James Vinson (London: St. James; New York: St. Martin's, 1973), as by Jerome Lawrence, is actually by Joan Lawrence.

## COLLABORATIONS WITH ROBERT E. LEE

ANNIE LAURIE: A STORY OF ROBERT BURNS. New York: Harms, 1954.

"A Musiplay in One Act."

DILLY. New York: Hart Stenographic Service, 1955.

Typescript at the Lincoln Center Library of the Performing Arts. Music by Vernon Duke.

INHERIT THE WIND. New York: Random House, 1955.

Their great success, dramatizing the clash of William Jennings Bryan and Clarence Darrow during the Scopes trial.

ROARING CAMP: A MUSIPLAY IN ONE ACT. New York: Harms, 1955.

Based on Bret Harte's famous short story (1870).

SHANGRI-LA. New York: Morris Music, 1956.

Book by Jerome Lawrence, Robert E. Lee, and James Hilton; an adaptation of Hilton's novel LOST HORIZONS (1933), music by Harry Warren.

AUNTIE MAME. New York: Vanguard Press, 1957.

Based on the novel by Patrick Dennis (1955), with a Foreword by Patrick Dennis.

AUNTIE MAME. Rev. New York: Dramatists Play Service, 1960.

THE GANG'S ALL HERE. Cleveland: World Publishing, 1960.

ONLY IN AMERICA. New York: Samuel French, 1960.

Based on the book by Harry Golden (1958).

A CALL ON KUPRIN. New York: Samuel French, 1962.

Based on the novel by Maurice Edelman (1959).

MAME. New York: Random House, 1967.

Adaptation of AUNTIE MAME, with music by Jerry Herman.

SPARKS FLY UPWARD. New York: Dramatists Play Service, 1969.

A typescript of an earlier version, DIAMOND ORCHID, is at the Lincoln Center Library of the Performing Arts.

THE NIGHT THOREAU SPENT IN JAIL. New York: Hill and Wang, 1970.

THE INCOMPARABLE MAX. New York: Hill and Wang, 1972.

JABBERWOCK: IMPROBABILITIES LIVED AND IMAGINED BY JAMES THURBER IN THE FICTIONAL CITY OF COLUMBUS, OHIO. New York: Samuel French, 1974.

## BIBLIOGRAPHY

Salem, James M., ed. A GUIDE TO CRITICAL REVIEWS. Part 1: AMERICAN DRAMA, 1909-1969. 2nd ed. Metuchen, N.J.: Scarecrow Press, 1973.

List of reviews, pages 281-84.

## CRITICISM

Leech, Michael T. "Jerome Lawrence and Robert E. Lee." In CONTEMPORARY DRAMATISTS. Ed. James Vinson. London: St. James; New York: St. Martin's, 1973, pp. 461-63.

# DORIS LESSING (1919- )

EACH HIS OWN WILDERNESS. In NEW ENGLISH DRAMATISTS. Ed. Elliott Martin Browne. Harmondsworth, Engl.: Penguin, 1959.

PLAY WITH A TIGER. London: Michael Joseph, 1962.

THE SINGING DOOR. In SECOND PLAYBILL 2. Ed. Alan Durband. London: Hutchinson, 1973.

## BIBLIOGRAPHY

Burkom, Selma R., with Margaret Williams, eds. DORIS LESSING: A CHECK-LIST OF PRIMARY AND SECONDARY SOURCES. Troy, N.Y.: Whitston, 1973.

Less complete than the Krause bibliography (below).

Krause, Agate Nesaule, ed. "A Doris Lessing Checklist." CONTEMPORARY LITERATURE, 14 (Autumn 1973), 590-97.

Includes a checklist of criticism and reviews of the two unpublished plays.

## SELECTED NONDRAMATIC WRITING

"A Small Private Voice." In DECLARATION. Ed. Tom Maschler. London: MacGibbon & Kee, 1957, pp. 12-27.

## CRITICISM

Brewster, Dorothy. DORIS LESSING. New York: Twayne, 1965.

Nicoll, Allardyce. "Somewhat in a New Dimension." In CONTEMPORARY THEATRE. Ed. John Russell Brown and Bernard Harris. London: Edward Arnold, 1968, pp. 82-83, 92.

Pratt, Annis, and L.S. Dembo, eds. DORIS LESSING: CRITICAL STUDIES. Madison: University of Wisconsin Press, 1974.

"Articles in this volume originally appeared in CONTEMPORARY LITERATURE, Autumn 1973."

Schlueter, Paul George. THE NOVELS OF DORIS LESSING. Preface by Harry T. Moore. Carbondale: Southern University Press, 1973.

Taylor, John Russell. "More Playwrights in the Provinces." In his ANGER AND AFTER: A GUIDE TO THE NEW BRITISH DRAMA. Rev. ed. Harmondsworth, Engl.: Penguin, 1963, pp. 195-96.

Wellwarth, George. "Doris Lessing: The Angry Young Cocoon." In his THE THEATER OF PROTEST AND PARADOX: DEVELOPMENTS IN THE AVANT-GARDE DRAMA. New York: New York University Press, 1964, pp. 248-50.

## BENN LEVY (1900- )

RETURN TO TYASSI. London: Victor Gollancz, 1951.

CUPID AND PSYCHE. London: Victor Gollancz, 1952.

THE GREAT HEALER. London: Samuel French, 1954.

THE ISLAND OF CIPANGO. London: Samuel French, 1954.

THE TRUTH ABOUT TRUTH. In THE BEST ONE-ACT PLAYS OF 1956-1957. Ed. Hugh Miller. London: Harrup, 1957.

THE RAPE OF THE BELT. London: MacGibbon & Kee, 1957.

THE MEMBER FOR GAZA. In PLAYS OF THE YEAR 32. Ed. J.C. Trewin. London: Elek Books, 1966.

THE MEMBER FOR GAZA. London: Evans Bros., 1968.

### BIBLIOGRAPHY

Salem, James M., ed. A GUIDE TO CRITICAL REVIEWS. Part 3: BRITISH AND CONTINENTAL DRAMA FROM IBSEN TO PINTER. Metuchen, N.J.: Scarecrow Press, 1968.

> Short list of reviews of the New York production of THE RAPE OF THE BELT. See page 148.

### SELECTED NONDRAMATIC WRITING

BRITAIN AND THE BOMB: THE FALLACY OF NUCLEAR DEFENCE. London: Campaign for Nuclear Disarmament, 1959.

## CRITICISM

Dobree, Bonamy. "Some Recent London Plays." SR, 66 (Autumn 1958), 649-52.

On THE RAPE OF THE BELT, and other plays.

Worsley, T.C. THE FUGITIVE ART. London: John Lehman, 1952.

On RETURN TO TYASSI. See pages 180-82.

# HENRY LIVINGS (1929- )

STOP IT, WHOEVER YOU ARE. In NEW ENGLISH DRAMATISTS 5. Ed. Tom Maschler. Harmondsworth, Engl.: Penguin, 1962.

NIL CARBORUNDUM. In NEW ENGLISH DRAMATISTS 6. Ed. Elliott Martin Browne. Harmondsworth, Engl.: Penguin, 1963.

KELLY'S EYE AND OTHER PLAYS. London: Methuen, 1964.

Also includes BIG SOFT NELLIE (once titled THACRED NIT), and THERE'S NO ROOM FOR YOU HERE FOR A START.

EH? London: Methuen, 1965.

THE DAY DUMBFOUNDED GOT HIS PYLON. In WORTH A HEARING. Ed. Alfred Bradley. Glasgow: Blackie, 1967.

GOOD GRIEF! London: Methuen, 1968.

A collection consisting of AFTER THE LAST LAMP, DOES IT MAKE YOUR CHEEKS ACHE?, PIE-EATING CONTEST, THE REASONS FOR FLYING, VARIABLE LENGTHS, and YOU'RE FREE.

HONOUR AND OFFER. London: Methuen, 1969.

THE LITTLE MRS. FOSTER SHOW. London: Methuen, 1969.

PONGO PLAYS 1-6. London: Methuen, 1971.

Consists of THE GAMECOCK, RATTEL, THE BOGGART, BEEWINE, THE RIFLE VOLUNTEER, and CONCILIATION.

THE FFINEST FFAMILY IN THE LAND. London: Methuen, 1972.

THE JOCKEY DRIVES LATE NIGHTS. London: Eyre Methuen, 1972.

Based on THE POWER OF DARKNESS by Tolstoy (1888).

BRAINSCREW. In SECOND PLAYBILL 3. Ed. Alan Durband. London: Hutchinson, 1973.

SIX MORE PONGO PLAYS. London: Eyre Methuen, 1974.

## SELECTED NONDRAMATIC WRITING

"Henry Livings: An Interview." EN, 10 (July-August 1963), 28-44.

"Let's Make a Theatre for Real People." TQ, 2 (April-June 1972), 5-7.

In a letter to director David Scase, on the opening of a new theatre, Livings deplores the absence of simplicity, the excesses of scenic realism, of "Director's Theatre."

## CRITICISM

Giannetti, Louis D. "Henry Livings: A Neglected Voice in the New Drama." MD, 12 (May 1969), 38-48.

Livings' unabashed farces and his work on television have kept him from enjoying critical success. EH? and KELLY'S EYE are his best works; they are examined in detail, and are compared thematically with Pinter and Osborne.

Taylor, John Russell. "Henry Livings." In his ANGER AND AFTER: A GUIDE TO THE NEW BRITISH DRAMA. Rev. ed. Harmondsworth, Engl.: Penguin, 1963, pp. 258-71.

Livings is "even at his funniest a serious writer whom serious people can enjoy."

# FREDERICK LONSDALE (1881-1954)

THE DAY AFTER TOMORROW. TA, 35 (April 1951), 57-88.

THE WAY THINGS GO. London: Samuel French, 1951.

LET THEM EAT CAKE. In PLAYS OF THE YEAR 19. Ed. J.C. Trewin. London: Elek Books, 1959.

A third title for 1937 HALF A LOAF (1937), which in 1938 was retitled ONCE IS ENOUGH.

## BIBLIOGRAPHY

Salem, James M., ed. A GUIDE TO CRITICAL REVIEWS. Part 3: BRITISH AND CONTINENTAL DRAMA FROM IBSEN TO PINTER. Metuchen, N.J.: Scarecrow Press, 1968.

A list of reviews, page 150, of the New York production of THE DAY AFTER TOMORROW.

## CRITICISM

Donaldson, Francis. FREDDY LONSDALE. London: Heinemann, 1957.

An affectionate clear-eyed reminiscence by his daughter.

Taylor, John Russell. THE RISE AND FALL OF THE WELL-MADE PLAY. New York: Hill and Wang, 1967.

Brief survey of Lonsdale's career, pages 120-23.

# ROBERT LOWELL (1917-1977)

PHAEDRA. In THE CLASSIC THEATRE, Vol. 4. Ed. Eric Bentley. Garden City, N.Y.: Doubleday, 1961.

PHAEDRA. In PHAEDRA AND FIGARO. New York: Farrar, Straus and Cudahy, 1961.

Racine's PHEDRE trans. by Robert Lowell and Beaumarchais' FIGARO'S MARRIAGE trans. by Jacques Barzun.

BENITO CERENO. S, 4 (August 1964), 82-96.

MY KINSMAN, MAJOR MOLINEUX. PR, 31 (Fall 1964), 495-514, 566-83.

THE OLD GLORY. New York: Farrar, Straus and Giroux, 1965.

Consists of ENDICOTT AND THE RED CROSS; MY KINSMAN, MAJOR MOLINEUX; and BENITO CERENO, with Robert Brustein's introduction and Jonathan Miller's director's note.

PROMETHEUS BOUND. NYRB, 13 July 1967, pp. 17-24

Derived from Aeschylus.

THE OLD GLORY. Rev. ed. New York: Farrar, Straus and Giroux, 1968.

The revision consists of an expansion of ENDICOTT AND THE RED CROSS.

PROMETHEUS BOUND. New York: Farrar, Straus and Giroux, 1969.

## BIBLIOGRAPHY

Mazzaro, Joseph, comp. "Checklist: 1939-1968." In ROBERT LOWELL: A

PORTRAIT OF THE ARTIST IN HIS TIME. Ed. Michael London and Robert Boyars. New York: David Lewis, 1970.

Superb bibliography in a fine collection of essays.

Salem, James M., ed. A GUIDE TO CRITICAL REVIEWS. Part 1: AMERICAN DRAMA, 1909-1969. 2nd ed. Metuchen, N.J.: Scarecrow Press, 1973.

Brief list of reviews, pages 301-02.

## CRITICISM

Crick, J.F. ROBERT LOWELL. Edinburgh: Oliver and Boyd, 1974.

Chapter 4 is on the plays.

Estrin, Mark W. "Robert Lowell's BENITO CERENO." MD, 15 (March 1973), 411-26.

Lowell transforms Melville's delineation of Delano, a man blind to evil in the world, into Delano, symbol of white America's racial obtuseness.

Fergusson, Francis. "Prometheus at Yale." NYRB, 3 August 1967, pp. 30-32.

Finds PROMETHEUS BOUND filled with a trendy resentment against authority.

Ferlita, Ernest. THE THEATRE OF PILGRIMAGE. New York: Sheed and Ward, 1971.

The abuse of biblical language by the Boston patriots in MY KINSMAN, MAJOR MOLINEUX typifies the interpenetration of good and evil in America's history. See pages 137-49.

Hochman, Baruch. "Robert Lowell's THE OLD GLORY." TDR, 11 (Summer 1967), 127-38.

Argues that the plays, while seemingly historical, are actually ahistorical studies of human barbarism and futility.

Hoffman, Daniel. "Robert Lowell's NEAR THE OCEAN: The Greatness and Honor of Empire." HOLLINS CRITIC, 4 (February 1967), 1-18.

Reviewing Lowell's recent writing, this is an extremely perceptive exploration of Lowell's use of his sources in PHAEDRA and OLD GLORY.

Ilson, Robert. "Benito Cereno from Melville to Lowell." SALMAGUNDI, 1, no. 4 (1966-1967), 78-86.

Useful notes on the changes Lowell has made in adapting Melville, focusing on Delano's character, politics, and the endings of the novella and the play.

Knauf, David. "Notes on Mystery, Suspense, and Complicity: Lowell's Theatricalization of Melville's BENITO CERENO." ETJ, 27 (March 1975), 40-55.

Excellent study of what is uniquely Lowell's in his adaptation of Melville.

Mazzaro, Jerome. "Robert Lowell's THE OLD GLORY: Cycle and Epicycle." WESTERN HUMANITIES REVIEW, 24 (Autumn 1970), 347-58.

_____. "National and Individual Psychohistory in Robert Lowell's ENDICOTT AND THE RED CROSS." UNIVERSITY OF WINDSOR REVIEW, 8 (Fall 1972), 99-113.

_____. "The Classicism of Robert Lowell's PHAEDRA." COMPARATIVE DRAMA, 7 (Summer 1973), 87-106.

Lowell's changes are interpreted to reveal his conception of classicism, and the presence in the play of Lowell's poetic and personal preoccupations.

_____. "PROMETHEUS BOUND: Robert Lowell and Aeschylus." COMPARATIVE DRAMA, 7 (Winter 1973-74), 278-90.

Price, Jonathan. "Jonathan Miller Directs PROMETHEUS." YT, 1 (Spring 1968), 40-50.

Behind the scenes at the first production.

Raizis, M. Byron. "Robert Lowell's PROMETHEUS BOUND." PAPERS ON LANGUAGE AND LITERATURE, 5, Supplement (Summer 1969), 154-68.

PROMETHEUS as "the tragedy of the modern intellectual per excellence."

Simon, John. "Abuse of Privilege: Lowell as Translator." HR, 20 (Winter 1967-68), 543-62.

Primarily about IMITATORS; PROMETHEUS BOUND suffers from being about nothing in particular.

Spurling, Hilary. "Poet Bites Poet." SPECTATOR, 17 March 1967, pp. 314-15.

Calls Lowell's version of BENITO CERENO a botched burglary of Melville.

Steiner, George. "Two Translations." KR, 23 (Autumn 1961), 714-18.

Lowell's PHAEDRA is a variation on themes from Racine, not a translation. See Eric Bentley's and Albert Bermel's comments in the next issue.

Weales, Gerald. "Robert Lowell as Dramatist." SH, 20 (Autumn 1968), 3-28.

Excellent, detailed consideration of PHAEDRA and OLD GLORY, most of which is to be found also in Weales's THE JUMPING OFF PLACE (New York: Macmillan, 1969). Characteristic of Weales is his note on Farrar, Straus and Giroux's sloppy text for OLD GLORY.

Yankowitz, Susan. "Robert Lowell's BENITO CERENO: An Investigation of American Innocence." YT, 1 (Summer 1968), 81-90.

# CHARLES LUDLAM ( - )

BLUEBEARD. In MORE PLAYS FROM OFF OFF BROADWAY. Ed. Michael Smith. Indianapolis: Bobbs-Merrill, 1972.

EUNUCHS OF THE FORBIDDEN CITY. SCRIPTS, 6 (April 1972).

## COLLABORATIONS

TURDS IN HELL. TDR, 14 (September 1970), 110-34.

In collaboration with Bill Vehr.

## CRITICISM

Gottfried, Martin. "Charles Ludlam." In CONTEMPORARY DRAMATISTS. Ed. James Vinson. London: St. James; New York: St. Martin's, 1973, pp. 487-88.

"As a manager, director, actor and playwright, he is doubtless the contemporary theatre person of whom Shakespeare would have been fondest."

# PETER LUKE (1919- )

HADRIAN THE SEVENTH. In PLAYS OF THE YEAR 33. Ed. J.C. Trewin. London: Elek Books, 1967.

Based on HADRIAN THE SEVENTH (1904) and other works by Frederick Rolfe (Baron Corvo).

THE PLAY OF HADRIAN THE SEVENTH. London: Andre Deutsch, 1968.

HADRIAN THE SEVENTH. New York: Knopf, 1969.

Despite the differences in titling, the play remains the same. Herbert Weinstock's introduction has a charm that is somewhat reminiscent of A.J. Symons' splendid classic, THE QUEST FOR CORVO.

## SELECTED NONDRAMATIC WRITING

"Peter Luke Used to Be a Television Producer, Then He Escaped." LISTENER, 12 September 1968, pp. 325-26.

Fond reminiscences of the BBC drama department.

## CRITICISM

Roose-Evans, James. "Peter Luke." In CONTEMPORARY DRAMATISTS. Ed. James Vinson. London: St. James; New York: St. Martin's, 1973, pp. 490-91.

The director of the first production of HADRIAN discusses Luke and the play.

# MICHAEL McCLURE (1932- )

THE GROWL. ER, 8 (April-May 1964), 75-76 ff.

THE BEARD. N.p., 1965.

A private printing, in the Library of Harvard University.

THE BEARD. Rev. ed. New York: Grove Press, 1967.

The controversial two-character play about Billy the Kid and Jean Harlow, with an introduction by Norman Mailer.

THE BLOSSOM; OR, BILLY THE KID. Milwaukee: Great Lakes Books, 1967.

THE SHELL. London: Cape Goliard, 1968.

LITTLE ODES & THE RAPTORS: POEMS AND A PLAY. Los Angeles: Black Sparrow, 1969.

THE CHERUB. Los Angeles: Black Sparrow, 1970.

GARGOYLE CARTOONS; OR, THE CHARBROILED CHINCHILLA. New York: Delacorte Press, 1971.

Collection including THE SHELL, THE PANSY, THE MEATBALL, THE BOW, SPIDER RABBIT, APPLE GLOVE, THE SAIL, THE DEAR, THE AUTHENTIC RADIO LIFE OF BRUCE CONNER AND SNOUTBURBLER, THE FEATHER, and THE CHERUB, most dating from the late sixties.

THE MAMMALS. San Francisco: Cranium Press, 1972.

Includes THE BLOSSOM, THE FEAST, and THE PILLOW.

## BIBLIOGRAPHY

Clements, Michael, ed. A CATALOGUE OF WORKS BY MICHAEL McCLURE, 1956-1965. New York: Phoenix Book Shop, 1965.

## SELECTED NONDRAMATIC WRITING

MEAT SCIENCE ESSAYS. San Francisco: City Lights Books, 1963.

MEAT SCIENCE ESSAYS. 2nd ed., enl. San Francisco: City Lights Books, 1966.

THE SERMONS OF JEAN HARLOW AND THE CURSES OF BILLY THE KID. San Francisco: Four Seasons Foundation, 1968.

## CRITICISM

Fadiman, Regina. "Of Mammals and Men: A Study of Means and Ends in THE BEARD." NTM, 10 (Winter 1969-70), 10-16.

> McClure affirms the primacy of the fleshy, violent, animal reality of man through a variety of sophisticated techniques, but does not explore this basic paradox.

Gilman, Richard. "The Beard." In his COMMON AND UNCOMMON MASKS: WRITINGS ON THEATRE 1961-1970. New York: Random House, 1971, pp. 183-87.

# CARSON McCULLERS (1917-1967)

THE MEMBER OF THE WEDDING. New York: New Directions, 1951.

THE SQUARE ROOT OF WONDERFUL. Boston: Houghton Mifflin, 1958.

## BIBLIOGRAPHY

Salem, James M., ed. A GUIDE TO CRITICAL REVIEWS. Part 1: AMERICAN DRAMA, 1909-1969. 2nd ed. Metuchen, N.J.: Scarecrow Press, 1973.

List of reviews, page 303.

## SELECTED NONDRAMATIC WRITING

THE BALLAD OF THE SAD CAFE; THE NOVELS AND STORIES OF CARSON McCULLERS. Boston: Houghton Mifflin, 1951.

The title story is the basis for the Albee play.

CLOCK WITHOUT HANDS. Boston: Houghton Mifflin, 1961.

Novel.

SWEET AS A PICKLE AND CLEAN AS A PIG. Boston: Houghton Mifflin, 1964.

Poetry.

## CRITICISM

Carr, Virginia Spencer. THE LONELY HUNTER: A BIOGRAPHY OF CARSON McCULLERS. Garden City, N.Y.: Doubleday, 1975.

Lengthy, sympathetic, not very critical biography.

Hamilton, Alice. "Loneliness and Alienation: The Work of Carson McCullers." DR, 50 (Summer 1970), 215-29.

Phillips, Louis. "The Novelist as Playwright: Baldwin, McCullers, and Bellow." In MODERN AMERICAN DRAMA: ESSAYS IN CRITICISM. Ed. William E. Taylor. Deland, Fla.: Everett-Edwards, 1968, pp. 145-62.

Williams, Tennessee. "This Book." Introduction to REFLECTIONS IN A GOLDEN EYE. By Carson McCullers. New York: New Directions, 1950.

Williams defends his friend against criticism, while explaining the characteristics of the southern Gothic writer.

# JOHN McGRATH (1935- )

EVENTS WHILE GUARDING THE BOFORS GUN. London: Methuen, 1966.

PLUGGED IN. P&P, 20 (November 1972), 39-50.

Three one-act plays: ANGEL OF THE MORNING, PLUGGED IN TO HISTORY, and THEY'RE KNOCKING DOWN THE PIE-SHOP.

RANDOM HAPPENINGS IN THE HEBRIDES; OR, THE SOCIAL DEMOCRAT AND THE STORMY SEA. London: Davis-Poynter, 1972.

BAKKE'S NIGHT OF FAME. London: Davis-Poynter, 1973.

Adapted from William Butler's novel, A DANISH GAMBIT (1966).

## CRITICISM

Hayman, Ronald. "John McGrath." In CONTEMPORARY DRAMATISTS. Ed. James Vinson. London: St. James; New York: St. Martin's, 1973, pp. 525-27.

## ARCHIBALD MacLEISH (1892- )

THE TROJAN HORSE. Boston: Houghton Mifflin, 1952.

"This play is intended for reading without scenery, or for radio."

THIS MUSIC CREPT BY ME UPON THE WATERS. BO, no. 11 (1953), 172-225.

THIS MUSIC CREPT BY ME UPON THE WATERS. Cambridge, Mass.: Harvard University Press, 1953.

J.B.: THE PROLOGUE TO THE PLAY. SATURDAY REVIEW OF LITERATURE, 34 (1 September 1956), 7-10.

This is from the work in progress; it is substantially revised in the first book publication.

J.B.: A PLAY IN VERSE. Boston: Houghton Mifflin, 1958.

J.B.: A PLAY IN VERSE. TA, 44 (February 1960), 33-64.

This, the final stage version, differs from the book text, particularly in the last scene, introduced on Broadway.

THE SECRET OF FREEDOM. ES, October 1959, pp. 153-54 ff.

THE SECRET OF FREEDOM. In THREE SHORT PLAYS: THE SECRET OF FREEDOM, AIR RAID, THE FALL OF THE CITY. New York: Dramatists Play Service, 1961.

The last two are radio plays of the thirties also by MacLeish.

OUR LIVES, OUR FORTUNES, AND OUR SACRED HONOR. THINK, 27 (July-August 1961), 2-23.

Written for the IBM magazine, July 4, 1961 issue, using the actual words of Adams, Jefferson, and others.

AN EVENING'S JOURNEY TO CONWAY, MASSACHUSETTS: AN OUTDOOR PLAY. Northhampton, Mass.: Gehenna Press, 1967.

AN EVENING'S JOURNEY TO CONWAY, MASSACHUSETTS: AN OUTDOOR PLAY. New York: Grossman, 1967.

"Written for the bicentennial of the Town of Conway, 1767-1967."

HERAKLES: A PLAY IN VERSE. Boston: Houghton Mifflin, 1967.

SCRATCH. Boston: Houghton Mifflin, 1971.

Based on Stephen Vincent Benet's "The Devil and Daniel Webster" (1937).

## BIBLIOGRAPHY

Mullaly, Edward J., ed. ARCHIBALD MacLEISH: A CHECKLIST. Kent, Ohio: Kent State University Press, 1973.

Lists MacLeish's works, with an excellent, full, annotated bibliography of criticism.

Salem, James M., ed. A GUIDE TO CRITICAL REVIEWS. Part 1: AMERICAN DRAMA, 1909-1969. 2nd ed. Metuchen, N.J.: Scarecrow Press, 1973.

A list of reviews, pages 308-10.

## SELECTED NONDRAMATIC WRITING

"The Poet as Playwright." ATLANTIC MONTHLY, 195 (February 1955), 49-52.

Poetry in the drama must express action.

"About a Trespass on a Monument." NEW YORK TIMES, 7 December 1958, Sec. 2, p. 5 ff.

On J.B.

Kazan, Elia, and Archibald MacLeish. "The Staging of a Play: The Notebooks and Letters behind Elia Kazan's Staging of Archibald MacLeish's J.B." ES, 51 (May 1959), 144-58.

## CRITICISM

Brustein, Robert. "The Theatre of Middle Seriousness." HARPER'S, March 1959, pp. 60-63.

J.B. is a popular, painless justification of American capitalism.

Campbell, Shannon O. "The Book of Job and MacLeish's J.B." ENGLISH JOURNAL, 61 (May 1972), 653-57.

Donoghue, Denis. THE THIRD VOICE: MODERN BRITISH AND AMERICAN VERSE DRAMA. Princeton, N.J.: Princeton University Press, 1959.

Defends J.B. as more Aristotelian than THIS MUSIC CREPT BY ME ON THE WATERS, which is a "mood play." See pages 195-212.

Eberhart, Richard. "Outer and Inner Verse Drama." VIRGINIA QUARTERLY REVIEW, 34 (Autumn 1958), 618-23.

On J.B. as plot and action, as well as language.

Falk, Signi Lenea. ARCHIBALD MacLEISH. New York: Twayne, 1965.

The only full-length study of MacLeish.

Gassner, John. "Broadway in Review." ETJ, 11 (March 1959), 29-32.

Interesting analysis of the differences between the Broadway-Kazan production of J.B. and the published text.

Gerstenberger, Donna. "Three Verse Playwrights and the American Fifties." In MODERN AMERICAN DRAMA: ESSAYS IN CRITICISM. Ed. William E. Taylor. Deland, Fla.: Everett-Edwards, 1968, pp. 117-28.

Despite the title, little social analysis.

MacLeish, Andrew. "The Poet's Three Comforters: J.B. and the Critics." MD, 2 (December 1959), 224-30.

Defends the play against those critics who see it as attempting to add to the Book of Job. Instead, he argues, the play uses it as a frame for a parable of man in the Christian tradition.

Marcus, S. "Power of the Audience." COMMENTARY, 18 (August 1954), 172-75.

On THIS MUSIC CREPT BY ME ON THE WATERS.

Sickels, Eleanor M. "MacLeish and the Fortunate Fall." AL, 35 (May 1963), 205-17.

The lost paradise existed in MacLeish's work long before J.B. There it receives its most affirmative statement.

Siegel, Ben. "Miracle on Broadway: And the Box-Office Magic of the Bible." MD, 2 (May 1959), 45-46.

A tongue-in-cheek account of J.B.'s Broadway success.

# JACKSON MAC LOW (1922- )

VERDUROUS SANGUINARIA: ACT 1. TDR, 10 (Winter 1965), 119-22.

Part of the "happenings" issue of TDR, with a brief explanatory note.

TWIN PLAYS: PORT-AU-PRINCE AND ADAMS COUNTY ILLINOIS. New York: Something Else Press, 1966.

## SELECTED NONDRAMATIC WRITING

MANIFESTOS. New York: Something Else Press, 1966.

22 LIGHT POEMS. Los Angeles: Black Sparrow Press, 1968.

## CRITICISM

Higgins, Dick. "Jackson Mac Low." In CONTEMPORARY DRAMATISTS. Ed. James Vinson. London: St. James; New York: St. Martin's, 1973, pp. 499-501.

"In recent years Jackson Mac Low has been recognized as America's leading dramatist of the aleatoric school...."

# TERRENCE McNALLY (1939- )

THE ROLLER COASTER. COLUMBIA REVIEW, 40 (Spring 1960), 42-60.

Unproduced undergraduate effort.

AND THINGS THAT GO BUMP IN THE NIGHT. In PLAYWRIGHTS FOR TOMORROW: A COLLECTION OF PLAYS. Vol. 1. Ed. Arthur H. Ballet. Minneapolis: University of Minnesota Press, 1966.

SWEET EROS. YT, 1 (Winter 1968), 41-50.

TOUR. In COLLISION COURSE. Ed. Edward Parone. New York: Random House, 1968.

NOON. In MORNING, NOON, AND NIGHT. With Israel Horovitz and Leonard Melfi. New York: Random House, 1969.

SWEET EROS, NEXT, AND OTHER PLAYS. New York: Random House, 1969.

Also includes BOTTICELLI, I CUBA SI!

THREE PLAYS: i CUBA SI!, BRING IT ALL BACK HOME, LAST GASPS. New York: Dramatists Play Service, 1970.

WHERE HAS TOMMY FLOWERS GONE? New York: Dramatists Play Service, 1972.

WHISKEY: A ONE-ACT PLAY. New York: Dramatists Play Service, 1973.

BAD HABITS. New York: Dramatists Play Service, 1974.

## COLLECTIONS

APPLE PIE. New York: Dramatists Play Service, 1969.

Consists of NEXT, TOUR, and BOTTICELLI.

## BIBLIOGRAPHY

Salem, James M., ed. A GUIDE TO CRITICAL REVIEWS. Part 1: AMERICAN DRAMA, 1909-1969. 2nd ed. Metuchen, N.J.: Scarecrow Press, 1973.

List of reviews, pages 311-13.

## CRITICISM

Simon, John. UNEASY STAGES. New York: Random House, 1975, pp. 81-82, 188-89.

THINGS THAT GO BUMP IN THE NIGHT is an overtly homosexual play filled with hysterical ugliness. NEXT is a brief, brilliant, and touching play.

# NORMAN MAILER (1923- )

THE DEER PARK (Scenes 2, 3, 4). In ADVERTISEMENTS FOR MYSELF. New York: Putnam, 1959.

ADVERTISEMENTS also contains BUDDIES; OR, IN THE HOLE AT THE SUMMIT: A FRAGMENT OF A ONE-ACT PLAY.

"Scenes from THE DEER PARK." PR, 26 (Fall 1959), 527-34.

Scenes 7 and 10.

THE DEER PARK: A PLAY. New York: Dial Press, 1967.

A reworking of the 1955 novel about Hollywood. Mailer's introduction is interesting, if only because it comes from one of our leading nondramatists; it is a plea for more complex theatre and a denunciation of what Mailer calls "Cactus Flower" drama.

## BIBLIOGRAPHY

Adams, Laura, comp. NORMAN MAILER: A COMPREHENSIVE BIBLIOGRAPHY. Introd. Robert F. Lucid. Metuchen, N.J.: Scarecrow Press, 1974.

Salem, James M., ed. A GUIDE TO CRITICAL REVIEWS. Part 1: AMERICAN DRAMA, 1909-1969. 2nd ed. Metuchen, N.J.: Scarecrow Press, 1973.

A listing of the reviews, page 313, for THE DEER PARK.

## CRITICISM

Kerr, Walter. "Believing." In his THIRTY PLAYS HATH NOVEMBER: PAIN AND PLEASURE IN THE CONTEMPORARY THEATER. New York: Simon and Schuster, 1968, pp. 237-41.

THE DEER PARK is a negative example of the need for believable, sympathetic characters.

Poirier, Richard. NORMAN MAILER. New York: Viking, 1972.

Thompson, John. "Catching Up on Mailer." NYRB, 20 April 1967, pp. 14-16.

Weales, Gerald. "The Park in the Playhouse." In WILL THE REAL NORMAN MAILER PLEASE STAND UP? Ed. Laura Adams. Port Washington, N.Y.: Kennikat Press, 1974.

In an excellent collection depicting the many careers of Norman Mailer, Weales reviews the New York production of DEER PARK, and finds the play garrulous, over-plotted, and hard to take seriously.

## WOLF MANKOWITZ (1924- )

THE BESPOKE OVERCOAT. London: Evans Bros., 1954.

FIVE ONE-ACT PLAYS. London: Evans Bros., 1955.

THE BESPOKE OVERCOAT, THE BABY, IT SHOULD HAPPEN TO A DOG, THE LAST OF THE CHEESECAKE, and THE MIGHTY HUNTER.

### COLLABORATION WITH JULIAN MORE

EXPRESSO BONGO: A MUSICAL PLAY. London: Evans Bros., 1960.

From an original story by Wolf Mankowitz, with the book by Wolf Mankowitz and Julian More and music and lyrics by David Heneker and Monty Norman. Production notes by William Chappell.

### SELECTED NONDRAMATIC WRITING

MAKE ME AN OFFER. London: Andre Deutsch, 1952.

Novel.

A KID FOR TWO FARTHINGS. London: Andre Deutsch, 1953.

Novel.

EXPRESSO BONGO: A WOLF MANKOWITZ READER. New York: Yoseloff, 1961.

### CRITICISM

Metcalf, John. "Wolf Mankowitz." ATLANTIC MONTHLY, 198 (October 1956), 86-88.

Praises Mankowitz' realism and irreverence.

Taylor, John Russell. "Wolf Mankowitz and the Cockney Improvisers." In his ANGER AND AFTER: A GUIDE TO THE NEW BRITISH DRAMA. Rev. ed. Harmondsworth, Engl.: Penguin, 1963, pp. 121-22.

The "simplicity and truth of THE BESPOKE OVERCOAT are by now, it seems, gone quite beyond recall."

# FRANK MARCUS (1928- )

THE FORMATION DANCERS. London: Elek Books, 1964.

THE KILLING OF SISTER GEORGE. London: Hamish Hamilton, 1965.

CLEO AND MAX. LONDON MAGAZINE, n.s. 5 (February 1966), 55-64.

THE WINDOW. London: Samuel French, 1968.

MRS. MOUSE, ARE YOU WITHIN? P&P, 15 (July 1968), 29-44 ff.

MRS. MOUSE, ARE YOU WITHIN? In PLAYS OF THE YEAR 35. Ed. J.C. Trewin. London: Elek Books, 1969.

NOTES ON A LOVE AFFAIR. P&P, 19 (July 1972), 35-50.

BLANK PAGES: A MONOLOGUE. London: Samuel French, 1973.

NOTES ON A LOVE AFFAIR. In PLAYS OF THE YEAR 42. Ed. J.C. Trewin. London: Elek Books, 1973.

## SELECTED NONDRAMATIC WRITING

"Unity to West End." P&P, 11 (June 1964), 17-18.

Introduces THE FORMATION DANCERS.

"I Ask Myself." In BEHIND THE SCENES: THEATER AND FILM INTERVIEWS FROM THE TRANSATLANTIC REVIEW. Ed. Joseph F.M. McCrindle, introd. Jean-Claude van Itallie. New York: Holt, Rinehart and Winston, 1971, pp. 149-54.

Brief auto-interview on influences on his work and the censor.

## CRITICISM

Young, B.A. "Frank Marcus." In CONTEMPORARY DRAMATISTS. Ed. James Vinson. London: St. James; New York: St. Martin's, 1973, pp. 508-09.

On Marcus' sympathetic portrayals of women.

# ELAINE MAY (1932- )

NOT ENOUGH ROPE. New York: Samuel French, 1964.

ADAPTATION. New York: Dramatists Play Service, 1971.

## BIBLIOGRAPHY

Salem, James M., ed. A GUIDE TO CRITICAL REVIEWS. Part 1: AMERICAN DRAMA, 1909-1969. 2nd ed. Metuchen, N.J.: Scarecrow Press, 1973.

A list of reviews for NOT ENOUGH ROPE. See pages 316-17.

# MURRAY MEDNICK (1939- )

THE HUNTER. Indianapolis: Bobbs-Merrill, 1969.

Illustrated by Domenick Capobianco.

THE DEER KILL. Indianapolis: Bobbs-Merrill, 1972.

CARTOON AND OTHER PLAYS. Indianapolis: Bobbs-Merrill, 1973.

Also includes THE MARK OF ZORRO, GUIDELINE, SAND, and WILLIE THE GERM.

THE SHADOW RIPENS. Indianapolis: Bobbs-Merrill, 1973.

## COLLABORATION WITH TONY BARSHA

KEYSTONE'S THE HAWK: AN IMPROVISATION PLAY. Indianapolis: Bobbs-Merrill, 1968.

## CRITICISM

Simon, John. UNEASY STAGES. New York: Random House, 1975, pp. 403-06.

The critical praise for THE HUNTER is an example of baffled critics not wanting to be considered old fogies.

Smith, Michael. "Murray Mednick." In CONTEMPORARY DRAMATISTS. Ed. James Vinson. London: St. James; New York: St. Martin's, 1973, pp. 530-31.

Murray Mednick is one of the most important younger American dramatists.

# LEONARD MELFI (1935- )

ENCOUNTERS: 6 ONE-ACT PLAYS. New York: Random House, 1967.

BIRDBATH, LUNCHTIME, HALLOWEEN, FERRYBOAT, THE SHIRT, and TIMES SQUARE.

STARS AND STRIPES. In COLLISION COURSE. Ed. Edward Parone. New York: Random House, 1968.

JACK AND JILL. In OH! CALCUTTA!: AN ENTERTAINMENT WITH MUSIC. New York: Grove Press, 1969.

NIGHT. In MORNING, NOON, AND NIGHT. With Israel Horovitz and Terrence McNally. New York: Random House, 1969.

NIAGRA FALLS. In NEW THEATRE FOR NOW. Ed. Edward Parone. New York: Dell, 1971.

CINQUE. In SPONTANEOUS COMBUSTION: EIGHT NEW AMERICAN PLAYS. Ed. Rochelle Owens. New York: Winter House, 1972.

## BIBLIOGRAPHY

Salem, James M., ed. A GUIDE TO CRITICAL REVIEWS. Part 1: AMERICAN DRAMA, 1909-1969. 2nd ed. Metuchen, N.J.: Scarecrow Press, 1973.

List of reviews for Melfi's plays, page 318.

## DAVID MERCER (1928-1980)

THE GOVERNOR'S LADY. STAND, 4 (Spring 1962).

Radio version.

THE GOVERNOR'S LADY. P&P, 12 (April 1965), 25-30.

THE GENERATIONS: A TRILOGY OF PLAYS. London: John Calder, 1964.

Although the first was originally written for the stage, these are three plays for television: WHERE THE DIFFERENCE BEGINS, A CLIMATE OF FEAR, and THE BIRTH OF A PRIVATE MAN.

RIDE A COCK HORSE. London: Calder and Boyars, 1966.

THREE T.V. COMEDIES. London: Calder and Boyars, 1966.

A SUITABLE CASE FOR TREATMENT (made into the 1966 film MORGANO, FOR TEA ON SUNDAY, and AND DID THOSE FEET.

BELCHER'S LUCK. London: Calder and Boyars, 1967.

THE PARACHUTE. WITH TWO MORE T.V. PLAYS: LET'S MURDER VIVALDI, IN TWO MINDS. London: Calder and Boyars, 1967.

THE GOVERNOR'S LADY. London: Methuen, 1968.

AFTER HAGGARTY. London: Methuen, 1970.

FLINT. London: Methuen, 1970.

ON THE EVE OF PUBLICATION AND OTHER PLAYS. London: Methuen, 1970.

Includes THE CELLAR AND THE ALMOND TREE and EMMA'S TIME.

THE BANKRUPT, AND OTHER PLAYS. London: Eyre Methuen, 1974.

Also includes YOU AND ME AND HIM, AN AFTERNOON AT THE FESTIVAL, and FIND ME.

DUCK SONG. London: Eyre Methuen, 1974.

## BIBLIOGRAPHY

Jarman, Francis, John Noyes, and Malcolm Page, comps. THE QUALITY OF MERCER: A BIBLIOGRAPHY. Brighton, Engl.: Smoothie Publications, 1974.

## SELECTED NONDRAMATIC WRITING

THE LONG CRAWL THROUGH TIME. In NEW WRITERS 3. London: John Calder, 1965.

"Birth of a Playwrighting Man." TQ, 3 (January-March 1973), p. 43-55.

An interview with the editors of TQ and Francis Jarman in which Mercer talks about his experiences as a pathology-lab technician doing post-mortems, about politics, and about his writing for television.

## CRITICISM

"David Mercer Interviewed by Giles Gordon." In BEHIND THE SCENES: THEATER AND FILM INTERVIEWS FROM THE TRANSATLANTIC REVIEW. Ed. Joseph F.M. McCrindle, introd. Jean-Claude van Itallie. New York: Holt, Rinehart and Winston, 1971, pp. 88-98.

On BELCHER'S LUCK, R.D. Laing, politics, and intellectuals.

Taylor, John Russell. "David Mercer." In THE SECOND WAVE. London: Methuen, 1971, pp. 36-58.

The drive for individuality is the underlying theme of all of Mercer's plays.

Worth, Katharine J. "Realism in New Directions: Arnold Wesker, David Storey, David Mercer." In her REVOLUTIONS IN MODERN ENGLISH DRAMA. London: G. Bell, 1973, pp. 40-44.

On Mercer's mixture of farce and realism.

## W[ILLIAM] S[TANLEY] MERWIN (1927- )

EUFEMIA. TDR, 3 (December 1958), 57-79.

Translation of Lope de Rueda (1567).

THE FALSE CONFESSION. In THE CLASSIC THEATRE. Vol. 4. Ed. Eric Bentley. Garden City, N.Y.: Doubleday, 1961.

Translation of Marivaux (1737).

TURCARET. In THE CLASSIC THEATRE. Vol. 4. Ed. Eric Bentley. Garden City, N.Y.: Doubleday, 1961.

Translation of Lesage (1709).

THE RIVAL OF HIS MASTER. TDR, 6 (June 1962), 130-55.

Translation of Lesage (1707).

### CRITICISM

Hoffman, Daniel. "The Gift of Tongues: W.S. Merwin's Poems and Translations." HC, 5 (June 1968), 1-12.

Howard, Richard. "W.S. Merwin." In his ALONE WITH AMERICA: ESSAYS ON THE ART OF POETRY IN THE UNITED STATES SINCE 1950. New York: Atheneum, 1971, pp. 349-81.

## RONALD MILLAR (1919- )

WAITING GILLIAN. London: Samuel French, 1954.

From the novel A WAY THROUGH THE WOOD by Nigel Balchin (1951).

THE BRIDE AND THE BACHELOR: A FARCICAL COMEDY IN THREE ACTS. London: Samuel French, 1958.

A TICKLISH BUSINESS: A LIGHT COMEDY IN THREE ACTS. London: Samuel French, 1959.

THE MORE THE MERRIER. London: Samuel French, 1960.

THE BRIDE COMES BACK. London: Samuel French, 1961.

Sequel to the successful THE BRIDE AND THE BACHELOR.

THE AFFAIR. London: Samuel French; New York: Charles Scribner, 1962.

From the novel by C.P. Snow (1960).

THE AFFAIR, THE NEW MEN, THE MASTERS: THREE PLAYS BASED ON THE NOVELS OF C.P. SNOW AND WITH A PREFACE BY C.P. SNOW. London: Macmillan, 1964.

ROBERT AND ELIZABETH. London: Samuel French, 1967.

Music by Ron Grainer. Lyrics and adaptation from Rudolph Besier's THE BARRETTS OF WIMPOLE STREET (1932) by Ronald Miller.

NUMBER 10. London: Heinemann, 1967.

Based on the novel by William Clark.

THEY DON'T GROW ON TREES. London: Samuel French, 1969.

ABELARD AND HELOISE. London: Samuel French, 1970.
Adapted from PETER ABELARD by Helen Wadell (1933).

THE CASE IN QUESTION. London: Samuel French, 1975.
Based on C.P. Snow's novel IN THEIR WISDOM (1974).

## CRITICISM

Dennis, Nigel. "Under the Combination Room." In his DRAMATIC ESSAYS. London: Weidenfeld and Nicolson, 1962, pp. 167-70.

THE AFFAIR "shows where professors go when they die."

# ARTHUR MILLER (1915- )

AN ENEMY OF THE PEOPLE. New York: Viking, 1951.

A liberalizing adaptation of the Ibsen play (1882), with a preface.

THE CRUCIBLE. New York: Viking, 1953.

THE CRUCIBLE. TA, 37 (October 1953), 35-67.

Contains an additional scene between Procter and Abigail, placed before the act 3 courtroom scene.

A VIEW FROM THE BRIDGE: TWO ONE-ACT PLAYS. New York: Viking, 1955.

Contains the verse, one-act version of A VIEW FROM THE BRIDGE, and A MEMORY OF TWO MONDAYS, with "On Social Plays" as a preface.

A VIEW FROM THE BRIDGE. In ARTHUR MILLER'S COLLECTED PLAYS. With introd. New York: Viking, 1957.

This is the revised, two-act version in prose of A VIEW, written for Peter Brook's 1956 London production. The introduction details the circumstances of the revision.

AFTER THE FALL. SATURDAY EVENING POST, 1 February 1964, pp. 32-59.

With a foreword by Miller and photographs from the original production by Inge Morath.

AFTER THE FALL. New York: Viking, 1964.

Differs only slightly from the magazine version.

AFTER THE FALL. Rev. Final Stage Version. New York: Viking, 1964.

After the rocky reception of the first production, Miller revised the text substantially. As Leonard Moss, in ARTHUR MILLER (New York: Twayne, 1967), p. 128, notes, this text includes "extensive deletion, rephrasing and rearrangement."

INCIDENT AT VICHY. New York: Viking, 1965.

THE PRICE. New York: Viking, 1968.

FAME. YALE LITERARY MAGAZINE, 140 (March 1971).

THE CREATION OF THE WORLD AND OTHER BUSINESS. New York: Viking, 1972.

## MANUSCRIPTS

Both the Library of Congress and the Research Center Library at the University of Texas posess Miller manuscripts and drafts. Both have early versions of THE CRUCIBLE and A VIEW FROM THE BRIDGE called, respectively, THOSE FAMILIAR SPIRITS, and FAR FROM THE SEA.

## COLLECTIONS

ARTHUR MILLER'S COLLECTED PLAYS. With introd. New York: Viking, 1957.

ALL MY SONS, DEATH OF A SALESMAN, THE CRUCIBLE, A MEMORY OF TWO MONDAYS, and the revised version of A VIEW FROM THE BRIDGE.

THE CRUCIBLE: TEXT AND CRITICISM. Ed. Gerald Weales. New York: Viking, 1971.

This estimable critical edition contains an excellent selection of contemporary reviews, subsequent criticism, historical sources, and literary parallels. Also included is the interpolated scene between Procter and Abigail, with a useful explanatory note.

## BIBLIOGRAPHY

Eissenstat, Martha Turnquist, ed. "Arthur Miller: A Bibliography." MD, 5 (May 1962), 93-106.

Unannotated, preponderantly reviews, with some serious omissions.

Hayashi, Tetsumaro, ed. ARTHUR MILLER CRITICISM: 1930-1967. Metuchen, N.J.: Scarecrow Press, 1969.

A bibliographical debacle that includes works by two other Arthur Millers, one a British playwright and the other a Hollywood cameraman. For a more detailed examination of this embarrassment, see Robert A. Martin's review in MD, 14 (December 1971), 448-49. The best Miller bibliography now available is Leonard Moss's in his ARTHUR MILLER (New York: Twayne, 1967), under CRITICISM below.

Salem, James M., ed. A GUIDE TO CRITICAL REVIEWS. Part 1: AMERICAN DRAMA, 1909-1969. 2nd ed. Metuchen, N.J.: Scarecrow Press, 1973.

List of reviews, pages 321-28.

## SELECTED NONDRAMATIC WRITING

"Journey to THE CRUCIBLE." NEW YORK TIMES, 8 February 1953, sec. 2, pp. 1, 3.

"A Boy Grew in Brooklyn." HOLIDAY, 17 (March 1955), 54-55 ff.

"On Social Plays." A VIEW FROM THE BRIDGE: TWO ONE-ACT PLAYS. New York: Viking, 1955.

Miller's major statement on drama and society.

"The Playwright and the Atomic World." COLORADO QUARTERLY, no. 5 (1956), 117-37. Rpt. in TDR, 5 (June 1961), 3-20.

A good example of Miller's well-intentioned, but ill-focused political writing.

"Introduction." ARTHUR MILLER'S COLLECTED PLAYS. New York: Viking, 1957, pp. 3-55.

Miller's most thorough and interesting examination of his own works; this is an invaluable source.

"Morality and Modern Drama." ETJ, 10 (October 1958), 190-202.

Transcript of a wide-ranging radio interview with Philip Gelb that gives us Miller on Shaw, Williams, and his own plays, especially DEATH OF A SALESMAN and THE CRUCIBLE.

THE MISFITS. New York: Viking, 1961.

Written in a style that is half screenplay and half novella, this is

Miller's redaction of the film that starred Marilyn Monroe and Clark Gable. The screenplay is based on Miller's short story, "The Misfits," from ESQUIRE, 48 (October 1957), 158-66.

"With Respect for Her Agony--but with Love." LIFE, 7 February 1964, p. 66.

Miller defends AFTER THE FALL as more than biography; the false antithesis of the title does not appear to be Miller's.

"Arthur Miller Talks." MICHIGAN QUARTERLY REVIEW, 6 (Summer 1967), 153-84.

Miller explains that there was another version of the interpolated scene in THE CRUCIBLE that has never been published.

I DON'T NEED YOU ANY MORE. New York: Viking, 1967.

Collected short stories.

IN RUSSIA. New York: Viking, 1969.

In collaboration with Inge Morath.

"Arthur Miller and the Meaning of Tragedy." MD, 13 (May 1970), 34-39.

Interviewed by Robert A. Martin, Miller discusses AFTER THE FALL and tragedy.

## CRITICISM

Baxandall, Lee. "Arthur Miller: Still the Innocent." EN, 11 (May-June 1964), 16-19. Also in THE CRUCIBLE: TEXT AND CRITICISM. Ed. Gerald Weales. New York: Viking, 1971, pp. 352-58 (hereafter cited as TEXT, Weales).

Miller and AFTER THE FALL are attacked for a retreat from socialism.

Bentley, Eric. "The American Drama 1944-1954." In his THE THEATRE OF COMMITMENT. New York: Atheneum, 1967, pp. 34-40. Also in his THE DRAMATIC EVENT: AN AMERICAN CHRONICLE. New York: Horizon Press, 1954, pp. 254-58.

In this much-travelled essay, THE CRUCIBLE is seen as symptomatic of liberalism's refusal to acknowledge the existence of communism.

_____. "The Innocence of Arthur Miller." In his WHAT IS THEATRE?; INCORPORATING THE DRAMATIC EVENT AND OTHER REVIEWS, 1944-1967. New York: Atheneum, 1968, pp. 62-65, 453-54. Also in TEXT, Weales, pp. 204-09.

Bentley's review of the original production of THE CRUCIBLE finds that Procter is too much the innocent. He feels that Miller also seems to have missed Elia Kazan's sense of guilt, as well as his directorial talent. THE NEW REPUBLIC, where the review was originally published, dropped nearly two paragraphs from Bentley's text, paragraphs that dealt with the political ironies of Kazan's and Miller's past.

_____. "On the Waterfront." In his WHAT IS THEATRE?: INCORPORATING THE DRAMATIC EVENT AND OTHER REVIEWS, 1944-1967. New York: Atheneum, 1968, pp. 258-61, 463-64.

A VIEW FROM THE BRIDGE is filled with rhetoric; its verse is typographic; its passion is operatic. Its politics, as is often the case with Miller, gets lost in sexual conflict.

_____, ed. THIRTY YEARS OF TREASON: EXCERPTS FROM HEARINGS BEFORE THE HOUSE COMMITTEE ON UN-AMERICAN ACTIVITIES, 1938-68. New York: Viking, 1971, pp. 789-825.

Selections from Miller's 1956 testimony in which he refused to name anyone who attended political meetings with him during the thirties and forties.

Bermel, Albert. "Right, Wrong and Mr. Miller." NEW YORK TIMES, 14 April 1968, sec. 2, pp. 1, 7.

Miller's major characters, who are supposed to be common men, are in fact most uncommon for their remarkable sense of right and wrong. No matter what, Miller's protagonists finally do the right thing. In THE PRICE, despite good reasons to do otherwise, Victor still behaves as an exemplary character.

Bigsby, C.W.E. "What Price Arthur Miller? An Analysis of THE PRICE." TCL, 16 (January 1970), 16-25.

Explains why THE PRICE is an improvement over INCIDENT AT VICHY and AFTER THE FALL.

Blumberg, Paul. "Sociology and Social Literature: Work Alienation in the Plays of Arthur Miller." AMERICAN QUARTERLY, 21 (Summer 1964), 291-310.

On the recurring theme in Miller of work and its alienating effects.

Bronson, David. "AN ENEMY OF THE PEOPLE: A Key to Arthur Miller's Art and Ethics." COMPARATIVE DRAMA, 2 (Winter 1968-69), 229-47.

A valuable, detailed examination of Miller's alterations of Ibsen, especially his reduction of Stockmann into a simple, noble figure.

Clurman, Harold. "Director's Notes: INCIDENT AT VICHY." TDR, 9 (Summer 1965), 77-90.

The director of Miller's play for the Lincoln Center Repertory Company here publishes excerpts from the notebooks from which he directed the play.

Cohn, Ruby. DIALOGUE IN AMERICAN DRAMA. Bloomington: Indiana University Press, 1971.

See pages 68-96.

Driver, Tom F. "Strengths and Weaknesses in Arthur Miller." TDR, 4 (May 1960), 45-52.

After acknowledging Miller's psychological acuteness, Driver expands upon Eric Bentley's criticism of Miller as a liberal optimist, and finds Miller's failure epitomized in his inability to decide whether Willy Loman's fate lies within the man or comes about through external circumstances.

Epstein, Arthur. "A Look at A VIEW FROM THE BRIDGE." TEXAS STUDIES IN LITERATURE AND LANGUAGE, 7 (Spring 1965), 109-22.

"Although Miller considers Eddie a tragic figure, he . . . never had a clearly defined outline of the emotions toward Eddie which he wanted to elicit from his audience."

Evans, Richard Isadore. PSYCHOLOGY AND ARTHUR MILLER. New York: E.P. Dutton, 1969.

These dialogues with a psychologist about the writer, society, and psychology are only very occasionally informative about Miller, his art, or the topics discussed.

Fender, Stephen. "Precision and Pseudo-Precision in THE CRUCIBLE." JOURNAL OF AMERICAN STUDIES, 1 (April 1967), 87-98. Also in TEXT, Weales, pp. 272-89.

Fender finds a conceptual confusion in Puritan theology that Miller, perhaps unawares, recreates quite faithfully. This essay may be seen as a counter to Warshow's influential reading, below.

Ferras, John H., ed. TWENTIETH CENTURY INTERPRETATIONS OF THE CRUCIBLE: A COLLECTION OF CRITICAL ESSAYS. Englewood Cliffs, N.J.: Prentice-Hall, 1972.

Findlater, Richard. "No Time for Tragedy." TWENTIETH CENTURY, 161 (January 1957), 56-66.

A VIEW FROM THE BRIDGE is another of Miller's unsparing attempts at tragedy that makes British drama seem pale. The censoring of the play, because of its sexual content, forcing the Peter Brook production into "club" performances, is absurd. The play's great flaws are that Eddie is simply too unintelligent to know what is happening to him, and that the choral figure of Alfieri is unnecessary.

Ganz, Arthur. "The Silence of Arthur Miller." DS, 3 (October 1963), 224-37.

The failure of THE MISFITS, after the long hiatus since A VIEW FROM THE BRIDGE, reveals basic flaws in Miller's dramatic conceptions; Miller has too simplistic a view of society and of character.

______. "Arthur Miller: After the Silence." DS, 3 (Spring-Fall 1964), 520-30.

For all its problems, AFTER THE FALL shows a new, more complex awareness of human guilt, in sharp contrast to the earlier plays' simplicities.

Goode, James. THE STORY OF THE MISFITS. New York and Indianapolis: Bobbs-Merrill, 1963.

Chatty, uncritical, behind-the-scenes story of the making of the Miller-Monroe-Gable-Huston film.

Hayman, Ronald. ARTHUR MILLER. New York: Frederick Ungar, 1972.

Prefaced with a 1969 interview with Miller, this study devotes a chapter that is largely plot summary to each play, and concludes by emphasizing the formal consequences of Miller's almost Sartrean concern with the results of man's past actions.

Heilman, Robert Bechtold. "Arthur Miller (1915--)." In his THE ICEMAN, THE ARSONIST, AND THE TROUBLED AGENT: TRAGEDY AND MELODRAMA ON THE MODERN STAGE. Seattle: University of Washington Press, 1973, pp. 142-61.

Miller, from THE CRUCIBLE to AFTER THE FALL, seemed to be moving from a melodramatic to a tragic interpretation of experience. But in THE PRICE he reverts to the earlier form.

Huftel, Sheila. ARTHUR MILLER: THE BURNING GLASS. New York: Citadel, 1965.

More an appreciation than criticism.

Koppenhaver, Allen J. "THE FALL and After." MD, 9 (September 1966), 206-09.

AFTER THE FALL is similar in subject and vision to Camus's THE FALL (1956). The same argument is pursued by C.W.E. Bigsby in CONFRONTATION AND COMMITMENT: A STUDY OF CONTEMPORARY AMERICAN DRAMA, 1959-66. Columbia: University of Missouri Press, 1968, pp. 44-46.

Lowenthal, Lawrence D. "Arthur Miller's INCIDENT AT VICHY." MD, 18 (March 1975), 29-41.

INCIDENT AT VICHY is a dramatic rendering of Sartre's ANTI-SEMITE AND JEW (1946).

McCarthy, Mary. "Naming Names: The Arthur Miller Case." In her ON THE CONTRARY: ARTICLES OF BELIEF, 1946-1961. New York: Farrar, Straus and Giroux, 1961, pp. 147-54.

The House Un-American Activities Committee's motive in asking Miller to inform them of what they already knew was to apply a loyalty test, to make informing a standard of good citizenship.

______. "The American Realist Playwrights." In her MARY McCARTHY'S THEATRE CHRONICLES, 1937-1962. New York: Noonday Press, 1963, pp. 209-29.

Realism, as the "depreciation of the real," never satisfies its practitioners, who are continually looking for something beyond the real. A VIEW FROM THE BRIDGE is typical of this paradox. When originally published in ENCOUNTER in July 1961, it was titled, "Americans, Realists, Playwrights."

Moss, Leonard. ARTHUR MILLER. New York: Twayne, 1967.

Excellent study arguing that Miller is at his best as a psychologist and at his weakest as a social and political critic. The volume also contains a very fine bibliography.

Nelson, Benjamin. ARTHUR MILLER: PORTRAIT OF A PLAYWRIGHT. New York: David McKay, 1970.

Traditional critical biography, emphasizing plot summaries and critical evaluations. The book's flaw is its earnestness, accepting an accidental mix-up in a bakery van as an "inkling into the meaning of tragedy" for the adolescent Miller and seeing his education as a "ceaseless, churning process."

Overland, Orm. "The Action and Its Significance: Arthur Miller's Struggle with Dramatic Form." MD, 18 (March 1975), 1-14.

Miller has long struggled to find a dramatic style that will enable him to synthesize the psychological and the social.

Popkin, Henry. "Arthur Miller: Strange Encounter." SR, 68 (Winter 1960), 34-60.

Each of Miller's plays centers on the confrontation between a common man and an extraordinary moral issue; in each case the little man cannot face the big issue.

______. "Arthur Miller's THE CRUCIBLE." CE, 26 (November 1964), 139-46.

Popkin repeats Bentley's argument that Miller's parallel between the atmosphere of Salem and McCarthyism founders because while there were Communists, there were no witches. THE CRUCIBLE succeeds best as a well-planned series of crises in the lives of people we are interested in.

Prudhoe, John. "Arthur Miller and the Tradition of Tragedy." ENGLISH STUDIES, 43 (October 1962), 430-39.

Defends Miller's theories of tragedy and Miller's attempts to find the stylistic means to express those theories.

Rahv, Philip. "Arthur Miller and the Fallacy of Profundity." NYRB, 14 January 1965, pp. 3-4.

The intellectual confusion of INCIDENT AT VICHY is unfortunately typical of America's retreat from political reality into mystification and pseudo-profundity.

Rogoff, Gordon. "Theater." NATION, 10 February 1964, pp. 153-54.

As a play that takes place in the mind of its protagonist, AFTER THE FALL is a failure because it is tediously self-justifying. It is also a gloomy portent for the development of Lincoln Center.

Rovere, Richard H. "Arthur Miller's Conscience." In his THE AMERICAN ESTABLISHMENT AND OTHER REPORTS, OPINIONS AND SPECULATIONS. New York: Harcourt, Brace and World, 1962, pp. 276-81. Also in TEXT, Weales, pp. 315-23.

Miller's refusal to inform before the House Committee reflects a confusion about the nature of social relations. Although Miller's scruples when dealing with this committee are commendable, refusing to inform cannot be raised to a universal legal principle.

Seager, Alan. "The Creative Agony of Arthur Miller." ES, October 1959, pp. 123-26. Also in TEXT, Weales, pp. 326-38.

A friend describes Miller's working methods and reproduces excerpts from Miller's notebooks.

Sontag, Susan. "Going to Theater, etc." In her AGAINST INTERPRETATION AND OTHER ESSAYS. New York: Farrar, Straus and Giroux, 1966, pp. 140-62.

Describes AFTER THE FALL's "intellectual weakmindedness" leading to "moral dishonesty."

Stampler, Henry. THE CRUCIBLE. New York: Highgate Press, 1961.

Stampler's libretto to Robert Ward's music for the Pulitzer Prize opera.

Stinson, John J. "Structure in AFTER THE FALL: The Relevance of the Maggie Episode to the Main Themes and the Christian Symbolism." MD, 10 (December 1967), 233-40.

Defends Miller against the charge that his play exploited the relationship with Marilyn Monroe for insufficiently serious reasons.

Tynan, Kenneth. "American Blues: The Plays of Arthur Miller and Tennessee Williams." In his CURTAINS: SELECTIONS FROM THE DRAMA CRITICISM AND RELATED WRITINGS. New York: Atheneum, 1961, pp. 257-66.

Both Miller and Williams depict the individual victimized by society. For Miller this preoccupation leads in his adaptation of AN ENEMY OF THE PEOPLE to a loss of objectivity and in THE CRUCIBLE to emotional oversimplification.

Warshow, Robert. "The Liberal Conscience in THE CRUCIBLE." In his THE IMMEDIATE EXPERIENCE: MOVIES, COMICS, THEATRE AND OTHER ASPECTS OF POPULAR CULTURE. Introd. Lionel Trilling. New York: Doubleday, 1962, pp. 189-203. Also in TEXT, Weales, pp. 210-26.

The much-admired essay that argues that Miller misunderstood and exploited the Salem trials, while evading the real issues of the contemporary witch hunts. Miller is "Odets without the poetry."

Weales, Gerald. "Arthur Miller: Man and His Image." TDR, 7 (September 1962), 165-80. Also in TEXT, Weales, pp. 333-51.

Miller's theme is "the relationship between a man's identity and the image that society demands of him."

______. "All About Talk: Arthur Miller's THE PRICE." OHIO REVIEW, 8 (Winter 1972), 74-84.

Welland, Dennis. ARTHUR MILLER. Edinburgh: Oliver and Boyd, 1961.

Brief survey of Miller's life and works that seeks intermittently to place his plays in an American tradition of individuals denied a community.

Wiegand, William. "Arthur Miller and the Man Who Knows." WESTERN REVIEW, 21 (Winter 1957), 85-102. Also in TEXT, Weales, pp. 290-314.

Miller's loss of faith in Marxism is connected with the theme in his plays of the need to know and the inevitable destruction of the man who does know. Miller is compared unfavorably with Odets and Ibsen.

Williams, Raymond. "The Realism of Arthur Miller." CRQ, 1 (Summer 1959), 140-49. Also in TEXT, Weales, pp. 313-25.

Miller's social drama attends to individuals, their alienation, and their desperate, fatal attempts to achieve meaning.

## HENRY MILLER (1891- )

JUST WILD ABOUT HARRY: A MELO-MELO IN SEVEN SCENES. New York: New Directions, 1963.

Miller's only published play, a farce, introduced by the author.

## CHARLES MORGAN (1894-1958)

THE RIVER LINE. London: Macmillan, 1952.

First conceived as a play, first published as a novel, finally realized here as a play, with the introductory essay, "On Transcending the Age of Violence."

THE BURNING GLASS. London: Macmillan; New York: St. Martin's, 1953.

With his essay, "On Power Over Nature."

### SELECTED NONDRAMATIC WRITING

DIALOGUE IN NOVELS AND PLAYS. Aldington, Engl.: Hand and Flower Press, 1954.

Lecture.

THE WRITER AND HIS WORLD: LECTURES AND ESSAYS. London: Macmillan, 1960.

SELECTED LETTERS OF CHARLES MORGAN. Ed., with memoir by Eiluned Lewis. London: Macmillan, 1967.

The memoir is an excellent biographical source.

### CRITICISM

Duffin, Henry Charles. THE NOVELS AND PLAYS OF CHARLES MORGAN. London: Bowes and Bowes, 1959.

Harding, Joan N. "Three Plays by Charles Morgan." CONTEMPORARY REVIEW, 1078 (October 1955), 244-48.

Weales, Gerald. "The Devil's Glass." ETJ, 10 (December 1958), 311-15.

Perceptive analysis of Morgan's theories about science's role in contemporary culture.

## JOHN MORTIMER (1923- )

THREE PLAYS: THE DOCK BRIEF, WHAT SHALL WE TELL CAROLINE?, I SPY. London: Elek Books, 1958; New York: Grove Press, 1962.

LUNCH HOUR, AND OTHER PLAYS. London: Methuen, 1960.

Includes COLLECT YOUR HANDBAGGAGE, DAVID AND BROCCOLI, and CALL ME A LIAR.

TRIANGLE, CONFERENCE, COLLECTOR'S PIECE, and CLEANING UP JUSTICE. In ONE TO ANOTHER. With N.F. Simpson and Harold Pinter. London: Samuel French, 1960.

Review sketches.

THE WRONG SIDE OF THE PARK. London: Samuel French, 1960.

TWO STARS FOR COMFORT. London: Methuen, 1962.

A FLEA IN HER EAR. London: Samuel French, 1967.

From the play by Feydeau (1907).

THE JUDGE. London: Methuen, 1967.

A CHOICE OF KINGS. In PLAYBILL 3. Ed. Alan Durband. London: Hutchinson, 1969.

CAT AMONG THE PIGEONS. London: Samuel French, 1970.

From a play by Feydeau (1899).

THE CAPTAIN OF KOPENICK. London: Methuen, 1971.

Adaptation of Carl Zuckmayer's comedy (1931).

COME AS YOU ARE! London: Methuen, 1971.

Consists of four short plays: MILL HILL, BERMONDSEY, GLOUCESTER ROAD, and MARBLE ARCH.

DESMOND. In BEST SHORT PLAYS 1971. Ed. Stanley Richards. Philadelphia: Chilton, 1971.

A VOYAGE ROUND MY FATHER. P&P, 18 (February 1971), 68-85.

A VOYAGE ROUND MY FATHER. London: Methuen, 1971.

I CLAUDIUS. P&P, 19 (September 1972), i-xvi.

COLLABORATORS. London: Eyre Methuen, 1973.

KNIGHTSBRIDGE. London: Samuel French, 1973.

## COLLECTIONS

FIVE PLAYS. London: Methuen, 1970.

THE DOCK BRIEF, WHAT SHALL WE TELL CAROLINE?, I SPY, LUNCH HOUR, and COLLECT YOUR HANDBAGGAGE.

## SELECTED NONDRAMATIC WRITING

ANSWER YES OR NO. London: Lane, 1950.

Novel published as THE SILVER HOOK in New York by Morrow in 1950.

LIKE MEN BETRAYED. London: Collins, 1953.

Novel.

THE NARROWING STREAM. London: Collins, 1953.

Novel.

THREE WINTERS. London: Collins, 1956.

Novel.

"Introduction." THREE PLAYS. London: Elek Books, 1958.

## CRITICISM

Hayman, Ronald. "Like a Woman They Keep Going Back To." DRAMA, n.s. 98 (Autumn 1970), 57-66.

> Mortimer, along with Peter Shaffer, Robert Bolt, and John Bowen, is continually abandoning naturalism, and then returning to it.

Taylor, John Russell. "John Mortimer." In his ANGER AND AFTER: A GUIDE TO THE NEW BRITISH DRAMA. Rev. ed. Harmondsworth, Engl.: Penguin, 1963, pp. 235-48.

> Mortimer "applies his exploratory techniques to the middle classes in decline rather than the working classes ascendant."

Wellwarth, George. "The Apotheosis of Failure." In his THE THEATRE OF PROTEST AND PARADOX. New York: New York University Press, 1964, pp. 253-57.

> Mortimer is at his best in one-act plays, where his failed characters can come into their own.

## TAD MOSEL (1922- )

JINXED. New York: Samuel French, n.d.

MY LOST SAINTS. In BEST TELEVISION PLAYS. Ed. Gore Vidal. New York: Ballantine, 1956.

OTHER PEOPLE'S HOUSES: SIX TELEVISION PLAYS. New York: Simon and Schuster, 1956.

> The title play, and ERNIE BARGER IS FIFTY, THE HAVEN, THE LAWN PARTY, STAR IN THE SUMMER NIGHT, and THE WAITING PLACE.

THE FIVE-DOLLAR BILL. In BEST TELEVISION PLAYS 1957. Ed. William I. Kauffman. New York: Harcourt Brace, 1957.

THE OUT-OF-TOWNERS. In TELEVISION PLAYS FOR WRITERS: EIGHT TELEVISION PLAYS. Ed. A.S. Burack. Boston: Writer, 1957.

THE FIVE DOLLAR BILL. Chicago: Dramatic Publishing, 1958.

PRESENCE OF THE ENEMY. In BEST SHORT PLAYS, 1957-1958. Ed. Margaret Mayorga. Boston: Beacon Press, 1958.

JINXED. In THEY FOUND ADVENTURE. Ed. Carver et al. Englewood Cliffs, N.J.: Prentice-Hall, 1960.

ALL THE WAY HOME. New York: Oblensky, 1961.

> Based on the novel A DEATH IN THE FAMILY by James Agee (1957).

IMPROMPTU. New York: Dramatists Play Service, 1961.

THAT'S WHERE THE TOWN'S GOING. New York: Dramatists Play Service, 1962.

ALL THE WAY HOME. New York: Avon Books, 1963.

Contains both the play and the screenplay by Philip Reisman, Jr.

## BIBLIOGRAPHY

Salem, James M., ed. A GUIDE TO CRITICAL REVIEWS. Part 1: AMERICAN DRAMA, 1909-1969. 2nd ed. Metuchen, N.J.: Scarecrow Press, 1973.

List of reviews of ALL THE WAY HOME. See page 331.

## CRITICISM

Burian, Jarka M. "Tad Mosel." In CONTEMPORARY DRAMATISTS. Ed. James Vinson. London: St. James; New York: St. Martin's, 1973, p. 559.

# DAVID MOWAT (1943-  )

ANN-LUSE AND OTHER PLAYS. London: Calder and Boyars, 1970.

The others are JENS and PURITY.

THE OTHERS. London: Calder and Boyars, 1973.

## CRITICISM

Marcus, Frank. "David Mowat." In CONTEMPORARY DRAMATISTS. Ed. James Vinson. London: St. James; New York: St. Martin's, 1973, pp. 560-61.

Mowat's plays, like Pinter's, are difficult but spellbinding.

## IRIS MURDOCH (1919- )

THE THREE ARROWS, AND, THE SERVANTS AND THE SNOW. London: Chatto and Windus, 1973.

### COLLABORATIONS

A SEVERED HEAD. London: Chatto and Windus, 1964.

Adapted from the 1961 novel by Murdoch and J.B. Priestley.

THE ITALIAN GIRL. P&P, 15 (March 1968), 27-42 ff.

THE ITALIAN GIRL. London: Samuel French, 1968.

Adapted from the 1964 novel by Murdoch and James Saunders.

### SELECTED NONDRAMATIC WRITING

A SEVERED HEAD. London: Chatto and Windus, 1961.

THE ITALIAN GIRL. London: Chatto and Windus, 1964.

### CRITICISM

Baker, Roger. "Iris Murdoch." In CONTEMPORARY DRAMATISTS. Ed. James Vinson. London: St. James; New York: St. Martin's, 1973, p. 563.

# VLADIMIR NABOKOV (1899-1977)

THE WALTZ INVENTION. Trans. Dmitri Nabokov. New York: Phaedra, 1966.

From the 1933 play in Russian.

LOLITA. New York: McGraw-Hill, 1974.

The screenplay, revised.

## BIBLIOGRAPHY

Field, Andrew, ed. NABOKOV: A BIBLIOGRAPHY. New York: McGraw-Hill, 1973.

Primary sources.

## CRITICISM

Appel, Alfred, Jr., and Charles Newman, eds. NABOKOV: CRITICISM, REMINISCENCES, TRANSLATIONS AND TRIBUTES. Evanston, Ill.: Northwestern University Press, 1970.

This is a reprint of the Winter 1970 issue of TRI-QUARTERLY. Nabokov's response to each item is in his STRONG OPINIONS, published in New York in 1973 by McGraw-Hill.

Karlinsky, Simon. "Illusion, Reality, and Parody in Nabokov's Plays." WS, 8 (Spring 1967), 268-79.

After a discussion of THE EVENT, a 1938 play not available in English, THE WALTZ INVENTION is summarized and its thematic relationship to Nabokov's other works is noted.

Rowe, William Wooden. NABOKOV'S DECEPTIVE WORLD. New York: New York University Press, 1971.

# Vladimir Nabokov

Nabokov's hilarious demolition of this symbolic reading of his work is reprinted from NYRB in Nabokov's STRONG OPINIONS, published in New York in 1973 by McGraw-Hill.

## BILL NAUGHTON (1910- )

MY FLESH, MY BLOOD. London: Samuel French, 1959.

See also SPRING AND PORT WINE, below.

ALFIE. London: Samuel French, 1963.

Based on the radio play, ALFIE ELKINS AND HIS LITTLE LIFE (1962).

ALL IN GOOD TIME. London: Samuel French, 1964.

ALL IN GOOD TIME. Rev. ed. London: Samuel French, 1965.

SHE'LL MAKE TROUBLE. In WORTH A HEARING. Ed. Alfred Bradley. Glasgow: Blackie, 1967.

Radio play from 1958.

SPRING AND PORT WINE. Rev. and rewritten version. London: Samuel French, 1967.

Revision of MY FLESH, MY BLOOD, Produced in New York as KEEP IT IN THE FAMILY.

### SELECTED NONDRAMATIC WRITING

ALFIE. London: MacGibbon & Kee, 1966.

Novel.

ALFIE DARLING. London: MacGibbon & Kee, 1970.

Novel.

## CRITICISM

Strachan, Alan. "Bill Naughton." In CONTEMPORARY DRAMATISTS. Ed. James Vinson. London: St. James; New York: St. Martin's, 1973, pp. 570-71.

# PETER NICHOLS (1927- )

PROMENADE. In SIX GRANADA PLAYS. London: Faber and Faber, 1960.

BEN SPRAY. In NEW GRANADA PLAYS. London: Faber and Faber, 1961.

A DAY IN THE LIFE OF JOE EGG. London: Faber and Faber, 1967.

A DAY IN THE LIFE OF JOE EGG. As JOE EGG. New York: Grove Press, 1967.

THE NATIONAL HEALTH; OR, NURSE NORTON'S AFFAIR. London: Faber and Faber, 1970.

FORGET-ME-NOT-LANE. London: Faber and Faber, 1971.

CHEZ NOUS: A DOMESTIC COMEDY IN TWO ACTS. London: Faber and Faber, 1974.

THE FREEWAY. London: Faber and Faber, 1975.

## CRITICISM

Kauffmann, Stanley. "THE NATIONAL HEALTH." In his PERSONS OF THE DRAMA. New York: Harper and Row, 1976, pp. 242-44.

> Nichols has talent and interesting theatrical ideas, but he is reluctant to work them out.

Taylor, John Russell. "Peter Nichols." In his THE SECOND WAVE. London: Methuen, 1971, pp. 16-35.

> Useful, particularly for the summaries of unpublished television plays.

# NORMAN NICHOLSON (1914- )

THE OLD MAN OF THE MOUNTAINS. Rev. ed. London: Faber and Faber, 1950.

Revision of the 1946 play.

PROPHECY TO THE WIND. London: Faber and Faber, 1950.

A MATCH FOR THE DEVIL. London: Faber and Faber, 1955.

BIRTH BY DROWNING. London: Faber and Faber, 1960.

## SELECTED NONDRAMATIC WRITING

"Modern Verse-Drama and the Folk Tradition." CQ, 2 (Summer 1960), 166-70.

On the crucial distinction between the verse theatre of Eliot and his followers, and the folk theatre.

## CRITICISM

Gardiner, Philip. NORMAN NICHOLSON. New York: Twayne, 1973.

Major attention is given to the life and the poetry, with one chapter on the verse plays.

Weales, Gerald. RELIGION IN MODERN ENGLISH DRAMA. Philadelphia: University of Pennsylvania Press, 1961, pp. 239-49.

# JOHN FORD NOONAN (1943- )

THE YEAR BOSTON WON THE PENNANT. New York: Grove Press, 1970.

RAINBOWS FOR SALE. In THE OFF-OFF-BROADWAY BOOK. Ed. Albert Poland and Bruce Mailman. Indianapolis: Bobbs-Merrill, 1972.

## CRITICISM

Kostelanetz, Richard. "John Ford Noonan." In CONTEMPORARY DRAMATISTS. Ed. James Vinson. London: St. James; New York: St. Martin's, 1973, pp. 579-81.

> "Especially for the quality of his characterizations and his prose, he ranks among the best American dramatists of that generation now about thirty."

Lahr, John. "Mystery on Stage." In his ASTONISH ME: ADVENTURES IN CONTEMPORARY THEATER. New York: Viking, 1973, pp. 150-56.

> THE YEAR BOSTON WON THE PENNANT depicts the obsessive, nonrational mythologies our society creates and then consumes.

## FRANK NORMAN (1930- )

FINGS AIN'T WOT THEY USED T'BE. London: Secker and Warburg, 1960.

> This proletarian musical, with music by Lionel Bart, was one of Joan Littlewood's most praised productions.

INSIDEOUT. P&P, 15 (February 1970), 61-78.

### SELECTED NONDRAMATIC WRITING

STAND ON ME: A TRUE STORY OF SOHO. With a Glossary of Slang, for Those Who Need it. New York: Simon and Schuster, 1961.

SOHO NIGHT AND DAY. With Jeffrey Bernard. London: Secker and Warburg, 1966.

### CRITICISM

Simmons, Judith Cooke. "Frank Norman." In CONTEMPORARY DRAMATISTS. Ed. James Vinson. London: St. James; New York: St. Martin's, 1973, pp. 582-83.

> On FINGS as the cockney equivalent of short-story writer Damon Runyon.

# CONOR CRUISE O'BRIEN (1917-  )

MURDEROUS ANGELS: A POLITICAL TRAGEDY AND COMEDY IN BLACK AND WHITE. Boston: Little, Brown, 1968.

This political drama by the former United Nations representative to the Congo is replete with an essay on "Hammarskjold's Role in Relation to the Downfall and Death of Lumumba," and ten pages of notes.

## CRITICISM

Hughes, Catharine. PLAYS, POLITICS AND POLEMICS. New York: Drama Book Specialists, 1973.

See pages 165-74.

Simon, John. UNEASY STAGES. New York: Random House, 1975.

MURDEROUS ANGELS makes all the mistakes possible for documentary drama. See pages 364-66.

# SEAN O'CASEY (1880-1964)

COLLECTED PLAYS. Vols. 3, 4. London: Macmillan, 1951.

First publications of HALL OF HEALING, BEDTIME STORY, and TIME TO GO.

THE BISHOP'S BONFIRE: A SAD PLAY WITHIN THE TUNE OF A POLKA. London: Macmillan, 1955.

RED ROSES FOR ME. New York: Dramatists Play Service, 1956.

PURPLE DUST. New York: Dramatists Play Service, 1957.

PURPLE DUST. In THE GENIUS OF THE IRISH THEATRE. Ed. Sylvan Barnet, Morton Berman, William Burto. New York: Mentor, 1960.

Final revision of the 1940 play.

THE DRUMS OF FATHER NED: A MICKROCOSM OF IRELAND. London: Macmillan, 1960.

BEHIND THE GREEN CURTAIN, FIGARO IN THE NIGHT, THE MOON SHINES ON KYLENAMOE: THREE PLAYS. London: Macmillan; New York: St. Martin's, 1961.

CATHLEEN LISTENS IN and NANNIE'S NIGHT OUT. In FEATHERS FROM THE GREEN CROW: SEAN O'CASEY 1905-1925. Ed. Robert Hogan. Columbia: University of Missouri Press, 1962.

Two early, hitherto unpublished plays.

RED ROSES FOR ME. In THREE MORE PLAYS. Introd. J.C. Trewin. London: Macmillan; New York: St. Martin's, 1965.

Final revision of the 1942 play.

## BIBLIOGRAPHY

Mikhail, E.H., ed. SEAN O'CASEY: A BIBLIOGRAPHY OF CRITICISM. Introd. Ronald Ayling. Seattle: University of Washington Press, 1972.

## CRITICISM

Ayling, Ronald. "A Note on Sean O'Casey's Manuscripts and His Working Methods." BULLETIN OF THE NEW YORK PUBLIC LIBRARY, 73 (June 1969), 359-67.

______, ed. SEAN O'CASEY. London: Macmillan, 1969.

Valuable, scholarly collection of essays and reviews, with an excellent bibliography.

Krause, David. SEAN O'CASEY: THE MAN AND HIS WORKS. 2nd ed. New York: Macmillan, 1975.

Best critical biography.

# CLIFFORD ODETS (1906-1963)

THE COUNTRY GIRL. New York: Viking, 1951.

THE FLOWERING PEACH. New York: Dramatists Play Service, 1954.

THE COUNTRY GIRL. As THE WINTER JOURNEY. London: Samuel French, 1955.

## COLLABORATION WITH WILLIAM GIBSON

GOLDEN BOY. New York: Atheneum, 1965.

The book of a musical by Clifford Odets and William Gibson based upon Mr. Odets' play. With lyrics by Lee Adams, to music by Charles Strouse. Gibson's preface, "A Memento," tells of the genesis of his posthumous "collaboration" with Odets.

## BIBLIOGRAPHY

Salem, James M., ed. A GUIDE TO CRITICAL REVIEWS. Part 1: AMERICAN DRAMA, 1909-1969. 2nd ed. Metuchen, N.J.: Scarecrow Press, 1973.

List of reviews, pages 342-48.

## CRITICISM

Becker, William. "Reflections on Three New Plays." HR, 8 (Summer 1955), 258-72.

THE FLOWERING PEACH is one of Odets' best plays. It draws upon his greatest strengths--the depiction of modern immigrant Jewish Life.

Bentley, Eric, ed. THIRTY YEARS OF TREASON: EXCERPTS FROM HEARINGS BEFORE THE HOUSE COMMITTEE ON UN-AMERICAN ACTIVITIES, 1938-1968. New York: Viking, 1971, pp. 498-531.

Excerpts from Odets' 1952 testimony before HUAC.

Mendelsohn, Michael J. "Odets at Center Stage." TA, 47 (May-June 1963), 16-19, 28-30 ff.

Valuable biographical interview.

_____. "Clifford Odets and the American Family." DS, 3 (October 1963), 238-43.

Traces the change in Odets' writing from anti-family to pro-family, a change culminating in THE FLOWERING PEACH.

_____. CLIFFORD ODETS: HUMANE DRAMATIST. Introd. Morris Freedman. Deland, Fla.: Everett-Edwards, 1969.

Thin.

Tynan, Kenneth. CURTAINS: SELECTIONS FROM THE DRAMA CRITICISM AND RELATED WRITINGS. New York: Atheneum, 1961, pp. 19-21.

Attacks those critics who snub THE COUNTRY GIRL as too theatrical.

Weales, Gerald. CLIFFORD ODETS: PLAYWRIGHT. New York: Bobbs Merrill, 1971.

In this affectionate scholarly study, Weales seeks to demythologize Odets' career. Weales's method is intensive research into the political and theatrical climate of the thirties and forties.

Willet, Ralph. "Clifford Odets and Popular Culture." SOUTH ATLANTIC QUARTERLY, 69 (Winter 1970), 68-78.

Argues that Odets eventually "succumbed to total despair."

## FRANK O'HARA (1926-1966)

AWAKE IN SPAIN. New York: American Theatre for Poets, 1960.

TRY! TRY! In ARTISTS' THEATRE. Ed. Herbert Machiz. New York: Grove Press, 1960.

THE GENERAL'S RETURN FROM ONE PLACE TO ANOTHER. New York: n.p., 1962.

Manuscript in the Library of Northwestern University.

THE GENERAL'S RETURN FROM ONE PLACE TO ANOTHER. In EIGHT PLAYS FROM OFF-OFF BROADWAY. Ed. Nick Orzel and Michael Smith. Indianapolis: Bobbs-Merrill, 1964.

LOVE'S LABOR: AN ECLOGUE. New York: American Theatre for Poets, 1964.

FOUR DIALOGUES FOR TWO VOICES AND TWO PIANOS. Words by Frank O'Hara, music by Ned Rorem. New York: Boosey and Hawkes, 1969.

THE SUBWAY, THE AIRPORT, THE APARTMENT, and IN SPAIN AND IN NEW YORK.

TWO PIECES. London: Long Hair Books, 1969.

THOSE WHO ARE DREAMING: A PLAY ABOUT ST. PAUL and the poem "Commercial Variations."

### SELECTED NONDRAMATIC WRITING

THE COLLECTED POEMS OF FRANK O'HARA. Ed. Donald Allen. Introd. John Ashbery. New York: Knopf, 1971.

ART CHRONICLES, 1954-1968. New York: G. Braziller, 1975.

## CRITICISM

Howard, Richard. "Frank O'Hara." In his ALONE WITH AMERICA: ESSAYS ON THE ART OF POETRY IN THE UNITED STATES SINCE 1950. New York: Atheneum, 1971, pp. 396-412.

Sontag, Susan. AGAINST INTERPRETATION AND OTHER ESSAYS. New York: Farrar, Straus and Giroux, 1966.

On Taylor Mead's performance in THE GENERAL'S RETURN FROM ONE PLACE TO ANOTHER; see pages 157-58.

# JOHN O'HARA (1905-1970)

PAL JOEY: THE LIBRETTO AND LYRICS. New York: Random House, 1952.

FIVE PLAYS. New York: Random House, 1961.

THE FARMERS HOTEL, THE SEARCHING SUN, THE CHAMPAGNE POOL, VERONIQUE, and THE WAY IT WAS--none produced on Broadway.

## BIBLIOGRAPHY

Bruccoli, Matthew J., comp. JOHN O'HARA: A CHECKLIST. With a previously unpublished speech by John O'Hara. New York: Random House, 1972.

## CRITICISM

Bruccoli, Matthew J. THE O'HARA CONCERN: A BIOGRAPHY OF JOHN O'HARA. New York: Random House, 1975.

An excellent biography with a lengthy bibliography of primary and secondary sources.

# EUGENE O'NEILL (1888-1953)

LOST PLAYS OF EUGENE O'NEILL. New York: New Fathoms, 1950.

First publication, unauthorized by O'Neill, of ABORTION, MOVIE MAN, THE SNIPER, SERVITUDE, and A WIFE FOR LIFE.

A MOON FOR THE MISBEGOTTEN. New York: Random House, 1952.

LONG DAY'S JOURNEY INTO NIGHT. New Haven, Conn.: Yale University Press, 1956.

A TOUCH OF THE POET. New Haven, Conn.: Yale University Press, 1957.

HUGHIE. New Haven, Conn.: Yale University Press, 1959.

THE ANCIENT MARINER. YALE UNIVERSITY LIBRARY GAZETTE, 35 (October 1960), 61-68.

First publication of a short play from the twenties, based on the Coleridge poem of 1798.

MORE STATELY MANSIONS. Shortened from the author's partly revised script by Karl Ragnar Gierow and editdd by Donald Gallup. New Haven, Conn.: Yale University Press, 1964.

TEN "LOST" PLAYS BY EUGENE O'NEILL. New York: Random House, 1964.

Adds five plays published in 1914 to the five first published in 1950 by New Fathoms, above.

## BIBLIOGRAPHY

Atkinson, Jennifer, ed. EUGENE O'NEILL: A DESCRIPTIVE BIBLIOGRAPHY.

Pittsburgh: University of Pittsburgh Press, 1971.

Primary sources.

Miller, Jordan Y., ed. EUGENE O'NEILL AND THE AMERICAN CRITIC: A BIBLIOGRAPHICAL CHECKLIST. 2nd ed. rev. Hampden, Conn.: Archon Books, 1973.

Annotated survey of secondary sources.

Salem, James M., ed. A GUIDE TO CRITICAL REVIEWS. Part 1: AMERICAN DRAMA, 1909-1969. 2nd ed. Metuchen, N.J.: Scarecrow Press, 1973.

See pages 348-72.

## CRITICISM

Bentley, Eric. "Trying to Like O'Neill." In his IN SEARCH OF THEATER. New York: Knopf, 1953, pp. 220-34.

"But the more he attempts, the less he achieves." This is the classic attack upon O'Neill's language and his cultural and intellectual pretentions.

______. "Eugene O'Neill's Pieta." In his THE DRAMATIC EVENT: AN AMERICAN CHRONICLE. New York: Horizon Press, 1954, pp. 30-37.

Bentley finds A MOON FOR THE MISBEGOTTEN's central image a "neurotic fantasy indulged rather than exploited and critically speaking, poetry strained after rather than achieved."

______. "Eugene O'Neill." In his THEATRE OF WAR: COMMENTS ON 32 OCCASIONS. New York: Viking, 1972, pp. 64-92.

A less polemical evaluation of O'Neill's status, focusing on O'Neill's relationship with his father and the problem of success. Bentley still denies O'Neill's ultimate greatness.

Bermel, Albert. "The Family as Villain." In his CONTRADICTORY CHARACTERS: AN INTERPRETATION OF THE MODERN THEATRE. New York: E.P. Dutton, 1973, pp. 105-21.

LONG DAY'S JOURNEY INTO NIGHT is Mary's tragedy, and her family embodies her fall from innocence. Thus the three men are not as guilty as they seem.

Cargill, Oscar, et al., eds. O'NEILL AND HIS PLAYS: FOUR DECADES OF CRITICISM. New York: New York University Press, 1961.

A valuable collection of essays and reviews that chart O'Neill's reputation, ideas, language, and life.

Cohn, Ruby. "Absurdity in English: Joyce and O'Neill." COMPARATIVE DRAMA, 3 (Fall 1969), 156-61.

HUGHIE and the Nighttown chapter of Joyce's ULYSSES (1922) are seen as absurdist dramas.

______. DIALOGUE IN AMERICAN DRAMA. Bloomington: Indiana University Press, 1971.

See pages 8-67.

Falk, Doris V. EUGENE O'NEILL AND THE TRAGIC TENSION: AN INTERPRETATIVE STUDY OF THE PLAYS. New Brunswick, N.J.: Rutgers University Press, 1958.

Tracing the philosophic and psychological antinomies of O'Neill's career, Falk argues that self-understanding leads to paralysis in both A MOON FOR THE MISBEGOTTEN and LONG DAY'S JOURNEY INTO NIGHT. Further, the latter is, in its character types and themes, a recapitulation of O'Neill's personal and dramatic obsessions.

______. "That Paradox O'Neill." MD, 6 (December 1963), 221-38.

Like Dion Anthony, O'Neill was a deeply divided personality and his plays, in their varied and often contradictory sources, reflect that dividedness.

Fitzgerald, John J. "Guilt and Redemption in O'Neill's Last Play: A Study of A MOON FOR THE MISBEGOTTEN." TEQ, 9 (Spring 1965), 146-58.

The play is a "triple purgation," for O'Neill, James Tyrone, and the audience.

Fleisher, Frederic, and Horst Frenz. "Eugene O'Neill and the Royal Dramatic Theater of Stockholm: The Later Phase." MD, 10 (December 1967), 300-311.

Traces O'Neill's remarkable posthumous career on the Swedish stage, concluding with the world premiere of MORE STATELY MANSIONS in 1962.

Gassner, John. O'NEILL: A COLLECTION OF CRITICAL ESSAYS. Englewood Cliffs, N.J.: Prentice-Hall, 1964.

Good introductory collection.

Hartman, Murray. "The Skeletons in O'Neill's MANSIONS." DS, 5 (Winter 1966-67), 276-79.

MORE STATELY MANSIONS recapitulates O'Neill's sexual and familial obsessions, but without artistic control.

Holtan, Orley I. "Eugene O'Neill and the Death of the 'Covenant.'" QJS, 56 (October 1970), 256-63.

American social history in A TOUCH OF THE POET and MORE STATELY MANSIONS.

Leech, Clifford. "Eugene O'Neill and His Plays, I and II." CQ, 3 (Autumn, Winter 1961), 242-56, 339-53.

This two-part survey of O'Neill's career emphasizes the biographical element and the role of an exterior pattern imposed on the drama. The second part notes the new theme of the terror of self-recognition in ICEMAN and the successful portrayal of character in LONG DAY'S JOURNEY INTO NIGHT.

McCarthy, Mary. "'Realism' in the American Theatre." HARPERS, June 1961, pp. 45-52.

The theatre, with the splendid exception of O'Neill and his LONG DAY'S JOURNEY INTO NIGHT, has failed to come to grips with realism.

Nethercot, Arthur H. "The Psychoanalyzing of Eugene O'Neill." MD, 3 (December 1960), 242-56; (February 1961), 357-72.

Tracing the critical evaluations of O'Neill's use of psychoanalytic theory in his plays, this two-part essay focuses on his early works and on Doris Falk's landmark study, EUGENE O'NEILL AND THE TRAGIC TENSION, above.

______. "O'Neill's MORE STATELY MANSIONS." ETJ, 27 (May 1975), 161-69.

The theme of dreams and ghosts in O'Neill's last play.

______. "Madness in the Plays of Eugene O'Neill." MD, 18 (September 1975), 259-79.

This survey of the plays seeks to demonstrate that the subject of madness had an irresistible fascination for O'Neill.

Parks, Edd Winfield. "Eugene O'Neill's Quest." TDR, 4 (March 1960), 99-107.

O'Neill was not a pessimist or a determinist, but a man seeking a belief he could accept, and finding it in human love.

Raleigh, John Henry. "O'Neill's LONG DAY'S JOURNEY INTO NIGHT and New England Irish-Catholicism." PR, 26 (Fall 1959), 573-92.

LONG DAY'S JOURNEY INTO NIGHT is more than autobiography;

it is "THE great cultural expression of American Irish Catholicism."

_____. THE PLAYS OF EUGENE O'NEILL. Carbondale: Southern Illinois University Press, 1965.

Excellent study.

Real, Jere. "The Brothel in O'Neill's MANSIONS." MD, 12 (February 1970), 383-89.

Traces the theme of sexual exploitation in MORE STATELY MANSIONS.

Reardon, William R. "O'Neill Since World War II: Critical Reception in New York." MD, 10 (December 1967), 289-99.

This is a survey of the varied critical reaction to the first performances of O'Neill's late plays and selected revivals. The full impact of what amounted to the rediscovery of a great American playwright is only hinted at.

Rothenberg, Albert, and Eugene D. Shapiro. "The Defense of Psychoanalysis in Literature: LONG DAY'S JOURNEY INTO NIGHT and A VIEW FROM THE BRIDGE." COMPARATIVE DRAMA, 7 (Spring 1973), 51-67.

LONG DAY'S JOURNEY INTO NIGHT is charted in terms of its characters' use of a variety of psychological defenses, such as denial, rationalization, displacement, retrojection, and more.

Scheibler, Rolf. "HUGHIE: A One-Act Play for the Imaginary Theatre." ENGLISH STUDIES, 54 (June 1973), 231-48.

HUGHIE, with its lengthy and often first-person stage directions, seems unsuitable for the stage. Yet the night clerk's dreams and asides are dramatic in nature and keep the play from being a closet drama.

Shawcross, John T. "The Road to Ruin: The Beginning of O'Neill's LONG DAY'S JOURNEY." MD, 3 (December 1960), 289-96.

AH, WILDERNESS! depicts, just a few years earlier, the same family as that in LONG DAY'S JOURNEY INTO NIGHT.

Sheaffer, Louis. O'NEILL: SON AND PLAYWRIGHT. Boston: Little, Brown, 1968.

_____. O'NEILL: SON AND ARTIST. Boston: Little, Brown, 1973.

The definitive, two-volume, critical biography.

Tornqvist, Egil. A DRAMA OF SOULS: STUDIES IN O'NEILL'S SUPER-NATURALISTIC TECHNIQUE. New Haven, Conn.: Yale University Press, 1969.

O'Neill's interest in religion and psychology could only be expressed in a nonnaturalistic drama. By examining O'Neill's lighting effects, masks, stage dialogue, settings, and directions, Tornqvist seeks the meaning behind what is often apparently realistic action. Typical is his treatment of the lighting effects in LONG DAY'S JOURNEY INTO NIGHT.

# JOE ORTON (1933-1967)

ENTERTAINING MR. SLOANE. London: Hamish Hamilton, 1964.

THE RUFFIAN ON THE STAIR. In NEW RADIO DRAMA. London: BBC, 1966.

The radio version.

CRIMES OF PASSION: THE RUFFIAN ON THE STAIR, THE ERPINGHAM CAMP. London: Methuen, 1967.

The author's note to these two plays gives the deletions insisted upon by the Lord Chamberlain prior to production, and the substitutions accepted by him. This terse listing has an impact quite as forceful as any tirade against censorship. The New York production typescript is available at the Lincoln Center Library of the Performing Arts.

LOOT. London: Methuen, 1967.

WHAT THE BUTLER SAW. London: Methuen, 1969.

FUNERAL GAMES, AND THE GOOD AND FAITHFUL SERVANT. Introd. Peter Willes. London: Methuen, 1970.

UNTIL SHE SCREAMS. ER, 14 (May 1970), 51-53.

ENTERTAINING MR. SLOANE. London: Methuen, 1973.

Uniform with the other Methuen publications of Orton, and with an introduction by John Lahr.

## SELECTED NONDRAMATIC WRITING

"The Biter Bit." P&P, 11 (August 1964), p. 16.

Introduces ENTERTAINING MR. SLOANE.

HEAD TO TOE. Drawings by Patrick Prockton and Interphot. London: Blond, 1971.

Novel.

## CRITICISM

Fox, James. "The Life and Death of Joe Orton." SUNDAY TIMES MAGAZINE (London), 22 November 1970, pp. 44-52, 78.

Anecdotal, journalistic account of Orton's career and his relationship with Kenneth Halliwell. This article also contains photographs and details about Orton's pseudonymous letter writing.

Fraser, Keath. "Joe Orton: His Brief Career." MD, 14 (February 1972), 413-19.

Brief, sympathetic treatment of the life and works.

"Joe Orton Interviewed by Giles Gordon." In BEHIND THE SCENES: THEATER AND FILM INTERVIEWS FROM THE TRANSATLANTIC REVIEW. Ed. Joseph F.M. McCrindle, introd. Jean-Claude van Itallie. New York: Holt, Rinehart and Winston, 1971, pp. 116-24.

On LOOT, bad taste, Oscar Wilde, and book defacing.

Lahr, John. "Joe Orton: Artist of the Outrageous." In his ASTONISH ME: ADVENTURES IN CONTEMPORARY THEATER. New York: Viking, 1973, pp. 83-101.

Orton's farces are a confrontation with contemporary schizophrenia. This essay also serves as the introduction to the Grove Press edition of WHAT THE BUTLER SAW.

Taylor, John Russell. "Joe Orton." In his THE SECOND WAVE. London: Methuen, 1971, pp. 125-40.

The key to Orton's work is the dislocation between the ever-genteel word and the outrageous deed.

Worth, Katharine J. "Forms of Freedom and Mystery: Beneath the Subtext." In her REVOLUTIONS IN MODERN ENGLISH DRAMA. London: G. Bell, 1973, pp. 148-56.

On Orton's macabre subversion of farce.

# JOHN OSBORNE (1929- )

THE ENTERTAINER. London: Faber and Faber, 1957.

LOOK BACK IN ANGER. London: Faber and Faber, 1957.

THE WORLD OF PAUL SLICKEY: A COMEDY OF MANNERS WITH MUSIC. London: Faber and Faber, 1959.

Music by Christopher Whelen.

LUTHER. London: Faber and Faber, 1961.

A SUBJECT OF SCANDAL AND CONCERN: A PLAY FOR TELEVISION. London: Faber and Faber, 1961.

PLAYS FOR ENGLAND: THE BLOOD OF THE BAMBERGS, UNDER PLAIN COVER. London: Faber and Faber, 1963.

TOM JONES: A SCREENPLAY. London: Faber and Faber, 1964.

TOM JONES: A SCREENPLAY. Rev. ed. New York: Grove Press, 1964.

Robert Hughes, in "A Note on the Revised Edition of TOM JONES," points out that the Faber edition excludes ten scenes from the finished film and includes "more than eighty shots cut from the picture," while the Grove edition omits the latter, includes the former, and arranges the text to follow the screen sequences. Thus the Faber edition emphasizes the Osborne script, and Grove the finished film.

INADMISSIBLE EVIDENCE. London: Faber and Faber, 1965.

A BOND HONORED. London: Faber and Faber, 1966.

A free adaptation of Lope de Vega's LA FIANZA SATISFICHA (1615).

A PATRIOT FOR ME. London: Faber and Faber, 1966.

TIME PRESENT, THE HOTEL IN AMSTERDAM. London: Faber and Faber, 1968.

THE RIGHT PROSPECTUS: A PLAY FOR TELEVISION. London: Faber and Faber, 1970.

VERY LIKE A WHALE. London: Faber and Faber, 1971.

Television play.

WEST OF SUEZ. London: Faber and Faber, 1971.

THE GIFTS OF FRIENDSHIP: A PLAY FOR TELEVISION. London: Faber and Faber, 1972.

HEDDA GABLER. London: Faber and Faber, 1972.

Adaptation of the 1890 Ibsen play.

THE PICTURE OF DORIAN GRAY: A MORAL ENTERTAINMENT. London: Faber and Faber, 1973.

Adaptation of Oscar Wilde's novel from 1891.

A PLACE CALLING ITSELF ROME. London: Faber and Faber, 1973.

Based on Shakespeare's CORIOLANUS.

A SENSE OF DETACHMENT. London: Faber and Faber, 1973.

THE END OF ME OLD CIGAR: A PLAY, AND, JACK AND JILL: A PLAY FOR TELEVISION. London: Faber and Faber, 1975.

WATCH IT COME DOWN. London: Faber and Faber, 1975.

## COLLABORATION WITH ANTHONY CREIGHTON

EPITAPH FOR GEORGE DILLON. London: Faber and Faber, 1958.

This is the earliest of Osborne's plays yet to be published.

## BIBLIOGRAPHY

Northouse, Cameron, and Thomas P. Walsh, eds. JOHN OSBORNE: A REFERENCE GUIDE. Boston: G.K. Hall, 1974.

Salem, James M., ed. A GUIDE TO CRITICAL REVIEWS. Part 3: BRITISH AND CONTINENTAL DRAMA FROM IBSEN TO PINTER. Metuchen, N.J.: Scarecrow Press, 1968.

See pages 178-81.

## SELECTED NONDRAMATIC WRITING

"Sex and Failure." OBSERVER, 20 January 1957, p. 11.

In a review of two English collections of Tennessee Williams' plays, Osborne claims that they are about failure, which is what makes people interesting. The review includes Osborne's notorious, "The female must come toppling down to where she should be--on her back."

"They Call it Cricket." In DECLARATION. Ed. Tom Maschler. London: MacGibbon & Kee, 1957, pp. 630-84.

This characteristically scatter-gun attack on the English church, royalty, and politics is particularly useful for the autobiographical material of its last pages.

"The Epistle to the Philistines." TRIBUNE (London), 13 May 1960, p. 5. Also in JOHN OSBORNE: LOOK BACK IN ANGER, A CASEBOOK. Ed. John Russell Taylor. London: Macmillan, 1968, pp. 63-67. (This volume will hereafter be cited as CASEBOOK, ed Taylor.)

A bitter and not particularly deft parody of a Pauline epistle.

"That Awful Museum." TWENTIETH CENTURY, 169 (February 1961), 212-16. Also in CASEBOOK, ed. Taylor, pp. 63-67.

This rambling conversation with Richard Findlater includes Osborne's suspicion that the National Theatre will probably become just another Royal Academy, and that the theatre of the sixties faces the same danger--of becoming a new Establishment. Television reduces the human spirit; LUTHER is not a costume drama; LOOK BACK IN ANGER now embarrasses him.

"A Letter to My Fellow Countrymen." TRIBUNE (London), 18 August 1961, p. 7. Also in CASEBOOK, ed. Taylor, pp. 67-69.

This, the "damn you, England" letter, is a remarkably melodramatic outburst in Osborne's very best Jimmy Porter style.

"The Pioneer at the Royal Court." OBSERVER, 23 January 1966, p. 11.

In this brief tribute to the recently deceased George Devine, Osborne praises his character and influence on writers, actors, and the two subsidized theatre companies.

"John Osborne Talks to Kenneth Tynan." OBSERVER, 30 June 1967, p. 21, and 7 July 1967, p. 21.

The theatre hasn't changed substantially since LOOK BACK IN ANGER. Happenings and light shows are "democracy gone mad." It took nine days to write LOOK BACK IN ANGER and eleven to write THE ENTERTAINER.

"Intellectuals and Just Causes: A Symposium." ENC, 29 (September 1967), 3-4.

Osborne rejects the "odour of psychopathic self-righteousness" of most protest demonstrations and urges the virtues of speaking modestly. He sees little to choose in Vietnam between "Communist police terrorism and shoddy American power politics," though the latter is "minimally less repugnant."

"John Osborne on the Thesis Business and the Seekers after the Bare Approximate; On the Rights of the Audience and the Wink and Promise of the Well-Made Play." TIMES SUNDAY REVIEW (London), 14 October 1967, p. 20.

A denunciation of theatre studies, most particularly THE OXFORD COMPANION TO THE THEATRE and John Russell Taylor's THE RISE AND FALL OF THE WELL-MADE PLAY.

## CRITICISM

Allsop, Kenneth. THE ANGRY DECADE: A SURVEY OF THE CULTURAL REVOLT OF THE NINETEEN-FIFTIES. Rev. introd. by the author. London: Peter Owen, 1964.

Osborne's commitment to change is too superficial. Jimmy Porter in LOOK BACK IN ANGER is a louse who is angry because of a frustrated nostalgia for the very things he so noisily despises. See pages 96-132.

Arden, John. "A BOND HONOURED." LONDON TIMES, 11 June 1966, p. 11.

Arden faults the critics for their superficial treatment of Osborne's play.

Brown, John Russell. "John Osborne: Theatrical Belief." In his THEATRE LANGUAGE: A STUDY OF ARDEN, OSBORNE, PINTER, WESKER. London: John Lane, Penguin Press, 1972, pp. 118-57.

Theatricality and role-playing are essential to Osborne's plays. From the bears and squirrels to Maitland's nightmarish obsessions, his characters wear masks to protect themselves, usually in vain.

Brustein, Robert. "Theatre Chronicle." HR, 12 (Spring 1959), 98-101.

EPITAPH FOR GEORGE DILLON is compared to Orwell's KEEP THE ASPIDISTRA FLYING (1936).

Carter, Alan. JOHN OSBORNE. Edinburgh: Oliver and Boyd, 1969.

This badly written, irritatingly simple-minded assessment classes all the plays as either public or private voice.

Deming, Barbara. "John Osborne's War against the Philistines." HR, 11 (Autumn 1958), 411-19.

Osborne's refusal to grant his Philistine opponents any virtues at all is his greatest failure as a dramatist. THE ENTERTAINER, so much like Beckett's ENDGAME, weakens its impact by forcing us, in a kind of snobbery in reverse, to make superficial choices between Osborne's favorites and his Philistines. Beckett also sees deeply into all his characters.

Dennis, Nigel. "Out of the Box." In his DRAMATIC ESSAYS. London: Weidenfeld and Nicolson, 1962, pp. 159-65.

On the Brechtian and Elizabethan antecedents for the form of LUTHER.

Dyson, A.E. "LOOK BACK IN ANGER." CRITICAL QUARTERLY, no. 1 (1959), 318-26. Rpt. in MODERN BRITISH DRAMATISTS: A COLLECTION OF CRITICAL ESSAYS. Ed. John Russell Brown. Englewood Cliffs, N.J.: Prentice-Hall, 1968, pp. 47-57.

As a corrective to a too simplistic identification of Osborne with Jimmy Porter, it is argued here that Porter is clearly presented as an ambiguous character.

Farber, M.D. "The Character of Jimmy Porter: An Approach to LOOK BACK IN ANGER." MD, 13 (May 1970), 67-77.

Jimmy Porter has an oral fixation neurosis.

Gersh, Gabriel. "The Theatre of John Osborne." MD, 10 (September 1967), 137-43.

Osborne has had an enormous impact, but no imitators. His sole stylistic contribution is the obsessed, masochistic tirade.

Hancock, Robert. "Anger." SPECTATOR, 5 April 1957, pp. 438-39.

A consistently snide, nasty interview with Osborne, typical of the sort of press treatment that led to some of Osborne's outbursts, one of which appears in the next week's issue.

Hardwick, Elizabeth. "Theater in New York." NYRB, 6 June 1966, pp. 5-6.

INADMISSIBLE EVIDENCE, which has a scabrous vitality lacking on the American stage, is used as a stick to beat the second Blau-Irving production at Lincoln Center, Wycherly's THE COUNTRY WIFE.

Hayman, Ronald. JOHN OSBORNE. London: Heinemann, 1968.

Brief, useful study of the life and work.

______. JOHN OSBORNE. New York: Frederick Ungar, 1972.

Expanded version of the English edition.

Hunter, G.K. "The World of John Osborne." CRQ, no. 3 (1961), 76-81.

Osborne's success in depicting the conflict between self-expression and repression, his central theme, varies as he avoids limiting that conflict to an individual, personal problem. THE WORLD OF PAUL SLICKEY, although it is sufficiently impersonal, is too small and parochial to sustain the kind of statement Osborne wishes to make.

Huss, Roy. "John Osborne's Backward Half-Way Look." MD, 6 (May 1963), 20-25.

LOOK BACK IN ANGER is a set of variations on the theme of sadomasochism. This a psychoanalytic reading, emphasizing Jimmy Porter's pre-Oedipal neurosis.

Karrfalt, David H. "The Social Theme in Osborne's Plays." MD, 13 (May 1970), 78-82.

Anger is the unvarying reaction of Osborne's heroes when faced with life's anguish and the absence of feeling in other people. Shared despair, Osborne believes, is the necessary prelude to an escape from despair.

Kitchin, Laurence. MID-CENTURY DRAMA. London: Faber and Faber, 1960, pp. 99-106.

______. "Redbrick Luther" and "The Wages of Sex." In his DRAMA IN THE SIXTIES. London: Faber and Faber, 1966, pp. 185-91.

Lahr, John. "Poor Johnny One-Note." In his UP AGAINST THE FOURTH WALL: ESSAYS ON MODERN THEATRE. New York: Grove Press, 1970, pp. 230-45.

HOTEL IN AMSTERDAM and TIME PRESENT are evidence of Osborne's theatrical enfeeblement and political irrelevance.

McCarthy, Mary. "A New Word." In her MARY McCARTHY'S THEATRE CHRONICLES, 1937-1962. New York: Noonday, 1963, pp. 186-98.

LOOK BACK IN ANGER and THE ENTERTAINER are nonparty protests against the hellish boredom of English life, as well as a revival of interest in the voice of the working class.

______. "Verdict on Osborne." OBSERVER, 4 July 1965, p. 17.

A PATRIOT FOR ME, typically, is without ideas; it is about a character whose "'problem' is simply being a homosexual."

Mander, John. THE WRITER AND COMMITMENT. London: Secker and Warburg, 1961, pp. 179-88.

Jimmy Porter is best understood in the light of Osborne's stage direction, "To be as vehement as he is, is to be almost noncommittal." The play's failure is due to the emptiness of all the other characters; there is no drama.

Marowitz, Charles. "The Ascension of John Osborne." TDR, 7 (Winter 1962), 175-79. Also in MODERN BRITISH DRAMATISTS: A COLLECTION OF CRITICAL ESSAYS. Ed. John Russell Brown. Englewood Cliffs, N.J.: Prenctice-Hall, 1968, pp. 117-21.

LUTHER, despite the Brechtian influence, is, for both good and ill, typical Osborne.

O'Brien, Charles H. "Osborne's LUTHER and the Humanities Tradition." RENASCENCE, 21 (Winter 1969), 59-63.

Osborne's treatment of Luther conforms to the humanist belief, as embodied in Erasmus, that Luther was driven to excess by an "inner irrational force."

Roberts, Mark. THE TRADITION OF ROMANTIC MORALITY. London: Macmillan, 1970.

The first chapter connects Jimmy Porter's "energy of soul" with a basic theme in the development of Romanticism into the twentieth century: the approval of vitality as a higher, overriding morality.

Scott-Kilvert, Ian. "The Hero in Search of a Dramatist: The Plays of John Osborne." ENC, 9 (December 1957), 26-30.

Osborne has broken through the "conspiracy of ghastly good taste," and the social impact of this breakthrough is of greater import than any purely literary judgment might indicate.

Seymour, Alan. "Maturing Vision." LONDON MAGAZINE, 5 (October 1965), 75-79.

A PATRIOT FOR ME moves beyond the earlier plays in acknowledging the protagonist's participation in society, and not, as before, settling for a simple choice between the individual and society.

Spacks, Patricia Meyer. "Confrontation and Escape in Two Social Plays." MD, 11 (May 1968), 61-72.

The characters in Ibsen's A DOLL'S HOUSE (1879), unlike those in LOOK BACK IN ANGER, seek to confront rather than escape an unpleasant social reality. Lacking Ibsen's irony, Osborne accepts his protagonist at his own valuation.

Spalter, Max. "Five Examples of How to Write a Brechtian play that is Not Really Brechtian." ETJ, 27 (May 1975), 220-35.

LUTHER is one of the examples.

Taylor, John Russell. "John Osborne." In his ANGER AND AFTER: A GUIDE TO THE NEW BRITISH DRAMA. Rev. ed. Harmondsworth, Engl.: Penguin, 1963, pp. 37-58.

Places Osborne's work in the context of the fifties, with a somewhat higher proportion of analysis to plot summary than is generally the case in this volume.

______, ed. JOHN OSBORNE: LOOK BACK IN ANGER, A CASEBOOK. London: Macmillan, 1968.

Extremely useful collection of reviews, criticism, and Osborne's own essays. Cited as CASEBOOK, ed. Taylor in this section.

Tschudin, Marcus. A WRITER'S THEATRE: GEORGE DEVINE AND THE ENGLISH STAGE COMPANY AT THE ROYAL COURT, 1956-1965. Bern, Switzerland: Herbert Lang, 1972.

Trussler, Simon. THE PLAYS OF JOHN OSBORNE. London: Gollancz, 1969.

Useful critical survey of the life and works, with a good bibliography and casts for first performances.

Tynan, Kenneth. "The Voice of the Young." OBSERVER, 13 May 1956, p. 11. Also in his CURTAINS: SELECTIONS FROM THE DRAMA CRITICISM AND RELATED WRITINGS. New York: Atheneum, 1961, pp. 130-32.

> Easily the single most famous review written during this period. Tynan adopts Porter as the embodiment of postwar youth, and suggests that the play has as its audience the nearly seven million people in England between the ages of twenty and thirty. Tynan's enthusiastic advocacy, his reputation as a youthful critic, together with a BBC broadcast of an extract from the play, all helped make LOOK BACK IN ANGER the focus of a "movement." It should be noted that Tynan's review did not stand alone in its praise, only in the degree of its enthusiasm.

______. "A Phony or a Genius." In his CURTAINS: SELECTIONS FROM THE DRAMA CRITICISM AND RELATED WRITINGS. New York: Atheneum, 1961, pp. 205-07.

> Osborne and Anthony Creighton couldn't decide whether George Dillon was a fraud or a real talent.

Wellwarth, George E. "Angry Young Man?" In his THE THEATER OF PROTEST AND PARADOX: DEVELOPMENTS IN THE AVANTE-GARDE DRAMA. New York: New York University Press, 1964, pp. 222-34.

> Porter's outbursts are "sophomoric piffle."

Worth, Katharine J. "The Angry Young Man: John Osborne." In EXPERIMENTAL DRAMA. Ed. William A. Armstrong. London: G. Bell, 1963, pp. 147-68. Also in CASEBOOK, ed. Taylor, pp. 101-16.

> Sympathetic treatment of Osborne as a playwright of suffering.

______. "John Osborne." In his REVOLUTIONS IN MODERN ENGLISH DRAMA. London: G. Bell, 1973, pp. 67-85.

> Osborne, like Bernard Shaw, demands performers capable of both verbal and physical acrobatics. They share Socialist sympathies, ambiguous feelings about England, and the urge to educate the audience. With specific comparisons of plays, this is a most interesting juxtaposition.

## ALUN OWEN (1926- )

THE ROUGH AND READY LOT. London: Encore, 1960.

THREE T.V. PLAYS. London: Jonathan Cape, 1961.

NO TRAMS TO LIME STREET; AFTER THE FUNERAL; and LENA, OH MY LENA.

PROGRESS TO THE PARK. P&P, 8 (July 1961), 25-33; (August 1961), 25-31.

PROGRESS TO THE PARK. In NEW ENGLISH DRAMATISTS 5. Ed. Tom Maschler. Harmondsworth, Engl.: Penguin, 1962.

THE ROSE AFFAIR. In ANATOMY OF A TELEVISION PLAY. London: Weidenfeld and Nicolson, 1962.

A LITTLE WINTER LOVE. London: Evans Bros., 1964.

DARE TO BE A DANIEL. In EIGHT PLAYS: BOOK I. Ed. Malcolm Stuart Fellows. London: Cassell, 1965.

GEORGE'S ROOM. London: Samuel French, 1968.

SHELTER. London: Samuel French, 1968.

NORMA. In MIXED DOUBLES. London: Methuen, 1970.

DOREEN. In THE BEST SHORT PLAYS 1971. Ed. Stanley Richards. Philadelphia: Chilton, 1971.

MALE OF THE SPECIES. In CAMERA THREE: THREE PLAYS FOR TELEVISION. Ed. Ronald Side and Ralph Greenfield. Toronto: Holt, Rinehart and Winston of Canada, 1972.

THE WAKE. In THEATRE CHOICE: A COLLECTION OF MODERN SHORT PLAYS. Ed. Michael Marland. London: Blackie, 1972.

## CRITICISM

Taylor, John Russell. "Alun Owen." In his ANGER AND AFTER: A GUIDE TO THE NEW ENGLISH DRAMA. Rev. ed. Harmondsworth, Engl.: Penguin, 1963, pp. 200-222.

> "Owen is not primarily a cerebral dramatist, and his plays present a point of view of the world more intuitive than reasoned. . . . Their structures are free and rhapsodic . . . and in his best work plot is replaced by incident and atmosphere."

# ROCHELLE OWENS (1936- )

FUTZ. New York: Hawk's Well Press, 1962.

Early version of her controversial first play.

FUTZ AND WHAT CAME AFTER. New York: Random House, 1968.

FUTZ, BECLCH, HOMO, THE STRING GAME, and ISTANBOUL.

HE WANTS SHIH. YT, 1 (Summer 1968), 72-74.

Brief excerpt.

THE QUEEN OF GREECE: A CURTAIN RAISER. YT, 2 (Summer 1969), 92-101.

Author's note: "It was originally conceived as a narrative poem, and was published as such, in an earlier version in the poetry magazine SOME/THING." Although performed at La Mama, the text still seems more a poem than a play.

THE KARL MARX PLAY. In THE BEST SHORT PLAYS 1971. Ed. Stanley Richards. Philadelphia: Chilton, 1971.

A short version.

KONTRAPTION. SCRIPTS, 2 (December 1971), 4-25.

HE WANTS SHIH! In SPONTANEOUS COMBUSTION: EIGHT NEW AMERICAN PLAYS. Ed. Rochelle Owens. New York: Winter House, 1972.

THE KARL MARX PLAY AND OTHERS. New York: E.P. Dutton, 1974.

Also includes KONTRAPTION, HE WANTS SHIH!, FARMER'S ALMANAC: A RITUAL, COCONUT FOLK-SINGER: A RADIO PLAY, O.K. CERTALDO, and an introduction by the author.

## BIBLIOGRAPHY

Young, Karl, ed. "Bibliography." MARGINS, 24, 25, 26 (September-November 1975), 132-33.

## SELECTED NONDRAMATIC WRITING

NOT BE ESSENCE THAT CANNOT BE. New York: Trobar Press, 1961.

Poetry.

SALT AND CORE. San Francisco: Black Sparrow Press, 1968.

Poetry.

"Without the Language . . . There is just Nothing." NTM, 10 (Summer 1970), 22-24.

## CRITICISM

Brustein, Robert. "A Theatre Slouches to be Born." In his THE THIRD THEATER. New York: Knopf, 1969, pp. 68-72.

> FUTZ is "a pornographic version of UNDER MILK WOOD, complete with an omniscient narrator, an episodic structure, and a radio-style loquacity, about a rural Christian community sick with repressed sexual longings."

Young, Karl, ed. "Symposium on Rochelle Owens." MARGINS, 24, 25, 26 (September-November 1975), 107-33.

> Fifteen articles and reviews, with a bibliography, about the work of Rochelle Owens. The critical materials are uniformly laudatory; of interest are Kenneth Bernard's "The Plays of Rochelle Owens," and Bonnie Marranca's "'Transformations' as Technique in the Recent Plays of Rochelle Owens."

## JOHN PATRICK (JOHN PATRICK GOGGAN) (1907- )

THE CURIOUS SAVAGE. New York: Dramatists Play Service, 1951.

LO AND BEHOLD! New York: Samuel French, 1952.

THE TEAHOUSE OF THE AUGUST MOON. New York: Putnam, 1954.

His most considerable success, adapted from the novel by Vern Sneider (1951).

EVERYBODY LOVES OPAL: A PRANK IN THREE ACTS. New York: Dramatists Play Service, 1962.

EVERYBODY'S GIRL. New York: Dramatists Play Service, 1968.

THE SCANDAL POINT. New York: Dramatists Play Service, 1969.

LOVE IS A TIME OF DAY. New York: Dramatists Play Service, 1970.

LOVELY LADIES, KIND GENTLEMEN. New York: Samuel French, 1970.

Unsuccessful musical adaptation of TEAHOUSE, music and lyrics by Stan Freeman and Franklin Underwood.

A BARREL FULL OF PENNIES. New York: Dramatists Play Service, 1971.

ANYBODY OUT THERE? New York: Dramatists Play Service, 1972.

THE DANCING MICE. New York: Dramatists Play Service, 1972.

MACBETH DID IT. New York: Dramatists Play Service, 1972.

OPAL IS A DIAMOND. New York: Dramatists Play Service, 1972.

THE SAVAGE DILEMMA. New York: Dramatists Play Service, 1972.

A sequel to THE CURIOUS SAVAGE.

ROMAN CONQUEST. New York: Samuel French, 1972.

THE ENIGMA. New York: Dramatists Play Service, 1974.

OPAL'S BABY: A NEW SEQUEL IN TWO ACTS. New York: Dramatists Play Service, 1974.

## BIBLIOGRAPHY

Salem, James M., ed. A GUIDE TO CRITICAL REVIEWS. Part 1: AMERICAN DRAMA 1909-1969. 2nd ed. Metuchen, N.J.: Scarecrow Press, 1973.

List of reviews, pages 378-81.

## CRITICISM

Moe, Christian H. "John Patrick." In CONTEMPORARY DRAMATISTS. Ed. James Vinson. London: St. James; New York: St. Martin's, 1973, pp. 598-600.

"John Patrick merits attention as a major craftsman of the American theatre."

## ROBERT PATRICK (1937-  )

STILL LOVE. INTERMISSION (Chicago), 1967.

CAMERA OBSCURA. In COLLISION COURSE. Ed. Edward Parone. New York: Random House, 1968.

CHEESECAKE. OFF-OFF MAGAZINE (New York), 1969.

ACTION. YT, 2 (Summer 1969), 88-91.

Part of the triple bill of LIGHTS, CAMERA, ACTION.

SEE OTHER SIDE. YT, 2 (Summer 1969), 85-87.

THE GOLDEN CIRCLE. In NEW AMERICAN PLAYS. Vol. 3. Ed. William H. Hoffman. New York: Hill and Wang, 1969.

### COLLECTIONS

CHEEP THEATRICKS! New York: Winter House, 1972.

Short plays from 1964-70: I CAME TO NEW YORK TO WRITE; THE HAUNTED HOST; JOYCE DYNEL; CORNERED; STILL LOVE; LIGHTS, CAMERA, ACTION; HELP, I AM; THE ARNOLD BLISS SHOW; ONE PERSON; PREGGIN AND LISS; and THE RICHEST GIRL IN THE WORLD FINDS HAPPINESS; introduced by Lanford Wilson.

### CRITICISM

Carragher, Bernard. "Robert Patrick." In CONTEMPORARY DRAMATISTS. Ed. James Vinson. London: St. James; New York: St. Martin's, 1973, pp. 602-03.

# S[IDNEY] J[OSEPH] PERELMAN (1904-1979)

THE BEAUTY PART. New York: Simon and Schuster, 1963.

The short-lived Bert Lahr vehicle.

THE BEAUTY PART. In BROADWAY'S BEAUTIFUL LOSERS. Ed. Marilyn Stasio. New York: Delacorte, 1972.

With a sympathetic analysis of the play's lack of success.

## CRITICISM

Brustein, Robert. SEASONS OF DISCONTENT: DRAMATIC OPINIONS 1959-1965. New York: Simon and Schuster, 1965.

THE BEAUTY PART satirized the "American culture industry," with a bitterness unusual for Perelman, but the play's stance is too ambiguous. See pages 149-51.

Simon, John. UNEASY STAGES. New York: Random House, 1975.

THE BEAUTY PART is weak satire, and Perelman's writing is simply not funny. See pages 4-6.

# DAVID PINNER (1940-  )

FANGHORN. Harmondsworth, Engl.: Penguin, 1966.

DICKON. In NEW ENGLISH DRAMATISTS 10. Harmondsworth, Engl.: Penguin, 1967.

THE DRUMS OF SNOW. In NEW ENGLISH DRAMATISTS 13. Harmondsworth, Engl.: Penguin, 1968.

## SELECTED NONDRAMATIC WRITING

RITUAL. London: Hutchinson, 1967.

Novel.

WITH MY BODY. London: Weidenfeld and Nicolson, 1968.

Novel.

## CRITICISM

Hayman, Ronald. "David Pinner." In CONTEMPORARY DRAMATISTS. Ed. James Vinson. London: St. James; New York: St. Martin's, 1973, pp. 607-08.

## HAROLD PINTER (1930- )

THE BIRTHDAY PARTY. London: Encore Publishing, 1959.

THE BIRTHDAY PARTY AND OTHER PLAYS. London: Methuen, 1960.

With THE DUMB WAITER and THE ROOM.

THE BLACK AND WHITE and TROUBLE IN THE WORKS. In ONE TO ANOTHER. With John Mortimer and F.N. Simpson. London: Samuel French, 1960.

Review sketches.

THE CARETAKER. London: Methuen, 1960.

A SLIGHT ACHE AND OTHER PLAYS. London: Methuen, 1961.

With A NIGHT OUT, THE DWARFS (which is based on an unpublished novel), and five review sketches: TROUBLE IN THE WORKS, THE BLACK AND WHITE, REQUEST STOP, LAST TO GO, and APPLICANT. According to John Russell Brown in his THEATRE LANGUAGE (London: John Lane, 1972), "The first stage version of THE DWARFS is in the 1966 reprint, the second stage version in that of 1968" (p. 252).

THE CARETAKER. Rev. ed. London: Methuen, 1962.

THE COLLECTION, AND THE LOVER. London: Methuen, 1963.

Also includes the short story, "The Examination."

DIALOGUE FOR THREE. STAND (London), 6 (1963).

Sketch.

THE BIRTHDAY PARTY. Rev. ed. London: Methuen, 1965.

Pinter's revisions, here and elsewhere, are nearly all deletions, tightening the dialogue, making it, if possible, more enigmatic.

THE HOMECOMING. London: Methuen, 1965.

THE HOMECOMING. London: H. Karnac, 1968.

A limited, signed edition.

THE DWARFS AND EIGHT REVIEW SKETCHES. New York: Dramatists Play Service, 1965.

INTERVIEW, THAT'S ALL, and THAT'S YOUR TROUBLE, with the five sketches collected in A SLIGHT ACHE AND OTHER PLAYS.

THE TEA PARTY. London: Methuen, 1965.

SPECIAL OFFER. In A.P. Hinchliffe, HAROLD PINTER. New York: Twayne, 1967.

Brief sketch.

THE TEA PARTY AND OTHER PLAYS. London: Methuen, 1967.

Includes THE BASEMENT and NIGHT SCHOOL.

LANDSCAPE. London: Pendragon, 1968.

THE TEA PARTY. Rev. ed. London: H. Karnac, 1968.

LANDSCAPE AND SILENCE. London: Methuen, 1969.

The two plays and NIGHT, a sketch first performed as part of MIXED DOUBLES.

FIVE SCREENPLAYS. London: Methuen, 1971.

Screenplays dating from 1963 to 1971: THE GO-BETWEEN, THE SERVANT, THE PUMPKIN EATER, ACCIDENT, and THE QUILLER MEMORANDUM.

OLD TIMES. London: Eyre Methuen, 1971.

MONOLOGUE. London: Covent Garden Press, 1973.

NO MAN'S LAND. London: Eyre Methuen, 1975.

## BIBLIOGRAPHY

Imhof, Rudiger, comp. PINTER: A BIBLIOGRAPHY. His Works and Occasional Writings, with a Comprehensive Checklist of Criticism and Reviews of the London Publications. London: TQ Publications, 1975.

Authoritative.

Schroll, Herman T. HAROLD PINTER: A STUDY OF HIS REPUTATION (1958-1969) AND A CHECKLIST. Metuchen, N.J.: Scarecrow Press, 1971.

An exhaustive eighty-six page essay on Pinter's critical reputation with some strictures on theatrical trendiness and critical over-interpretation. This excellent research tool concludes with a forty-eight page bibliographical index of reviews and criticism.

## SELECTED NONDRAMATIC WRITING

"Harold Pinter Replies." NTM, 2 (January 1961), 8-10.

This interview with Harry Thompson is interesting for Pinter's remarks on the influence of Samuel Beckett, on political thinking, and on himself as a director of his own work.

"Writing for Myself." TWENTIETH CENTURY, 169 (February 1961), 172-75.

Important, early statement, notable for Pinter's explanation of the origins of THE ROOM: "I went into a room one day and saw a couple of people in it." It also contains a brief allusion to his autobiographical novel, THE DWARFS.

"Between the Lines." SUNDAY TIMES (London), 4 March 1962, p. 25.

This is a valuable statement of Pinter's feelings about language, its deceptiveness, its function as a "stratagem to cover nakedness." If one were to read but one Pinter statement, this should be it.

"Harold Pinter." In WRITERS AT WORK: THE PARIS REVIEW INTERVIEWS. 3rd series. Introd. Alfred Kazin. New York: Viking Press, 1967.

On directing, politics, his early experiences of violence, that burdensome word "Pinteresque," and his sense of himself as a very traditional playwright.

POEMS. Rev. ed. Ed. Alan Clodd. London: Enitharmon Press, 1970.

"Filming THE CARETAKER: Harold Pinter and Clive Donner Interviewed by Kenneth Cavander." In BEHIND THE SCENES: THEATRE AND FILM INTERVIEWS FROM THE TRANSATLANTIC REVIEW. Ed. Joseph F.M. McCrindle, introd. Jean-Claude van Itallie. New York: Holt, Rinehart and Winston, 1971, pp. 211-22.

Pinter and the film's director discuss their collaboration.

"Speech: Hamburg 1970." TQ, 1 (July-September 1971), 3-4.

In an acceptance speech, after receiving the Shakespeare Prize for LANDSCAPE and SILENCE, Pinter recounts the practical, non-intellectual work of directing and writing, his distrust of generalizations, and his pain during a period of creative inactivity.

## CRITICISM

Allison, Ralph, and Charles Wellborn. "Rhapsody in an Anechoic Chamber: Pinter's LANDSCAPE." ETJ, 25 (May 1973), 215-25.

The ambiguities and silences in LANDSCAPE are compared to such contemporary, aperiodic music as John Cage's.

Amend, Victor E. "Harold Pinter--Some Credits and Debits." MD, 10 (September 1967), 165-74.

Laments Pinter's vagueness and the absence of a "positive approach."

Arden, John. "Book Review: THE CARETAKER." NTM, 1 (July 1960), 29-30.

Pinter is a new kind of realist, neither an Ibsenite nor a symbolist. His orchestrated verbal patterns alone convey a great deal.

Benedictus, David. "Pinter's Errors." SPECTATOR, 11 June 1965, p. 755.

This review of THE HOMECOMING sees the work as autobiography, with Pinter as Teddy.

Bermel, Albert. "The Monarch as Beggar." In his CONTRADICTORY CHARACTERS: AN INTERPRETATION OF MODERN THEATRE. New York: E.P. Dutton, 1973, pp. 228-42.

A SLIGHT ACHE is a Frazerian fertility ritual of one kingship supplanted by another.

Brody, Alan. "The Gift of Realism: Hitchcock and Pinter." JOURNAL OF MODERN LITERATURE, 3 (April 1973), 149-72.

Compares Hitchcock's film SHADOW OF A DOUBT with THE BIRTHDAY PARTY.

Brown, John Russell. "Mr. Pinter's Shakespeare." CQ, 5 (Autumn 1963), 251-65.

"Exposition has become Development, and Conclusion as well." This characteristic of Pinter, Beckett, and Ionesco is then applied to Shakespeare.

______. THEATRE LANGUAGE: A STUDY OF ARDEN, OSBORNE, PINTER AND WESKER. London: Alan Lane, 1972.

Pinter receives three chapters of perceptive analysis. The first, "Words and Silence," treats his use of language as a smokescreen for manipulation, a use related to the Stanislavskian subtext. The second, "Gestures, Spectacle and Performance," concerns physical movement, without and under dialogue, particularly in THE CARETAKER and THE DWARFS, in its evolution from radio to the stage. The third, "Action and Control," focuses on THE HOMECOMING and Pinter's mixture of astringency and density. See pages 15-118.

Burkman, Katherine H. "Pinter's A SLIGHT ACHE as Ritual." MD, 11 (December 1968), 326-35.

The play is a fertility ritual celebrating, ironically, the death of the old god-king and the birth of the new.

Carpenter, Charles A. "The Absurdity of Dread: Pinter's THE DUMB WAITER." MD, 16 (December 1973), 279-85.

THE DUMB WAITER is a farce, not a soulful exercise in metaphysical alienation.

Cohn, Ruby. "The World of Harold Pinter." TDR, 6 (March 1962), 55-68. Also in PINTER: A COLLECTION OF CRITICAL ESSAYS. Ed. Arthur Ganz. Englewood Cliffs, N.J.: Prentice-Hall, 1972, pp. 78-92. (Hereafter cited as COLLECTION, ed. Ganz.)

An analysis of Pinter's early work that places him between Beckett and Osborne and emphasizes the theme of victimization.

Coward, Noel. "These Old-Fashioned Revolutionaries." SUNDAY TIMES (London), 15 January 1961, p. 23.

THE CARETAKER, despite its depiction of the lower social stratum, is a well-written work whose "basic premise is victory."

Dawick, John. "'Punctuation' and Patterning in THE HOMECOMING." MD, 14 (May 1971), 37-46.

The varied uses of hesitation, the pause, the silence, the blackout, and the curtain are distinguished in the text of THE HOMECOMING.

Dennis, Nigel. "Pintermania." NYRB, 17 December 1970, pp. 21-22.

Dennis criticizes Esslin's and Hollis' books (see below) for discovering profundities where none exist. He suggests that Pinter's puzzles are less philosophical excursions and more the result of an actor's cagey sense of what will play on a stage.

Eigo, James. "Pinter's LANDSCAPE." MD, 16 (September 1973), 179-83.

The "intersecting themes" of the monologues of Beth and Duff are traced.

Esslin, Martin. THE PEOPLED WOUND: THE WORK OF HAROLD PINTER. Garden City, N.Y.: Doubleday, 1970.

This excellent study, for which Esslin had access to some of Pinter's unpublished materials, is admirably tentative in its interpretations. The volume is prefaced by a meticulous chronology of Pinter's career; each play is analyzed, with a separate section for the poetry and the screenplays.

Ganz, Arthur. "A Clue to the Pinter Puzzle: The Triple Self in THE HOMECOMING." ETJ, 21 (May 1969), 180-87.

The play is seen as a psychomachia.

_____, ed. PINTER: A COLLECTION OF CRITICAL ESSAYS. Englewood Cliffs, N.J.: Prentice-Hall, 1972.

Good introductory collection of essays. Cited as COLLECTION, ed. Ganz, in this section.

Hinchliffe, Arnold P. "Mr. Pinter's Belinda." MD, 11 (September 1968), 173-79.

Pinter's post-CARETAKER plays show a gradual evolution of theme, culminating in the sexual identity games of THE HOMECOMING.

Hoefer, Jacqueline. "Pinter and Whiting: Two Attitudes Towards the Alienated Artist." MD, 4 (February 1962), 402-08.

Hoefer compares THE BIRTHDAY PARTY and SAINT'S DAY (1952), finding in one the artist as victim, in the other the artist as destroyer.

Hollis, James R. HAROLD PINTER: THE POETICS OF SILENCE. Carbondale: Southern Illinois University Press, 1970.

Kaufman, Michael W. "Actions that a Man Might Play: Pinter's THE BIRTHDAY PARTY." MD, 16 (September 1973), 167-78.

Review of Pinter's first "gentle" works.

Lahr, John. "Pinter the Spaceman." In his UP AGAINST THE FOURTH WALL: ESSAYS ON MODERN THEATER. New York: Grove Press, 1970, pp. 175-94.

Pinter and arbitrary nature.

______. "Pinter and Chekhov: The Bond of Naturalism." In his ASTONISH ME: ADVENTURES IN CONTEMPORARY THEATER. New York: Viking, 1973, pp. 67-82. Also in COLLECTION. Ed. Arthur Ganz, pp. 60-71.

Both playwrights explore a subtle dynamism between surface naturalism and a poetry beyond physical objects.

Lesser, Simon O. "Reflections on Pinter's THE BIRTHDAY PARTY." CONTEMPORARY LITERATURE, 13 (Winter 1972), 34-43.

Pinter and THE BIRTHDAY PARTY are deeply indebted to Kafka, but Pinter's play is his own, and Lesser finds it is about social exploitation.

Mast, Gerald. "Pinter's HOMECOMING." DS, 6 (Spring 1968), 266-77.

The ending of THE HOMECOMING is defended as a reasonable result of the play's characters in action.

Milne, Tom. "The Hidden Faces of Violence." In THE ENCORE READER: A CHRONICLE OF THE NEW DRAMA. Ed. Charles Marowitz, Tom Milne, and Owen Hale. London: Methuen, 1965, pp. 115-25. Also in MODERN BRITISH DRAMATISTS: A COLLECTION OF CRITICAL ESSAYS. Ed. John Russell Brown. Englewood Cliffs, N.J.: Prentice-Hall, 1968, pp. 38-46.

THE BIRTHDAY PARTY, John Whiting's SAINT'S DAY (1952), and John Arden's SERJEANT MUSGRAVE'S DANCE (1960) "share a common theme: the nature of violence."

Minogue, Valerie. "Taking Care of THE CARETAKER." TWENTIETH CENTURY, 168 (September 1960), 243-48. Also in COLLECTION. Ed. Arthur Ganz, pp. 72-76.

The critics are paying too much attention to the stylistic niceties of Pinter's art, and are neglecting the plain contemporary meaning of his plays' contents.

Morris, Kelly. "THE HOMECOMING." TDR, 11 (Winter 1966), 185-91.

The play is a comedy of manners in which stage action itself is the only reality, all linked to Ruth's speech that begins, "Don't be too sure though."

Murphy, Robert P. "Non-Verbal Communications and the Overlooked Action in Pinter's THE CARETAKER." QJS, 58 (February 1972), 41-47.

The stage directions are evidence that Davies' psyche is maliciously destroyed by the brothers.

Nelson, Hugh. "THE HOMECOMING: Kith and Kin." In MODERN BRITISH DRAMATISTS: A COLLECTION OF CRITICAL ESSAYS. Ed. John Russell Brown. Englewood Cliffs, N.J.: Prentice-Hall, 1968, pp. 145-63.

The homecoming is Ruth's; it is her self-discovery. The play demonstrates the superiority of function over blood ties. The play is compared with TROILUS AND CRESSIDA and the BOOK OF JOB.

Pesta, John. "Pinter's Usurpers." DS, 6 (Spring-Summer 1967), 54-67. Also in COLLECTION. Ed. Arthur Ganz, pp. 123-35.

Each of Pinter's plays features a usurper, an intruder who can be either victim or victimizer.

Powlick, Leonard. "A Phenomenological Approach to Harold Pinter's A SLIGHT ACHE." QJS, 60 (February 1974), 25-32.

The threat to Edward is internal, and comes from the person he is becoming.

Roberts, Patrick. "Pinter: The Roots of the Relationship." In his THE PSYCHOLOGY OF TRAGIC DRAMA. London: Routledge and Kegan Paul, 1975, pp. 69-101.

This psychoanalytic reading emphasizes the "primitive, infantile self" that is concealed in and dominates the adult in THE BIRTHDAY PARTY, THE COLLECTION, and THE HOMECOMING.

Schechner, Richard. "Puzzling Pinter." TDR, 11 (Winter 1966), 176-84.

Schiff, Ellen F. "Pancakes and Soap Suds: A Study of Childishness in Pinter's Plays." MD, 16 (June 1973), 91-101.

Pinter's characters behave like children, fascinated with language, vulnerable, afraid of the outside world, and locked into a highly dangerous relationship with the mother.

States, Bert O. "Pinter's HOMECOMING: The Shock of Nonrecognition." HR, 21 (August 1968), 474-86. Also in COLLECTION. Ed. Arthur Ganz, pp. 147-60.

This essay in historical aesthetics identifies Pinter and his characters as ironists in a literary world only marginally connected with reality.

Storch, R.F. "Harold Pinter's Happy Families." MR, 8 (Autumn 1967), 703-12.

The source of Pinter's power is that he depicts that most quintessential of all bourgeois institutions--the family.

Sykes, Arlene. "Harold Pinter's DWARFS." KOMOS, 1 (June 1967), 70-75.

The dwarfs represent, not the poetic imagination or unseen monsters, but the turmoil of the relationship among Len, Mack, and Peter. THE DWARFS is derived largely from "Extract from WATT," published in IRISH WRITING in 1951.

Walker, Augusta. "Messages from Pinter." MD, 10 (May 1967), 1-10.

The loss of God, of "innerness," is the source of the emptiness in Pinter's plays and the modern world.

Wardle, Irving. "The Comedy of Menace." In THE ENCORE READER: A CHRONICLE OF THE NEW DRAMA. Ed. Charles Marowitz, Tom Milne, and Owen Hale. London: Methuen, 1965, pp. 86-91.

Pinter is "a writer dogged by one image--the womb." "Menace . . . stands for something more substantial: destiny." This review is the source for the much used and abused title phrase.

Worth, Katharine J. "Joyce via Pinter." In her REVOLUTIONS IN MODERN ENGLISH DRAMA. London: G. Bell, 1973, pp. 46-54.

Joyce's EXILES (1918), as directed by Pinter and compared to Pinter's own works, illustrates the continuity of English realism.

Wray, Phoebe. "Pinter's Dialogue: The Play on Words." MD, 13 (February 1971), 418-22.

Pinter is praised for his use of silences, pauses, and jargon that, paradoxically, returns to language a power it seemed to have lost.

## ALAN PLATER (1935- )

THE MATING SEASON. In WORTH A HEARING: A COLLECTION OF RADIO PLAYS. Ed. Alfred Bradley. London: Blackie, 1967.

A QUIET NIGHT. In Z CARS: FOUR SCRIPTS FROM THE TELEVISION SERIES. Ed. Michael Marland. London: Longmans, 1968.

CLOSE THE COALHOUSE DOOR. London: Methuen, 1969.

> With an introduction by Plater, this was a musical documentary about coal mining, based on stories by Sid Chaplin, with songs by Alex Glasgow.

EXCURSION. In PLAYBILL 3. Ed. Alan Durband. London: Hutchinson, 1969.

THE VIRGIN AND THE GIPSY. London: Kenwood Films, 1969.

> Technical shooting script by Christopher Miles, screenplay by Plater.

SEE THE PRETTY LIGHTS. In THEATRE CHOICE: A COLLECTION OF MODERN SHORT PLAYS. Ed. Michael Marland. London: Blackie, 1972.

YOU AND ME: FOUR PLAYS. Ed. Alfred Bradley. London: Blackie, 1973.

> Contains EXCURSION, CHRISTMAS DAY IN THE MORNING, AND A LITTLE LOVE BESIDES, SEVENTEEN PER CENT SAID PUSH OFF, and a note on the media by the author.

### SELECTED NONDRAMATIC WRITING

"The Writer in the Provinces." NTM, 5 (October-December 1964), 3-5.

Why Plater lives in Hull, and what regional theatre, television, and radio can offer.

"The Playwright and His People." TQ, 1 (April-June 1971), 67-70.

Plater discusses his work in the theatre, films, and television in terms of the audience he seeks. He laments the absence of virtually any drama descriptive of the role of work in an individual's life.

## CRITICISM

Taylor, John Russell. "Three Social Realists: John Hopkins, Alan Plater, Cecil P. Taylor." In his THE SECOND WAVE. London: Methuen, 1971, pp. 181-86.

Plot summaries.

Worth, Katharine J. "New Forms of Melodrama and Epic Theatre." In her REVOLUTIONS IN MODERN ENGLISH DRAMA. London: G. Bell, 1973, pp. 124-26.

Music hall techniques in CLOSE THE COALHOUSE DOOR.

# DENNIS POTTER (1935- )

THE NIGEL BARTON PLAYS: TWO TELEVISION PLAYS. Harmondsworth, Engl.: Penguin, 1967.

Consists of STAND UP, NIGEL BARTON, and VOTE VOTE VOTE FOR NIGEL BARTON.

SON OF MAN. London: Andre Deutsch, 1970.

## CRITICISM

Raynor, Henry. "Dennis Potter." In CONTEMPORARY DRAMATISTS. Ed. James Vinson. London: St. James; New York: St. Martin's, 1973, pp. 621-22.

# EZRA POUND (1885-1972)

SOPHOCLES' WOMEN OF TRACHIS. HR, 5 (Winter 1954), 487-523.

Pound's adaptation of Sophocles.

SOPHOCLES' WOMEN OF TRACHIS. London: Neville Spearman, 1956.

With critical essays on the translation and Pound's stay in Italy.

## BIBLIOGRAPHY

Gallup, Donald, ed. A BIBLIOGRAPHY OF EZRA POUND. London: Rupert Hart-Davis, 1963.

Exemplary primary source bibliography.

## CRITICISM

Carter, Thomas H. "That Hard Sophoclean Light." KR, 19 (Autumn 1957), 658-61.

Pound has altered Sophocles' emphasis and also placed his own style too much in the forefront.

Mason, H.A. "THE WOMEN OF TRACHIS and Creative Translation." In EZRA POUND: A CRITICAL ANTHOLOGY. Ed. J.P. Sullivan. Harmondsworth, Engl.: Penguin, 1970, pp. 279-310.

While Pound has in some ways altered the essence of Sophocles and diminishes the role of Deianeira, he has performed a miracle of recreation in his heroic treatment of Heracles. Most importantly, his translation is judgable by only the highest of standards and compels a critical reassessment of the play itself.

Sullivan, J.P. "Ezra Pound's Classical Translations." TEXAS QUARTERLY, 10 (Winter 1967), 57-60.

Sutherland, Donald. "Ezra Pound or Sophocles." COLORADO QUARTERLY, 8 (Autumn 1959), 182-91.

Pound's version does no service to Sophocles or to today's audience.

## J[OHN] B[OYNTON] PRIESTLEY (1894- )

BRIGHT SHADOW: A PLAY OF DETECTION IN THREE ACTS. London: Samuel French, 1950.

SUMMER DAY'S DREAM. London: Samuel French, 1950.

MOTHER'S DAY. London: Samuel French, 1953.

PRIVATE ROOMS: A ONE ACT COMEDY IN THE VIENNESE STYLE. London: Samuel French, 1953.

TREASURE ON PELICAN. London: Evans Bros., 1953.

TRY IT AGAIN. London: Samuel French, 1953.

A GLASS OF BITTER. London: Samuel French, 1954.

THE SCANDALOUS AFFAIR OF MR. KETTLE AND MRS. MOON. London: Samuel French, 1956.

THE GLASS CAGE. Toronto: Kingswood House, 1957.

THE GLASS CAGE. London: Samuel French, 1958.

A PAVILION OF MASKS. London: Samuel French, 1958.

### COLLABORATIONS

DRAGON'S MOUTH: A DRAMATIC QUARTET IN TWO PARTS. London: Heinemann, 1952.

A collaboration with Jacquetta Hawkes.

DRAGON'S MOUTH. In THE OFF-BROADWAY THEATRE. Ed. Richard A. Cordell and Lowell Matson. New York: Random House, 1959.

A SEVERED HEAD. London: Chatto and Windus, 1964.

A collaboration with Iris Murdoch.

## BIBLIOGRAPHY

Salem, James M., ed. A GUIDE TO CRITICAL REVIEWS. Part 3: BRITISH AND CONTINENTAL DRAMA FROM IBSEN TO PINTER. Metuchen, N.J.: Scarecrow Press, 1968.

List of reviews of the New York production of A SEVERED HEAD. See page 185.

## SELECTED NONDRAMATIC WRITING

THE ART OF THE DRAMATIST: A LECTURE TOGETHER WITH APPENDICES AND DISCURSIVE NOTES. London: Heinemann, 1957.

## CRITICISM

Brown, Ivor. J.B. PRIESTLEY. New York: Longmans, 1957.

Cooper, Susan. J.B. PRIESTLEY: PORTRAIT OF AN AUTHOR. London: Heinemann, 1970.

Adulatory, with a lengthy chapter on the plays.

Dews, Peter. "Coming Again, Like Parkin." DRAMA, n.s. 115 (Winter 1974), 28-32.

A tribute to J.B. Priestley as a dramatist.

Evans, Gareth Lloyd. J.B. PRIESTLEY--THE DRAMATIST. London: Heinemann, 1964.

The focus is on the earlier works; the post-fifties plays are barely mentioned.

Hughes, David. J.B. PRIESTLEY: AN INFORMAL STUDY OF HIS WORK. London: Hart-Davis, 1958.

Very informal, with a cursory treatment of the postwar plays in chapter 8.

Trewin, J.C. "Bradford Enchanted." In his DRAMATISTS OF TODAY. London: Staples Press, 1953, pp. 111-23.

Survey of Priestley's early work.

# TERENCE RATTIGAN (1911- )

ADVENTURE STORY. London: Samuel French, 1950.

WHO IS SYLVIA? A LIGHT COMEDY. London: Hamish Hamilton, 1951.

THE DEEP BLUE SEA. London: Hamish Hamilton, 1952.

THE SLEEPING PRINCE. London: Hamish Hamilton, 1954.

SEPARATE TABLES: TWO PLAYS. London: Hamish Hamilton, 1955.

TABLE NUMBER SEVEN and TABLE BY THE WINDOW.

THE SLEEPING PRINCE: AN OCCASIONAL FAIRY TALE. London: Samuel French, 1956.

THE PRINCE AND THE SHOWGIRL: THE SCRIPT FOR THE FILM. New York: New American Library, 1957.

Rattigan's screenplay based on his THE SLEEPING PRINCE.

VARIATIONS ON A THEME. London: Hamish Hamilton, 1958.

ROSS: A DRAMATIC PORTRAIT. London: Hamish Hamilton, 1960.

MAN AND BOY. New York: Samuel French, 1963.

ALL ON HER OWN. In THE BEST SHORT PLAYS OF 1970. Ed. Stanley Richards. Philadelphia: Chilton, 1970.

A BEQUEST TO THE NATION. London: Hamish Hamilton, 1970.

IN PRAISE OF LOVE: A PLAY; WITH A CURTAIN RAISER, BEFORE DAWN. London: Hamish Hamilton, 1973.

## COLLECTIONS

THE COLLECTED PLAYS. Vol. 2. London: Hamish Hamilton, 1953.

Includes, along with earlier works, ADVENTURE STORY, WHO IS SYLVIA?, and THE DEEP BLUE SEA.

THE COLLECTED PLAYS. Vol. 3. London: Hamish Hamilton, 1964.

THE SLEEPING PRINCE, SEPARATE TABLES, VARIATIONS ON A THEME, ROSS, and the only published text of HEART TO HEART.

## BIBLIOGRAPHY

Salem, James M., ed. A GUIDE TO CRITICAL REVIEWS. Part 3: BRITISH AND CONTINENTAL DRAMA. Metuchen, N.J.: Scarecrow Press, 1968.

List of reviews of the New York productions. See pages 197-201.

## CRITICISM

Taylor, John Russell. "Terence Rattigan." In his THE RISE AND FALL OF THE WELL-MADE PLAY. New York: Hill and Wang, 1967, pp. 146-65.

Rattigan is a "wilfull and self-conscious neo-classicist," who also makes use of the new subjects and opportunities won by the newer dramatists.

Trewin, J.C. "Diplomatist." In his DRAMATISTS OF TODAY. London: Staples Press, 1953, pp. 182-91.

Tynan, Kenneth. "Rattigan in Two Volumes." In his CURTAINS: SELECTIONS FROM THE DRAMA CRITICISM AND RELATED WRITINGS. New York: Atheneum, 1961, pp. 74-76.

This review of THE COLLECTED PLAYS is very critical of Rattigan's preface containing the Aunt Edna character, the personification of middle-class good sense.

______. "Separate Tables." In his CURTAINS: SELECTIONS FROM THE DRAMA CRITICISM AND RELATED WRITINGS. New York: Atheneum, 1961, pp. 79-81.

An imaginary dialogue between "Aunt Edna" and a "Young Perfectionist" that attacks Rattigan's attempt simultaneously to shock and reassure all segments of his audience.

Weintraub, Stanley. "How History Gets Rewritten: Lawrence of Arabia in the Theatre." DS, 5 (February 1963), 269-75.

Contrasts the legendary Lawrence of ROSS with the facts of Lawrence's life.

# RONALD RIBMAN (1932- )

THE JOURNEY OF THE FIFTH HORSE, AND HARRY, NOON AND NIGHT: TWO PLAYS. Boston: Little, Brown, 1967.

THE CEREMONY OF INNOCENCE. New York: Dramatists Play Service, 1968.

THE FINAL WAR OF OLLY WINTER. In GREAT TELEVISION PLAYS. Ed. William I. Kaufman. New York: Dell, 1969.

PASSING THROUGH FROM EXOTIC PLACES: THREE SHORT PLAYS. New York: Dramatists Play Service, 1970.

THE SON WHO HUNTED TIGERS IN JAKARTA, SUNSTROKE, and THE BURIAL OF ESPOSITO.

FINGERNAILS AS BLUE AS FLOWERS. In PLAYS OF THE AMERICAN PLACE THEATER. Ed. Richard Shotter. New York: Dell, 1973.

## CRITICISM

Gottfried, Martin. A THEATER DIVIDED: THE POSTWAR AMERICAN STAGE. Boston: Little, Brown, 1967, pp. 72-75.

Kaufman, Stanley. "The Journey of the Fifth Horse." In his PERSONS OF THE DRAMA. New York: Harper and Row, 1976, pp. 173-75.

Ribman's play never rises above its basic device.

Weales, Gerald. THE JUMPING-OFF PLACE: AMERICAN DRAMA IN THE 60S. New York: Macmillan, 1969, p. 229.

Weales picks Ribman as the most exciting of the new playwrights.

# JACK RICHARDSON (1935- )

THE PRODIGAL. New York: E.P. Dutton, 1960.

GALLOWS HUMOR. Preface by the author. New York: E.P. Dutton, 1961.

XMAS IN LAS VEGAS. New York: Dramatists Play Service, 1966.

XMAS IN LAS VEGAS. In BROADWAY'S BEAUTIFUL LOSERS. Ed. Marilyn Stasio. New York: Delacorte, 1972.

JUAN FELDMAN. In PARDON ME, SIR, BUT IS MY EYE HURTING YOUR ELBOW? New York: Bernard Geis, 1968.

Segment of an unproduced film.

## BIBLIOGRAPHY

Salem, James M., ed. A GUIDE TO CRITICAL REVIEWS. Part 1: AMERICAN DRAMA, 1909-1969. 2nd ed. Metuchen, N.J.: Scarecrow Press, 1973.

List of reviews, pages 400-401.

## CRITICISM

Weissman, Philip. "MOURNING BECOMES ELECTRA and THE PRODIGAL: Electra and ORESTES." MD, 3 (December 1960), pp. 257-59.

A psychoanalyst views Richardson's Orestes in THE PRODIGAL as a spokesman for the youth of today, trying to keep equally free of excessive parental domination and excessive rebellion.

## ANNE RIDLER (1912- )

HENRY BLY AND OTHER PLAYS. London: Faber and Faber, 1950.

Includes THE MASK and THE MISSING BRIDEGROOM.

THE TRIAL OF THOMAS CRANMER. London: Faber and Faber, 1956.

WHO IS MY NEIGHBOR? AND, HOW BITTER THE BREAD. London: Faber and Faber, 1963.

THE JESSE TREE: A MASQUE IN VERSE. Music by Elizabeth Maconchy. London: Lyrebird Press, 1972.

### CRITICISM

Kliewer, Warren. "Theological Form in Anne Ridler's Plays." APPROACH, 52 (Summer 1964), 22-32.

Spanos, William V. THE CHRISTIAN TRADITION IN MODERN BRITISH VERSE DRAMA. Foreword by E. Martin Browne. New Brunswick, N.J.: Rutgers University Press, 1967.

See pages 253-69.

Weales, Gerald. RELIGION IN MODERN ENGLISH DRAMA. Philadelphia: University of Pennsylvania Press, 1961, pp. 227-33.

# DAVID RUDKIN (1936- )

AFORE NIGHT COME. In NEW ENGLISH DRAMATISTS 7. Harmondsworth, Engl.: Penguin, 1963.

MOSES AND AARON. London: Friends of Covent Garden, 1965.

A translation of the libretto with music by Arnold Schoenberg.

THE GRACE OF TODD. Music by Gordon Cross. London: Oxford University Press, 1970.

CRIES FROM CASEMENT AS HIS BONES ARE BROUGHT TO DUBLIN. London: 1973.

Radio play.

PENDA'S FEN. London: Davis-Poynter, 1975.

Originally a television play.

## CRITICISM

Milne, Tom. "AFORE NIGHT COME." In THE ENCORE READER: A CHRONICLE OF THE NEW DRAMA. Ed. Charles Marowitz, Tom Milne, and Owen Hale. London: Methuen, 1965, pp. 234-38.

This review asserts that the play's "theme is that of LORD OF THE FLIES--the incredible, primitive savagery and blood-lust latent in mankind, so easily brought to the surface by fear or isolation."

Taylor, John Russell. "David Rudkin." In his ANGER AND AFTER: A GUIDE TO THE NEW ENGLISH DRAMA. Rev. ed. Harmondsworth, Engl.: Penguin, 1963, pp. 275-80.

Like Artaud, "Rudkin sees dramatic performance as something which acts subliminally, releasing from the subconscious mind forces of which the conscious, civilized mind is virtually unaware."

# HOWARD SACKLER (1929- )

NINE O'CLOCK MAIL. In NEW THEATRE IN AMERICA. Ed. Edward Parone. New York: Dell, 1965.

THE GREAT WHITE HOPE. New York: Dial Press, 1968.

A FEW INQUIRIES. New York: Dial Press, 1970.

Consists of SARAH, MR. WELK AND JERSEY JIM, SKIPPY, and a reprint of THE NINE O'CLOCK MAIL, with an introduction by Martin Gottfried.

## BIBLIOGRAPHY

Salem, James M., ed. A GUIDE TO CRITICAL REVIEWS. Part 1: AMERICAN DRAMA, 1909-1969. 2nd ed. Metuchen, N.J.: Scarecrow Press, 1973.

List of reviews for THE GREAT WHITE HOPE. See pages 410-11.

## CRITICISM

Kenny, Brendan. "The Great Black Hope." PL, 45 (December-January 1970), 64-67.

A tepid comparison of THE GREAT WHITE HOPE and Eldridge Cleaver's SOUL ON ICE (1968).

Simon, John. UNEASY STAGES. New York: Random House, 1975, pp. 160-64.

THE GREAT WHITE HOPE succeeds despite its attempt at poetry, and its evasiveness about Johnson's last fight.

Trousdale, Marion. "Ritual Theater: THE GREAT WHITE HOPE." WESTERN HUMANITIES REVIEW, 23 (Autumn 1969), 295-303.

## ARTHUR SAINER (1924- )

THE BITCH OF WAVERLY PLACE: A SHORT PLAY. New York: n.p., 1964.

Typescript at the Lincoln Center Library of the Performing Arts.

THE THING ITSELF. In PLAYWRIGHTS FOR TOMORROW: A COLLECTION OF PLAYS. Vol. 6. Ed. Arthur H. Ballet. Minneapolis: University of Minnesota Press, 1969.

### CRITICISM

Ballet, Arthur H. "Arthur Sainer." In CONTEMPORARY DRAMATISTS. Ed. James Vinson. London: St. James; New York: St. Martin's, 1973, pp. 662-64.

> "Sainer's work is uncompromising, or demanding or even unproducible, in the same way that the best of Strindberg's plays are. No more, no less."

## WILLIAM SAROYAN (1908-1981)

THE SLAUGHTER OF THE INNOCENTS. TA, 36 (November 1952), 33-56.

THE OYSTER AND THE PEARL: A PLAY FOR TELEVISION. PERSPECTIVES USA, 4 (September 1953), 86-104.

CAT, MOUSE, MAN, WOMAN; THE ACCIDENT. CONTACT (Sausalito, Calif.), no. 1 (1958), 146-60.

Two incomplete plays, with notes and corrections.

THE CAVE DWELLERS. New York: Putnam, 1958.

His most highly regarded work of this period.

SAM, THE HIGHEST JUMPER OF THEM ALL; OR, THE LONDON COMEDY. London: Faber and Faber, 1961.

FOUR PLAYS: THE PLAYWRIGHT AND THE PUBLIC, THE HANDSHAKERS, THE DOCTOR AND THE PATIENT, THIS I BELIEVE. ATLANTIC MONTHLY, 211 (April 1963), 50-52.

DENTIST AND PATIENT, HUSBAND AND WIFE. In THE BEST SHORT PLAYS 1968. Ed. Stanley Richards. Philadelphia: Chilton, 1968.

THE DOGS; OR, THE PARIS COMEDY AND TWO OTHER PLAYS: CHRIS SICK; OR, HAPPY NEW YEAR ANYWAY; MAKING MONEY AND 19 OTHER VERY SHORT PLAYS. New York: Phaedra, 1969.

THE NEW PLAY. In BEST SHORT PLAYS 1970. Ed. Stanley Richards. Philadelphia: Chilton, 1970.

## BIBLIOGRAPHY

Salem, James M., ed. A GUIDE TO CRITICAL REVIEWS. Part 1: AMERICAN DRAMA, 1909-1969. 2nd ed. Metuchen, N.J.: Scarecrow Press, 1973.

List of reviews, pages 411-16.

## CRITICISM

Fisher, William J. "What Ever Happened to William Saroyan?" CE, 16 (March 1955), 336-40.

Saroyan's optimism has been ill-suited to a world in which evil and man's limitations are readily apparent.

Floan, Howard R. WILLIAM SAROYAN. New York: Twayne, 1966.

Argues, very briefly, that THE CAVE DWELLERS lacks conflict.

Gassner, John. THEATRE AT THE CROSSROADS: PLAYS AND PLAYWRIGHTS OF THE MID-CENTURY AMERICAN STAGE. New York: Holt, Rinehart and Winston, 1960.

On THE CAVE DWELLERS. See pages 151-53.

Shinn, Thelma J. "William Saroyan: Romantic Existentialism." MD, 15 (September 1972), 185-94.

Saroyan's plotless, symbolic dramas, even when most optimistic, offer more than sentimental romanticism; his willingness to affirm the values of beauty and love is a kind of courage.

## JAMES A. SAUNDERS (1925- )

ALAS, POOR FRED: A DIALOGUE IN THE STYLE OF IONESCO. Scarborough, Yorkshire: Studio Theatre, 1960.

BARNSTABLE. London: Samuel French, 1961.

BARNSTABLE. In NEW DIRECTIONS: FIVE ONE ACT PLAYS IN THE MODERN IDIOM. Ed. Alan Durband. London: Hutchinson, 1961.

NEXT TIME I'LL SING TO YOU. London: Andre Deutsch, 1963.

Based on themes from A HERMIT DISCLOSED by Raleigh Trevelyan.

DOUBLE, DOUBLE. London: Samuel French, 1964.

A SCENT OF FLOWERS. P&P, 12 (December 1964), 23-28; (January 1965), 23-30 ff.

A SCENT OF FLOWERS. London: Andre Deutsch, 1965.

NEIGHBORS. P&P, 14 (September 1967), 19-27.

NEIGHBORS AND OTHER PLAYS. London: Andre Deutsch, 1968.

Includes TRIO; ALAS, POOR FRED; RETURN TO A CITY; A SLIGHT ACCIDENT; and THE PEDAGOGUE.

THE TRAVAILS OF SANCHO PANZA: A PLAY FOR THE YOUNG. London: Heinemann, 1970.

A MAN'S BEST FRIEND. In MIXED DOUBLES. London: Methuen, 1970.

THE BORAGE PIGEON AFFAIR. London: Andre Deutsch, 1970.

GAMES, AND, AFTER LIVERPOOL. London: Samuel French, 1973.

## COLLABORATION WITH IRIS MURDOCH

THE ITALIAN GIRL. P&P, 15 (March 1968), 27-42 ff.

Based on a novel by Iris Murdoch.

THE ITALIAN GIRL. London: Samuel French, 1968.

## SELECTED NONDRAMATIC WRITING

"A Trembling in the Air." P&P, 12 (December 1964), 22.

Serves as an introduction to A SCENT OF FLOWERS.

## CRITICISM

Billington, Michael. "Novel into Play." P&P, 15 (March 1968), 26.

On Saunders' adaptation of THE ITALIAN GIRL.

Hammond, Jonathan. "James A. Saunders." In CONTEMPORARY DRAMATISTS. Ed. James Vinson. London: St. James; New York: St. Martin's, 1973, pp. 671-73.

"Saunders has always been concerned essentially with the same themes; but his desire for experiment is likely to lead him into exciting new forms of writing."

Taylor, John Russell. "More Playwrights in the Provinces." In his ANGER AND AFTER: A GUIDE TO THE NEW BRITISH DRAMA. Rev. ed. Harmondsworth, Engl.: Penguin, 1963, pp. 179-85.

Saunders "has not yet established a consistent style and personality as a dramatist, and this has probably militated up to now against his wide recognition."

# DORE SCHARY (1905- )

LONELYHEARTS. Hollywood: n.p., 1958.

Based on the novel MISS LONELYHEARTS (1933) by Nathaniel West and the play by Howard Teichmann. The typescript for the screenplay is located at the Russell Sage Library of the City College of New York.

SUNRISE AT CAMPOBELLO. New York: Random House, 1958.

THE HIGHEST TREE. New York: Random House, 1960.

THE DEVIL'S ADVOCATE. New York: Morrow, 1961.

A dramatization of the novel by Morris L. West.

ONE BY ONE. New York: n.p., 1964.

Typescript in the Lincoln Center Library of the Performing Arts.

BRIGHTOWER. New York: n.p., 1970.

Typescript in the Lincoln Center Library of the Performing Arts.

## COLLABORATION WITH SINCLAIR LEWIS

STORM IN THE WEST. New York: Stein and Day, 1963.

Original, unproduced screenplay.

## BIBLIOGRAPHY

Salem, James M., ed. A GUIDE TO CRITICAL REVIEWS. Part 1: AMERICAN DRAMA, 1909-1969. 2nd ed. Metuchen, N.J.: Scarecrow Press, 1973.

List of reviews, pages 417-18.

## JAMES SCHEVILL (1920- )

HIGH SINNERS, LOW ANGELS. Music by James Schevill, Arranged by Robert Commanday. San Francisco: Bern Porter, 1953.

THE BLOODY TENET. In RELIGIOUS DRAMA I. Ed. Marvin Halverson. New York: Meridian Books, 1957.

VOICES OF MASS AND CAPITAL A: A PLAY FOR VOICES. New York: Friendship Press, 1962.

THE BLACK PRESIDENT AND OTHER PLAYS. Denver: Swallow Press, 1965.

Includes the double-bill AMERICAN POWER: THE SPACE FAN AND THE MASTER, and a reprint of THE BLOODY TENET.

THE DEATH OF ANTON WEBERN. In his VIOLENCE AND GLORY: POEMS 1962-1968. Chicago: Swallow Press, 1969.

### COLLABORATION WITH ROBERT AND ANGELA GOLDSBY

THE CID. In THE CLASSIC THEATRE. Vol. 4. Ed. Eric Bentley. Garden City, N.Y.: Doubleday, 1961.

Translation of the Corneille classic (1637).

### CRITICISM

Cohn, Ruby. "James Schevill." In CONTEMPORARY DRAMATISTS. Ed. James Vinson. London: St. James; New York: St. Martin's, 1973, pp. 677-78.

"A post has reached out to embrace the many possibilities of the theatre."

Robbins, Martin. "James Schevill: Poet with Music, and Playwright with a Message." VOYAGES, 3 (Winter 1970), 85-87.

# MURRAY SCHISGAL (1926- )

THE TYPISTS, AND THE TIGER: TWO PLAYS. New York: Coward-McCann, 1963.

With an introduction by the author.

FRAGMENTS, WINDOWS, AND OTHER PLAYS. Introd. Michael J. Arlen. New York: Coward-McCann, 1965.

Includes REVERBERATIONS, MEMORIAL DAY, THE OLD JEW.

LUV. New York: Coward-McCann, 1965.

With an introduction by Walter Kerr and an interview with the author by Ira Peck.

JAX, MAX, BAXTER & MAX: TWO ONE-ACT PLAYS. New York: Lansbury and Merson, 1966.

Typescript of apparently unperformed works in the Central Collection of the Harvard College Library.

JIMMY SHINE. New York: Atheneum, 1969.

THE CHINESE, AND DR. FISH. New York: Dramatists Play Service, 1970.

Two short plays.

DUCKS AND LOVERS. New York: Dramatist Play Service, 1972.

AN AMERICAN MILLIONAIRE. New York: Dramatists Play Service, 1974.

ALL OVER TOWN. New York: Dramatists Play Service, 1975.

## BIBLIOGRAPHY

Salem, James M., ed. A GUIDE TO CRITICAL REVIEWS. Part 1: AMERICAN DRAMA, 1909-1969. 2nd ed. Metuchen, N.J.: Scarecrow Press, 1973.

List of reviews, pages 418-20.

## SELECTED NONDRAMATIC WRITING

"An Interview with Murray Schisgal." In THE AMERICAN THEATER TODAY. Ed. Alan S. Downer. New York: Basic Books, 1967, pp. 124-35.

## CRITICISM

Arlen, Michael J. "Portrait of the Playwright in the Catbird Seat." S, 5 (April 1965), 69-71.

Simon, John. UNEASY STAGES. New York: Random House, 1975, pp. 66-68.

LUV has enough material for a not very good twenty-minute sketch.

# DAVID SELBOURNE (1937- )

THE PLAY OF WILLIAM COOPER AND EDMUND DEW-NEVETT. London: Methuen, 1968.

THE TWO-BACKED BEAST. London: Methuen, 1969.

DORABELLA. London: Metheun, 1970.

THE DAMNED. London: Methuen, 1971.

SAMPSON, AND ALISON MARY FAGAN. London: Calder and Boyars, 1971.

Two plays.

CLASS PLAYS. London: Calder and Boyars, 1973.

Three plays.

## CRITICISM

Brown, John Russell. "David Selbourne." In CONTEMPORARY DRAMATISTS. Ed. James Vinson. London: St. James; New York: St. Martin's, 1973, pp. 681-82.

Taylor, John Russell. "The Dark Fantastic." In his THE SECOND WAVE. London: Methuen, 1971, pp. 211-12.

Very brief look at Selbourne's works.

# ANTHONY SHAFFER (1926- )

SLEUTH. New York: Dodd, Mead, 1970.

## CRITICISM

Glenn, Jules. "Anthony and Peter Shaffer's Plays: The Influence of Twinship on Creativity." AMERICAN IMAGO, 31 (Fall 1974), 270-94.

# PETER SHAFFER (1926- )

FIVE FINGER EXERCISE. London: Hamish Hamilton, 1958.

THE PRIVATE EAR, AND THE PUBLIC EYE: TWO ONE ACT PLAYS. London: Hamish Hamilton, 1962.

THE ROYAL HUNT OF THE SUN: A PLAY CONCERNING THE CONQUEST OF PERU. London: Hamish Hamilton, 1964.

BLACK COMEDY, INCLUDING WHITE LIES: TWO PLAYS. New York: Stein and Day, 1967.

THE WHITE LIARS, BLACK COMEDY: TWO PLAYS. London: Hamish Hamilton, 1968.

> "THE WHITE LIARS is a new play. It is loosely based on my play, WHITE LIES."

EQUUS. London: Deutsch, 1973.

SHRIVINGS. London: Deutsch, 1974.

## BIBLIOGRAPHY

Salem, James, ed. A GUIDE TO CRITICAL REVIEWS. Part 3: BRITISH AND CONTINENTAL DRAMA FROM IBSEN TO PINTER. Metuchen, N.J.: Scarecrow Press, 1969.

> List of reviews of New York productions. See pages 211-13.

## SELECTED NONDRAMATIC WRITING

"Labels Aren't for Playwrights." TA, 44 (February 1960), 20-21.

Shaffer rejects such labels as drawing room or kitchen sink, deplores the arty politics of the theatre, and affirms that his own uncertainty is a virtue in an overly categorized time.

"In Search of a God." P&P, 12 (October 1964), 22.

Introduces THE ROYAL HUNT OF THE SUN.

## CRITICISM

Glenn, Jules. "Anthony and Peter Shaffer's Plays: The Influence of Twinship on Creativity." AMERICAN IMAGO, 31 (Fall 1974), 270-94.

Hayman, Ronald. "Like a Woman They Keep Going Back To." DRAMA, n.s. 98 (Autumn 1970), 57-66.

Peter Shaffer, like John Mortimer, Robert Bolt, and John Bowen, is continually abandoning naturalism, and then returning to it.

Pennel, Charles A. "The Plays of Peter Shaffer: Experiment in Covention." KANSAS QUARTERLY, 3 (Spring 1971), 100-109.

"Peter Shaffer Interviewed by Barry Pree." In BEHIND THE SCENES: THEATER AND FILM INTERVIEWS FROM THE TRANSATLANTIC REVIEW. Ed. Joseph F.M. McCrindle, introd. Jean-Claude van Itallie. New York: Holt, Rinehart and Winston, 1971, pp. 205-10.

Taylor, John Russell. "Shaffer and the Incas." P&P, 11 (April 1964), 12-13.

## IRWIN SHAW (1913- )

CHILDREN FROM THEIR GAMES. New York: Samuel French, 1962.

### BIBLIOGRAPHY

Salem, James M., ed. A GUIDE TO CRITICAL REVIEWS. Part 1: AMERICAN DRAMA, 1909-1969. 2nd ed. Metuchen, N.J.: Scarecrow Press, 1973.

List of reviews of CHILDREN FROM THEIR GAMES. See page 425.

## ROBERT SHAW (1927-1978)

THE MAN IN THE GLASS BOOTH. London: Chatto and Windus, 1967.

Directed in London and New York by Harold Pinter.

CATO STREET. London: Chatto and Windus, 1972.

### CRITICISM

Hughes, Catharine. PLAYS, POLITICS AND POLEMICS. New York: Drama Book Specialists, 1973, pp. 145-54.

Taylor, John Russell. "The Legacy of Realism." In his THE SECOND WAVE. London: Methuen, 1971, pp. 200-202.

THE MAN IN THE GLASS BOOTH succeeds because it is more than a problem play.

# SAM SHEPARD (1943- )

CHICAGO. In EIGHT PLAYS FROM OFF-OFF BROADWAY. Ed. Nick Orzel and Michael Smith. Indianapolis: Bobbs-Merrill, 1966.

FIVE PLAYS. Indianapolis: Bobbs-Merrill, 1967.

Contains CHICAGO, ICARUS'S MOTHER, RED CROSS, FOURTEEN HUNDRED THOUSAND, and MELODRAMA PLAY. Each play is prefaced by a brief statement by its director, except MELODRAMA PLAY, which has a statement by Shepard.

COWBOYS NO. 2. In COLLISION COURSE. Ed. Edward Parone. New York: Random House, 1968.

FORENSIC AND THE NAVIGATORS. In THE BEST OF OFF-OFF BROADWAY. Ed. Michael Smith. New York: E.P. Dutton, 1968.

LA TURISTA. Indianapolis: Bobbs-Merrill, 1968.

OPERATION SIDEWINDER. ES, May 1969, pp. 152 ff.

OPERATION SIDEWINDER. Indianapolis: Bobbs-Merrill, 1970.

MAD DOG BLUES AND OTHER PLAYS. New York: Winter House, 1971.

With COWBOY MOUTH, written with singer Patti Smith, and COWBOYS #2.

THE UNSEEN HAND AND OTHER PLAYS. Indianapolis: Bobbs-Merrill, 1971.

Includes FORENSIC AND THE NAVIGATORS, BACK BOG BEAST BAIT, SHAVED SPLITS, HOLY GHOSTLY, and ROCK GARDEN, all from the sixties.

THE TOOTH OF CRIME, AND, GEOGRAPHY OF A HORSE DREAMER: TWO PLAYS. New York: Grove Press, 1974.

ACTION AND THE UNSEEN HAND. London: Faber and Faber, 1975.

## BIBLIOGRAPHY

Salem, James M., ed. A GUIDE TO CRITICAL REVIEWS. Part 1: AMERICAN DRAMA, 1909-1969. 2nd ed. Metuchen, N.J.: Scarecrow Press, 1973.

Short list of reviews, page 423.

## CRITICISM

Davis, Richard A. "'Get Up Out a' Your Homemade Beds': The Plays of Sam Shepard." PL, 47 (October-November 1971), 12-19.

Davis summarizes Shepard's plays and concludes that he is repeating himself and needs new themes.

Frutkin, Ren. "Sam Shepard: Paired Existence Meets the Monster." YT, 2 (Summer 1969), 22-30.

Shepard's contribution "has been to reclaim for the imagination certain territories lost in a variety of recent cultural floodings."

Hardwick, Elizabeth. "Word of Mouth." NYRB, 6 April 1967, pp. 6-8.

Praise for the literary and dramatic talents that give form to LA TURISTA's images of despair.

Lahr, John. "Jules Feiffer and Sam Shepard: Spectacles of Disintegration." In his ASTONISH ME: ADVENTURES IN THE CONTEMPORARY THEATER. New York: Viking, 1973, pp. 102-19.

OPERATION SIDEWINDER is based on conflicting mythologies and images of death.

Madden, David. "The Theatre of Assault." MR, 8 (Autumn 1967), 713-25.

This breathless account of the horrors of Off Off Broadway finds LA TURISTA a prime culprit, claiming that it was apparently written "out of the conviction that Aristotle was a fascist."

Valgemae, Mardi. "Expressionism and the New American Drama." TCL, 17 (October 1971), 227-34.

LA TURISTA is an instance of contemporary expressionism.

## R[OBERT] C[EDRIC] SHERRIFF (1896-1975)

HOME AT SEVEN. London: Gollancz, 1950.

MR. KNOW-ALL. In TRIO: ORIGINAL STORIES BY W. SOMERSET MAUGHAM. London: Heinemann, 1950.

Screenplays by W. Somerset Maugham, R.C. Sherriff, and Noel Langley.

THE KITE. In ACTION: BEACON LIGHTS OF LITERATURE. Ed. Georgia G. Winn et al. Syracuse, N.Y.: Iroquois Press, 1952.

THE WHITE CARNATION. London: Heinemann, 1953.

THE LONG SUNSET. In PLAYS OF THE YEAR 12. Ed. J.C. Trewin. London: Elek Books, 1955.

THE TELESCOPE. London: Samuel French, 1957.

THE LONG SUNSET. London: Longmans, 1960.

With an introduction and notes by Elizabeth Haddon.

A SHRED OF EVIDENCE. London: Samuel French, 1961.

BADGER'S GREEN. Rev. ed. London: Samuel French, 1962.

Revision of the 1930 play.

### SELECTED NONDRAMATIC WRITING

NO LEADING LADY: AN AUTOBIOGRAPHY. London: Gollancz, 1968.

## R[obert] C[edric] Sherriff

### CRITICISM

Dennis, Nigel. "Abide with Me." In his DRAMATIC ESSAYS. London: Weidenfeld and Nicolson, 1962, pp. 181-82.

THE LONG SUNSET is full of hope, unfortunately.

Trewin, J.C. "The Ordinary Man." In his DRAMATISTS OF TODAY. London: Staples Press, 1953, pp. 143-50.

Brief summary and survey of Sherriff's work.

# ROBERT E. SHERWOOD (1896-1955)

SECOND THRESHOLD. New York: Harper and Row, 1951.

Sherwood's completion of Philip Barry's last play, with revisions and a preface by Sherwood.

SMALL WAR ON MURRAY HILL. New York: Dramatists Play Service, 1957.

## BIBLIOGRAPHY

Salem, James M., ed. A GUIDE TO CRITICAL REVIEWS. Part 1: AMERICAN DRAMA, 1909-1969. 2nd ed. Metuchen, N.J.: Scarecrow Press, 1973.

List of reviews of SMALL WAR ON MURRAY HILL. See page 437.

## SELECTED NONDRAMATIC WRITING

"Most Terrible Drama of All Times." SATURDAY REVIEW, 33 (October 21, 1950), 22-23.

"Credo." SURVEY, 87 (March 1951), 118.

"There is No Alternative to Peace." FORTUNE, 52 (July 1955), 84-85 ff.

## CRITICISM

Meserve, Walter J. ROBERT SHERWOOD: RELUCTANT MORALIST. New York: Pegasus, 1970.

Rice, Elmer. "A Personal Memoir." NEW YORK TIMES, 30 November 1955, sec. 2, pp. 1, 3.

Schuman, R. Baird. ROBERT EMMET SHERWOOD. New York: Twayne, 1964.
On SMALL WAR ON MURRAY HILL. See pages 46-51.

# NEIL SIMON (1937- )

COME BLOW YOUR HORN. New York: Samuel French, 1961.

BAREFOOT IN THE PARK. New York: Random House, 1964.

THE ODD COUPLE. New York: Random House, 1966.

SWEET CHARITY. New York: Random House, 1966.

Based on the Fellini film NIGHTS OF CABIRIA (1956). Book by Neil Simon, music by Cy Coleman, and words by Dorothy Fields.

THE STAR-SPANGLED GIRL. New York: Random House, 1967.

Simon's only failure during this decade.

PLAZA SUITE. New York: Random House, 1969.

Three one-act plays: VISITOR FROM MAMARONECK, VISITOR FROM HOLLYWOOD, and VISITOR FROM FOREST HILLS.

PROMISES, PROMISES. New York: Random House, 1969.

Based on the film THE APARTMENT by Billy Wilder and I.A.L. Diamond (1960). Book by Neil Simon and music and lyrics by Burt Bacharach and Hal David.

LAST OF THE RED HOT LOVERS. New York: Random House, 1970.

THE GINGERBREAD LADY. New York: Random House, 1971.

THE PRISONER OF SECOND AVENUE. New York: Random House, 1972.

THE SUNSHINE BOYS. New York: Random House, 1973.

THE GOOD DOCTOR: A NEW COMEDY WITH MUSIC. New York: Random House, 1974.

Adapted from Chekhov short stories.

GOD'S FAVORITE. New York: Random House, 1975.

## COLLABORATION

ADVENTURES OF MARCO POLO: A MUSICAL FANTASY. New York: Samuel French, 1959.

Book by Neil Simon with William Friedburg, music by Clay Warnick and Mel Pahl (based on themes by Rimsky-Korsakov), and lyrics by Edgar Esser.

HEIDE. New York: Samuel French, 1959.

Based on the novel by Johanna Spyri. Book by William Friedberg and Neil Simon, lyrics by Carolyn Leigh, and music by Clay Warnick based on themes by Robert Schuman.

## COLLECTIONS

THE COMEDY OF NEIL SIMON. New York: Random House, 1972.

COME BLOW YOUR HORN; BAREFOOT IN THE PARK; THE ODD COUPLE; THE STAR-SPANGLED GIRL; PROMISES, PROMISES; PLAZA SUITE; and LAST OF THE RED HOT LOVERS; with an introduction by Simon.

## BIBLIOGRAPHY

Salem, James M., ed. A GUIDE TO CRITICAL REVIEWS. Part 1: AMERICAN DRAMA, 1909-1969. 2nd ed. Metuchen, N.J.: Scarecrow Press, 1973.

List of reviews, pages 445-46.

## CRITICISM

Lahr, John. "Neil Simon and Woody Allen: Images of Impotence." In his ASTONISH ME: ADVENTURES IN THE CONTEMPORARY THEATER. New York: Viking, 1973, pp. 120-36.

Simon's plays are social documents of the silent majority, "the castrati of capitalism."

McMahon, Helen. "A Rhetoric of American Popular Drama: The Comedies of Neil Simon." PL, 51 (October-November 1975), 10-15.

Simon's comedies continually raise serious human issues, only to duck them in vaudeville routines and gags.

## N[ORMAN] F[REDERICK] SIMPSON (1919- )

THE HOLE. London: Samuel French, 1958.

A RESOUNDING TINKLE. In THE OBSERVER PLAYS. London: Faber and Faber, 1958.

The volume has a preface by Kenneth Tynan.

A RESOUNDING TINKLE. London: Samuel French, 1958.

CAN YOU HEAR ME? and GLADY OTHERWISE. In ONE TO ANOTHER. With John Mortimer and Harold Pinter. London: Samuel French, 1960.

Review sketches.

ONE WAY PENDULUM. London: Faber and Faber, 1960.

THE FORM. P&P, 9 (May 1962), 31-35.

THE HOLE AND OTHER PLAYS AND SKETCHES. London: Faber and Faber, 1964.

Also includes a shortened version of A RESOUNDING TINKLE, THE FORM, GLADLY OTHERWISE, OH, and ONE BLAST AND HAVE DONE.

THE CRESTA RUN. London: Faber and Faber, 1966.

SOME TALL TINKLES: TELEVISION PLAYS. London: Faber and Faber, 1968.

WAS HE ANYONE? London: Faber and Faber, 1973.

## BIBLIOGRAPHY

Salem, James M., ed. A GUIDE TO CRITICAL REVIEWS. Part 3: BRITISH AND CONTINENTAL DRAMA FROM IBSEN TO PINTER. Metuchen, N.J.: Scarecrow Press, 1968.

Short list of reviews of New York productions, page 268.

## SELECTED NONDRAMATIC WRITING

"Making Nonsense of Nonsense." TR, 21 (Summer 1966), 5-13.

Characteristically chaotic auto-interview.

## CRITICISM

Dennis, Nigel. "The Fully Considered Page." In his DRAMATIC ESSAYS. London: Weidenfeld and Nicolson, 1962, pp. 23-31.

ONE WAY PENDULUM is wonderful nonsense, but its fantasy is insufficiently controlled.

Fothergill, C.Z. "Echoes of A RESOUNDING TINKLE: N.F. SIMPSON." MD, 16 (December 1973), 299-306.

Simpson's characters are systematically deranged; yet he is not a satirist or an absurdist.

Swanson, Michele A. "ONE WAY PENDULUM: A New Dimension in Farce." DS, 2 (February 1963), 322-32.

Simpson's farces in the context of absurdist philosophy.

Taylor, John Russell. "N.F. Simpson." In his ANGER AND AFTER: A GUIDE TO THE NEW BRITISH DRAMA. Rev. ed. Harmondsworth, Engl.: Penguin, 1963, pp. 58-64.

"Whether one likes or dislikes N.F. Simpson's work, it seems to me, there is very little to be said about it. It is uniquely all of a piece, all written in pretty well the same style, and all based on one principle, the non sequitur."

Worth, Katharine J. "Avante Garde at the Royal Court Theatre: John Arden and N.F. Simpson." In EXPERIMENTAL DRAMA. Ed. William A. Armstrong. London: G. Bell, 1963, pp. 214-23.

## MICHAEL SMITH (1935- )

I LIKE IT. KULCHUR, 3 (Spring 1963), 3-10.

THE NEXT THING. In THE BEST OF OFF-BROADWAY. Ed. Michael Smith. New York: E.P. Dutton, 1969.

COUNTRY MUSIC. In THE OFF-OFF-BROADWAY BOOK. Ed. Albert Poland and Bruce Mailman. Indianapolis: Bobbs-Merrill, 1972.

### CRITICISM

Hoffman, William M. "Michael Smith." In CONTEMPORARY DRAMATISTS. Ed. James Vinson. London: St. James; New York: St. Martin's, 1973, pp. 710-11.

# JOHNNY SPEIGHT (1912- )

IF THERE WEREN'T ANY BLACKS YOU'D HAVE TO INVENT THEM. London: Methuen, 1968.

Television play adapted to the stage.

TIL DEATH US DO PART. London: Woburn Press, 1973.

Television scripts from the popular Alf Garnett series, the English source for Archie Bunker.

## CRITICISM

Taylor, John Russell. "Johnny Speight." In his ANGER AND AFTER: A GUIDE TO THE NEW BRITISH DRAMA. Rev. ed. Harmondsworth, Engl.: Penguin, 1963, pp. 271-75.

Survey, focusing on the unpublished THE KNACKER'S YARD, "arguably the nastiest comedy yet to have reached the stage in this country."

# COLIN SPENCER (1933- )

SPITTING IMAGE. P&P, 16 (November 1968), 27-45.

## CRITICISM

"Colin Spencer Interviewed by Peter Burton." TR, 35 (Spring 1970), 61-67.

On the American production of SPITTING IMAGE, the Oedipus myth, and his quartet of novels.

Taylor, John Russell. "The Dark Fantastic." In his THE SECOND WAVE. London: Methuen, 1971, pp. 208-10.

SPITTING IMAGE works as fantasy because it is firmly grounded in realistic detail.

# JOHN SPURLING (1936- )

MACRUNE'S GUEVARA. London: Calder and Boyars, 1969.

The Beckett critic's first commercial production.

IN THE HEART OF THE BRITISH MUSEUM. London: Calder and Boyars, 1972.

SHADES OF HEATHCLIFF, AND DEATH OF CAPTAIN DOUGHTY. London: Calder and Boyars, 1975.

## CRITICISM

Young, B.A. "John Spurling." In CONTEMPORARY DRAMA. Ed. James Vinson. London: St. James; New York: St. Martins, 1973, pp. 723-24.

MACRUNE'S GUEVARA "is a pioneering example of what has come to be known as 'multi-viewpoint' drama."

# DAVID STARKWEATHER (1935- )

THE POET'S PAPERS: NOTES FOR AN EVENT. In NEW AMERICAN PLAYS 3. Ed. William H. Hoffman. New York: Hill and Wang, 1970.

YOU MAY GO HOME AGAIN. In THE OFF-OFF-BROADWAY BOOK. Ed. Albert Poland and Bruce Mailman. Indianapolis: Bobbs-Merrill, 1972.

> This play, as was typical of Off Off Broadway, waited nine years for publication.

## CRITICISM

Hoffman, William M. "David Starkweather." In CONTEMPORARY DRAMATISTS. Ed. James Vinson. London: St. James; New York: St. Martin's, 1973, pp. 726-27.

> "In the plays of David Starkweather we have a most complete view of what in olden times would have been called a saint. . . ."

# BARRIE STAVIS (1906- )

THE MAN WHO NEVER DIED: A PLAY ABOUT JOE HILL. New York: Haven Press, 1954.

With notes on Joe Hill and his time.

BANNERS OF STEEL: A PLAY ABOUT JOHN BROWN. South Brunswick, N.J.: A.S. Barnes, 1967.

With an introduction by Tyrone Guthrie.

LAMP AT MIDNIGHT: A PLAY ABOUT GALILEO. Rev. ed. South Brunswick, N.J.: A.S. Barnes, 1967.

COAT OF MANY COLORS: A PLAY ABOUT JOSEPH IN EGYPT. South Brunswick, N.J.: A.S. Barnes, 1968.

With an introduction by John Levin.

THE MAN WHO NEVER DIED: A PLAY ABOUT JOE HILL. Rev. ed. South Brunswick, N.J.: A.S. Barnes, 1972.

LAMP AT MIDNIGHT: A PLAY ABOUT GALILEO. Chicago: Dramatic Publishing Co., 1973.

A shortened version.

## CRITICISM

Shore, Herb. "Barrie Stavis: The Humanist Alternative." ETJ, 25 (December 1973), 520-24.

# JOHN STEINBECK (1902-1968)

BURNING BRIGHT. New York: Dramatists Play Service, 1951.

Acting version of the 1950 novel, BURNING BRIGHT: A PLAY IN STORY FORM.

VIVA ZAPATA! ARGOSY, 33 (February 1952).

Merle Miller's abridgement of the Steinbeck screenplay.

PIPE DREAM. New York: Viking, 1954.

Oscar Hammerstein's adaptation of SWEET HONESTY (1954) for the musical stage.

## BIBLIOGRAPHY

Hayashi, Telsumaro, ed. A NEW JOHN STEINBECK BIBLIOGRAPHY 1929-1971. Metuchen, N.J.: Scarecrow Press, 1973.

With unannotated secondary sources.

Salem, James M., ed. A GUIDE TO CRITICAL REVIEWS. Part 1: AMERICAN DRAMA, 1909-1969. 2nd ed. Metuchen, N.J.: Scarecrow Press, 1973.

List of reviews of BURNING BRIGHT, page 462.

## CRITICISM

Anon. "Staging a Story." TIMES LITERARY SUPPLEMENT, 18 August 1951, p. 513.

Review of BURNING BRIGHT.

French, Warren. JOHN STEINBECK. New York: Twayne, 1961, pp. 148-52.

On BURNING BRIGHT.

Weales, Gerald. AMERICAN DRAMA SINCE WORLD WAR II. New York: Harcourt, Brace and World, 1962.

See pages 198-99.

# TOM STOPPARD (1937- )

ALBERT'S BRIDGE. P&P, 15 (October 1967), 21-30.

ROSENCRANTZ AND GUILDENSTERN ARE DEAD. London: Faber and Faber, 1967.

ENTER A FREE MAN. London: Faber and Faber, 1968.

> This play, surprisingly realistic for Stoppard, was originally written for the stage, but was first performed on television as A WALK ON THE WATER in 1963 and then was staged in Hamburg in 1964. It was on television again in 1964 as THE PRESERVATION OF GEORGE RILEY. It was revised and staged in 1968 under its published title.

THE REAL INSPECTOR HOUND. London: Faber and Faber, 1968.

TANGO. London: Jonathan Cape, 1968.

> Slawomir Mrozek's play (1964), adapted by Stoppard, and translated by Nicholas Bethell.

ALBERT'S BRIDGE AND IF YOU'RE GLAD I'LL BE FRANK: TWO PLAYS FOR RADIO. London: Faber and Faber, 1969.

A SEPARATE PEACE. In PLAYBILL 2. Ed. Alan Durband. London: Hutchinson, 1969.

> Television play.

AFTER MAGRITTE. London: Faber and Faber, 1971.

ENTER A FREE MAN. New York: Grove Press, 1972.

JUMPERS. London: Faber and Faber, 1972.

ARTIST DESCENDING A STAIRCASE, AND, WHERE ARE THEY NOW?: TWO PLAYS FOR RADIO. London: Faber and Faber, 1973.

TRAVESTIES. London: Faber and Faber, 1975.

## BIBLIOGRAPHY

Ryan, Randolph, comp. "Theatre Checklist No. 2: Tom Stoppard." TF, 2 (May-July 1974), 2-9.

## SELECTED NONDRAMATIC WRITING

INTRODUCTION 2: STORIES BY NEW WRITERS. London: Faber and Faber, 1964.

Stoppard's contributions are three: "Reunion," "Life, Times, Fragments," and "The Story."

LORD MALQUIST AND MR. MOON. London: Anthony Blond, 1968.

Novel.

## CRITICISM

Anderson, Michael. "The Unnatural Scene: Plays and Plays." NTM, 8 (Spring 1968), 28-31.

Contrasts ROSENCRANTZ AND GUILDENSTERN with Gunter Grass's THE PLEBIANS REHEARSE THE UPRISING (1966), much to the advantage of the latter.

Babula, William. "The Play-Life Metaphor in Shakespeare and Stoppard." MD, 15 (December 1972), 279-81.

As Hamlet is confronted by the role of revenger, a role he is not comfortable in, so Ros and Guil are trapped in a script of HAMLET.

Berlin, Normand. "ROSENCRANTZ AND GUILDENSTERN ARE DEAD: Theater of Criticism." MD, 16 (December 1973), 269-77.

Stoppard, an intellectual playwright, is at his best when creating a kind of theatrical criticism, not of life, but of art itself.

Callen, Anthony. "Stoppard's Godot: Some French Influences on Post-War English Drama." NTM, 10 (Winter 1969-70), 22-30.

Traces ROSENCRANTZ AND GUILDENSTERN's extensive debt to WAITING FOR GODOT.

Keyssar-Franke, Helene. "The Strategy of ROSENCRANTZ AND GUILDENSTERN ARE DEAD." ETJ, 27 (March 1975), 85-97.

Stoppard's creation and manipulation of dramatic material is considered in terms of the relationship to the audience and the audience's response.

Levinson, Jill. "Views from a Revolving Door: Tom Stoppard's Canon to Date." QUEEN'S QUARTERLY, 78 (Autumn 1971), 431-42.

Taylor, John Russell. "Tom Stoppard." In his THE SECOND WAVE. London: Methuen, 1971, pp. 94-107.

Stoppard embodies fancy rather than imagination.

"Tom Stoppard Interviewed by Giles Gordon." In BEHIND THE SCENES: THEATER AND FILM INTERVIEWS FROM THE TRANSATLANTIC REVIEW. Ed. Joseph F.M. McCrindle, introd. Jean-Claude van Itallie. New York: Holt, Rinehart and Winston, 1971, pp. 37-87.

Excellent interview ranging over Stoppard's reticence, productions of ROSENCRANTZ AND GUILDENSTERN, and his style.

# DAVID STOREY (1933- )

THE RESTORATION OF ARNOLD MIDDLETON. London: Cape, 1967.

IN CELEBRATION. London: Cape, 1969.

THE CONTRACTOR. P&P, 17 (December 1969), 63-86.

THE CONTRACTOR. London: Cape, 1970.

HOME. London: Cape, 1970.

THE CHANGING ROOM. London: Cape, 1972.

CROMWELL. London: Cape, 1973.

THE FARM. London: Cape, 1973.

LIFE CLASS. London: Cape, 1975.

## SELECTED NONDRAMATIC WRITING

FLIGHT INTO CAMDEN. London: Longmans, 1960.
Novel.

THIS SPORTING LIFE. London: Longmans, 1960.
Novel, later made into a film.

RADCLIFFE. London: Longmans, 1963.

## CRITICISM

Bygrave, Mike. "David Storey: Novelist or Playwright?" TQ, 1 (April-June 1971), 31-36.

Storey's novels, and RADCLIFFE in particular, are impassioned, pessimistic, even apocalyptic, but the plays are dry, realistic, and tame.

"David Storey Interviewed by Brendan Hennessy." TR, 33 and 34 (Winter 1969-70), 5-11.

Just prior to the first performance of THE CONTRACTOR, Storey discusses the relationship between his novels and his plays.

Free, William J. "The Ironic Anger of David Storey." MD, 16 (December 1973), 307-16.

This examination of IN CELEBRATION and THE CONTRACTOR seeks to demonstrate Storey's differences from Pinter and Osborne.

Hayman, Ronald. "David Storey." In his PLAYBACK. London: Davis-Poynter, 1973, pp. 7-20.

Interview-essay in which Storey surveys his past writing and says that the novel seems like a dead end.

Kaufmann, Stanley. "Notes on Naturalism: Truth is Stranger as Fiction." In his PERSONS OF THE DRAMA. New York: Harper and Row, 1976, pp. 329-35.

Variations on the theme of stage realism, suggested by Storey's THE CONTRACTOR and THE CHANGING ROOM.

Taylor, John Russell. "David Storey." In his THE SECOND WAVE. London: Methuen, 1971, pp. 141-54.

Filled with interesting quotations from Storey.

Worth, Katharine J. "Realism in New Directions: Arnold Wesker, David Storey, David Mercer." In her REVOLUTIONS IN MODERN ENGLISH DRAMA. London: G. Bell, 1973, pp. 26-30.

On the physical focus of Storey's work.

# GEORGE TABORI (1914- )

FLIGHT INTO EGYPT. New York: Dramatists Play Service, 1953.

THE EMPEROR'S CLOTHES. New York: Samuel French, 1953.

BRECHT ON BRECHT: AN IMPROVISATION. New York: Samuel French, 1968.

Brecht compilation.

THE GUNS OF CARRAR. New York: Samuel French, 1970.

Brecht adaptation.

THE CANNIBALS. London: Davis-Poynter, 1973.

## BIBLIOGRAPHY

Salem, James M., ed. A GUIDE TO CRITICAL REVIEWS. Part 3: BRITISH AND CONTINENTAL DRAMA FROM IBSEN TO PINTER. Metuchen, N.J.: Scarecrow Press, 1968.

List of reviews, pages 246-47.

## CRITICISM

Bentley, Eric. "Hans Anderson's Boomerang." In his THE DRAMATIC EVENT: AN AMERICAN CHRONICLE. New York: Horizon, 1954, pp. 95-96.

Bentley says of THE EMPEROR'S CLOTHES, "As a mere script, it puts us uncomfortably in mind of the emperor's new clothes."

# RONALD TAVEL (1941- )

CHRISTINA'S WORLD. CHICAGO REVIEW, 16 (Winter-Spring 1963), 1-79.

This early play by a charter member of the "Theatre of the Ridiculous" is in verse and, more surprising, it appears to be in earnest.

TARZAN OF THE FLICKS. BLACKLIST, 6 (1965).

THE LIFE OF JUANITA CASTRO. TRI-QUARTERLY, 6 (1966), 119-26.

VINYL. CLYDE, 2 (1966), 22-27.

Adapted from a shooting script for Andy Warhol's film VINYL. A typescript is at the Lincoln Center Library of the Performing Arts.

KITCHENETTE. PR, 34 (Spring 1967), 233-50.

CLEOBIS AND BITO: A DANCE ORATORIO. New York: n.p., 1968.

Typescript at the Lincoln Center Library of the Performing Arts.

THE LIFE OF LADY GODIVA. In NEW UNDERGROUND THEATRE. Ed. Robert Schroeder. New York: Bantam, 1968.

GORILLA QUEEN. In THE BEST OF OFF-OFF BROADWAY. Ed. Michael Smith. New York: E.P. Dutton, 1969.

ARENA OF LUTETIA. In EXPERIMENTS IN PROSE. Ed. Eugene Wildman. Chicago: Swallow Press, 1969.

VINYL VISITS AN FM STATION. TDR, 14 (September 1970), 72-92.

SECRETS OF THE CITIZEN'S CORRECTION COMMITTEE. SCRIPTS, 1 (January 1972), 4-23.

BIGFOOT AND OTHER PLAYS. New York: Winter House, 1973.

Announced for 1973 but never published.

## COLLABORATION WITH HARRY FAINLIGHT AND BILLY LINICK

HARLOT. FILM CULTURE, 40 (Spring 1966), 57-66.

Screenplay for an Andy Warhol film.

## SELECTED NONDRAMATIC WRITING

"The Theatre of the Ridiculous." TRI-QUARTERLY, no. 6 (1966), 93-109.

Manifesto.

## CRITICISM

Brustein, Robert. "Notes from the Underground." In his THE THIRD THEATRE. New York: Knopf, 1969, pp. 47-50.

"Tavel uses the theatre exclusively for the purposes of advertizing queerdom."

Epstein, Leslie. "Beyond the Baroque: The Role of the Audience in the Modern Theater." TRI-QUARTERLY, 12 (Spring 1968), 213-34.

Isaac, Dan. "Ronald Tavel: Ridiculous Playwright." TDR, 13 (Fall 1968), 106-15.

An approving description of the origin and character of Tavel's pansexual parodies.

Madden, David. "The Theatre of Assault: Four Off-Off-Broadway Plays." MR, 8 (Autumn 1967), 713-25.

GORILLA QUEEN is one of the stops along a horrified tour of Off Off Broadway.

Michelson, Peter. "The Pop Scene and the Theatre of the Ridiculous." TRI-QUARTERLY, 6 (1966), 111-17.

Tavel has a talent larger than the pop milieu can allow.

# CECIL P. TAYLOR (1929- )

ALLERGY. In TRAVERSE PLAYS. Ed. Jim Haynes. Harmondsworth, Engl.: Penguin, 1966.

BREAD AND BUTTER. P&P, 14 (October 1966), 31-46, 72.

THE BALLACHULISH BEAT: A PLAY WITH SONGS. London: Rapp and Carroll, 1967.

Music by Taylor.

BREAD AND BUTTER. In NEW ENGLISH DRAMATISTS 10. Harmondsworth, Engl.: Penguin, 1967.

FABLE. Edinburgh: Edinburgh University Drama Society, 1967.

HAPPY DAYS ARE HERE AGAIN. In NEW ENGLISH DRAMATISTS 12: RADIO PLAYS. Harmondsworth, Engl.: Penguin, 1968.

MAKING A TELEVISION PLAY: A COMPLETE GUIDE FROM CONCEPTION TO BBC PRODUCTION. Newcastle-upon-Tyne: Oriel Press, 1970.

Based on the making of the play CHARLES AND CROMWELL, includes script.

THANK YOU VERY MUCH. London: Methuen, 1970.

THE TRUTH ABOUT SARAJEVO: A PLAY FOR TRAVERSE THEATRE. Kirknewton, Midlothian: Scottish Theatre Editions, 1970.

BLOCH'S PLAY. Kirknewton, Midlothian: Scottish Theatre Editions, 1971.

WORDS. In SECOND PLAYBILL 2. Ed. Alan Durband. London: Hutchinson, 1973.

## CRITICISM

Taylor, John Russell. "Three Social Realists: John Hopkins, Alan Plater, Cecil P. Taylor." In his THE SECOND WAVE. London: Methuen, 1971, pp. 186-90.

On the great emphasis Taylor places on plot.

## MEGAN TERRY (1932- )

CALM DOWN MOTHER: A TRANSFORMATION FOR THREE WOMEN. In EIGHT PLAYS FROM OFF-OFF-BROADWAY. Ed. Nick Orzel and Michael Smith. Indianapolis: Bobbs-Merrill, 1966.

CALM DOWN MOTHER: A TRANSFORMATION FOR THREE WOMEN. New York: Samuel French, 1966.

EX-MISS COPPER QUEEN ON A SET OF PILLS. In PLAYWRIGHTS FOR TO-MORROW: A COLLECTION OF PLAYS. Vol. 1. Ed. Arthur Ballet. Minneapolis: University of Minnesota Press, 1966.

KEEP TIGHTLY CLOSED IN A COOL, DRY PLACE. TDR, 10 (Summer 1966), 177-200.

VIET ROCK. TDR, 11 (Fall 1966), 196-207.

VIET ROCK AND OTHER PLAYS. New York: Simon and Schuster, 1967.

> Also contains COMINGS AND GOINGS: A THEATRE GAME, KEEP TIGHTLY CLOSED IN A COOL, DRY PLACE, and THE GLOAMING, OH MY DARLING. Each script is preceded by production notes; Marianne de Pury's music for VIET ROCK and COMING AND GOINGS is at the end of the volume, and the volume opens with an introduction by Richard Schechner.

THE MAGIC REALISTS. In BEST SHORT PLAYS OF 1968. Ed. Stanley Richards. Philadelphia: Chilton Books, 1968.

THE PEOPLE VS. RACHMAN, EX-MISS COPPER QUEEN ON A SET OF PILLS: TWO PLAYS. New York: Samuel French, 1968.

MASSACHUSETTS TRUST. In THE OFF-OFF-BROADWAY BOOK. Ed. Albert Poland and Bruce Mailman. Indianapolis: Bobbs-Merrill, 1970.

THE TOMMY ALLEN SHOW. SCRIPTS, 1 (December 1971).

APPROACHING SIMONE. New York: Feminists Press, 1972.
With an introduction by Phyllis Jane Wagner.

HOME. New York: Samuel French, 1972.

THREE ONE-ACT PLAYS. New York: Samuel French, 1972.
Consists of SANIBAL AND CAPTIVA, THE MAGIC REALISTS, and ONE MORE LITTLE DRINKIE.

COUPLINGS AND GROUPINGS. New York: Pantheon, 1973.

HOTHOUSE. New York: Samuel French, 1974.

TWO ONE-ACT PLAYS. Holly Springs, Miss.: Ragnarok Press, 1975.

## CRITICISM

Sainer, Arthur. "Megan Terry." In CONTEMPORARY DRAMATISTS. Ed. James Vinson. London: St. James; New York: St. Martin's, 1973, pp. 754-55.

## PETER TERSON (1932- )

MIGHTY RESERVOY. P&P, 14 (August 1967), 19-32.

A NIGHT TO MAKE THE ANGELS WEEP. In NEW ENGLISH DRAMATISTS 11. Harmondsworth, Engl.: Penguin, 1967.

THE APPRENTICES. P&P, 16 (October 1968), 27-55.

THE APPRENTICES. Harmondsworth, Engl.: Penguin, 1970.

THE KNOTTY: A MUSICAL DOCUMENTARY. London: Methuen, 1970.

> "Created by the Victoria Theatre Company, working from historical research by Peter Terson under the direction of Peter Cheeseman," with an introduction and notes by Peter Cheeseman.

MIGHTY RESERVOY. In NEW ENGLISH DRAMATISTS 14. Harmondsworth, Engl.: Penguin, 1970.

SPRING-HEELED JACK. P&P, 18 (November 1970), 62-85.

ZIGGER ZAGGER, MOONEY AND HIS CARAVANS: TWO PLAYS. Harmondsworth, Engl.: Penguin, 1970.

BUT FRED, FREUD IS DEAD. P&P, 19 (March 1972), 62-78.

THE ADVENTURES OF GERVASE BECKET; OR, THE MAN WHO CHANGED PLACES. Introd. by Peter Cheeseman. Ed. Peter Cheeseman. London: Eyre Methuen, 1973.

## COLLABORATION WITH MIKE BUTLER

THE SAMARITAN. P&P, 18 (July 1971), 72-84.

## CRITICISM

Croft, Michael. "Introduction." In Terson's THE APPRENTICES. Harmondsworth, Engl.: Penguin, 1970.

On the collaborative work that made THE APPRENTICES.

Elvgren, Ira Gillette. "Peter Terson's Vale of Eversham." MD, 18 (June 1975), 173-88.

Terson's Eversham plays, most of which are unpublished and are summarized here, depict a Chekhov-like decline of the countryside. The plays' often violent conflict is usually between earthy primitives and rootless educated characters.

Taylor, John Russell. "Peter Terson." In his THE SECOND WAVE. London: Methuen, 1971, pp. 108-24.

Prefers the Vale of Eversham plays to the more well-known, but less personal works for the National Youth Theatre.

# DYLAN THOMAS (1914-1953)

LLAREGGUB: A PIECE FOR RADIO PERHAPS. BO, 9 (1952), 134-53.

With an explanatory "From a Letter," this is, with some revisions toward the end, the first half of UNDER MILK WOOD.

THE DOCTOR AND THE DEVILS. London: J.M. Dent, 1953.

Written in 1944, this screenplay is based on the crimes of Burke and Hare from a story by Donald Taylor.

UNDER MILK WOOD: A PLAY FOR VOICES. MADEMOISELLE, February 1954, pp. 110-22, 144-56.

Preceded by "Dylan Thomas and His Village" by John Malcolm Brinnin, this is a slightly abbreviated text.

UNDER MILK WOOD: A PLAY FOR VOICES. London: J.M. Dent, 1954.

The standard text, with a preface by Daniel Jones.

THE BEACH OF FALESA. New York: Stein and Day, 1963.

Filmscript, "based on a story by Robert Louis Stevenson."

A FILM SCRIPT OF TWENTY YEARS A-GROWING. London: J.M. Dent, 1964.

From the story by Maurice O'Sullivan (1933).

ME AND MY BIKE: AN UNFINISHED SCREENPLAY. New York: McGraw-Hill, 1965.

REBECCA'S DAUGHTERS. London: Triton Publishers, 1965.

Unproduced, original screenplay.

THE DOCTOR AND THE DEVILS AND OTHER SCRIPTS. New York: New Directions, 1966.

Includes TWENTY YEARS A-GROWING, and THE LONDONER, which is a possible source for UNDER MILK WOOD.

## BIBLIOGRAPHY

Maud, Ralph N. DYLAN THOMAS IN PRINT: A BIBLIOGRAPHICAL HISTORY. Pittsburgh: University of Pittsburgh Press, 1970.

Salem, James M., ed. A GUIDE TO CRITICAL REVIEWS. Part 2: BRITISH AND CONTINENTAL DRAMA FROM IBSEN TO PINTER. Metuchen, N.J.: Scarecrow Press, 1968.

List of reviews of the New York production of UNDER MILK WOOD. See pages 248-49.

## CRITICISM

Agee, James. "A Dylan Thomas Screen Play." NEW YORK TIMES BOOK REVIEW, 6 December 1953, p. 38.

On THE DOCTOR AND THE DEVILS.

Claverton, Douglas. THE GROWTH OF MILK WOOD: WITH TEXTUAL VARIANTS OF UNDER MILK WOOD. London: J.M. Dent, 1969.

The director of the BBC and of subsequent first stage productions of MILK WOOD traces the complex textual history of the play. This is an extremely useful and scholarly narrative.

Manly, Frank. "The Text of Dylan Thomas' UNDER MILK WOOD." EMORY UNIVERSITY QUARTERLY, 20 (Summer 1964), 131-44.

A valiant elucidation of the complex provenance of UNDER MILK WOOD. Of particular interest are the variants the Thomas estate prohibited from publication in the Dent text.

Rea, J. "A Topological Guide to UNDER MILK WOOD." CE, 25 (April 1964), 535-42.

A geographical outline of UNDER MILK WOOD with explanatory notations about the actual village of Laugharne, as well as occasional comments by Thomas culled from various publications. A map is provided of the imaginary Llarregub.

Wells, Henry W. "Voice and Verse in Dylan Thomas' Play." CE, 15 (May 1954), 438-44.

UNDER MILK WOOD, "folk art in a modern key," is compared with

Louis MacNeice's THE DARK TOWER (1947) to demonstrate how innovative the Thomas play is.

Williams, Raymond. "Dylan Thomas's Play for Voices." In his DRAMA FROM IBSEN TO BRECHT. New York: Oxford University Press, 1969, pp. 211-19.

The verse describing character and action is superior to the purely atmospheric verse, which seems a carry-over from Thomas' bad habits as a poet. The Circe section of ULYSSES is examined as an influence, and Williams concludes that UNDER MILK WOOD is a miscellany of dreams of self-enclosed voices.

# GWYN THOMAS (1913-  )

THE KEEP. London: Elek Books, 1962.

JACKIE THE JUMPER. In PLAYS OF THE YEAR 26. Ed. J.C. Trewin. London: Elek Books, 1963.

THE LOOT. In EIGHT PLAYS. Book 2. Ed. Malcolm Stuart Fellows. London: Cassell, 1965.

## SELECTED NONDRAMATIC WRITING

"After the Chip-Soup." P&P, 10 (February 1963), 26-27.

Introduces the magazine publication of JACKIE THE JUMPER.

A FEW SELECTED EXITS: AN AUTOBIOGRAPHY OF SORTS. Boston: Little, Brown, 1968.

## CRITICISM

Raynor, Henry. "Gwyn Thomas." In CONTEMPORARY DRAMATISTS. Ed. James Vinson. London: St. James; New York: St. Martin's, 1973, pp. 759-61.

"The world of Gwyn Thomas is inhabited by exploiters and exploited."

# BEN TRAVERS (1886-1980)

WILD HORSES:. A FARCIAL COMEDY IN THREE ACTS. London: Samuel French, 1953.

NUN'S VEILING. London: Samuel French, 1956.

Revision of an unpublished 1936 farce, O MISTRESS MINE.

## SELECTED NONDRAMATIC WRITING

VALE OF LAUGHTER: AN AUTOBIOGRAPHY. London: G. Bles, 1957.

## CRITICISM

Trewin, J.C. "Green Cheese." In his DRAMATISTS OF TODAY. London: Staples Press, 1953, pp. 84-90.

# DAVID TURNER (1927- )

SEMI-DETACHED. London: Heinemann, 1962.

WAY OFF BEAT. In CONFLICTING GENERATIONS: FIVE TELEVISION PLAYS. Ed. Michael Marland. London: Longmans, 1968.

## COLLABORATION WITH PAUL LAPWORTH

THE SERVANT OF TWO MASTERS. London: Evans, 1973.

Adaptation of the Goldoni play.

## CRITICISM

Taylor, John Russell. "David Turner." In his ANGER AND AFTER: A GUIDE TO THE NEW BRITISH DRAMA. Rev. ed. Harmondsworth, Engl.: Penguin, 1963, pp. 169-79.

"SEMI-DETACHED is that great rarity in English theatre, a play about the lower middle class which does not patronize or condemn, but simply accepts. . . ."

## PETER USTINOV (1921- )

PLAYS ABOUT PEOPLE. London: Jonathan Cape, 1950.

Three plays from the forties: THE TRAGEDY OF GOOD INTENTIONS, BLOW YOUR OWN TRUMPET, and THE INDIFFERENT SHEPERD.

THE LOVE OF FOUR COLONELS. London: English Theatre Guild, 1951.

THE MOMENT OF TRUTH. London: English Theatre Guild, 1953.

ROMANOFF AND JULIET. London: English Theatre Guild, 1957.

PHOTO FINISH: AN ADVENTURE IN BIOGRAPHY IN THREE ACTS. London: Heinemann, 1962.

THE UNKNOWN SOLDIER AND HIS WIFE. New York: Random House, 1967.

HALFWAY UP THE TREE. New York: Random House, 1968.

THE UNKNOWN SOLDIER AND HIS WIFE: TWO ACTS OF WAR SEPARATED BY A TRUCE. London: Heinemann, 1968.

THE UNKNOWN SOLDIER AND HIS WIFE: TWO ACTS OF WAR SEPARATED BY A TRUCE FOR REFRESHMENT. London: Samuel French, 1968.

### COLLECTION

FIVE PLAYS. London: Heinemann, 1965.

Contains the introduction, "Peter Ustinov Speaking," and ROMANOFF AND JULIET, THE MOMENT OF TRUTH, THE LOVE OF FOUR COLONELS, BEYOND, and the only published version of NO SIGN OF THE DOVE.

## BIBLIOGRAPHY

Salem, James M., ed. A GUIDE TO CRITICAL REVIEWS. Part 3: BRITISH AND CONTINENTAL DRAMA FROM IBSEN TO PINTER. Metuchen, N.J.: Scarecrow Press, 1968.

List of reviews of New York productions, pages 251-52.

## CRITICISM

Bentley, Eric. "Guilding the Lilli." In his DRAMATIC EVENT: AN AMERICAN CHRONICLE. New York: Horizon, 1954, pp. 86-89.

In reviewing THE LOVE OF FOUR COLONELS, Bentley argues that Ustinov should eschew moralizing and stay frivolous.

Trewin, J.C. "Up-and-Coming." In his DRAMATISTS OF TODAY. London: Staples Press, 1953, pp. 192-97.

# JEAN-CLAUDE VAN ITALLIE (1936- )

IT'S ALMOST LIKE BEING. TDR, 9 (Summer 1965), 171-78.

AMERICA HURRAH: A MASQUE FOR THREE DOLLS. In EIGHT PLAYS FROM OFF-OFF BROADWAY. Ed. Nick Orzel and Michael Smith. Indianapolis: Bobbs-Merrill, 1966.

> This is the one-act puppet play, later retitled MOTEL, which forms the third part of AMERICA HURRAH, the next item.

AMERICA HURRAH. New York: Coward-McCann, 1967.

> Consists of three one-act plays: INTERVIEW (earlier called PAVANE), T.V., and MOTEL. MOTEL is inaccurately titled HOTEL in the Union Catalogue of the Library of Congress.

AMERICA HURRAH: FIVE SHORT PLAYS. Harmondsworth, Engl.: Penguin, 1967.

> Includes, in addition to the three plays in the American edition, WAR and IT'S ALMOST LIKE BEING.

WAR AND FOUR OTHER PLAYS. New York: Dramatists Play Service, 1967.

> Also includes IT'S ALMOST LIKE BEING, THE HUNTER AND THE BIRD, I'M REALLY HERE, and WHERE IS DE QUEEN?

THE SERPENT: A CEREMONY BY JEAN-CLAUDE VAN ITALLIE IN COLLABORATION WITH THE OPEN THEATRE UNDER THE DIRECTION OF JOSEPH CHAIKIN. New York: Atheneum, 1969.

TAKE A DEEP BREATH. TOUCAN (Kent, Ohio), 2nd supplement (1970).

> Sketch for Eric Bentley's DMZ cabaret.

MYSTERY PLAY: A FARCE. New York: Dramatists Play Service, 1973.

SEVEN SHORT AND VERY SHORT PLAYS. New York: Dramatists Play Service, 1973.

THE KING OF THE UNITED STATES. New York: Dramatists Play Service, 1975.

## COLLABORATION WITH SHARON THIE

THOUGHTS ON THE INSTANT OF GREETING A FRIEND ON THE STREET. In COLLISION COURSE. Ed. Edward Parone. New York: Random House, 1969.

## BIBLIOGRAPHY

Brittain, Michael J., ed. "A Checklist of Jean-Claude van Itallie." SERIF, 9 (Winter 1972), 75-77.

Also includes a valuable chronology of his work.

Salem, James M., ed. A GUIDE TO CRITICAL REVIEWS. Part 1: AMERICAN DRAMA, 1909-1969. 2nd ed. Metuchen, N.J.: Scarecrow Press, 1973.

List of reviews, pages 497-98.

## SELECTED NONDRAMATIC WRITING

"Francois Yattend." TR, 7 (Fall 1961), 114-18.

Short story.

"Playwright at Work: Off-Off Broadway." TDR, 10 (Summer 1966), 154-58.

Van Itallie recounts his association with the Open Theater of Joseph Chaikin. He denies that OOB is a training ground for playwrights; instead it is a school for audiences.

## CRITICISM

Berk, Philip R. "Memories of John." SERIF, 9 (Winter 1972), 9-11.

High school and Harvard reminiscences.

Gaisner, Rhea. "Jean-Claude van Itallie: Playwright of the Ensemble: Open Theater." SERIF, 9 (Winter 1972), 14-17.

Brief recollections by a former member of the company about van Itallie as a collaborative playwright with the Open Theater.

Hirsch, Foster. "Performance Theatre: DIONYSUS IN 69 and THE SERPENT." KANSAS QUARTERLY, 3 (Spring 1971), 41-49.

Performance theatre cannot replace drama as literature.

Jackson, Esther M. "American Theater in the Sixties: The Drama of Internal Crisis." PL, 48 (Summer 1973), 236-49.

AMERICA HURRAH is an instance of the Living Theatre's influence, helping to create a new production language for the contemporary stage.

Kerr, Walter. "God on the Gymnasium Floor." In his GOD ON THE GYMNASIUM FLOOR AND OTHER THEATRICAL ADVENTURES. New York: Simon and Schuster, 1971, pp. 21-27.

Grudging praise for the power of THE SERPENT.

Lahr, John. "The Open Theater's SERPENT." In his UP AGAINST THE FOURTH WALL: ESSAYS ON THE MODERN THEATER. New York: Grove Press, 1970, pp. 158-74.

Praises van Itallie and Chaikin's affirmative exploration of myths for the modern stage.

Novick, Julius. "About the One That Succeeds: Interview with van Itallie." NEW YORK TIMES, 15 November 1969, Sec. 2, p. 1.

Valgemae, Mardi. "Expressionism and the New American Drama." TCL, 17 (October 1971), 227-34.

AMERICA HURRAH uses American subject matter and an imaginative style of subjective distortion.

Wagner, Phyllis Jane. "Jean-Claude van Itallie: Political Playwright." SERIF, 9 (Winter 1972), 19-74.

This lengthy, well-documented analysis of van Itallie's work incorporates a valuable interview.

# GORE VIDAL (1925- )

VISIT TO A SMALL PLANET. In BEST TELEVISION PLAYS. Ed. Gore Vidal. New York: Ballantine Books, 1956.

VISIT TO A SMALL PLANET AND OTHER TELEVISION PLAYS. Foreword by the author. Boston: Little, Brown, 1956.

Also includes BARN BURNING, DARK POSSESSION, THE DEATH OF BILLY THE KID, A SENSE OF JUSTICE, SMOKE, SUMMER PAVILION, and THE TURN OF THE SCREW.

HONOR. In TELEVISION PLAYS FOR WRITERS: EIGHT TELEVISION PLAYS. Ed. A.S. Burack. Boston: By the author, 1957.

A VISIT TO A SMALL PLANET: A COMEDY AKIN TO A VAUDEVILLE. Boston: Little, Brown, 1957.

Stage version.

THE BEST MAN: A PLAY ABOUT POLITICS. Boston: Little, Brown, 1960.

ROMULUS. New York: Dramatists Play Service, 1962.

Adapted from a play by Friedrich Duerrenmatt. See also the 1966 Grove Press edition containing both Vidal's adaptation, with a preface, and a translation of the Duerrenmatt play, ROMULUS THE GREAT.

WEEKEND. New York: Dramatists Play Service, 1968.

AN EVENING WITH RICHARD NIXON. New York: Random House, 1972.

## COLLECTIONS

THREE PLAYS. London: Heinemann, 1962.

Includes THE BEST MAN, the stage version of A VISIT TO A SMALL PLANET, and a revised version of HONOR, called ON THE MARCH TO THE SEA: A SOUTHRON COMEDY.

## BIBLIOGRAPHY

Salem, James M., ed. A GUIDE TO CRITICAL REVIEWS. Part 1: AMERICAN DRAMA, 1909-1969. 2nd ed. Metuchen, N.J.: Scarecrow Press, 1973.

List of reviews, pages 502-03.

## CRITICISM

Brustein, Robert. "Politics and the Higher Gossip." In his SEASONS OF DISCONTENT: DRAMATIC OPINIONS 1959-1965. New York: Simon and Schuster, 1965, pp. 108-10.

THE BEST MAN contains not a single political idea as it panders to a trivial sophistication.

"Gore Vidal Interviewed by Eugene Walter." In BEHIND THE SCENES: THEATER AND FILM INTERVIEWS FROM THE TRANSATLANTIC REVIEW. Ed. Joseph F.M. McCrindle, introd. Jean-Claude van Itallie. New York: Holt, Rinehart and Winston, 1971, pp. 327-41.

# KURT VONNEGUT, JR. (1922- )

VERY FIRST CHRISTMAS MORNING. BETTER HOMES AND GARDENS, 40 (December 1962), 14 ff.

FORTITUDE. PLAYBOY, 15 (September 1968), 99-100 ff.

HAPPY BIRTHDAY, WANDA JUNE. New York: Delacorte, 1970.

With "About this Play" by Vonnegut.

HAPPY BIRTHDAY, WANDA JUNE. Rev. ed. New York: Samuel French, 1971.

FORTITUDE. In WAMPETERS, FOMA & GRANFALLOONS: OPINIONS. New York: Delacorte, 1974.

## BIBLIOGRAPHY

Hudgens, Betty Linhardt, ed. KURT VONNEGUT, JR.: A CHECKLIST. Detroit: Gale Research Co., 1972.

Primary sources only.

Pieratt, Asa B., Jr., and Jerome Klinkowitz, eds. KURT VONNEGUT, JR.: A DESCRIPTIVE BIBLIOGRAPHY AND ANNOTATED CHECKLIST. Hamden, Conn.: Archon Books, 1974.

Most complete bibliography available.

## CRITICISM

Klinkowitz, Jerome. "The Dramatization of Kurt Vonnegut, Jr." PL, 50 (February-March 1975), 62-64.

The corrected typescript is used to show how the dramatic form affected Vonnegut's vision in HAPPY BIRTHDAY, WANDA JUNE.

Klinkowitz, Jerome, and John Somer, eds. THE VONNEGUT STATEMENT: ORIGINAL ESSAYS ON THE LIFE AND WORK OF KURT VONNEGUT, JR. New York: Delacorte, 1973.

Also contains a good bibliography of secondary sources.

# ROBERT PENN WARREN (1905- )

ALL THE KING'S MEN: A PLAY. New York: Random House, 1960.

Warren's adaptation of his 1946 novel, which in turn was based on the verse drama, PROUD FLESH (1946).

## BIBLIOGRAPHY

Huff, Mary Nance, comp. ROBERT PENN WARREN: A BIBLIOGRAPHY. New York: David Lewis, 1968.

Salem, James M., ed. A GUIDE TO CRITICAL REVIEWS. Part 1: AMERICAN DRAMA, 1909-1969. 2nd ed. Metuchen, N.J.: Scarecrow Press, 1973.

List of reviews, page 509.

## SELECTED NONDRAMATIC WRITING

"A Note to ALL THE KING'S MEN." SR, 61 (Summer 1953), 476-80.

Reprinted in revised form as the introduction to the 1953 Modern Library edition of the novel, this consists of remarks on PROUD FLESH and the composition of the novel.

"ALL THE KING'S MEN: The Matrix of Experience." YALE REVIEW, 53 (December 1963), 161-64. Also in ROBERT PENN WARREN: A COLLECTION OF CRITICAL ESSAYS. Ed. John Lewis Longley. New York: New York University Press, 1965.

# JEROME WEIDMAN (1913- )

I CAN GET IT FOR YOU WHOLESALE: A MUSICAL PLAY. New York: Random House, 1962.

The book by Jerome Weidman is based on his novel. The music and lyrics are by Harold Rome.

ASTERISK! A COMEDY OF TERRORS. New York: Dramatists Play Service, 1970.

## COLLABORATIONS

FIORELLO. New York: Random House, 1960.

Book by Jerome Weidman and George Abbott, music by Jerry Bock, and lyrics by Sheldon Harnick.

TENDERLOIN. New York: Random House, 1963.

The book by Jerome Weidman and George Abbott is based on the novel by Samuel Hopkins Adams. The music is by Jerry Bock and lyrics by Sheldon Harnick.

IVORY TOWER. New York: Dramatists Play Service, 1969.

With James Yaffe.

## CRITICISM

Aronson, Erica. "Jerome Weidman." In CONTEMPORARY DRAMATISTS. Ed. James Vinson. London: St. James; New York: St. Martin's, 1973, pp. 796-97.

"Weidman is generally most successful in musical comedy where his talent to dramatize the big city atmosphere can be augmented by music and lyrics."

# ARNOLD WEINSTEIN (1927- )

RED EYE OF LOVE. New York: Grove Press, 1961.

FORTUNA: A MUSICAL PLAY. New York: n.p., 1962.

Adapted from a play by Eduardo de Filippo and Armando Curcio. English book and lyrics by Arnold Weinstein and music by Francis Thorne. Typescript at the Lincoln Center Library of the Performing Arts.

DYNAMITE TONITE. New York: Trio Music, 1964.

Book and lyrics by Arnold Weinstein and music by William Bolcom.

REG. U.S. PAT. OFF. In PARDON ME, SIR, BUT IS MY EYE HURTING YOUR ELBOW? New York: Bernard Geis, 1968.

Part of the unproduced film.

THEATRE POEMS AND PLAYS. YT, 1 (Spring 1968), 64-68.

MAHAGONNY. YT, 1 (Summer 1968), 53-65.

Selections from adaptation of the Brecht work.

## CRITICISM

Gottfried, Martin. "Arnold Weinstein." In CONTEMPORARY DRAMATISTS. Ed. James Vinson. London: St. James; New York: St. Martin's, 1973, pp. 799-800.

Gottfried believes Weinstein "has been hurt by a combination of critical rejection and changing taste, and though the author of charming plays and libretti, his career seems frustrated."

## Arnold Weinstein

Gruen, John. "Arnold Weinstein." In his CLOSE-UP. New York: Viking, 1968, pp. 54-57.

Brief interview.

# MICHAEL WELLER (1942- )

AND NOW THERE'S JUST THREE OF US. P&P, 17 (November 1969), 68-78.

CANCER: A COMEDY. P&P, 18 (December 1970), 65-84.

CANCER: A COMEDY. London: Faber and Faber, 1971.

Performed, and published in New York in 1972 by Delacorte, as MOONCHILDREN.

THE BODYBUILDERS, AND TIRA TELLS EVERYTHING THERE IS TO KNOW ABOUT HERSELF. New York: Dramatists Play Service, 1972.

GRANT'S MOVIE AND TIRA. London: Faber and Faber, 1972.

TIRA is a shortened title for TIRA TELLS EVERYTHING THERE IS TO KNOW ABOUT HERSELF.

FISHING. New York: Samuel French, 1975.

## CRITICISM

Hammond, Jonathan. "Michael Weller." In CONTEMPORARY DRAMATISTS. Ed. James Vinson. London: St. James; New York: St. Martin's, 1973, pp. 801-02.

Marowitz, Charles. "Introduction." In OFF-BROADWAY PLAYS 2. Harmondsworth, Engl.: Penguin, 1972.

# ARNOLD WESKER (1932- )

CHICKEN SOUP WITH BARLEY. In NEW ENGLISH DRAMATISTS. Ed. Elliott Martin Browne. Harmondsworth, Engl.: Penguin, 1959.

The first part of the Wesker trilogy.

ROOTS: THE SECOND PLAY OF THE "CHICKEN SOUP" TRILOGY. Harmondsworth, Engl.: Penguin, 1959.

I'M TALKING ABOUT JERUSALEM. Harmondsworth, Engl.: Penguin, 1960.

The third part of THE TRILOGY.

THE KITCHEN. In NEW ENGLISH DRAMATISTS 2. Ed. Tom Machler. Harmondsworth, Engl.: Penguin, 1960.

The one-act version.

THE KITCHEN: A PLAY IN TWO ACTS. London: Cape, 1961.

The revised, expanded version.

CHIPS WITH EVERYTHING. London: Cape, 1962.

THE FOUR SEASONS. In NEW ENGLISH DRAMATISTS. 9. Introd. Michael Billington. Harmondsworth, Engl.: Penguin, 1966.

This version contains the "Epilogue," which was not included in the 1966 Jonathan Cape edition.

THEIR VERY OWN AND GOLDEN CITY: A PLAY IN TWO ACTS AND TWENTY-NINE SCENES. London: Cape, 1966.

THE FRIENDS. London: Cape, 1970.

THE OLD ONES. P&P, 20 (October 1972), i-xv.

THE JOURNALIST. London: Cape, 1973.

THE OLD ONES. London: Cape, 1973.

THE OLD ONES. Edited by Michael Marland. Rev. ed. London: Blackie, 1974.

## COLLECTIONS

THE WESKER TRILOGY. London: Cape, 1960.

CHICKEN SOUP WITH BARLEY, ROOTS, and I'M TALKING ABOUT JERUSALEM.

## BIBLIOGRAPHY

Salem, James M., ed. A GUIDE TO CRITICAL REVIEWS. Part 3: BRITISH AND CONTINENTAL DRAMA FROM IBSEN TO PINTER. Metuchen, N.J.: Scarecrow Press, 1968.

List of reviews of New York productions. See pages 259-60.

## SELECTED NONDRAMATIC WRITING

"Let Battle Commence!" EN, 5 (November 1958), 18-24. Also in THE NEW BRITISH DRAMA. Ed. Henry Popkin. New York: Grove Press, 1964.

"I cannot simply write plays, I have to write them in such a way as to suggest a play is worthwhile writing for something more than telling a tale."

"The Modern Playwright." GEMINI, 3 (Spring 1960), 5-7.

The trade union movement and the Labour Party must support the arts and educate the worker culturally.

"Discovery." TR, 5 (December 1960), 16-18.

On his feelings after completing THE TRILOGY.

"One Room Living: Breaking the Barrier to a New Audience." NTM, 3 (January 1962), 11-14.

On art, the human spirit, and the founding of Centre 42.

"THEIR VERY OWN AND GOLDEN CITY." QUEST (London), 1 (September 1965), 58-65.

Contains the rough draft of scenes 2-5 of act 2 of THEIR VERY OWN AND GOLDEN CITY, with notes by Wesker on his intentions.

"Casual Condemnations: A Brief Study of the Critic as Censor." TQ, 1 (April-June 1971), 16-30.

A lengthy defense of the FRIENDS and a denunciation of the unsympathetic criticism it received. In particular, John Russell Taylor and Ronald Bryden are attacked.

## CRITICISM

Anderson, Michael. "Arnold Wesker and the Workers." NTM, 2 (October 1960), 3-7.

Wesker's proposals in "The Modern Playwright" have not been taken seriously because they assume that the working class has no existing educational opportunities; Wesker also neglects the inevitable cheapening of art that must follow any attempt to construct theatres exclusively for the working classes.

______. "Arnold Wesker: The Last Humanist?" NTM, 8 (Summer 1968), 10-27.

This detailed consideration of Wesker's work argues that he is a unique combination of faith in human possibility and a surprising willingness to face up to the possible failure of his own ideas.

Brien, Alan. "Country of the Blind." SPECTATOR, 10 July 1959, pp. 27-28.

A vividly affirmative review of ROOTS.

Brown, John Russell. "Theatrical Demonstration." In his THEATRE LANGUAGE: A STUDY OF ARDEN, OSBORNE, PINTER AND WESKER. London: Alan Lane, 1971, pp. 158-89.

Brown takes as his theme Wesker's statement that he is "no longer satisfied if the characters are simply on the stage talking to each other. . . . What I try to have them do is DEMONSTRATE an idea, live it out, act it out."

Garforth, John. "Arnold Wesker's Mission." In THE ENCORE READER: A CHRONICLE OF THE NEW DRAMA. Ed. Charles Marowitz, Tom Milne, and Owen Hale. London: Methuen, 1965, pp. 223-30.

"Wesker brings no startling solutions to the problems of our time. . . but by God he cares!"

Goodman, Henry. "The New Dramatists, 2: Arnold Wesker." DS, 1 (October 1961), 215-22

Wesker is in the mold of the social well-made dramas of the thirties; his is an optimistic and, when compared to Brecht's, sentimental theatre.

Gordon, Giles. "Arnold Wesker: An Interview by Giles Gordon." In BEHIND THE SCENES: THEATER AND FILM INTERVIEWS FROM THE TRANSATLANTIC REVIEW. Ed. Joseph F.M. McCrindle, introd. Jean-Claude van Itallie. New York: Holt, Rinehart and Winston, 1971, pp. 137-48.

On the hostile reception of THE FOUR SEASONS and the prospects for Centre 42.

Hayman, Ronald. ARNOLD WESKER. London: Heinemann, 1970.

Brief, informative study.

______. "Arnold Wesker and John Dexter Talking to Ronald Hayman." TR, 48 (Winter 1973-74), 89-99.

The author and director, old friends and collaborators, reminisce.

Jones, A.R. "The Theatre of Arnold Wesker." CQ, 2 (Winter 1960), 366-70.

THE TRILOGY is a rewriting of the myth of our time from the point of view of "those who suffered and, somehow, survived the crises and disillusionments of the last twenty-five years."

Kitchin, Laurence. "Drama with a Message: Arnold Wesker." In EXPERIMENTAL DRAMA. Ed. William A. Armstrong. London: G. Bell, 1963, pp. 169-85. Also in MODERN BRITISH DRAMATISTS: A COLLECTION OF CRITICAL ESSAYS. Ed. John Russell Brown. Englewood Cliffs, N.J.: Prentice-Hall, 1968, pp. 71-82.

This sympathetic treatment of THE KITCHEN and the TRILOGY looks for the human questions beneath the overt political content.

Latham, Jacqueline. "ROOTS: A Reassessment." MD, 8 (September 1965), 192-97.

Wesker treats the Bryants a good deal more sympathetically than is usually understood. They are, for all their very real faults, close to the natural world.

Leech, Clifford. "Two Romantics: Arnold Wesker and Harold Pinter." In CONTEMPORARY THEATRE. Ed. John Russell Brown and Bernard Harris. London: Edward Arnold, 1962, pp. 10-31.

A cautious treatment of Wesker's and Pinter's early works, with a comparison between them and Wordsworth and Coleridge.

Mander, John. THE WRITER AND COMMITMENT. London: Secker and Warburg, 1961, pp. 194-211.

ROOTS is the great achievement of the "New Drama," dramatizing the conflict between a conservative working class and a personalized Socialist vision.

Marland, Michael, ed. TIMES AUTHORS SERIES 1--ARNOLD WESKER. London: London Times, 1971.

A package of clippings and other materials about Wesker.

O'Connor, Garry. "Production Casebook No. 2: Arnold Wesker's THE FRIENDS." TQ, 1 (April-June 1971), 78-92.

The diaries and notes of the assistant director written during the rehearsals for Wesker's own production of his play provide an invaluable look at the playwright and his difficulties as a director.

Page, Malcolm. "Whatever Happened to Arnold Wesker?: His Recent Plays." MD, 11 (December 1968), 317-35.

Sympathetically examines Wesker's plays since 1960 and notes his attempts to expand his range of theatrical and linguistic expression.

Ribalow, Harold U. ARNOLD WESKER. New York: Twayne, 1965.

Rothenberg, Abraham. "Waiting for Wesker." ANTIOCH REVIEW, 24 (Winter 1964-65), 492-505.

Report of an interview with Wesker, with information about Centre 42.

Trussler, Simon. "Interview with Simon Trussler." In THEATRE AT WORK. Ed. Charles Marowitz and Simon Trussler. London: Methuen, 1967, pp. 78-95.

How the plays were written and Wesker's opinion of the changes in his work.

Worth, Katharine J. "Realism in New Directions: Arnold Wesker, David Storey, David Mercer." In her REVOLUTIONS IN MODERN ENGLISH DRAMA. London: G. Bell, 1973, pp. 19-21, 30-38.

ROOTS demonstrated "how much untapped vitality there was . . . in the whole convention of realism." His works combine "clowning and pain . . . wordiness and physicality."

# HUGH WHEELER (1916- )

BIG FISH, LITTLE FISH. New York: Random House, 1961.

LOOK: WE'VE COME THROUGH. New York: Dramatists Play Service, 1963.

RICH LITTLE RICH GIRL. New York: Studio Duplicating Service, 1964.

Typescript at the Lincoln Center Library of the Performing Arts.

WE HAVE ALWAYS LIVED IN THE CASTLE: A MELODRAMA IN THREE ACTS. New York: Dramatists Play Service, 1967.

Adapted from the novel by Shirley Jackson.

LOOK: WE'VE COME THROUGH. In BROADWAY'S BEAUTIFUL LOSERS. Ed. Marilyn Stasio. New York: Delacorte Press, 1972.

A LITTLE NIGHT MUSIC. New York: Dodd, Mead, 1974.

Libretto for Stephen Sondheim's musical treatment of the Ingmar Bergman film SMILES OF A SUMMER NIGHT (1955).

## BIBLIOGRAPHY

Salem, James M., ed. A GUIDE TO CRITICAL REVIEWS. Part 3: BRITISH AND CONTINENTAL DRAMA FROM IBSEN TO PINTER. Metuchen, N.J.: Scarecrow Press, 1968.

Reviews of the first two plays above. See page 260.

# JOHN WHITE (1919- )

BUGS AND VERONICA: TWO PLAYS. New York: Dramatists Play Service, 1966.

## CRITICISM

Gottfried, Martin. "John White." In CONTEMPORARY DRAMATISTS. Ed. James Vinson. London: St. James; New York: St. Martin's, 1973, pp. 807-08.

A lament for White's abortive career.

# JOHN WHITING (1918-1963)

SAINT'S DAY. In PLAYS OF THE YEAR 6. Ed. J.C. Trewin. London: Elek Books, 1952.

MARCHING SONG. London: Samuel French, 1954.

THE PLAYS OF JOHN WHITING. London: Heinemann, 1957.

Reprints of SAINT'S DAY and MARCHING SONG, with the first publication of A PENNY FOR A SONG, and an introduction by Whiting.

MADAME DE. London: Samuel French, 1959.

A translation of Anouilh's adaptation of Louise de Vilmorin's MADAM DE (1951).

SACRIFICE TO THE WIND. In PLAYS FOR RADIO AND TELEVISION. Ed. Nigel Samuel. Harlow, Engl.: Longmans, 1959.

A translation of Obey's UNE FILLE POUR DU VENT (1953).

TRAVELLER WITHOUT LUGGAGE. London: Samuel French, 1959.

A translation of Anouilh's LE VOYAGEUR SANS BAGAGE (1937).

THE DEVILS. London: Heinemann, 1961.

Based on Aldous Huxley's THE DEVILS OF LOUDUN (1952).

NO WHY. London: Samuel French, 1961.

A PENNY FOR A SONG. Rev. ed., introd. E.R. Wood. London: Heinemann, 1964.

## COLLECTIONS

THE COLLECTED PLAYS. 2 vols. Ed. Ronald Hayman. London: Heinemann, 1969.

Includes CONDITIONS OF AGREEMENT (first publication), SAINT'S DAY, A PENNY FOR A SONG (the earlier of the two versions), MARCHING SONG, THE GATE OF SUMMER (first publication), NO WHY, A WALK IN THE DESERT (first publication of this television play), THE DEVILS, and drafts and notes for NOMAN and its revision, THE NOMADS. Obviously this is a most valuable textual source.

## SELECTED NONDRAMATIC WRITING

JOHN WHITING ON THEATRE. London: Alan Ross, 1966.

Theatre reviews from LONDON MAGAZINE.

THE ART OF THE DRAMATIST. Ed., introd. Ronald Hayman. London: London Magazine Editions, 1970.

In addition to reviews, this volume includes a narrative for television, a film scenario, a play fragment, short stories, and several lectures and articles.

## CRITICISM

Burgess, Anthony. "The Blackness of Whiting." SPECTATOR, 21 May 1965, p. 664.

Praises SAINT'S DAY, during a revival, for creating its own innocent world, despite its many inconsistencies.

Clurman, Harold. "THE DEVILS." NATION, 13 December 1973, pp. 483-84.

Clurman calls the play an "indigestible mess."

Hamilton, Iain. "Theatre." SPECTATOR, 14 September 1951, p. 328.

Rude reaction to the first run of SAINT'S DAY.

Hoefer, Jacqueline. "Pinter and Whiting: Two Attitudes Towards the Alienated Artist." MD, 4 (February 1962), 402-08.

THE BIRTHDAY PARTY and SAINT'S DAY are compared, with the former showing the artist as victim, and the latter the artist as destroyer.

Hurrell, John Dennis. "John Whiting and the Theme of Self-Destruction." MD, 8 (September 1965), 134-41.

SAINT'S DAY presents several parallel treatments of the theme of self-destruction, without any attempt to make the play "real" or logical.

Lyons, Charles R. "Futile Encounter in the Plays of John Whiting." MD, 11 (December 1968), 283-98.

The desire of the self to confront a reality beyond the self is, in Whiting, invariably in vain.

Mangham, Ian Leslie. "Plays of a Private Man." NTM, 6 (April-June 1965), 21-25.

Whiting's protagonists are disillusioned, solitary figures whose isolation best prepares them for the nothingness of death. MARCHING SONG is his best play; THE DEVILS, despite its popularity, is his most compromised play.

Milne, Tom. "The Hidden Face of Violence." In THE ENCORE READER: A CHRONICLE OF THE NEW DRAMA. Ed. Charles Marowitz, Tom Milne, and Owen Hale. London: Methuen, 1965, pp. 115-24. Also in MODERN BRITISH DRAMATISTS: A COLLECTION OF CRITICAL ESSAYS. Ed. John Russell Brown. Englewood Cliffs, N.J.: Prentice-Hall, 1968, pp. 38-46.

SAINT'S DAY, Pinter's THE BIRTHDAY PARTY, and Arden's SERJEANT MUSGRAVE'S DANCE "share a common theme: the nature of violence."

Milne, Tom, and Clive Goodwin. "Interview with Tom Milne and Clive Goodwin." In THEATRE AT WORK. Ed. Charles Marowitz and Simon Trussler. London: Methuen, 1967, pp. 21-35.

Whiting discusses his biography, the origins of his plays, his feelings about them, and his conception of himself as a disengaged artist.

Page, Malcolm. "The Two Versions of John Whiting's A PENNY FOR A SONG." NOTES ON CONTEMPORARY LITERATURE, 1 (January 1971), 8-9.

Robinson, Gabriele Scott. "A Private Mythology: The Manuscripts and Plays of John Whiting." MD, 14 (May 1971), 23-36.

Having access to Whiting's unpublished manuscripts and drafts, Robinson notes Whiting's tendency to make his work less explicit and more symbolic as he revised. Whiting's only novel, in a 1945 manuscript, contains the thematic material he was to spin out in his plays.

______. "Beyond the Waste Land: An Interpretation of John Whiting's SAINT'S DAY." MD, 14 (February 1972), 463-77.

Salmon, Eric. "John Whiting's Unpublished Novel." LONDON MAGAZINE, 12 (February-March 1973), 44-69.

Trussler, Simon. "The Plays of John Whiting." PROMPT, 1 (Summer 1963), 23-27.

This highly affirmative survey, with plot summaries, compares Whiting with William Blake, and finds his plays "masterpieces of dramatic construction."

# THORNTON WILDER (1897-1975)

THE DRUNKEN SISTERS. ATLANTIC MONTHLY, 200 (November 1957), 92-95.

THE DRUNKEN SISTERS. New York: Samuel French, 1957.

This is the "satyr" play (the comic afterpiece) for Wilder's version of the Alcestis myth, A LIFE IN THE SUN, first published in English in 1977 by Harper and Row.

THREE PLAYS: OUR TOWN, THE SKIN OF OUR TEETH, THE MATCHMAKER. New York: Harper and Row, 1957.

THE MATCHMAKER is a revised version of the 1939 MERCHANT OF YONKERS. Like the early version, it is dedicated to Max Reinhardt. THE MATCHMAKER was later transformed into the musical HELL, DOLLY (1964).

CHILDHOOD. New York: Samuel French, 1960.

INFANCY. New York: Samuel French, 1961.

SOMEONE FROM ASSISI. New York: n.p., 1961.

Available in manuscript from Samuel French.

## BIBLIOGRAPHY

Kosok, Heinz, ed. "Thornton Wilder: A Bibliography of Criticism." TCL, 9 (July 1963), 93-100.

## CRITICISM

Burbank, Rex. THORNTON WILDER. New York: Twayne, 1961.

Turgid.

Goldstein, Malcolm. THE ART OF THORNTON WILDER. Lincoln: University of Nebraska Press, 1965.

This admirably straightforward critical biography is most notable for the absence of any highly interpretive glosses on Wilder's texts. It has a brief well-selected bibliography.

Haberman, Donald. THE PLAYS OF THORNTON WILDER: A CRITICAL STUDY. Middletown, Conn.: Wesleyan University Press, 1967.

A diffuse, primarily literary study made valuable by the author's access to Wilder's manuscript of A LIFE IN THE SUN.

Hewitt, Barnard. "Thornton Wilder says 'Yes.'" TDR, 4 (December 1959), pp. 110-20.

THE MATCHMAKER is a farcical affirmation of life and adventure.

Nixon, Douglas Charles, Jr. "Dramatic Techniques of Thornton Wilder and Bertolt Brecht: A Study in Comparison." MD, 15 (September 1972), 112-24.

The focus is on the similarities in Wilder's and Brecht's theatricalism, characterization, staging, and dramatic structure, with the emphasis on Wilder's pre-1950 plays.

Tynan, Kenneth. "Greek and Roman." OBSERVER, 28 August 1955, p. 11.

This negative review of A LIFE IN THE SUN suggests that the departure from the style of OUR TOWN for "timeless prose" was a fatal error.

# EMLYN WILLIAMS (1905- )

ACCOLADE. London: Heinemann, 1951.

VIGIL. In THE SECOND BOOK OF ONE-ACT PLAYS. London: Heinemann, 1954.

SOMEONE WAITING. New York: Dramatists Play Service, 1956.

BETH. London: Heinemann, 1959.

THE MASTER BUILDER. London: Heinemann, 1967.

Adaptation of Ibsen's 1892 play.

## BIBLIOGRAPHY

Salem, James M., ed. A GUIDE TO CRITICAL REVIEWS. Part 3: BRITISH AND CONTINENTAL DRAMA FROM IBSEN TO PINTER. Metuchen, N.J.: Scarecrow Press, 1968.

List of reviews of the New York production of SOMEONE WAITING. See page 264.

## CRITICISM

Trewin, J.C. "Theatre Theatrical." In his DRAMATISTS OF TODAY. London: Staples Press, 1953, pp. 162-69.

Survey of Williams' work up to ACCOLADE.

# HEATHCOTE WILLIAMS (1941- )

THE LOCAL STIGMATIC. In TRAVERSE PLAYS. Ed. Jim Haynes. Harmondsworth, Engl.: Penguin, 1965.

THE LOCAL STIGMATIC. ER, 11 (December 1967), 33-43.

AC/DC. London: Calder and Boyars, 1972.

## SELECTED NONDRAMATIC WRITING

THE SPEAKERS. London: Hutchinson, 1964.

THE SPEAKERS. New York: Grove, 1967.

A recreation of the world of Hyde Park corner.

## CRITICISM

Taylor, John Russell. "Heathcote Williams." In CONTEMPORARY DRAMATISTS. Ed. James Vinson. London: St. James; New York: St. Martin's, 1973, p. 823.

A re-write of his brief treatment of Williams in THE SECOND WAVE.

## TENNESSEE [THOMAS LANIER] WILLIAMS (1911- )

SUMMER AND SMOKE. New York: Dramatists Play Service, 1950.

Revised, acting edition of the 1948 play; see THE ECCENTRICITIES OF A NIGHTINGALE, below, for a further-revised version of this same play.

I RISE IN FLAME, CRIED THE PHOENIX, A PLAY ABOUT D.H. LAWRENCE. Norfolk, Conn.: New Directions, 1951.

With a note by Frieda Lawrence.

THE ROSE TATTOO. New York: New Directions, 1951.

Prefaced by "The Timeless World of a Play."

CAMINO REAL. Norfolk, Conn.: New Directions, 1953.

This "revised and published version" is based on the one-act TEN BLOCKS ON THE CAMINO REAL from the 1948 collection AMERICAN BLUES. This full-length version, with foreword and afterword, is, as is often the case with Williams, quite different from the version actually performed during the Broadway run; from the unsigned editor's note to this edition, "three characters, a prologue and several scenes that were not in the Broadway production have been added or reinstated from earlier, preproduction versions, while other scenes have been deleted."

27 WAGONS FULL OF COTTON AND OTHER ONE-ACT PLAYS. Norfolk, Conn.: New Directions, 1953.

With its thirteen plays, this, not the 1946 edition, is the most complete text. It includes TALK TO ME LIKE THE RAIN AND LET ME LISTEN, and SOMETHING UNSPOKEN.

CAT ON A HOT TIN ROOF. New York: New Directions, 1955.

Prefaced by "Person-to-Person," this Pulitzer Prize play of 1955 contains two versions of its third act, with a "Note of Explanation" of how the Broadway version was written at the suggestion of the play's director, Elia Kazan. In 1975 Williams published a version that combines the two previous endings; i.e., Big Daddy reappears in the last act, but Brick remains passive.

LORD BYRON'S LOVE LETTER. New York: Ricordi, 1955.

Libretto for an opera by Raffaelo de Banfield; it is not identical with the short play in 27 WAGONS FULL OF COTTON.

BABY DOLL; THE SCRIPT FOR THE FILM INCORPORATING THE TWO ONE-ACT PLAYS WHICH SUGGESTED IT: 27 WAGONS FULL OF COTTON AND THE LONG STAY CUT SHORT; OR, THE UNSATISFACTORY SUPPER. New York: New Directions, 1956.

ORPHEUS DESCENDING, WITH BATTLE OF ANGELS. New York: New Directions, 1958.

Prefaced by "The Past, the Present and the Perhaps," a major biographical source, Williams' first major play is here reprinted with the later revision of ORPHEUS DESCENDING. ORPHEUS was itself reprinted in 1960 in paperback by the New American Library and retitled THE FUGITIVE KIND. This is not the unpublished screenplay of the same name by Williams and Meade Roberts.

A PERFECT ANALYSIS GIVEN BY A PARROT. ES, October 1958, pp. 131-34.

A PERFECT ANALYSIS GIVEN BY A PARROT. New York: Dramatists Play Service, 1958.

SUDDENLY LAST SUMMER. New York: New Directions, 1958.

GARDEN DISTRICT, TWO PLAYS: SOMETHING UNSPOKEN AND SUDDENLY LAST SUMMER. London: Secker and Warburg, 1959.

THE ENEMY: TIME. THEATRE, 1 (March 1959), 14-17.

Sketch for SWEET BIRD OF YOUTH.

SWEET BIRD OF YOUTH. ES, April 1959, pp. 114-55.

SWEET BIRD OF YOUTH. New York: New Directions, 1959.

PERIOD OF ADJUSTMENT: HIGH POINT OVER A CAVERN, A SERIOUS COMEDY. New York: New Directions, 1960.

THE NIGHT OF THE IGUANA. ES, February 1962, pp. 47-62, 115-30.

THE MILK TRAIN DOESN'T STOP HERE ANYMORE. New York: New Directions, 1964.

After two different Broadway productions, that of 17 February 1963 and that of 1 January 1964, MILK TRAIN was further transmogrified into the film BOOM!

THE ECCENTRICITIES OF A NIGHTINGALE AND SUMMER AND SMOKE. New York: New Directions, 1964.

SLAPSTICK TRAGEDY. ES, August 1965, pp. 95-102, 130-34.

Two one-act plays, THE MUTILATED and GNADIGES FRAULEIN; a preface contains an explanation of the full-length CAMINO REAL.

I CAN'T IMAGINE TOMORROW. ES, March 1966, pp. 76-79.

KINGDOM OF EARTH. ES, February 1967, pp. 98-100, 132, 134.

KINGDOM OF EARTH: THE SEVEN DESCENTS OF MYRTLE. New York: New Directions, 1968.

A much expanded version of the ESQUIRE text, with a subtitle.

IN THE BAR OF A TOKYO HOTEL. New York: New Directions, 1969.

THE TWO-CHARACTER PLAY. New York: New Directions, 1969.

SMALL CRAFT WARNINGS. New York: New Directions, 1972.

OUT CRY. New York: New Directions, 1973.

Retitled, revised version of the 1969 THE TWO-CHARACTER PLAY.

BATTLE OF ANGELS. Rev. ed. New York: Dramatists Play Service, 1975.

CAT ON A HOT TIN ROOF. New rev. ed. New York: New Directions, 1975.

## COLLECTIONS

DRAGON COUNTRY: A BOOK OF PLAYS. New York: New Directions, 1970.

Contains IN THE BAR OF A TOKYO HOTEL; I RISE IN FLAME, CRIED THE PHOENIX; THE MUTILATED; I CAN'T IMAGINE TOMORROW; GNADIGES FRAULEIN; A PERFECT ANALYSIS GIVEN BY A PARROT; CONFESSIONAL; and THE FROSTED GLASS COFFIN. The last two titles received their first publication in this volume.

THE THEATRE OF TENNESSEE WILLIAMS. 4 vols. New York: New Directions, 1971-72.

With the exception of SUDDENLY LAST SUMMER, this collection contains only full-length plays, and none post-1964.

## BIBLIOGRAPHY

The most useful bibliographies, though neither is complete nor extending past 1965, are those of Signi Falk's TENNESSEE WILLIAMS (Twayne, 1961), pp. 206-21, and Gerald Weales's TENNESSEE WILLIAMS (University of Minnesota, 1965), pp. 43-46. See also Nadine Dony's "Tennessee Williams: A Selected Bibliography," MD, 1 (December 1958), 181-91 and Charles A. Carpenter, Jr., and Elizabeth Cook's "Addenda to 'Tennessee Williams: A Selected Bibliography,'" MD, 2 (December 1959), 220-23.

## SELECTED NONDRAMATIC WRITING

"This Book." Introduction to Carson McCullers' REFLECTIONS IN A GOLDEN EYE. New York: New Directions, 1950.

In this introduction, Williams defends his friend, while explaining the characteristics of the southern Gothic writer.

THE ROMAN SPRING OF MRS. STONE. New York: New Directions, 1950.

Novel.

"Concerning the Timeless World of a Play." NEW YORK TIMES, 14 January 1951, sec. 2, pp. 1, 3.

Art, like contemplation and repose, allows us to escape the pressures and insecurities of a time-dominated life. This essay, shorn of the first word of its title, is the foreword to THE ROSE TATTOO.

HARD CANDY: A BOOK OF STORIES. New York: New Directions, 1955.

Contains "Two Players of a Summer Game," the short story source for CAT ON A HOT TIN ROOF.

"Person-to-Person." Foreword to CAT ON A HOT TIN ROOF. New York: New Directions, 1955.

One of Williams' most successful statements on the writer's need to communicate. This volume also contains the "Note of Explanation" with which Williams prefaces the stage version of the third act, and in which he tells of Kazan's suggested revisions and his own reactions.

IN THE WINTER OF CITIES. New York: New Directions, 1956.

The most complete edition of this poetry collection is, according to Weales, the 1964 paperback edition, also published by New Directions.

"The World I Live In." OBSERVER, 7 April 1957, p. 14.

Questions and answers, both by Williams, in which he calls himself "a minor artist who has happened to write one or two major works." He denies any belief in guilt, original sin, heroes, or villains.

"Tennessee Williams on the Past, the Present and the Perhaps." NEW YORK TIMES, 17 March 1957, sec. 2, pp. 1, 3. Also as preface to ORPHEUS DESCENDING, WITH BATTLE OF ANGELS. New York: New Directions, 1958.

A major biographical reminiscence about the failure of BATTLE OF ANGELS in Boston.

"The Writing is Honest." NEW YORK TIMES, 16 March 1958, sec. 2, pp. 1, 3. Rpt. as introd. to William Inge's DARK AT THE TOP OF THE STAIRS. New York: Random House, 1958.

William Inge's world is one of sincerity and an unashamed realism; Williams also recalls his first meeting with Inge.

"Williams' Wells of Violence." NEW YORK TIMES, 8 March 1959, sec. 2, pp. 1, 3. Rpt. as preface to SWEET BIRD OF YOUTH. New York: New Directions, 1959.

Williams describes his continual battle with writer's block, from his first adolescent efforts until present time. He is surprised at audiences' willingness to applaud the violence he describes, and he acknowledges that the violence and weaknesses have some relationship to his insight into his own character.

"Tennessee Williams Presents his POV." NEW YORK TIMES MAGAZINE, 12 June 1960, pp. 19, 78.

Williams defends his plays as having extended the perimeters of dramatic possibility.

THE KNIGHTLY QUEST: A NOVELLA AND FOUR SHORT STORIES. New York: New Directions, 1967. See also THE KNIGHTLY QUEST: A NOVELLA AND TWELVE SHORT STORIES. London: Secker and Warburg, 1968.

MEMOIRS. Garden City, N.Y.: Doubleday, 1975.

Indispensable, with rather more candor than is usual with such reminiscences.

## CRITICISM

Adler, Thomas P. "The Dialogue of Incompletion: Language in Tennessee Williams's Later Plays." QJS, 61 (February 1975), 48-58.

Williams' new theatre language, despite apparent similarities, is quite distinct from that of Beckett, Ionesco, and Pinter, and is based on the need for the "other."

Barthelme, Donald. "A Note on Elia Kazan." FORUM, 1 (January 1957), 19-22.

The poetry of playwrights like Williams and Inge "falls under its own weight."

Bentley, Eric. "Camino Unreal." In his THE DRAMATIC EVENT: AN AMERICAN CHRONICLE. New York: Horizon, 1954, pp. 106-10.

Finds Kazan irresistible, CAMINO REAL considerably less so.

Buell, John. "The Evil Imagery of Tennessee Williams." THOUGHT, 38 (Summer 1963), 167-89.

Provocative analysis of how Williams might have rewritten OEDIPUS REX, with an examination of the "victim" and the "victimizer" as Williams' central myth.

Callaghan, Berry. "Tennessee Williams and the Cocolooney Birds." TAMARACK REVIEW, 39 (Winter 1966), 52-58.

Praises THE GNADIGES FRAULEIN for its "stoic grace."

Cohn, Ruby. DIALOGUE IN AMERICAN DRAMA. Bloomington: Indiana University Press, 1971. See pages 97-129.

Cole, Charles W., and Carole I. Franco. "Critical Reaction to Tennessee Williams in the Mid-1960's." PLAYERS, 49 (Fall-Winter 1974), 18-24.

A survey of the reviewers' responses to SLAPSTICK TRAGEDY and THE SEVEN DESCENTS OF MYRTLE.

Costello, Donald P. "Tennessee Williams' Fugitive Kind." MD, 15 (May 1972), 26-43.

ORPHEUS DESCENDING provides in concentrated form the very essence of Williams' work, his symbols, and his themes.

Da Ponte, Durant. "Tennessee's Tennessee Williams." TENNESSEE STUDIES IN LITERATURE, no. 1 (1956), 11-17.

On Williams' father and the father's reactions to the son's work.

Donahue, Francis. THE DRAMATIC WORLD OF TENNESSEE WILLIAMS. New York: F. Ungar, 1964.

Pedestrian critical study, long on plot summary, short on critical analysis.

Dukore, Bernard F. "The Cat Has Nine Lives." TDR, 8 (Fall 1963), 95-100.

The play's theme is not homosexuality, but Brick's willingness or unwillingness to enter the procreative cycle of birth, aging, and death.

Dusenbury, Winifred. "BABY DOLL and THE PONDER HEART." MD, 3 (February 1961), 393-96.

Eudora Welty's novella is a possible source for the screenplay.

Falk, Signi. "The Profitable World of Tennessee Williams." MD, 1 (December 1958), 172-80.

After noting the remarkable disparity between Williams' pretentious prefatory comments and the plays themselves, Falk charts Williams' limited range of character, his sentimentality, and his very theatrical, very "tawdry success."

______. TENNESSEE WILLIAMS. New York: Twayne, 1961.

Intelligent, well-researched, treats the plays out of chronological order, grouping them around recurring character types: the southern gentlewoman, desperate heroes, and the degenerate artist.

Fedder, Norman J. THE INFLUENCE OF D.H. LAWRENCE ON TENNESSEE WILLIAMS. The Hague: Mouton and Co., 1966.

This is an attractive analysis of a real literary influence, but it is also a good instance of the limitations of a purely literary analysis of drama as it plays on the stage.

Ferlita, Ernest. THE THEATRE OF PILGRIMAGE. New York: Sheed and Ward, 1971.

CAMINO REAL is unconvincingly portrayed as the Stations of the Cross, a dream-like road to redemption. See pages 95-110.

Fritscher, John J. "Some Attitudes and a Posture: Religious Metaphor and Ritual in Tennessee Williams' Query of the American God." MD, 13 (September 1970), 201-15.

This theological and psychological reading of Williams' life and works argues that Williams' equivocal relationship to his father (God) is the key to his theatre.

Gelb, Arthur. "Williams and Kazan and the Big Walkout." NEW YORK TIMES, 1 March 1960, sec. 2, pp. 1, 3.

An interview with Williams is interspersed with comments from Elia Kazan, after Kazan withdrew as director of PERIOD OF ADJUSTMENT. Williams admits that Kazan never had to jazz up "my cornpone melodrama," for the hysteria is already in the plays, perhaps to excess.

Gerard, Albert. "The Eagle and the Star: Symbolic Motifs in THE ROMAN SPRING OF MRS. STONE." ENGLISH STUDIES, 36 (August 1955), 145-53.

Although not a major novel, THE ROMAN SPRING OF MRS. STONE is an interesting instance of the use of symbolic motifs in contemporary fiction.

Hays, Peter L. "Tennessee Williams' Use of Myth in SWEET BIRD OF YOUTH." ETJ, 18 (October 1966), 255-58.

Chance Wayne as Adonis.

Hurley, Paul J. "SUDDENLY LAST SUMMER as 'Morality Play.'" MD, 8 (February 1966), 392-402.

Williams is not Sebastian; in fact, Williams depicts Sebastian as a metaphor for an obsession with evil and the failure to participate in society.

Hurt, James R. "SUDDENLY LAST SUMMER: Williams and Melville." MD, 3 (February 1961), 396-400.

SUDDENLY LAST SUMMER is more than a homosexual horror story; it is about good and evil, and it derives much of its power from themes of Melville's MOBY DICK (1851) and THE ENCANTADAS (1856).

Jackson, Esther Merle. THE BROKEN WORLD OF TENNESSEE WILLIAMS. Madison: University of Wisconsin Press, 1965.

An abstract and often pretentious study.

Kalson, Albert E. "Tennessee Williams Enters DRAGON COUNTRY." MD, (June 1973), 61-67.

This comparison of I RISE IN FLAME, CRIED THE PHOENIX and IN THE BAR OF A TOKYO HOTEL reveals Williams' loss of faith in the powers of the relationship between art and life.

Leon, Ferdinand. "Time, Fantasy, and Reality in NIGHT OF THE IGUANA." MD, 11 (May 1968), 87-96.

In no other Williams play is memory so crucial a part.

Maxwell, Gilbert. TENNESSEE WILLIAMS AND FRIENDS. Cleveland: World, 1965.

The sometimes adoring and sometimes petulant memoirs of a close friend and poet.

Nelson, Benjamin. TENNESSEE WILLIAMS: THE MAN AND HIS WORK. New York: Ivan Oblensky, 1961.

Without scholarly apparatus, this is at best a routine study.

Peterson, William. "Williams, Kazan and the Two Cats." NTM, 7 (Summer 1967), 14-19.

Tracing the patterns and repetitions of CAT ON A HOT TIN ROOF, the author finds Williams' original ending is far superior to that shown on Broadway.

Popkin, Henry. "The Plays of Tennessee Williams." TDR, 4 (March 1960), 45-64.

A critical survey of Williams' works shows a recurring, symbolic conflict between an aging woman (the Gargoyle) and a superlatively handsome young man (the Adonis), with both hungry for love and trying to fend off time.

Rogoff, Gordon. "The Restless Intelligence of Tennessee Williams." TDR, 10 (Summer 1966), 78-92.

While the crisis in Williams' art is a real one, attributing it simply to his sexual preferences is a grave distortion. Rogoff finds that Williams' plays, after A STREETCAR NAMED DESIRE (1947), lack over-all vision or unity: he cites the incompatability of each act of SWEET BIRD OF YOUTH, and the conflicting endings of CAT ON A HOT TIN ROOF. The recurring theme of "the fugitive kind," suggestive as it is of Williams' own like, is more usefully understood as a creative problem: the absence of purposive direction.

Sacksteder, William. "The Three Cats: A Study in Dramatic Structure." DS, 5 (Winter 1966-67), 252-66.

Comparing the unpublished filmscript for CAT ON A HOT TIN ROOF with the two stage versions, Sacksteder finds the film's affirmations more consistent with the play's basic materials than either of the stage versions.

Sharp, William. "An Unfashionable View of Tennessee Williams." TDR, 6 (March 1962), 160-71.

Williams is a modern artist whose attempts at tragedy center on a conflict between what the individual and what society thinks is or ought to be. The article also contains an interesting comparison of ORPHEUS DESCENDING and A BATTLE OF ANGELS.

Starnes, Leland. "The Grotesque Children of THE ROSE TATOO." MD, 12 (February 1970), 357-69.

Williams uses farcical folk comedy to transcend realism and create aesthetic distance, while retaining, in the case of Serafina, respect for the character's stature.

Steen, Mike. A LOOK AT TENNESSEE WILLIAMS. New York: Hawthorne Books, 1969.

Recorded interviews with artistic collaborators and personal friends of the playwright.

Tischler, Nancy M. TENNESSEE WILLIAMS: REBELLIOUS PURITAN. New York: Citadel Press, 1961.

Tischler naively accepts Williams' own evaluation of events and character, and lards her book with plot summaries.

Tynan, Kenneth. "American Blues: The Plays of Arthur Miller and Tennessee Williams." In his CURTAINS: SELECTIONS FROM THE DRAMA CRITICISM AND RELATED WRITINGS. New York: Atheneum, 1961, pp. 257-66.

Williams' plays "thus have the static quality of dream rather than the dynamic quality of fact; they bring the drama of mood to what may be its final hothouse flowering."

_____. "Valentine to Tennessee Williams." In his CURTAINS: SELECTIONS FROM THE DRAMA CRITICISM AND RELATED WRITINGS. New York: Atheneum, 1961, pp. 266-71.

A personal portrait of the vagabond playwright.

Vowles, Richard B. "Tennessee Williams and Strindberg." MD, 1 (December 1958), 166-71.

CAMINO REAL, no matter what Williams may say, is a lineal descendant of Strindberg's pilgrimage plays.

______. "Tennessee Williams: The World of His Imagery." TDR, 3 (December 1958), 51-58.

Water imagery is seen as the central motif of Williams' art; it is used to explicate CAT ON A HOT TIN ROOF.

Weales, Gerald. TENNESSEE WILLIAMS. Minneapolis: University of Minnesota Press, 1965.

Exemplary introductory pamphlet.

______. "Tennessee Williams Borrows a Little Shaw." SHAW REVIEW, 8 (1965), 63-64.

______. "Tennessee Williams's 'Lost' Play." AL, 37 (November 1965), 321-23.

On AT LIBERTY, a 1941 play that has been ignored since then.

Williams, Edwina (Dobkins). REMEMBER ME TO TOM. As told to Lucy Freeman. New York: Putnam, 1963.

Williams' mother's anecdotal reminiscences of her son, herself, and her family are a valuable, if partial, biographical source.

# WILLIAM CARLOS WILLIAMS (1883-1963)

MANY LOVES AND OTHER PLAYS: THE COLLECTED PLAYS OF WILLIAM CARLOS WILLIAMS. Norfolk, Conn.: New Directions, 1961.

Of the five plays in this volume, only two were first published post-1950: TITUBA'S CHILDREN and THE CURE. The volume also contains useful brief "Notes on William Carlos Williams as Playwright" by John C. Thirlwall.

## BIBLIOGRAPHY

Wallace, Emily Mitchell, ed. A BIBLIOGRAPHY OF WILLIAM CARLOS WILLIAMS. Middletown, Conn.: Wesleyan University Press, 1968.

## CRITICISM

Atkinson, Clinton J. "In Search of Theatre." MR, 3 (Winter 1962), 331-36.

A plea for consideration of Williams as a playwright.

Donohue, H.E.F. "An Occasion for Tremendous Music." MR, 3 (Winter 1962), 338-44.

Brief survey of the plays.

Wagner, Linda Welshimer. THE PROSE OF WILLIAM CARLOS WILLIAMS. Middletown, Conn.: Wesleyan University Press, 1970.

Full-length study stressing the relationship between his poetry and his prose.

Witaker, Thomas R. WILLIAM CARLOS WILLIAMS. New York: Twayne, 1968.

General survey treating the plays only in passing.

# ANGUS WILSON (1913- )

THE MULBERRY BUSH. London: Secker and Warburg, 1956.

The first production of the English Stage Company.

SKELETONS AND ASSEGAIS: FAMILY REMINISCENCES. TR, 9 (Spring 1962), 19-43.

A play for radio.

# EDMUND WILSON (1895-1972)

THE LITTLE BLUE LIGHT. New York: Farrar, Straus and Co., 1950.

AN INTERVIEW WITH EDMUND WILSON. NEW YORKER, 38 (2 June 1962), 118-28.

EVERYMAN HIS OWN ECKERMANN. NYRB, 1 (Spring 1963), 1-4.

EVERYMAN HIS OWN ECKERMANN. In THE BIT BETWEEN MY TEETH: A LITERARY CHRONICLE 1950-1965. New York: Farrar, Straus and Giroux, 1965.

A discourse in dialog form.

AN INTERVIEW WITH EDMUND WILSON. In THE BIT BETWEEN MY TEETH: A LITERARY CHRONICLE 1950-1965. New York: Farrar, Straus and Giroux, 1965.

Another discourse in dialog form.

THE LAMENTABLE TRAGEDY OF THE DUKE OF PALERMO BY HENRY CHETTLE AND WILLIAM SHAKESPEARE NOW FIRST DISCOVERED AND TRANSCRIBED BY HOMER R. WINSLOW, M.A. HILLSDALE, Ph.D. HARVARD, PRESENTED BY EDMUND WILSON. NYRB, 7 (12 January 1967), 13-23.

This play within a play is part of Wilson's diatribe against fads in scholarship and teaching.

DR. McGRATH. COMMENTARY, 43 (May 1967), 60-67.

## COLLECTIONS

FIVE PLAYS. London: W.H. Allen, 1954.

With a prefatory essay, this volume includes the first publication of CYPRIAN'S PRAYER, and reprints of THE CRIME IN THE WHISTLER ROOM, THIS ROOM AND THIS GIN AND THESE SANDWICHES (a 1937 play formerly titled A WINTER IN BEECH STREET), BEPPO AND BETH, and THE LITTLE BLUE LIGHT.

THE DUKE OF PALERMO AND OTHER PLAYS WITH AN OPEN LETTER TO MIKE NICHOLS. New York: Farrar, Straus and Giroux, 1969.

THE LAMENTABLE TRAGEDY OF THE DUKE OF PALERMO, DR. McGRATH, OSBERT'S CAREER: OR THE POET'S PROGRESS, and the essay-letter in praise of Mike Nichols, urging him to revive a variety of notable, but now forgotten, American plays.

## BIBLIOGRAPHY

Ramsey, Richard David, comp. EDMUND WILSON: A BIBLIOGRAPHY. New York: David Lewis, 1971.

## CRITICISM

Berthoff, Warner. EDMUND WILSON. Minneapolis: University of Minnesota Press, 1968.

Introductory pamphlet.

Frank, Charles F. EDMUND WILSON. New York: Twayne, 1970.

Chapter 3 is devoted to the poems and plays.

# LANFORD WILSON (1937- )

BALM IN GILEAD, AND OTHER PLAYS. New York: Hill and Wang, 1965.

Includes HOME FREE! and LUDLOW FAIR.

THE MADNESS OF LADY BRIGHT. In EIGHT PLAYS FROM OFF-OFF BROADWAY. Ed. Nick Orzel and Michael Smith. Indianapolis: Bobbs-Merrill, 1966.

THE RIMERS OF ELDRITCH, AND OTHER PLAYS. New York: Hill and Wang, 1967.

Includes THIS IS THE RILL SPEAKING, WANDERING, DAYS AHEAD, and a reprint of THE MADNESS OF LADY BRIGHT.

THE GINGHAM DOG. New York: Hill and Wang, 1970.

LEMON SKY. New York: Hill and Wang, 1970.

THE SANDCASTLE, AND THREE OTHER PLAYS. New York: Dramatists Play Service, 1970.

STOOP: A TURN; SEXTET (YES): A PLAY FOR VOICES; and a reprint of WANDERING.

THE GREAT NEBULA IN ORION AND THREE OTHER PLAYS. New York: Dramatists Play Service, 1972.

Also includes IKKE, IKKE, NYE, NYE, NYE; THE FAMILY CONTINUES, and VICTORY ON MRS. DANDYWINE'S ISLAND.

SUMMER AND SMOKE. New York: Belwin Mills, 1972.

Adaptation, with music by Lee Hoiby, of the Tennessee Williams play (1948).

THE HOT L BALTIMORE. New York: Hill and Wang, 1973.

## BIBLIOGRAPHY

Salem, James M., ed. A GUIDE TO CRITICAL REVIEWS. Part 1: AMERICAN DRAMA, 1909-1969. 2nd ed. Metuchen, N.J.: Scarecrow Press, 1973.

List of reviews, omitting those in the VILLAGE VOICE. See pages 532-34.

## CRITICISM

Sainer, Arthur. "Lanford Wilson." In CONTEMPORARY DRAMATISTS. Ed. James Vinson. London: St. James; New York: St. Martin's, 1973, pp. 831-33.

# CHARLES WOOD (1933- )

COCKADE. P&P, 11 (December 1963), 23-30; (January 1964), 23-30 ff.

COCKADE. In NEW ENGLISH DRAMATISTS 8. Introd. John Russell Taylor. Harmondsworth, Engl.: Penguin, 1965.

> Consists of three short plays: PRISONER AND ESCORT, JOHN THOMAS, and SPARE.

DINGO. P&P, 14 (July 1967), 23-38.

FILL THE STAGE WITH HAPPY HOURS. In NEW ENGLISH DRAMATISTS 11. Harmondsworth, Engl.: Penguin, 1967.

THE LONG DAY'S DYING. London: Junction Films Ltd., 1968.

> An unpublished screenplay based on the short novel by Alan White; located at the Library of the University of California at Los Angeles.

DINGO. Harmondsworth, Engl.: Penguin, 1969.

"H": BEING MONOLOGUES AT FRONT OF BURNING CITIES. London: Methuen, 1970.

> With a preface by Michael Edwardes, the author's introduction, and a glossary.

VETERANS, OR, HAIRS IN THE GATES OF THE HELLESPONT. London: Eyre Methuen, 1972.

## SELECTED NONDRAMATIC WRITING

"My Boyhood Life." LONDON MAGAZINE, 7 (October 1965), 72-75.

Impressionist memories, mixed with a Brechtian contempt for lazy or overly emotional audiences.

## CRITICISM

Page, Malcolm. "Charles Wood: HOW I WON THE WAR and DINGO." LITERATURE OF FILM QUARTERLY, 1 (July 1973), 256-62.

Compares the film to the play.

Rudlin, John. "Charles Wood: An Actor's Writer?" NTM, 6 (April-June 1965), 2-5.

Wood's work, despite its lack of box-office appeal and difficulties with the Lord Chamberlain, is a valuable, collage-like alternative to well-made drama.

Taylor, John Russell. "Charles Wood." In his THE SECOND WAVE. London: Methuen, 1971, pp. 59-76.

Wood is fascinated with the army as a way of life, quite beyond any propagandistic purposes.

Worth, Katharine J. "New Forms of Melodrama and Epic Theatre." In her REVOLUTIONS IN MODERN ENGLISH DRAMA. London: G. Bell, 1973, pp. 135-40.

Discusses the use in "H" of Victorian melodrama, of O'Casey's "world on wallpaper."

# OLWEN WYMARK ( - )

THREE PLAYS. London: Calder and Boyars, 1967.

CODA, LUNCHTIME CONCERT, and THE INHABITANTS.

THE GYMNASIUM AND OTHER PLAYS. London: Calder and Boyars, 1972.

Also includes THE TECHNICIANS, STAY WHERE YOU ARE, JACK THE GIANT KILLER, and NEITHER HERE NOR THERE.

## CRITICISM

Brown, John Russell. "Olwen Wymark." In CONTEMPORARY DRAMATISTS. Ed. James Vinson. London: St. James; New York: St. Martin's, 1973, pp. 840-41.

"A sense of reality comes and goes in Olwen Wymark's plays, but it bites sharply and stimulates unexpected reactions."

# SUSAN YANKOWITZ (1941- )

SLAUGHTERHOUSE PLAY. YT, 2 (Summer 1969), 109-60.

SLAUGHTERHOUSE PLAY. In NEW AMERICAN PLAYS 4. Ed. William M. Hoffman. New York: Hill and Wang, 1971.

TERMINAL. SCRIPTS, 1 (November 1971), 17-45.

THE HA-HA PLAY. SCRIPTS, 10 (October 1972), 81-92.

TERMINAL. In THREE WORKS BY THE OPEN THEATER. Ed. Karen Malpede. New York: Drama Book Specialists, 1974.

> Revised version described as "the final evolution of the piece as it was being performed by the company during their final tour" (p. 38).

## CRITICISM

Sainer, Arthur. "Susan Yankowitz." In CONTEMPORARY DRAMATISTS. Ed. James Vinson. London: St. James; New York: St. Martin's, 1973, pp. 842-43.

# INDEXES

# AUTHOR INDEX

This index includes all authors, editors, compilers, translators, and other contributors to works cited in the text. References are to page numbers and alphabetization is letter by letter.

## A



## B

# Author Index

## E



## F

G



H

K



L

## M

## N



## O



## P

## R



## S

## Y



## Z

# — TITLE INDEX

This index includes all titles of books, reports, and proceedings cited in the text. In some cases titles have been shortened. References are to page numbers and alphabetization is letter by letter.

## A

## B

## D

## E

## F

## G

## H

## I

## J

## K



## L

## M

## N

# O

## Q



## R

## S

## T

## U

## V



## W

X



Y



Z

# SUBJECT INDEX

This index is alphabetized letter by letter and references are to page numbers. Major areas of emphasis have been underlined.

## G

## H

## J



## K



## L

## Q



## R

## W

Harris, Richard Hough.

Modern drama in America and England, 1950-1970



| DATE | | | |
|---|---|---|---|
| | | | |
| | | | |
| | | | |
| | | | |
| | | | |
| | | | |
| | | | |
| | | | |
| | | | |
| | | | |
| | | | |
| | | | |